AFRICAN ISSUES

Volunteer
Economies

T0319625

AFRICAN ISSUES

AFRICAN ISSUES

Volunteer Economies

The Politics & Ethics of Voluntary Labour in Africa

Edited by
Ruth Prince
& Hannah Brown

JAMES CURREY

James Currey
an imprint of
Boydell & Brewer Ltd
PO Box 9, Woodbridge
Suffolk IP12 3DF (GB)
www.jamescurrey.com
and of
Boydell & Brewer Inc.
668 Mt Hope Avenue
Rochester, NY 14620-2731 USA
www.boydellandbrewer.corn

© Contributors 2016
First published 2016

British Library Cataloguing in Publication Data
A catalogue record for this book is available on request from the British Library

ISBN 978-1-84701-139-8 (James Currey paper)
ISBN 978-1-84701-140-4 (James Currey hardback)

The publisher has no responsibility for the continued existence or accuracy of URLs for
external or third-party internet websites referred to in this book, and does not guarantee
that any content on such websites is, or will remain, accurate or appropriate.

This publication is printed on acid-free paper

Typeset in 9/11 Melior with Optima display
by Kate Kirkwood Publishing Services

CONTENTS

NOTES ON CONTRIBUTORS

Hannah Brown is a Lecturer in Anthropology at Durham University. She has a longstanding research interest in Kenya, where she has worked on issues of health care and health governance, caring relations within and beyond institutions, modes of developmental governance, and health systems bureaucracies. Her current research centres on zoonotic diseases and epidemic management in Sierra Leone, with a particular focus on Lassa fever and Ebola virus disease. She has recently published a focus on 'Volunteer Labour in East Africa' with Ruth Prince in *African Studies Review*.

Birgitte Bruun is a Postdoctoral Fellow at the Institute of Anthropology, University of Copenhagen, and holds a PhD in anthropology from the London School of Hygiene and Tropical Medicine where she was a member of the Anthropologies of African Biosciences research group. She has carried out ethnographic research on health in Ghana, Malawi and Zambia, where her doctoral research explored trajectories of lay engagement in transnational medical research projects.

Prosper Chaki is an entomologist based at the Ifakara Health Institute in Dar es Salaam. His research interests include urban malaria control. He has written about community-based programmes for malaria control in Tanzania and published in *Human Resources for Health and Malaria Journal*.

Christopher J. Colvin is a Senior Research Officer and Head of the Division of Social and Behavioural Sciences at the School of Public Health and Family Medicine at the University of Cape Town. He has a PhD in sociocultural anthropology and an MPH in epidemiology. His research interests include HIV and masculinity; community health worker and task shifting initiatives; health diplomacy, education and activism in the context of global health; and evidence synthesis of health social-science research.

Susan L. Erikson is an anthropologist and Associate Professor at the Faculty of Health Sciences, Simon Fraser University. She currently conducts ethnographic research on global health futures, reproductive imaging technologies, biomedical knowledge production and expertise, governmentality, and the political economy of clinical credibility. Research has focused on Sierra Leone.

Bjørn Hallstein Holte is a PhD candidate at Diakonhjemmet University College, Norway.

Michael Jennings is Senior Lecturer at the Department of Development Studies and Director of the Centre of African Studies, SOAS, University of London. His research focuses on the role of non-state actors in development and service provision in Africa, the emergence and evolution of development narratives in and about Africa, and synergies between power, politics and development in the North and South. His publications include the book *Surrogates of the State: NGOs, Development and Ujamaa in Tanzania* (2008, Kumarian Press) as well as articles in *African Affairs*, *Journal of Modern African Studies*, *Politique africaine*, *Development and Change* and *Social Science & Medicine* among others.

Ann H. Kelly is Senior Lecturer in the Department of Sociology, Anthropology and Philosophy. Her work focuses on the practices of medical research and scientific production, focusing on the built environment, material artefacts and practical labours of experimentation in sub-Saharan Africa. She has published in *Science as Culture, Journal of Cultural Economy, Medical Anthropology Quarterly, American Ethnologist* and the *Journal of the Royal Anthropological Institute*, among others, and has co-edited with J. Mair & C. High, *The Anthropology of Ignorance* (Palgrave Macmillan, 2012) and with P. Wenzel Geissler, *The Value of Transnational Medical Research* (Routledge, 2012).

Thomas G. Kirsch is Professor of Social and Cultural Anthropology at the University of Konstanz. He has published two monographs on African Christianity, one of them entitled *Spirits and Letters: Reading, Writing and Charisma in African Christianity* (Berghahn Books, 2008), and articles in the journals *American Anthropologist, American Ethnologist, Visual Anthropology* and *Journal of Southern African Studies*. He has conducted fieldwork on issues of violence, security and crime prevention in South Africa and is co-editor with T. Grätz of *Domesticating Vigilantism in Africa* (James Currey, 2010).

Ruth Prince is Associate Professor in Medical Anthropology at the Institute of Health and Society, University of Oslo. Recent publications include an edited book (with Rebecca Marsland) *Making and Unmaking Public Health in Africa: Ethnographic and Historical Perspectives* (Ohio

University Press, 2013) and the monograph with P. Wenzel Geissler, *The Land is Dying: Contingency, Creativity and Conflict in Western Kenya* (Berghahn Books, 2012).

Peter Redfield is Professor of Anthropology at University of North Carolina at Chapel Hill. His recent publications include *Life in Crisis: The Ethical Journey of Doctors Without Borders* (University of California Press, 2013) and, co-edited with Erica Bornstein, *Forces of Compassion: Humanitarianism between Ethics and Politics* (School of Advanced Research Press, 2010).

Noelle Sullivan is a Lecturer in Global Health Studies and the Department of Anthropology at Northwestern University. She has a PhD in medical anthropology. Her work focuses on the politics of global health, tracing what issues or challenges become 'in vogue' and the other possibilities that such prioritizations foreclose. Her interests include HIV/AIDS, malaria, health sector reform and health policy, diabetes and volunteerism.

Claire Wendland is Associate Professor at the Department of Anthropology, University of Wisconsin-Madison. She focuses on the globalization of biomedicine, particularly in Africa. Her first book, *A Heart for the Work: Journeys through an African Medical School*, was published by the University of Chicago Press in 2010 and explores the experiences of medical students learning to be doctors in Malawi.

Ståle Wig is a doctoral student at the Department of Social Anthropology at the University of Oslo. He has conducted field research in Lesotho, aiming to bring back renewed ethnographic attention towards development practitioners to a nation known among anthropologists, more than any other, for its politics and 'anti-politics' of development. He is currently conducting doctoral research on the uses and meanings of money in Cuba.

ACKNOWLEDGEMENTS

This volume originated as two workshops on volunteer labour and citizenship in Africa, which took place in October 2011 at Gonville & Caius College, University of Cambridge, and at the London School of Hygiene and Tropical Medicine. We are grateful to the participants who, in addition to some of the contributors to this volume, included Feliticas Becker, Tracey Chantler, Ela Drążkiewicz-Grodzicka, Wenzel Geissler, Emma Hunter, Sian Lazar, Hayley MacGregor and Tom Yarrow and, at LSHTM, Martin Gorsky, Alex Mold, Gareth Millward, Suzanne Taylor and Virginia Berridge. Conversations with members of the Anthropologies of African Biosciences group, especially Wenzel Geissler, and with Peter Redfield and Maia Green provided additional intellectual stimulation to this project. We wish to thank Robinson College, University of Cambridge, the Leverhulme Trust (Research Leadership Award Wenzel Geissler F/02 116/D) and the Mellon foundation for financially supporting the workshops. The editing of the volume and writing of the introduction were undertaken with the financial support of the Leverhulme Trust (Research Leadership Award F/02 116/D); the ESRC (ES/L010690/1), the Wellcome Trust (Grant number WT092699MF), the Norwegian Research Council FRISAM fellowship (Grant number 213670), Durham University and the University of Oslo. Jaqueline Mitchell has provided immense encouragement along the way. We are also grateful to the anonymous reviewers of the manuscript. Finally the journal *African Studies Review* and its reviewers supported a parallel project on a related theme.

Introduction ▌ The Politics & Ethics of Voluntary Labour in Africa

RUTH PRINCE
& HANNAH BROWN

In recent years the concept of 'volunteering' and the figure of the volunteer have become increasingly prominent in political ideologies, social movements and individual experience across the globe (Allahyari 2000; Eliasoph 2011; Hilton & McKay 2011; Milligan & Conradson 2006). The ethic of volunteering drives the work of charities, philanthropic groups, religious organizations and non-government organizations (NGOs) concerned with global inequalities, poverty alleviation, development, disaster response and emergency relief. Not only does volunteerism underpin an organizational ethic, heard for example in the term 'voluntary sector', but many of these organizations themselves also rely upon voluntary labour. Volunteer medical professionals are central to the work of humanitarian organizations such as Médicins Sans Frontières (MSF), the Red Cross and the Red Crescent, while NGOs such as the UK-based Oxfam or the North American World Vision grew out of the work of volunteers. Meanwhile 'gap-year' volunteering among Western youth has become popular alongside other kinds of volunteer tourism within ecological or development projects (e.g. Mostafanezhad 2013b; Parreñas 2012; Simpson 2004; 2005; Smith & Laurie 2011). While the direction of volunteer action within international development and humanitarian projects is predominantly from global North to global South (McWha 2011), there are South–South volunteering programmes organized by the United Nations (UN) and other international, including religious, organizations.[1] International volunteers work in Israeli kibbutzim, or join Palestinians in occupied territories as a display of solidarity. From South Africa to Egypt, Germany to India, Indonesia to Nicaragua, volunteers are involved in civic action, political activism, poverty alleviation, humanitarian aid and disaster relief within as well as beyond their own societies (see e.g. Watts 2002; Nading 2012, 2013; Mittermaier 2014).

---

[1] The UN runs a Volunteer programme, which, according to its website, mobilizes more than 7,000 volunteers to work in development and peace projects, 80 per cent of them from developing countries. www.unv.org/en/about-us.html (accessed 26 November 2015).

1

Voluntary labour and volunteerism is not only a prominent mode of engagement within global humanitarianism, development and philanthropy, political activism and social justice. As states withdraw from twentieth-century promises of work, care and social redistribution (Eliasoph 2011) 'voluntary organizations become key to the shifting social architecture in post-welfare societies and the new forms of citizenship that accompany it' (Muehlebach 2012:10). Voluntary labour is being positioned within an 'economy of affect' (Hardt 1999), which relies on unpaid labour and non-profit infrastructure to do the work of the state (Archambault & Boumendil 2002; Adams 2012). Neoliberal politicians in post-welfare Europe espouse voluntary work and volunteering as the kernel of a new, kinder, 'big society' in which ordinary citizens form voluntary groups that, instead of state employees, run social services for their communities (Rose 2000; Alcock 2011; Hilton & McKay 2011). In these political visions, volunteering is seen as a central means of promoting the public good in the context of global recession and cuts in welfare and social services (Muehlebach 2012). Within these 'experiments in citizenship', the volunteer has emerged as a 'central symbolic figure through which people are imagining social solidarity and collective life more generally' (ibid.: 11). It is not only governments and the non-profit voluntary sector that use volunteers; in some cases, private companies under contract to the state to provide welfare services or disaster relief, recruit and organize volunteers (Adams 2012) or deploy volunteers in 'corporate social responsibility' projects (Muthuri et al. 2009). Less explicitly celebrated by politicians is the use of the 'voluntary' labour of the unemployed as a pool of free labour, promoted as a means of giving people work experience and an advantage in the job market. Companies make use of state-organized volunteering schemes to take on young workers, often giving them less than a minimal wage. This use of cheap labour, which may or may not lead to (insecure) employment, reflects a growing presence (and often abuse) of 'internship' (Perlin 2012). As Muehlebach argues, what is at stake in these developments is not just a matter of cheap labour extraction by the state and the private sector but a reconceptualization of the larger social collective, in which the burden of solidarity is shifted onto citizens (2012: 7–8, 70–71).

Africa – as a prominent site of global humanitarian efforts and development interventions involving national and transnational volunteers – offers insights into such shifts and experiments in citizenship and governmentality (Bonneuil 2000; Jennings 2008; Rottenburg 2009; Redfield 2010). In many African countries the volunteer has been an important figure during the past fifty years, particularly in the field of development, although the popularity of volunteering as a tool of governance and a mode of citizenship has waxed and waned (Hyden 1995). During the 1960s and 1970s, newly independent governments in East Africa promoted the voluntary labour of citizens as the backbone of national development (Newell 1975; Hunter, 2015), and during the 1980s and 1990s the volunteer occupied an important role in the NGO-dominated move towards 'community-led development' and its espousal of 'grassroots' participation (Maes & Kalofonos 2013; Mercer & Green 2013). While each country has specific histories of voluntary action, activism and labour, volunteering in Africa is also configured by global movements and circulations. For example, in early 2000 in South Africa, volunteer activists, linked up by national and global NGOs, campaigned against 'big pharma' for greater access to anti-retroviral treatment for HIV-positive people (Robins 2004). A more controversial iteration of the volunteer is the medical research subject (Petryna 2009). In many African countries, voluntary participation in clinical trials takes shape in a contradictory space created by a poor public health system, volunteers' material needs and the demand for clinical trial subjects (Crane 2013; Geissler 2013; see also Bruun, this volume, Chapter 4). Meanwhile Africa remains a favoured site of volunteer organizations and individuals from the global North involved in development interventions, humanitarian relief and disaster management.

While volunteerism is usually considered to be an unmitigated public good, the position of voluntary action as a mode of engagement with widening global and national inequalities, and within development and humanitarian emergencies, calls for critical scrutiny (Redfield 2012, 2013). Volunteering is emerging as a key site of encounters 'between privilege and poverty' (Muehlebach 2013: 300) within a 'global moral economy of compassion' (Mittermaier 2014: 518; see Boltanski 1999; Berlant 2004; Fassin 2012). The questions of whether voluntary labour benefits the giver or receiver and whether it addresses or reinforces inequalities remain the subject of debate (e.g. Bornstein & Redfield 2010; Adams 2012; Roy 2012). The prominence of the voluntary sector in global disaster relief, humanitarian action and emergency response has critical political implications (Fisher 1997). During the aftermaths of the tsunami of 2006 and the Haitian earthquake of 2010, volunteers from MSF, the Red Cross, and the Red Crescent worked with UN agencies and national governments to provide emergency relief, shelter and medical care. After Hurricane Katrina devastated New Orleans, relief efforts relied upon the work of volunteers and voluntary organizations, filling in not just for the state but for the corporate for-profit sector contracted by the government to provide homes for the homeless (Adams 2012). The 2014–15 Ebola crisis in Guinea, Sierra Leone and Liberia focused worldwide attention on the place of voluntary action – both local and international – in emergency humanitarian action and disaster relief. MSF took responsibility for the treatment of sufferers and containment of the virus, in a situation where both the West African states and the international community were too slow to respond. As Peter Redfield's Epilogue to this volume argues, this situation raises serious questions about a model of global health governance in which the containment of a major public health epidemic was left to a voluntary organization (MSF), which was apparently the only international institution with the organizational skills and expertise to deal with it (Lachenal 2014).

While volunteerism has extensive national and international histories within and beyond Africa, the examples given above suggest that it is taking on a particular traction within the political and economic landscapes of the twenty-first century. Volunteering is a powerful concept, one that is capable of mobilizing individuals and groups and of marking out the possibilities of acting in the service of a greater good by addressing social inequalities or perceived deprivation. It can be framed as a means to act upon suffering, and used to promote a vision of a better integrated society or a more equal world As a moral act, volunteering is tied to religious sentiments as well as political projects (Holden 1997; Allahyari 2000; Mittermaier 2014). Yet the examples in this volume also reveal the heterogeneity of the projects that call or draw upon volunteers, and of the social forms they take. Volunteerism is shaped by transformations in labour markets, political economies and humanitarian emergencies. It is implicated in neo-liberal political projects, and the making of global as well as national citizens (Muehlebach 2011, 2012; Simpson 2004, 2005; Eliasoph 2011; Smith & Laurie 2011). It is clear that volunteering is not a neutral act. It takes place in a politically and economically loaded field, and it can be controversial, creating tensions.

The recent proliferation in the meanings and social practices of volunteerism in Africa and elsewhere, and the significance of volunteering and volunteerism to social, political and economic transformation – both historically and at the present time, make it an important subject to study. While there is a sizeable body of literature on volunteerism in the global North, we know rather little about voluntary labour as a mode of political, ethical and social action in African countries, even though volunteering has an extensive colonial and post-colonial history on the continent. This volume offers a rich ethnographic and historical assessment of the role of voluntary labour in African societies. Here, we build on our contribution in the recent issue of African Studies Review on voluntary labour in East Africa (Brown & Prince 2015) to argue that a focus on voluntary labour provides new perspectives on issues such as citizenship, the labour market, work, development and identity, as well as forms of belonging and collective futures across the African continent. We argue that voluntary labour also offers insights into aspirations and trajectories of African youth, individual ethical and political action, and religious identities. Considering both local and international voluntary labour in Africa, the volume examines the mobility and exchange of ideas and practices through volunteering as well as the perpetuation of post-colonial inequalities and hierarchies of opportunity, vulnerability and value. The studies of volunteering in this volume foreground issues of value and justice, forms of governmentality and notions of 'the social'. They open up a study of personal trajectories and careers, of class and mobility, as well as imaginations of individual agency, social collectives and the future.

This volume also outlines the contributions of anthropology to the study of voluntary labour, with each chapter using ethnographic or historical approaches to examine this ambiguous and paradoxical yet also compelling realm of social, political, ethical and economic action. By following the trajectories, encounters and exchanges of volunteers and the implications of voluntary action and labour, the authors in this volume approach voluntary labour as a field of dense meanings, tensions and contradictions. Contributing chapters, from South Africa, Lesotho, Zambia, Kenya, Tanzania, Malawi and Sierra Leone follow volunteers working within their own countries, as well as historical and contemporary configurations of international volunteer action. By situating voluntary action within post-colonial relations and situations, the volume opens up the politics, ethics and economics of volunteer action to critical debate.

In the first part of this Introduction, we explore theoretical questions raised by the broad range of practices and associations in circulation around the concept of volunteering. We suggest that although volunteerism consists of a diverse set of practices and organizational configurations there are nevertheless some common elements underlying these forms. We discuss five issues that lie at the kernel of volunteering: (i) the idea that volunteering is a gift, and the related notion of the volunteer as an independent agent who freely gives something of herself to a common project or a greater good; (ii) the relationship between the individual and larger collectives; (iii) the relations between volunteering, identity and the fashioning of the self; (iv) the relation between volunteering and an emerging global moral economy of compassion; and (v) the ways in which the relationship between voluntary labour and other forms of 'work' destabilizes conventional boundaries between paid/unpaid and formal/informal work.

In the second part we consider how the five issues we outlined above have played out in both historical and contemporary trajectories of volunteerism, volunteering and voluntary labour in Africa during the twentieth century and up to the present day, our aim being to specify the forms that volunteering takes in contemporary African society and to situate these forms within a changing political, economic and global landscape. At the end of the Introduction, we include a summary of the contributing chapters.

Theorizing volunteerism and voluntary labour

Volunteering as giving
Defining the figure of the volunteer and the sphere of volunteering is a difficult task. Both are historically specific – tied to particular political eras, religious trajectories and economic developments. The closer we

get to these spheres, the less clear they are. There is much slippage in the term 'volunteer', which is perhaps why it is so politically useful.[2] The Oxford English Dictionary (OED) defines as 'voluntary' actions that are 'performed or done of one's own free will, impulse, or choice; not constrained, prompted, or suggested by another'. 'Voluntarism' is action rooted in the will of the individual and not coerced. With regard to organizations, voluntarism is 'the principle of relying on voluntary action rather than compulsion'. In the UK (as in this volume), 'volunteerism' is more commonly used; both terms denote 'the involvement of voluntary organizations in social welfare'. The 'volunteer', meanwhile, is 'one who voluntarily offers his services in any capacity; one who of his own free will takes part in any enterprise' (OED).

This definition places emphasis on the freedom and choice embedded in the act of giving: it is an act of will (*voluntas*) which involves 'the act of offering free help', 'of doing something by choice' and 'without being asked' (OED). Volunteering is construed as a moral act because it is borne out of free will in a situation of choice (see Laidlaw 2000). There are underlying assumptions about freedom and morality here such as the idea that freedom is only possible in the total absence of constraint or relations of power (see Mahmood 2005). We know from Mauss (1967) that there is no such thing as a free gift; giving is always embedded in social relations of obligation and reciprocity. Yet volunteering is idealized as altruistic action that helps others beyond any expectation of return. As such, volunteering can be construed also as a sacrifice of one's labour, energies and time; it indicates a giving up of oneself to a cause, or to 'something bigger' (Bruun, Chapter 4).

As the contributions to this volume highlight, these assumptions about freedom and altruism do not hold in clear-cut ways when we consider voluntary labour ethnographically. Volunteers do not always work for 'the greater good', nor necessarily as free agents. For example, Birgitte Bruun's Chapter 4 on volunteers who sign up as clinical trial subjects in Lusaka shows that a decision to volunteer can be shaped by the need to maintain interpersonal networks of care and support within one's neighbourhood rather than as a 'gift' to future generations or unknown others. Nor do assumptions about volunteers' autonomy vis-à-vis economic issues and motivations hold when one considers specific acts – and economies – of volunteering. Defined in terms of altruism and self-sacrifice, voluntary work appears disconnected from economic and personal interests. However, while volunteering may often be altruistic, it is not necessarily done without any expectation of return. Volunteers may indeed have

---

[2] The idea of doing voluntary work underlay the philanthropic societies and charitable work of Victorian gentlefolk and the Christian philanthropy of nineteenth-century American capitalists. It continues to play a large role in Christian churches and charities, and it figures in Islamic, Hindu and Buddhist organizations. Military service has relied on the patriotic feelings of volunteers as well as conscripts. Nationalist and nation-building projects, from the Russian Revolution to wartime Britain to post-independence Tanzania, have drawn upon and promoted voluntary labour and the figure of the volunteer.

economic motivations and volunteering may form part of a livelihood, as Ståle Wig explores through an analysis of the differential logics of social assistance engaged by international and local volunteers working for an NGO in Lesotho (Chapter 4). As we will show, acts of volunteering are embedded in particular economies (and political contexts) and are shaped by a range of divergent motivations.

Clearly, there is a direct link between these conceptions of volunteering as defined by altruism, giving and helping, and religious ideas of the gift and of sacrifice. Christianity construes the giver as a Good Samaritan, motivated by compassion and pity for the other; one becomes good by doing good. Yet at the same time, as Bjørn Hallstein Holte argues in his Chapter 8 on elite Kenyan volunteers, this act emphasizes difference: I give to you. In Islam, giving is a religious duty. The Egyptian volunteers studied by Mittermaier, who distribute food and clothes to the needy, regard volunteering as part of a cultivation of a properly pious self: giving to the poor is a way of giving to God (Mittermaier 2014: 535). For the volunteer it is her ethical relationship to God rather than to society that is important; thus the act of giving does not inscribe difference between giver and recipient. Volunteering, and the ways in which it is understood as a gift, are thus constructed differently within different religious traditions of practice (see also Becker 2015). What may appear a globalized form of charitable action takes place within specific religious traditions, even while it is shaped by a shared compassionate response to globalized humanitarian discourses and images of suffering (Mittermaier 2014).

The individual and the collective
Another central feature of volunteering is the relation, intimate and value-laden, that it both assumes and establishes between an individual and larger collectives. In its idealized form, volunteering implies the giving of something of the self – labour, time or body – to a greater good. This establishes a relation between the individual and a collective, and as such, it has been used as a political tool – a position Richard Titmuss famously argued for in relation to blood donation and the UK's National Health Service (Titmuss 1997). This relationship to larger collectives is often mediated by organizations. For example, providing care to an elderly family member is not volunteering, but providing these same forms of care to a stranger might be, if carried out through an organization rather than simply an act of friendship or neighbourliness.

The relationship between the individual and broader collectives may be based upon shared identity or difference. Volunteering can arise out of identification of the self with the collective (the obvious example is the nation-state – volunteering one's life for the nation at war, or donating one's blood for fellow citizens), or it may arise out of difference: the volunteer is better off and wishes to aid those who are not so fortunate through charitable acts. Volunteering is often explicitly associated with an ideological commitment to equality and solidarity, emphasized in the vision of MSF – 'A life is a life anywhere – there is no difference in the value of a life' (Fassin 2012; Redfield 2013). Yet, while it may seek to overcome inequality, the act of giving often reinforces the difference between donor and recipient, giver and receiver. The collectives to which volunteers attach themselves are varied. During much of the twentieth century in Europe and also in newly independent African nations, the nation-state provided the overarching frame within which much voluntary work was conceived and valued, and voluntary labour was closely linked to citizenship (Hilton & McKay 2011; Hunter 2015). However, voluntary societies and volunteer associations have a long tradition of attachment to religious collectives, whether they are Christian churches and charities, Islamic organizations or Hindu and Buddhist groups (Redfield & Bornstein 2010). With globalization and the promotion of non-governmental intervention, these collectives have become more prominent. The voluntary sector, which includes religious as well as secular organizations, has gained increasing influence in both service delivery in wealthy countries and international development in the global South (Fisher 1997; Stewart 1997). Within this organizational infrastructure, volunteering contributes to improving lives and relieving human suffering (Fassin 2012), but rather than being directed towards national wellbeing or development, it is directed towards specific collectives and the good of certain groups of people ('the community' or 'the poor') rather than society as a whole (Rose 1996).

In an article tracing transformations in the political use of volunteers and voluntary action during the past fifty years, Lacey and Ilcan (2006) argue that whereas European welfare states used to be invested in shifting risks from individuals to society, during the past 20 to 30 years, risk has been shifted in the other direction, as today 'a range of authorities establish voluntary labour as a site for providing answers and solutions to social and economic problems that now lie outside the formal reach of the state' (ibid.: 35). During much of the twentieth century in Europe and in the post-independence era in Africa, the state implicated volunteers primarily as citizens working towards producing a more just and fair society. However, acts of volunteering under neoliberalism have been intrinsically influenced by its agendas: the production of 'responsibilized' and 'active' subjects, the reduction of state services, and the devolution of progress to market forces. Individuals are encouraged to take on duties previously the responsibility of the state and the role of the volunteers has shifted towards being citizens who are primarily responsible for the delivery of public services. In this way, voluntary labour is depoliticized and, despite the language of empowerment, the agency of the volunteer is 'effectively negated' (ibid.: 38). Framed as a charitable, rather than a political practice, volunteering becomes a 'highly individualized act' (ibid.). There are other political consequences:

assembling volunteers as responsible citizens in the delivery of public services has enormous implications for: the long-term viability of those services, given the donated nature of voluntary labor; the quality of services, given the precarious nature of voluntary labor supply, and; for the relationship between volunteers and local communities, given the potential for agenda-setting by either the volunteers themselves or the NGOs that act as overseers. (Lacey & Ilcan 2006: 47)

Lacey and Ilcan make an important link between volunteering in the neo-liberal North and volunteering as it is configured within international development in the global South. However they do not consider the contexts in which these ideas and practices circulate. Nor do they consider how volunteering practices articulate with earlier histories of volunteering, both religious and political, in relation to both state and non-state initiatives and the trajectories of political action and citizenship. In Africa as elsewhere, the productive power of volunteering and the way it gains traction in individual lives derives from it being situated outside of, as well as within, neo-liberal rationalities (Muehlebach 2012; see also Prince 2013). These issues are taken up by contributors to this volume, who situate volunteering in development economies (Bruun; Jennings; Wig) and civic action (Chaki & Kelly) and in relation to apartheid and its aftermath (Kirsch; Colvin).

As the above discussion underlines, the relationship between individual voluntary action and larger collectives raises questions about the contours of voluntary action as it produces personal as well as societal or national futures (Muehlebach 2012), and as it is enacted within specific figurations of or yearnings for belonging, attachment and care (Geissler 2011; Ferguson 2013; Prince 2015). These issues are discussed particularly in the chapters by Birgitte Bruun, Michael Jennings, Thomas Kirsch and Bjørn Hallstein Holte. As we argue elsewhere (Brown & Prince 2015), in Africa in particular, volunteer opportunities emerge from uneasy partnerships among state, transnational and non-governmental actors (Ferguson 2006). In this context, while volunteers like other African citizens may yearn to be 'part of a public of care and protection', and to be 'bearers of civic rights and responsibilities' (Geissler et al. 2013: 531) and participate in developmental futures, the opportunities, trajectories and institutional forms that connect them to such destinations are uncertain, transient and precarious (Manton 2013; Prince 2013; Tousignant 2013).

Volunteering as identity
As an act of giving one's labour freely for the benefit of a larger collective, volunteering emerges as closely tied to the politics of identity and citizenship. Yet as visions of welfare and understandings of the role of the nation-state have changed, so too the contours and responsibilities of citizenship have shifted along with the place of volunteerism. Within these shifting contexts volunteering has figured as a practice of self-fashioning, tied up with varied forms of public recognition and presence,

and situated within particular regimes of governmentality (e.g. Nading 2012, 2013; Brown 2013; Prince 2013, 2014). However, the motivations driving voluntary work are diverse, as are the relationships it fosters. Altruism and public service can coexist with the politics of self-expression and self-development.

The capacity to volunteer is linked both to the availability of time to dedicate to unpaid work and the desire to help others who may be perceived as less fortunate than oneself. Volunteering is therefore often associated with groups of people who are relatively wealthy. For example, in twentieth-century Britain, volunteering had a strong association with middle-class women. Often free from the constraints of the labour market and drawn to charitable work, their voluntary labour was caught up within the politics of social distinction relating to both gender and class (Hilton & McKay 2011). Some of these forms of volunteering were exported to Africa under colonialism though the voluntary work of the middle-class wives of colonial officers (Davin 1978; Lewis 2000). Although these class-based associations are complicated by other forms of volunteering (including activism and nationalist projects) there is little doubt that volunteer labour takes place within political and economic contexts that have a profound effect upon the individual status and identity of the person volunteering.

While volunteering can act as a means of fashioning particular kinds of identity this is often more complicated than simply becoming seen as a 'good person' who 'helps others'. For young Africans with education but no job, volunteering with a development project may be an opportunity to fashion a professional or 'working' identity (Brown & Green 2015; Prince 2015) or to position oneself within social or global networks (Colvin, Chapter 1; Bruun, Chapter 4). For young gap-year volunteers, their voluntary work can help them appear 'well-rounded' and worldly wise (Simpson 2005). As we stated above, these kinds of embodied qualities have economic traction in formal labour markets.

The embodied nature of volunteering as a mode of self-fashioning means that the gift of voluntary labour has specific meaning within the individual's life history and construction of the moral self, which is itself intimately part of national histories. Thomas Kirsch's Chapter 9, on volunteering as 'repentance', situates voluntary work in the juncture between individual life histories and political action. In post-apartheid South Africa, volunteers strive both to heal society and to make reparations for the part they played in the country's violent racialized past. Kirsch's volunteers display a strong belief in the significance of an individual's moral choices and actions in healing racial and social divisions, and constructing a better society. The positive response of many German volunteers to the 2015 refugee crisis in Europe can similarly be read as an attempt to link humanitarian action with a national conscience regarding 'doing the right thing', arising partly at least out of the nation's past.

Volunteering and the global moral economy of compassion
Volunteering as a mode of action and the figure of the volunteer are crucial nodes within what has been described as a 'global moral economy of compassion' (Mittermaier 2014: 518; Redfield & Bornstein 2010). This moral economy has emerged over the past half-century as central to international humanitarianism (and international development), itself bound up with an increasingly mediated experience of 'distant suffering' (Boltanski 1999), in which the suffering of others, whether strangers or fellow citizens, has become an important concern within the public sphere (Redfield & Bornstein 2010:4). While explicitly secular, global humanitarian action has roots in a Christian approach to suffering, based on Christian ethics of compassion and pity producing charitable action and 'doing good', and on an assumption that an individual moral choice lies at the roots of action (Fassin 2012).

While the framing of global humanitarianism assumes 'an emergent global voluntarism that is the same everywhere' (Mittermaier 2014: 518), our discussions of voluntary labour and volunteering in African countries suggest that volunteering is underpinned not only, nor always, by the Christian ethos of compassion and the response to suffering. The contributions to this volume highlight that, while volunteering work is often associated with visions of compassion, altruism and self-sacrifice (Holte), it also involves a wide range of other ethical concerns, for example around hospitality (Sullivan; Wig), care (Bruun; Colvin), reparations for the past (Kirsch), forms of civic engagement (Chaki & Kelly) and visions of developmental futures (Jennings). Analysing the modalities through which the global economy of compassion is 'engaged' (Tsing 2000, 2005) in these specific contexts draws attention to the diversity of ways in which this ethic can be reconfigured and re-appropriated. Perhaps more importantly, opening up an ethnographic analysis of this 'rhetoric of moral celebration' provides an important vantage point for attending to the ways that those who celebrate this global economy of compassion become complicit in the silencing of critical analyses of its enactment (Wendland, Erikson & Sullivan, Chapter 7).

Voluntary labour is becoming increasingly prominent in our 'age of poverty' (Roy 2012: 105), as one response to widening structures of national and global inequality. As Bjørn Hallestein Holte's chapter on elite Kenyan boarding school students argues, volunteer action has become a key zone of 'affect-laden encounters between privilege and poverty' (Muehlebach 2013: 300; Simpson 2004; Bornstein 2003; Bornstein & Redfield 2010; Parreñas 2012; Redfield 2012). Encounters between international volunteers and locals likewise bring into view 'global' lifestyles, mobility and comparative affluence, which contrast with 'local' experiences of disadvantage and immobility, often reinforcing rather than addressing inequalities, as Ståle Wig's chapter in this volume demonstrates. These encounters are also crucial sites of self-making (Roy

2012; Parreñas 2012).[3] As suggested in the chapters by Sullivan and by Wendland et al. on the flow of medical students from the global North to volunteer in African hospitals, studying these encounters opens up insights into the connection and disconnection, the mobility and immobility that are integral features of our present global condition (see Redfield 2012; Wendland 2012).

The relations between voluntary labour and paid work
Finally, we consider how volunteering is situated in relation to labour, work, and leisure or 'free' time. Volunteering is usually viewed as 'free labour', on the assumption that the volunteer gains income from another source (his job, the salary of a husband, etc.). Indeed volunteering becomes conceivable only within the modern configuration of work versus free time, which is itself part of capitalist modernity. The relation between labour and leisure or more specifically, free time, has been fundamental to industrial modernity and the eventual compromise reached between labour and capital within the nation-state. Volunteering today, however, is situated less in the leisure/free time of the employed (or groups such as middle-class housewives) than in the more ambiguous space that now exists between paid and unpaid work and between formal and informal economies. In a context of rising long-term unemployment, volunteering becomes more like 'internship', a route into a career or, as unpaid but socially valued work, it offers those on the margins of the economy a sense of social value and public recognition (Prince 2015). For many people in the global South, and for the growing body of the unemployed in the global North, volunteering is more an economic, livelihood strategy, a way of inserting oneself into networks of patronage, gaining experience, positioning oneself as qualified, and thus as employable, than a gift of free labour. In a situation of chronic unemployment, volunteering thus becomes a space in which those who are excluded from arenas of work, or in a marginal position in relation to labour markets, can gain public recognition and presence and build up particular kinds of relationships to the sphere of salaried labour (Brown & Green 2015) and, indeed, citizenship (Muehlebach 2012).

Volunteering, then, takes place across vastly unequal economies, bringing together people with different motivations and orientations to into a rather murky space that is, as underlined in many of the contributions to this volume, rife with misinterpretation. This opaqueness, and the heterogeneity surrounding economies and ideologies of volunteering, have political consequences. The fact that volunteering is clothed in an ideology of autonomous action, of free giving and free labour, can conceal relations of inequality and dependence, authoritarianism and coercion. At the same time, volunteering in the name of a common or public good

---

[3] Ananya Roy argues that the circulation of volunteers from affluent global North to the Global South "produce[s] "zones of intimacy" where poverty is encountered through volunteerism, philanthropy and other acts of (neo)liberal development' (Roy 2012: 241).

also allows people to articulate a common set of goals and shared interests and to create other kinds of valued relationships and opportunities, as discussed for example by Birgitte Bruun in her Chapter 4, but also by other contributions. We should pay heed to the plural horizons of moral practices bound up with voluntary work. Practices of giving or 'gifting' free labour may be bound up with forms of self-fashioning as well as with establishing relationships, often hierarchical ones, between donor and recipient, but they also include and evoke experiences of participation, of 'togetherness', of discovery and pleasure as volunteering opens up opportunities to learn specific knowledge and skills, to work together with others, and to inhabit a new identity and make new connections.

African volunteers: from nation building to 'participation' and 'community empowerment'

Having outlined some key theoretical issues surrounding its deployment, we now turn to voluntary labour as it took shape in the post-colonial period in Africa. We begin by situating contemporary practices of volunteering in historical context, paying particular attention to the relationships between voluntary labour, citizenship and nation building, especially in the post-independence period. In this section, the African nations of Kenya and Tanzania are used as case studies. Although volunteering has been an important political force across the continent, these East African countries have been the subject of more sustained historical analyses than other parts of Africa. The extensive scholarship on volunteering in Kenya and Tanzania provides useful insights into the political and economic traction of volunteering in colonial and post-colonial contexts. We then describe how these historical precedents have shaped new forms of African volunteering through intersections with global economies and projects of international development, and with religious and political organizations and influences. We draw attention to the diversity of forms of voluntary labour that African people are currently engaged in and the changing meanings and opportunities that are associated with this work. Finally, we turn to the question of non-Africans who travel to the continent to engage in voluntary labour, ranging from 'gap-year' students and medical students on hospital placements to professional voluntary-based organizations such as Voluntary Services Overseas (VSO) and Peace Corps. We thus situate African experiences within international networks and global movements of resources, ideas and ways of acting upon the world. While we treat African volunteers (people who volunteer within their own societies) and international volunteers separately it is important to underline that both forms of voluntary labour respond to and have been shaped by common processes: colonialism, post-colonial nation building, humanitarianism and development, globalization and neoliberalism.

Voluntary labour has a chequered history in modern Africa, from nineteenth-century mission philanthropy to twentieth-century nation building. In the early twentieth century, the colonial state called upon chiefs and headmen to induce (which often meant coerce) volunteers to build infrastructural projects such as roads. Meanwhile both rural and urban-based Africans formed voluntary welfare associations, often based on ethnic or religious affiliations (Little 1965; Parkin 1978; Barkan & Holmquist 1989; Barkan, McNulty & Ayeni. 1991). Late colonial welfare and development policies in British Africa explicitly promoted the use of volunteers, but the colonial state was ambiguous about voluntary welfare societies, suspecting them to be involved in political agitation (Lewis 2000). In late colonialism, Christian charity converged with the colonial state's concerns about welfare and development in the work of colonial wives who, in both Kenya and Nigeria, for example, set up women's development clubs and activities, as well as charitable associations (Wipper 1975; Callaway 1987). These charitable works provided a model for local charities and were often forerunners of nation-wide organizations. Like missionary work, they introduced Christian virtues of helping the poor. At the same time, they promoted self-development and self-reliance (Aubrey 1997).

Across colonial and post-colonial periods, voluntary labour also figured strongly within religious activities and charities, organized by churches, missions, mosques and Islamic organizations. Today, Christian churches – both national churches and the increasingly globalized Pentecostal churches – as well as Islamic organizations are heavily involved in charitable activities. Driven by the ethos of compassion and empathy for the poor, and the desire to build a better society or 'help the community', many organize social-welfare and development activities and run their own NGOs, much on the basis of voluntary labour (Dilger 2009; Freeman 2012; Becker 2015).

Historically, then, voluntary labour has been used as a tool to build social and political collectives, to support development, and within religious and charitable action. Both African and foreign volunteers have been driven by diverse motivations. While we keep this diversity in mind, below we focus on the importance of voluntary labour to post-colonial nation building.

Harambee *and* Ujamaa: *volunteering as citizenship*
To take one well-known example, in the Kenyan context, discourses of self help and nation-building were so important in the period of early independence that the call, '*harambee!*' (a Swahili term meaning, 'Let's pull together') became short-hand for this political era (Widner 1992). *Harambee* was President Kenyatta's rallying cry and combined notions of nation building with ideals of African traditionalism that emphasized communal labour. *Harambee* activities were central to the building of community facilities, especially rural health facilities and schools in the

period immediately following independence (Thomas 1985: 8; Maxon 1995: 137–8; Hill 1991). *Harambee* included physical labour (for example through work parties to build schools and clinics) and the donation of money or non-monetary goods – especially food – to fund such projects and/or feed those who donated their labour to these projects.

However *harambee* arrangements were not simple representations of an egalitarian communalism and often underlined hierarchies of power and wealth (e.g. Shipton 1989: 17; Parkin 1978: 216). Moreover, as elsewhere the practices of *harambee* grew out of a colonial tradition of forced labour as much as indigenous forms of self help (Hill 1991: 13–48), and include practices of clientelism, providing a mechanism for elites to channel resources to the poor and for the poor to make claims on those resources (Barkan & Holmquist 1989; Haugerud 1993: 46, 48). Thus, although the notion of 'voluntary labour' was and to some degree remains central to these self-help projects (which persist in Kenya now primarily as fundraising projects), the nature of this volunteerism has always been highly ambiguous, speaking to the inequalities of an emerging political system and new forms of engagement with the state, as much as to egalitarianism or communitarianism (see also Thomas 1985, 1987; Widner 1992).

Although *harambee* in Kenya emerged within the context of a very specific political culture, the power of the 'self-help' discourse to transcend modes of governance should not be underestimated. Similar nation-building projects based upon volunteerism existed across the continent and indeed the same 'self-help' discourse which underpins *harambee* has also been used as a marker of socialist government, for example in post-independence Tanzania (Holmquist 1984). Here, voluntary labour underpinned the national development programme of *ujamaa*, which focused on self-reliance, participation in development and nation-building, and included 'voluntary' resettlement of villages, as well as the participation of ordinary citizens in building projects. As such, voluntary labour was a central pillar of the developmentalist state's aspirations and policies and of 'developmentalism' itself as a project of improving standards of living and the country's education, health and agricultural capacities (Hunter 2015). National development relied upon building citizenship, which meant building relations not only between ordinary people and the state but with each other. Thus the goal of self-reliance through *ujamaa* meant building something together, rather than being individualistic; it meant sustainability, rather than dependency.

For President Nyerere, self-reliance as a socialist 'attitude of mind' and 'code of conduct' (Lal 2012: 213) was rooted in African tradition and humanistic universalism. As with *harambee* in Kenya, Tanzanian discourses of ujaama and self help were rooted in nostalgic ideals of African communitarianism and its ability to create self-sufficient and cooperative communities. Politicians and government officials as well as ordinary citizens and villagers referred to pre-colonial and 'African' traditions of forming cooperative work groups for agricultural labour and house-building. Yet, as with *harambee*, there was also continuity with colonial governance. Late British colonial policy promoted voluntary labour and 'self help' in rural development (Lewis, 2000; Jennings 2003; Burton & Jennings 2007). This partly 'echoed a missionary ethic of voluntarism-as-uplift' but it also 'served a practical purpose of legitimizing uncompensated labour and low state capital expenditure on local-level development especially in the construction and maintenance of infrastructure'. (Lal 2012: 216). While development ambitions were scaled up during the post-independence era, the promotion of voluntary participation has continued to be a convenient tool in the face of reduced development aid and national budgets – particularly since structural adjustment in the 1980s.

Recent scholarship reveals the contradictions within the 1960s and 1970s projects of national development and nation building, arguing that self-reliance became merely a condition of necessity for rural people as the state was unable to deliver on its developmental promises (Lal 2012). Moreover, the egalitarian and cooperative ideals underpinning *ujamaa* met increasingly authoritarian government and the imposition of bureaucratic hierarchies (Jennings 2003, 2007; Marsland 2006). Still, the ways in which ordinary people responded to *ujamaa* and the meanings it had for them were diverse. Tanzanian villagers approached 'self-reliance' and voluntary labour in relation to their own experiences and interests, with some emphasizing its rooting in personal independence and adulthood rather than its associations with political citizenship (Lal 2012: 221).

These East African examples underline that voluntary labour has been part of both colonial and post-colonial political projects, and used for contradictory purposes: to allow colonial states to cut back on costly development activities and divest themselves of social responsibilities, and also as citizenship projects after independence, which purported to draw upon 'African' communitarianism and 'natural' social solidarity (Hunter 2015). The use of volunteers was central to the struggle to create new societies, to establish and extend ideas about citizenship, nationhood and its development. At the same time it was a convenient way for the state to evade responsibilities for social-welfare services and to manage expectations surrounding development. As historical work has moved away from the ideals espoused by *ujamaa* and *harambee* to the activities of volunteers themselves, we begin to understand volunteering as a site of multiple, sometimes contradictory motivations and practices. The contributions to this volume show that these are issues that play out in different ways across the continent.

Volunteering in development
Ideas relating to volunteerism as 'participation' have been central to developmental projects in Africa since the colonial period. In East Africa,

and especially in Tanzania, the reframing of compulsory labour for the colonial state as voluntary work for the building of the nation (*kazi ya kujitolea*) was accompanied by broader changes in understandings about participation in development. Influenced by emerging ideas about grassroots participation (Paolo Freire in the 1970s and Robert Chambers in the 1980s) and amidst critiques of large-scale 'white elephant' development and disillusionment with the increasingly authoritarian undertones of developmental African states, the voluntary participation of communities in their own development was promoted as part of a turn towards the grassroots and the small-scale. In Tanzania, these early forms of participatory models of development were open, iterative attempts to place disadvantaged groups at the heart of research processes (e.g. Hall 1992), promoted by Nyerere as part of a commitment to engaging the knowledge of the poor (see Green 2010: 1246–7). These approaches included both forms of labour and other forms of engagement such as public meetings (Marsland 2006). However, the open experimental nature of early approaches soon gave way to a standardization of participatory methods and the gradual incorporation of participation approaches in mainstream development (e.g. Chambers 1994; Green 2003).

During the 1980s, participatory approaches were adopted within neo-liberal approaches to development, including by large organizations such as the World Bank and used to endorse a form of development divorced from the state. Funding was channelled through NGOs rather than through national governments (e.g. Hearn 1998; Ndegwa 1994; Semboja & Therkildsen 1995), and there was a promotion of voluntary labour in 'grassroots' development projects, and a growing emphasis on supporting civil society movements which were regarded as representing the interests of citizens in the face of authoritarian and over-powerful states (Comaroff & Comaroff 1999). These shifts can be seen as a devolving of responsibilities for development from the state to NGOs and the market, and onto self-reliant, 'empowered' individuals and communities (Rajak 2012; Prince 2013).

While voluntary participation in development was understood as a means to achieve sustainability and community 'ownership', those who engaged in these projects were not necessarily understood as volunteers. However, during the 2000s as part of an increased focus on poverty reduction agendas, the state has returned as an important actor in development (Craig & Porter 2006) and is increasingly responsible for scaling up discrete development projects and having an overview of development initiatives, some parts of which may be delivered by NGOs. These models frequently formalize the roles of volunteers as actors who can mediate between communities and development projects, building upon older visions of community development and participation. They usually provide some remuneration to volunteers in the form of an allowance or stipend which is less than the minimum wage but is often a significant income in terms of local economies.

This has led to a professionalization of volunteering, where volunteers increasingly distinguish themselves from the communities where they work and volunteering is no longer a participatory form of development engagement which is open to all (as in the post-colonial visions of nation building), but has become a semi-professional role for those who aspire to develop skills in development work and build skills and relational networks which may create possibilities for salaried labour in the future (Brown & Green 2015).

Voluntary labour as work
Recent anthropological literature on volunteers in the development sector provides a thick description of various forms of volunteer work as 'participation' and 'empowerment' (e.g. Swidler & Watkins 2009; Boesten et al. 2011; Maes 2012; Maes & Kalofonos 2013). While these studies situate voluntary labour in the context of neo-liberal development, they also discuss the diverse motivations of volunteers: to 'help the community' and to develop oneself, to position the self strategically and seek out relations of patronage with state and NGO actors, and to gain some kind of livelihood. An important issue that emerges from this literature is the ambiguous relation between voluntary labour and 'work' in a situation of high unemployment (Prince, 2015).

It is clear that despite the use of terms such as 'token', 'stipend' and 'lunch allowance', the resources gained through volunteer work are highly valued in contexts where formal employment is scarce (see chapters by Bruun, Colvin, Chaki & Kelly, and Wig). In a situation of scarcity, volunteers often survive on this income, some combining different volunteer positions in order to make ends meet, or supplementing this income with other kinds of income generation. The receipt of allowances and stipends is also often a marker of status, associated with the work of government personnel and consultants. Moreover, volunteer labour provides access to the world of NGOs and development; it is a way of learning the skills and cultures associated with development institutions, often through training courses which offer people certificates of attendance (see Bruun, Chapter 4; Colvin, Chapter 1; Prince 2014). In contexts where there are few labour opportunities in other industries, for young people struggling to enter the world of work, gaining skills in development work can be invaluable, and volunteer opportunities act as a form of internship.

Volunteering can be thought of as a kind of work, then, that renders possible new kinds of relationships to paid labour, for both national and international volunteers. Jones (2008) identifies the work of international volunteers as part of the emergence of forms of work shaped by increasingly 'distanciated' rather than physically proximate relationships, and coins the term 'global work' to describe these new forms of labour. These distanciated relationships and hybrid globalized networks create the possibility for volunteers to travel to sites where they undertake voluntary labour but they also have economic and practical effects – for example changing ideas about teaching practices in Tanzanian schools. For Jones, these working relationships are partly wider transformations associated with the growth of a global workforce in which both global space and the ability of the volunteer to have an influence upon that space are both being reconfigured.

From this perspective, the workplace of international volunteers cannot be understood as 'localized' in sites of the global South. International volunteering has become bound into networks of 'distanciated' relationships, organizational practices and mobile labour and ideas (ibid.: 24). The national volunteers who gain skills and connections that offer them engagements with NGOs and state-led development projects are similarly embedded in globalized relationships. Although they are not usually as mobile as their international counterparts, they volunteer for development projects which are often supported by international organizations and may come into contact with non-African nationals through their voluntary labour. African nationals may not find it as easy as international volunteers to convert their voluntary experience into cultural capital and strategic position with traction in relation to the labour market. However, as we discuss further below, national and international volunteers working in development projects in Africa share similar concerns about future careers and paid work.

International volunteers

While we have thus far foregrounded national/local volunteers in African contexts, international and foreign volunteers have had a prominent presence in African countries since the early decades of the twentieth century, drawn there by both political and religious motivations. From the nineteenth century, a sense of Christian vocation and the desire to convert others led Europeans to volunteer for missionary societies. Christian missions depended on committed volunteers both at home and in the missions, where missionaries and converts undertook works of charity. The latter included social work and expanded into medical intervention. For example, many of the first school, hospitals and medical centres in countries like Tanzania were set up in the early decades of the twentieth century by Christian missions. Hospitals continued to be serviced by volunteer Christian doctors into the post-colonial period, while newly independent governments began to take over the running of the schools (Jennings, Chapter 5). Missionaries introduced notions and practices of Christian love, involving compassion and charity, teaching that these practices lay at the heart of Christian community and were the foundation of the Christian self. Whatever the refractions that such ideas met in different cultural and social contexts, it is clear that Christian ideas and practices concerning voluntary action as being bound up with charity, compassion and love inform the practices of much voluntary work in Africa (see Holte, Chapter 8; Kirsch, Chapter 9). Voluntary work also informs the practices of both national and international churches, many of which have expanded their activities into poverty alleviation, social welfare and development (Dilger 2009: Freeman 2012). Meanwhile many of the large Western-based NGOs, such as Christian Aid and World Vision, have Christian roots and some continue to have an explicit Christian ethos (see e.g. Bornstein 2005).

With its roots in humanism and the late colonial concern about the welfare of colonized peoples, international development emerged after the Second World War alongside humanitarianism and human rights (see Redfield & Bornstein 2010). In the immediate post-colonial period, international volunteers were attracted to African countries. They were motivated by a desire to build a fairer and better world, to alleviate poverty and bring development, as well as a desire for adventure. Some were drawn by the socialist ethos of Nyerere's *ujamaa* or President Kaunda's Zambian Socialism (see Jennings this volume). At the same time the routes they took followed in the steps of their colonial predecessors and their involvement in development projects as foreign experts often continued colonial-era racial hierarchies.[4]

International volunteering has always been closely associated with international organizations (usually NGOs) amidst concerns to address poverty and promote economic and social progress. Alongside the rise of charities such as Oxfam and Christian aid (sending volunteers to Africa), during the 1970s and 1980s European and North American organizations such as VSO and the Peace Corps organized the provision of volunteers to the developing world, and continue to do so. These organizations at first sent young volunteers who lacked particular skills but it was soon obvious that these were often more of a burden than a contribution to the societies and communities they landed in (see Jennings, Chapter 5), and organizations began to limit their intake to people with specific and needed skills and professional qualifications.

In his (1995) historical study of black Peace Corps volunteers who served in Africa at the height of the civil rights movement in the United States, Jonathan Zimmerman explores the varied constructions of race that underpinned understandings of volunteering for this cohort of volunteers. He describes processes of recruitment and training – black volunteers were encouraged to help their 'Brothers and Sisters abroad' – but some faced prejudice from family and friends in the US who felt they were neglecting the fight for racial equality in their own country. Meanwhile, assumptions about race shaped training processes – volunteers were sent to live in black communities as part of their 'practical training', on the assumption that these communities and their living conditions resembled those of Sub-Saharan Africa. During placements however,

[4] International volunteers were not only from Northern and Western nations: Cuba has exported doctors and healthcare workers to the developing world as (minimally paid) 'volunteers', providing care and representing the benefits of Cuban socialism.

black volunteers often felt closer to white Peace Corps volunteers than to black Africans with whom they worked; some were not viewed as 'black' in the African communities where they worked, and many were shocked by inter-ethnic prejudice. Meanwhile, as news of the civil rights atrocities reached the African communities where these volunteers worked, these volunteers were sometimes ridiculed and accused of running away from their own problems, or betrayal of the cause.

Michael Jennings' Chapter 5 offers a rich account of the activities of and reception of foreign volunteers in Tanzania. He challenges many of the assumptions we make about international volunteering in the 1960s and 1970s, showing how volunteers were bound up, wittingly and unwittingly, with local and national politics concerning development, and associated struggles over power and prestige. Volunteers, he argues, enjoyed a powerful 'politics of presence' and occupied positions of influence as 'brokers' between donors, national governments and local communities. However, as guests, they were also vulnerable to political manoeuvrings.

Aided by the development of media and increasing ease of global travel, international volunteering by citizens of wealthy countries to countries in the global South continues to be an important, if largely overlooked, phenomenon (McWha 2011; Milligan 2007; Smith & Laurie 2011), and international volunteers continue to wield influence and power, as the chapters by Wig, Sullivan and Wendland et al. demonstrate. Professional volunteering is, moreover, an important component of global humanitarian action. MSF, for example, uses volunteers who are ready to respond to humanitarian emergencies, anywhere and at any time (Redfield 2013b). Unlike the VSO and Peace Corps models of sending volunteers for extended periods of several years, to build something up, these professional volunteers come for short periods of intense intervention (partly because of the nature of the situations – of war and humanitarian emergency – in which they act) creating a 'double bind' between the necessity for mobility and the urgency of local engagement (Redfield 2012). As Peter Redfield argues in the epilogue to this volume, volunteers working under conditions of emergency are particularly vulnerable, yet these very conditions serve to highlight hierarchies of risk and value concerning the bodies, health and lives of local and international volunteers.

Aside from the continuing activities of international voluntary organizations (some of which have become professionalized bureaucracies wielding huge amounts of funding power), there has been a proliferation of all kinds of outfits furnishing volunteers to work on projects in the global South – from ecological and environmental projects (Duffy 2008), to building schools, to providing professional medical services. Often these projects and experiences blur the distinction between volunteering and tourism, which has led to a growing literature on 'voluntourism' (Mostafanezhad 2013a). While some projects furnish young people with the experience of 'Third-World' conditions, others encourage middle-class professionals to combine vacation and volunteering for a good cause. Professionals may spend large sums of money on this kind of work, which often involves hard physical labour. Such projects work by providing affective and meaningful encounters for volunteer tourists, but nevertheless underline political asymmetries and international inequalities (Parreñas 2012; Lorimer 2010).

The phenomenon of gap-year volunteers – usually students and young people who are taking a 'year out' between school and university – is a significant growing category of volunteering in Africa (Fechter 2012a; Jones 2011). Gap-year volunteering is shaped by mixed motivations. The volunteers often want to travel and have fun, and they see voluntary labour as a way of enabling these goals, while also 'doing good' of some kind. However, framed in terms of alleviating poverty rather than addressing inequality, gap-year volunteering appears to support political-economic structures, rather than challenge them. Organized by private, often profit-making companies, gap-year experiences encourage school leavers to believe that paying several thousand pounds to cross the world to build a school is not only a good use of their money but beneficial to the receiving community. Recent critical analyses show how gap-year volunteering is also inflected by the corporate values of individualism and by the desire among young people to improve their career prospects (Simpson 2005; Smith and Laurie 2011). These authors relate the commercialization and popularization of the gap year and other forms of international volunteering to emerging forms of neo-liberal citizenship within which Third-World travel and doing good can demonstrate an interesting well-rounded identity and cultural capital. Meanwhile, gap-year projects perpetuate images of the Third World as sites of 'otherness' and need (Simpson 2004). In this sense the gap year plays upon two distinct registers of difference simultaneously: the geographical and cultural difference between home and the sites of volunteering work, and the difference between the gap-year volunteer and his/her competitors in a future job market, in a labour market shaped by internships and youth travel where the experience gained in jobs such as restaurant and shop work is increasingly viewed as irrelevant (cf. Perlin 2012: xiii).

Economic issues thus saturate practices of international volunteering even while they are submerged by dominant understandings of volunteering as an altruistic, noble act (see Redfield 2012; Wendland et al. Chapter 7). Many of the tensions to which Michael Jennings (Chapter 5) and Ståle Wig (Chapter 3) draw attention – the disparities in economic power and access to resources between international volunteers and local communities, differential power over setting agendas, and the ambiguous role of the volunteer as 'broker' between NGO, state and community, as well as the ambiguous status of volunteer as guest – continue to plague projects using international volunteers.

These tensions are explored by Sullivan (Chapter 6) and Wendland et al. (Chapter 7) with reference to the phenomenon of medical volunteering, or 'clinical tourism' (see also Wendland 2012) by medical students from the global North in African countries – in these cases, Sierra Leone, Malawi and Tanzania. Sullivan points to the ways in which the desire of medical volunteers in Tanzania to 'make a difference' and to see or even participate in medical work, comes into conflict with both the realities of working conditions in hospitals and Tanzanian ideas about the roles of volunteers and the scope of their contributions. Wendland et al. draw attention to the difficulty of talking about these inequalities, and discuss how the moral celebration of 'doing good' silences critical accounts of medical volunteering and flattens out political discussion, limiting possibilities for reflection upon the successes and failures of the diverse projects that fall under the umbrella of medical volunteering.

Conclusion

This volume offers several important perspectives on voluntary labour. First, while volunteering is often surrounded by the rhetoric of service and self-sacrifice, it may benefit the giver as much as the recipient. Second, while the creation of an intimate and value-laden tie between the individual and larger collectives may be central to understandings of volunteering, this tie is often opaque. Volunteering may be driven by political ideals, but the ways in which these relate individual action to larger collectives may be deeply ambiguous. Third, the political value of volunteerism cannot be separated from its economic value: it is presented as a form of unremunerated labour, yet its relation to paid work is ambiguous and its utility within the labour market may be significant. It may be driven more by economic necessity or by hopes to increase one's value in the labour market. Fourth, as volunteering often takes shape across inequalities, it can reinforce differences, between 'us' and 'them'; conceived as a gift, it can reinforce the hierarchy between giver and receiver.

The contributions to this volume highlight the complexities, ambiguities and political importance of voluntary involvements in Africa and they demonstrate the value of an ethnographic approach in exploring volunteer identities and actions within broader political and economic contexts. Studying voluntary work provides insights into the ambiguous separation between paid and unpaid labour, which is particularly significant to those on the peripheries of (or excluded from) the formal labour market. It sheds light upon changing conceptualizations of difference and duty to others, whether difference is configured through relationships between international volunteers and those with whom they work, or between African nationals and the 'communities' they serve. Studying the work of volunteers in development, humanitarianism and emergency response, in 'global health' interventions, and in educational, religious, political and ethical projects, perspectives are offered on changing forms of governance and governmentality, and the ways these relate to struggles around work, identity, professional practice and forms of belonging. The narrative that situates voluntary labour in the immediate post-colonial period within nation building and solidarity is challenged by showing the continuity of earlier forms into the present, and the multiple frameworks underpinning people's desire to volunteer that extend beyond deterministic conceptualizations of a neo-liberal world order.

Volunteering can be a means to shape a new identity, to become more employable, more experienced or a 'better' person. 'Doing good' can transform one's relationship to one's own biography, or help shape a religious orientation and relationship to God. By drawing attention to the diverse motivations of volunteers and the ways in which 'doing good' through the gift of free labour can be promoted to different political and moral causes, this volume makes the case for studying voluntary action as an important social form.

Outline of the book

Part I: Citizenship & Civic Participation
Voluntary labour is often imagined and promoted as an opportunity for citizens to give to each other, nurturing social solidarity, community and citizenship. The first two chapters in this volume explore shifting relationships between states, communities, citizens and volunteers – in post-colonial Tanzania and post-apartheid South Africa. They explore the civic capacities of voluntary labour in contexts where state investment in health care, disease control and sanitation systems is unstable, and where public health problems – malaria control or HIV/AIDS – are increasingly managed by partnerships with transnational institutions.

Christopher Colvin's Chapter 1 examines health volunteerism and HIV/AIDS in South Africa. Looking 'beyond altruism', it asks what other purposes volunteering serves for those with a stake in it, including volunteers themselves, recipients of care, the state, civil society, donors and academics. It also considers the health, social and political effects of health volunteering in South Africa. Like many states in Africa, the South African state remains in ambivalent relationship to civil society and its largely volunteer work force. While health volunteerism has certainly flourished as a result of the HIV epidemic, and played an important part in some of the key political struggles against stigma and for treatment access, it has also unfolded in a fragmented, sometimes chaotic, manner. Colvin concludes that, while volunteers represent a potentially critical resource to states and communities alike, they also represent an important political challenge – how to shape a diverse set of actors and complex mix of intentions towards instrumental health and social goals.

Chapter 2 by Prosper Chaki and Ann Kelly takes the case of community-based malaria control in Dar es Salaam to explore historical shifts in the civic contours of the urban volunteer across the past sixty years, from the early post-colonial period to the present day. They trace the circulation of ideals concerning voluntary action – as 'solidifying imagined communities by nurturing the common good' – from post-war Britain to newly independent Tanzania, where volunteer participation in grassroots development was directed at shaping Tanzanian citizens' relations to each other as well as to the state. Following the work of volunteers responsible for locating, mapping, and eliminating mosquito habitats in the city, they investigate how these participatory – and labour-intensive – activities are being situated within the imperatives of global health research, the structures of municipal governance and the vicissitudes of informal service provision. Volunteers' efforts to knit together these distinct social, political and economic resources elucidate shifting configurations of 'the public' implicit in efforts to bring community-based public health projects to scale.

Part II: Unequal Economies
Part II explores the ambiguities of volunteering when it takes place in low-income settings, where it may provide a valued opportunity to make a livelihood.

Chapter 3 by Ståle Wig explores the contested meanings and uses of money and volunteerism in development assistance. Based on ethnography of a 'rights-based' NGO in Lesotho, Wig describes tensions between Basotho and foreign NGO workers over the provision of cash to members of development projects. While expatriates argue that material inducements corrupt the spirit of volunteerism, Basotho practitioners insist that they are legitimate and necessary. The case shows how certain ambitions for volunteerism face trouble in transnational development encounters, challenging us to consider radically different logics of volunteerism and social assistance.

Drawing on ethnographic fieldwork in Lusaka, Zambia, Birgitte Bruun's Chapter 4 discusses participation in transnational clinical trials and medical research projects. Volunteering in medical research is formally framed by a set of international codes of conduct. Here, altruism figures centrally as an underlying moral assumption; it is imagined that individuals volunteer because they wish to make a contribution to science and public health. At the same time, there are concerns that in resource-poor settings, volunteers may be induced to participate because of perceived material benefits. Following the engagements of low-income Zambian women who volunteer in medical research, Bruun shows that becoming a clinical trial subject is indeed a matter of trying to make a livelihood. However, this extends beyond material concerns to a search for livelihoods in the widest, social sense. Amidst the profound insecurity and contingency that saturate urban life, where a stable income is rare and government healthcare provision tenuous, volunteering presents a possibility both to position oneself as a favoured recipient of care, and to channel this care onwards by sharing knowledge, material benefits, contacts and project openings with one's family, friends and neighbours. In Lusaka, volunteering in transnational medical research is not so much about altruism in the universal sense as it is about the possibility to be cared for and to care for others – and to extend this possibility beyond the time-limitation of a clinical trial.

Part III: Hosts & Guests
This section extends the discussion on the forms of exchange involved in volunteering in Africa and the complex relationships between those who volunteer and those with whom they work. These issues become politically loaded when volunteers from the affluent global North travel to 'resource-poor' settings in the global South, to participate in development or humanitarian projects. Focusing on international volunteers who come to work in Africa, the contributions in this section explore the political and moral economies of volunteering across geographical borders and often sharp gradients of inequality.

In Chapter 5 Michael Jennings interrogates the politics of voluntary work in early independent Tanzania. This period saw an influx of international volunteers into Tanzania, inspired by the radical development philosophy expounded by President Julius Nyerere and his government. Jennings' chapter shows how these volunteers became an important resource for development projects and a site of conflict over how development should be carried out and under whose management. Using archival material to describe conflicts over the control of volunteer labour, Jennings' contribution underlines the significant influence of international volunteering within domestic Tanzanian politics in this period.

Moving to the contemporary period, the next two chapters in this section discuss international volunteering in medical settings. Noelle Sullivan's Chapter 6 offers an extended case study of medical volunteering projects in Tanzania. Drawing attention to the motivations and perspectives of both hosts (Tanzanian medical staff) and guests (Northern medical students) Sullivan shows that, for Tanzanians, interacting with volunteers is tied closely to values of hospitality and hopes for particular imagined futures. Meanwhile, the motivations of foreign clinical volunteers reveal the ways that future medical professionals have internalized the popular discourses and narratives of global health. Analysing the tensions inherent in these different perspectives, Sullivan shows how claims that a foreign volunteer can individually 'make a difference' silence political conversations about global inequalities, aid industry cultures, and the kinds of people and institutions that merit investment.

Chapter 7 by Claire Wendland, Susan Erikson and Noelle Sullivan provides an overview to the complex issues raised by the practices that

Sullivan describes and that Wendland has elsewhere (2012) termed 'clinical tourism'. Their chapter highlights the modalities by which dominant rhetorics of doing good obscure many of the costs and problems of volunteering in these settings. The authors argue that these rhetorics about medical volunteering flatten diverse practices into a single narrative, thus limiting possibilities for learning from both successes and failures in volunteering projects.

Part IV: Moral Journeys
The chapters in the final section turn the perspective towards volunteers themselves, and the kinds of moral journeys and explorations of the self that volunteering makes possible. Bjørn Hallstein Holte's Chapter 8 focuses on elite Kenyan students studying at an international boarding school who volunteer at a Christian Bible Club for children from poor families. These encounters take place across vast socio-economic differences. Holte shows how the practice of volunteering with poor children acts upon the identities of the students, feeding into their formation as elite subjects by affirming the students' privilege and instilling in them dispositions for loving and responsible exercise of it.

Chapter 10 by Thomas Kirsch is an ethnographic account of volunteering work within non-state crime-prevention interventions in post-apartheid South Africa. He explores how the motivation to engage in this kind of volunteer work is discursively framed in the volunteers' autobiographical narratives. Kirsch argues that, rather than thinking about volunteerism through the classic anthropological concepts of helping and/or gift-giving, in this context it is more helpful to explore 'volunteering as repentance', that is, as a public display of expiatory feelings of remorse for actions of the past. Kirsch's analysis underlines how these individual biographies of volunteering shed an important light on challenges to post-Apartheid nation building that concern the contested issue of reconciliation as well as the moralization of citizenship in South Africa.

Epilogue: The Vulnerable Volunteer
Peter Redfield's Epilogue offers a timely reflection on the role played by a voluntary organization, Médecins Sans Frontières (MSF) in the 2014–15 Ebola epidemic in Sierra Leone, Guinea and Liberia. Redfield argues that concerns and dilemmas surrounding volunteers' bodily vulnerability and risk of infection reflect a scaling of risk along lines of geography and a hierarchy of lives valued. This case underlines the complexities, ambiguities and unresolved paradoxes that saturate the field of voluntary labour and its deployment across the globe. Redfield pulls together the volume through the interrogation of a theme that, in different ways, runs through all the contributions to this book. He reminds us that organized volunteering has significant limits as a tool oriented towards the public good. We should be wary of an unmitigated celebration of the multi-faceted moral and political dimensions of volunteer economies.

PART ONE ▌ Citizenship & Civic Participation

1

The Many Uses of Moral Magnetism

CHRISTOPHER J. COLVIN[1]

Volunteer Caregiving
& the HIV/AIDS
Epidemic in South Africa

Getting on the map

I first met Nolwazi Skweyiya several years ago during an evaluation of government efforts in South Africa's Western Cape Province to support the community-based response to the HIV/AIDS epidemic. The provincial government had money from the Global Fund to Fight AIDS, Tuberculosis and Malaria to provide seed funding for projects run by small community-based organizations (CBOs) and larger NGOs. These projects were supposed to mobilize volunteer support within communities to aid those infected and affected by HIV.

When we first met, Nolwazi was managing a relatively large volunteer operation from her two-roomed shack in a township on the edge of Cape Town. Her CBO, Sinethemba Support Organisation, had fourteen home-based carers (HBCs) who cared for HIV-positive community members in their homes, a team of eight young sexual health peer educators who counselled friends at school about HIV, sexually transmitted infections (STIs) and pregnancy, and three women who managed an informal day-care centre for local mothers who could not afford formal childcare. These volunteers also distributed 150 food parcels each month: packages of flour, sugar, rice and oil that were provided by the Department of Social Development (DSD) to qualifying families in the area.

Nolwazi had been running Sinethemba since 1999, long before the Global Fund initiative had arrived. When she started the group, she was living in an even smaller shack in the backyard of a neighbour's plot. The effects of the HIV epidemic were just starting to be felt in her impoverished community and in the absence of any coherent government or civil society response to the growing catastrophe, she and many women

[1] I am grateful to the many CBO, NGO and activist organisations and volunteers with whom I have worked, to Steven Robins, Alison Swartz and Natalie Leon for comments on earlier drafts, and to the National Institutes of Health in the United States for financial support (Award #: R24HD077976).

like her started caring for their sick neighbours and enlisting others, often from their churches, to help.

At first, her efforts were informal and took place amidst her other obligations to her husband and two children and the domestic cleaning work she did three times a week for a family in a middle-class suburb. Her volunteer work grew rapidly, however, and she soon started working nearly full time along with two other women from her church. They in turn recruited others who helped out on a more part-time basis. These volunteers often left as soon as opportunities for paid work came along but as soon as one person left, Nolwazi told me, there always seemed to be someone else 'with a heart for the community, for the suffering people'.

She received occasional support and donations from her employer in the suburbs and after a couple years, developed a formal working relationship with the local government clinic in her area. There was no funding available for her project work but the relationship did make referrals easier for the people she was caring for and her volunteers were offered trainings by clinic staff in infection control, first aid, nutrition, and adherence counselling for antiretroviral therapy (ART).

Her first contact with the Global Fund programme was through a new consultative body set up by the initiative called the Multi-Sectoral Action Team (or MSAT). The MSATs were set up as a way of getting CBOs, NGOs and local government representatives together on a monthly basis to coordinate the community-level response to the epidemic. Although these meetings were intended to be a form of 'grassroots participation', government officials often didn't show up and, when they did, it was mostly to recruit volunteers to participate in one of the regularly scheduled 'health theme days' (such as National Tuberculosis Day or AIDS Day). These meetings did, however, bring Nolwazi into fruitful engagement with a wide range of other civil society, faith-based and activist organizations she had not met previously. These contacts in turn translated into further training opportunities, a series of project collaborations, and the occasional chance to apply for funding.

The Global Fund project did eventually fund some of her HBC volunteers, offering them small daily stipends, some basic supplies like gloves and condoms, and transport money. When I first met her, the DSD had also started giving stipends to volunteers who distributed the food parcels. Six months later, however, DSD officials abruptly ended their stipend programme at about the same time that the Global Fund project cycle was over. Nolwazi was left unable to fund the more than a dozen HBCs who had been receiving small but significant payments for the last year. She told me she didn't know what she was going to do but that perhaps she could find some different work for them. She knew the clinic was looking for lay counsellors to do pre- and post-test counselling for HIV testing. She thought that maybe some researchers she had met the previous year would be looking for translators or field assistants.

During our last visit, about a year after we first met, Nolwazi told me that she had managed to keep most of her volunteers on but that they were now involved in a sewing project designed to generate income for both volunteers and the HIV-positive community members they helped. Before I left, she took me back to her bedroom in the back of her house and pulled a thick binder off a bookshelf. Opening it up, she showed me pages and pages of certificates of completion from workshops, letters of appreciation from local business, clinics, and NGOs, workbooks from training courses, and consent forms from research projects in which she had participated.

After I had paged through these accomplishments, with a final flourish, she pointed proudly to photographs on her wall of her standing with the Premier of the Western Cape (the provincial political leader), with U2's lead singer Bono, and with President Bill Clinton, each of whom had visited her small project during different tours of HIV community initiatives. She said she didn't know how they found her. She also said she didn't know the funding she received was from the Global Fund but thought rather than it was merely from the municipal health budget. When I asked how her project was going to survive in the coming year without Global Fund or DSD money, she pointed to the photographs and said that she now felt she was 'on the map' and she was sure that they would remember her and her project when the time came.

Beyond altruism

Nolwazi's story condenses the complicated experiences of many health volunteers working in South Africa after the end of apartheid. Driven by a mix of longstanding crises of social and economic reproduction and the new catastrophe of HIV/AIDS, volunteers like Nolwazi have cobbled together a wide range of responses to meet the urgent needs in their communities. In the context of health systems and labour markets that have failed to sustain their lives and their livelihoods, they offer care, support, encouragement, advice and often money from their own pockets to help those around them.

These initiatives have also brought volunteers into contact with a wide range of actors, many of whom they may otherwise have never have met, including patients and other community members, churches, government officials and politicians, healthcare workers, academics, NGO staff, foreign students, and even celebrities. Though these new relationships are numerous and often novel, for most volunteers, they are also not that durable, and they are shot through with a complicated mix of agendas and motives.

There is a similar ambivalence in volunteers' engagement with trainings, workshops, and meetings. They often have the opportunity to participate in these events and are optimistic that their newly acquired knowledge will translate into new work opportunities. But these efforts rarely seem to help volunteers gain a foothold in what is an increasingly professionalized civil society. These workshops may help them in their daily volunteer work with those with HIV but the jump to more sustainable, and paid, work is generally too far to manage.

When volunteers discover that their new relationships or training opportunities don't readily translate into tangible personal gain, they have a ready consolation at hand. They remind themselves, and others, that they are not doing this for personal benefit but out of a desire to serve their community. This is, of course, the most common and most socially acceptable explanation one can give about why volunteers do what they do. Altruism is at the core of the modern Western notion of volunteerism. Even in African contexts, where the potential material and political valences of volunteering are so much more apparent, this rhetoric of altruism still holds great sway. Others chapters in this volume, including those from Chaki & Kelly, from Wig and from Bruun, attest to the power of this altruistic imperative, to the 'moral magnetism' of volunteer work (Eliasoph, 2011), even in contexts where the material needs of volunteers are as desperate as those of the people they are serving.

To be sure, much of Nolwazi's motivation and her success over time is driven by her altruism, by what I can only assume is a sincere empathy for and commitment to alleviate the suffering of others. Volunteers like Nolwazi frame these altruistic intentions through a number of discourses. They refer to *ubuntu*, constructed as an African form of community-minded humanism, or to Christian or Islamic principles of service and sacrifice, or to gendered assumptions about the inability of women to ignore suffering (Swartz 2012).

But altruism is clearly an insufficient explanation for the complex forms of social relationship, political practice, and moral meaning-making that can be seen in Nolwazi's story. Volunteerism may often be underpinned by an altruistic impulse but altruism cannot adequately account for how volunteerism emerges, what it signifies and how it articulates with other moral, social and political projects in the lives of volunteers. To really understand what drives volunteerism, what shapes its forms, and its wider significance, we need to look much more closely at how those involved in volunteerism make use of this novel form of caring practice.

This chapter therefore examines the many uses volunteering is put to by the various actors involved. After a sketch of the recent past and present of volunteering in South Africa, it is divided into several sections that explore some of the functions that volunteering serves for those with a stake in it, including the volunteers themselves, the recipients of care, the state, civil society, donors and academics. It concludes by asking what effect these forms of health volunteering have had in South Africa and what the shape of health volunteerism after apartheid tells us about the broader context in South Africa, Africa as a whole, and globally. In particular, it examines how volunteering operates both as a site and as a mechanism of neo-liberal forms of governance.

The chapter's interpretations of volunteering are rooted in a reflection on and synthesis of a wide range of experiences I have had with health volunteers and volunteering in South Africa over the last fourteen years. Most of this engagement has been in my role as an anthropologist and public health researcher examining community and health system responses to HIV/AIDS. I have worked with very small CBOs such as two-person soup kitchens, a men's HIV support group and informal day-care centres, with faith-based organizations that run HIV workshops and support groups, with larger service-oriented NGOs that manage home-based care groups and peer educators, and with activist NGOs like the Treatment Action Campaign (TAC), the People's Health Movement (PHM) and the Social Justice Coalition (SJC). I have also participated as a board member of several of these organizations. Finally, as the director of a community health-themed study abroad programme, I have hosted and supervised numerous student volunteers from overseas.

Most of this experience has been in Cape Town, but I have also worked in rural areas in the Western Cape as well as extensive periods in rural areas in Mpumalanga and Limpopo Province as well as the cities of Johannesburg and Bloemfontein. A limitation of many of the shorter-term studies and volunteering experiences reviewed here is that they are focused largely on the organizational and institutional contexts in which volunteers work. They therefore speak less to how volunteering articulates with the everyday lives of volunteers in family and community contexts. (See Le Marcis, 2012 for a discussion of the relationships between the organizational and the everyday.) With the exception of the longer-term ethnographic work I have done with volunteers, I have generally spent more time with volunteers in these work settings and less time in other settings. Though my conclusions are drawn from this broad range of research projects and personal experiences, much of the narrative below is illustrated with examples from Nolwazi's group, Sinethemba, and, to a lesser extent, examples from Khululeka, a men's HIV support group with whom I have done ethnographic work off and on for several years.

Health volunteerism, past and present

Organized health-related volunteering during most of the twentieth century primarily took the form of community health workers (CHWs) in primary health care programmes. The 1930s and 1940s saw a range of progressive health reforms that brought effective preventive and curative health care closer to communities. CHWs and other community-based healthcare workers were an important part of these initiatives (Jeeves 2000; Marks 1997). Sidney and Emily Kark, for example, developed rural health centres in the Natal Province that were staffed by nurses, nurse assistants and CHWs; they were early pioneers in what would later come to be called the primary health care movement (Marks & Andersson 1992; Tollman & Pick 2002).

The rise of the National Party to government leadership in 1948, however, spelt the reversal of these reforms and an increasing segregation and neglect of healthcare for black communities. The 1950s and 1960s represented a long period of decline for community-oriented public health and medical care efforts (ibid.). CHW programmes and other progressive public health initiatives languished or disappeared.

In the 1970s and 1980s, however, the growing sense of militancy and crisis that was developing within South African communities and the government itself led to a renewed phase of CHW programmes. This new phase was inspired in large part by political resistance to apartheid and a sense that the conflict would soon be over; (this description of CHW programmes in the 1970s and 1980s is drawn largely from van Ginneken et al.'s very useful 2010 survey of CHWs in this period). These CHW programmes were generally initiated by white medical professionals in South Africa who saw their commitment to improving public health in black communities as part of the broader struggle against the apartheid government. Despite the impact of international sanctions that restricted the flow of information and technology into the country, many of these initiatives were able to develop appropriate training programmes and make effective use of available technology to improve health. Their funding came from both local and international sources but generally had few strings attached. Programmes were thus able to use their resources creatively and flexibly.

Many of those involved in the progressive public health movements in the 1970s and 1980s had great hopes that with the end of apartheid, these innovative approaches to community health would be taken up by the new government. They saw a window of opportunity for the development of not only an effective CHW cadre country-wide but also a comprehensive primary health care system that was decentralized, locally responsive and holistic in its approach. Unfortunately, the new government incorporated relatively few of these core primary health care principles. Post-apartheid health system reform took a primarily technicist and vertical (disease-specific) approach and CHWs were left out of health policy (Coovadia et al. 2010).

Rather than disappearing again, however, as they had done in the 1950s and 1960s, CHWs soon mushroomed in South Africa, driven by both the explosive impact of the HIV epidemic and the near non-response to the epidemic on the part of the Mbeki administration. As the Department of Health under Mbeki dragged its feet on HIV prevention, care and treatment, and got caught in a long-running battle with AIDS activists over AIDS denialism and the provision of ART, a huge health need emerged in communities hit by the disease. CBOs, NGOs and foreign donors quickly rushed in to fill the gap. In the space of a few years, thousands of CBOs and NGOs emerged performing all kinds of volunteer work and millions of Rand were funnelled directly to programmes working with communities affected by the epidemic, often bypassing the national government entirely.

While this response was responsible for filling the vacuum left by the government at a critical stage and brought relief to millions of people, it has also had a range of less beneficial effects. CHW and other health-related NGO and CBO programmes rapidly proliferated during the 2000s, resulting in the fragmentation and verticalisation of care, the duplication of services, competition between providers for funding and for patients, and rapidly increasing numbers of CHWs, often poorly trained and ineffectively supervised (Schneider et al. 2008). Recent estimates are that there were 60,000 CHWs in the country in 2009. This is in contrast to only 40,000 professional nurses working in the public sector. Most of these CHWs (up to 80 per cent according to some accounts) are working on HIV- and tuberculosis-specific programmes, performing a wide range of duties including HIV test counselling, awareness raising and education, adherence counselling, and home-based and hospice care (Lehmann et al. 2009).

Of course, CHWs are not the only kind of volunteers to have emerged in response to the HIV epidemic. There are many other types of volunteers engaged in the 'new struggle' against HIV including peer educators, child welfare volunteers, HIV and gender activists, life and jobs skills trainers, and school gardeners promoting good nutrition and food security, to name just a few. Many of these volunteers come from affected communities but many also come from without. Middle-class student volunteers from South Africa and, even more so, from abroad, are a familiar presence at many organizations. So too are researchers who volunteer their expertise in support of NGO and community initiatives. Churches with congregants from wealthy suburbs have also developed a strong volunteer presence in a number of townships through their HIV programming. There are even for-profit small businesses in Cape Town and Johannesburg that will, for a fee, arrange a packaged volunteer experience for foreign students.

While some of these programmes have tried to market themselves as addressing more than just HIV – in order to avoid stigma or promote a broader notion of public health – it really is the HIV epidemic that has been behind this burgeoning of volunteer energy and activity in South Africa in the last fifteen years. The result has been a rapid proliferation of civil-society initiatives from numerous sectors that make use of a diverse set of volunteers to address the dramatic toll of the epidemic.

If HIV was the catalyst for most of this work, and altruism was the motive that underpinned much of it, there is still a great deal more we can learn about what volunteering has meant in this context, why it has taken the particular forms it has, what impacts it has had on individuals, communities and the state, and what all of this signifies about the broader social and political conditions of possibility in post-apartheid South Africa. The remainder of this chapter addresses these questions by asking how volunteering has proven useful to those involved in this complex and wide-ranging enterprise.

Crises of social and economic reproduction: the productive power of volunteering

If altruism is the most commonly cited – and most socially acceptable – answer to the question of why people volunteer, the second most common answer, especially in African contexts, is that volunteers see their engagement as a means of developing skills, networks, experience and job opportunities. Volunteering here is (also) strategic, motivated by personal benefit and the urgent need in many of these contexts to secure social and economic reproduction in any way possible (see Ståle Wig's Chapter 3 for an example of how these material logics of volunteering came into sharp relief in the encounter between local and foreign NGO staff in Lesotho).

In most of the programmes I have worked with, the material benefits of volunteering represent a strong incentive. With the exception of adult, middle-class volunteers, most of those I have engaged with have material needs that volunteering provides some response to. These benefits include not only longer-term advantages such as on-the-job training or widening of social networks; they also include the small 'stipends' sometimes paid to volunteers, meals and refreshment offered at meetings, airtime for their phone, transport subsidies, access to reading materials or equipment and supplies, and sometimes just a safe social environment in which to spend time.

While the material benefits in many programmes can be considerable for volunteers coming from the same impoverished communities, this incentive is nonetheless often strongly downplayed by the volunteers I have met. For one, despite the justification volunteers from poor communities might rightly feel in taking advantage of these few benefits, the social pressure to prove the purity of one's moral intent is strong. Moreover, as described above, volunteers make use of a wide range of discursive frameworks to locate this altruism, including Christian service, kinship commitments, community values, gender and *ubuntu* (Swartz 2013; de Wet 2012).

This need to demonstrate one's good moral intention, however, does not simply reflect a conceptual conflict between the moral ends of altruism and personal benefit. In a context of scarce resources and frequent social conflict and mistrust, expressions of altruism become a way both to insulate one from charges of greed and self-advancement as well as to compete for scarce volunteer opportunities. In the Khululeka Men's Support Group, for example, where HIV-positive men gathered twice a week to discuss their treatment, support each other and do community outreach, there was a constant fear that member-volunteers in the group would secretly attend other HIV support groups in the area, especially ones that had access to food parcels or money for refreshments or transport. The group's leader, Phumzile Nywagi, expressed concern that these men were not in the group for altruistic reasons but rather were simply looking for access to material resources. He questioned their commitment to the support group and worried that this kind of behaviour would ultimately undermine the solidarity of its members. He also worried that better-funded support groups might siphon off volunteers who were weak in their commitment to the service principles of Khululeka. He described his best members as those who would 'never take a food parcel' from another organization. Though Phumzile's moral commitment to selfless service was a vital component of his work with Khululeka, he also used the moral discourse of altruism to both promote social cohesion within the group of volunteers and ensure that he maintained sufficient numbers of active members (an important element when it came time to fundraise for the group).

Nolwazi demonstrated a similar logic when the DSD sharply reduced their funding for volunteers who were delivering food parcels. Faced with the choice of cutting stipends completely to all but two of her senior volunteers, or cutting the stipends for everyone by 80 per cent, she chose to cut everyone's stipend by the same amount. She ended up losing only one volunteer out of twelve, instead of the ten she feared would leave if offered no stipend. The one who left was described as someone who 'didn't have that feeling of other people in her heart'. Social cohesion among the group members proved more important a resource for Nolwazi and her members than the short-term benefit of a few senior volunteers.

Material conditions and deprivations therefore are both a powerful inducement for individuals to volunteer as well as a powerful constraint on how much that motivation can be expressed. In a context where everyone is looking for access to resources and everyone is strongly dependent on and vulnerable to each other, expressions of personal gain and ambition are dangerous. By contrast, expressions of altruism have both a moral magnetism as well as a strategic usefulness.

Volunteering also had strategic powers, however, beyond just the material needs of the individual and the small group of volunteers. I have described elsewhere (Colvin 2012) how activist volunteers for the TAC sometimes clashed in community settings with volunteers from the AIDS denialist group, the Matthias Rath Foundation. I first heard about this conflict from Phumzile, when he warned members of Khululeka not to be taken in by Rath and his promises of miracle vitamin cures for HIV. He argued that Rath was promoting his alternative to ART in order to make money out of people's desperation and implied that some Khululeka members had already been seen talking with 'Rath's people'. He warned that this 'war' between TAC and Rath was dangerous and that only TAC and Khululeka really felt the people's suffering. He later described to me two confrontations between groups of TAC and Rath volunteers where supporters from one side cornered supporters from the other in a house and chanted and danced outside, threatening violence. What was at stake here was not merely the policing of personal gain or the promotion of solidarity within close social networks. It also wasn't just an expression of ideological conflict between HIV activists and denialists. This dramatic clash over AIDS science was indeed playing itself out in the streets and newspapers and courts across the country. But these local-level conflicts between volunteers were about something else as well. They were expressions of local political tensions between communities, between internal factions in the African National Congress (ANC), and between different governance structures in communities that were competing for access to power at the community level. Local dynamics and tensions around political patronage and social and economic obligation were therefore being played out by these volunteers. Participation as a volunteer was taken as a form of support for one side or the other in these conflicts.

Just as Nolwazi's volunteers maintained cohesion and mutuality in their relationships with each other by all taking a deep cut in their stipends, both individuals and organizations use volunteering as a way to establish a broad array of relationships of dependence and obligation. Some of these relationships could be glossed generically as forms of bonding social capital, relationships to others within immediate social networks that act as resources for people in times of need (Putnam 2000). Or they might, as James Ferguson has argued (2007), reflect more culturally and historically specific modes of service, and servitude, between individuals. But these relationships of dependence and obligation are not just between individuals. Broader community structures and forces are at play here and volunteering in this context proves useful in building and defending a range of social and political allegiances and claims.

Re-inventing self and other: identity work and relationship building through volunteering

In addition to fulfilling motives of altruism, and responding to the daily struggle for social and economic reproduction in families and communities, volunteering has also served a range of other functions for individuals. For many, volunteering is a way to rehabilitate stigmatized and spoiled identities and produce and support new forms of relationship that otherwise would be hard to sustain.

Probably the most striking example of this has been how volunteering in HIV programmes offered a way for those infected with the virus to transform, to some extent, a stigmatized social identity into a positive one. Many NGOs working in HIV actively sought out HIV-positive volunteers as both a moral imperative to support those with the virus and because HIV-positive volunteers were thought to be better able to understand and connect with the people they were caring for. For many individuals, participation in volunteer activities gave them a strong sense of purpose and contribution, a visible, positive role to play in the community, and a group of people to belong to and draw comfort and meaning from. These were precisely the elements that were so often withdrawn from and denied to those with HIV, leading to the kind of 'social death' (Robins, 2006) that could long precede physical death.

TAC's famous purple tee-shirts emblazoned with the words 'HIV-POSITIVE' are probably the most prominent example of how volunteering could help transform damaged identities but this dynamic was also expressed in a range of other ways in most of the projects with which I worked. Sometimes this identity work was explicit, as in the case of TAC members, or with Khululeka volunteers who adopted an open and proud display of their group membership through tee-shirts, banners and singing. In other contexts, it was more implicit, as with Nolwazi's volunteers who earned a quiet but significant satisfaction in the ways community members treated and spoke about them differently after they started performing home-based care work.

There were, of course, limits to these transformations. TAC members were sometimes attacked despite the prominence, popularity and power of their movement. Khululeka members confidently performed their membership in the group and their HIV status while on outreach activities in other townships but were significantly more subdued when around close family and friends in the neighbourhoods where they lived. Stigma has certainly not disappeared from South Africa in spite of the sea change in government policy and rhetoric, and the transformative powers of ART (Campbell et al. 2005; Robins 2006). Nonetheless, volunteering for an HIV CBO or NGO provided for many people one of the few avenues for rehabilitation of social identities damaged by infection.

Volunteering could also serve as a way of restoring some dignity to damaged masculine identities. The men in Khululeka, in particular, expressed frustration at the ways they were stigmatized by family, friends and community members as pathological vectors of the HI virus, as 'typical men' who were irresponsible, promiscuous and disease-spreading. Most members did not deny that their previous sexual behaviour put them at great risk of both contracting and transmitting the disease and led to a great deal of unnecessary suffering. But their participation in the group centred in large part on providing them ways to perform a new role and identity, one that was newly responsible, avoided alcohol and unprotected sex, and respected the rights of women.

Volunteering also sometimes helped these men compensate for another damaged part of their identity as men – their status as unemployed and their inability to contribute financially to their families. The material benefits of participating in Khululeka were few and far between but men spoke often of how even being able to bring home a few vegetables or 10 Rand of airtime or a plate of food from a community awareness event brought them some small measure of recognition in their families as a positive contribution (Colvin et al. 2010).

Finally, volunteering provided a powerful way to resist old identities and build new relationships across lines of race and class. One feature of many of the CBOs I have worked with is the presence of a 'champion', usually a white woman from a middle-class suburb who takes responsibility for sustaining the programme by training and energizing volunteers, raising funds, writing business plans and dealing with government paperwork. Many of the smallest CBOs in rural communities, at least the ones that were sustainable over time, often had such a champion working in the background. In these cases, one can see the operation of the logic of 'volunteering as repentance' that Thomas Kirsch explores at length in Chapter 9.

Nolwazi's neighbour down the street, Sisanda, ran a small CBO that had such a champion. Sisanda had worked as a domestic cleaner for a woman named Evelyn for sixteen years. During the first five years of their relationship, Sisanda would tell Evelyn about the needs in her community and occasionally receive donations of old clothing, dishes or appliances. Eventually, however, Evelyn, along with members of her church, decided to help Sisanda set up a 'community project' that would offer low-cost day care and a soup kitchen to needy families in her area. Though Evelyn initially conceived of the money she gave as a way to kick-start something that Sisanda would take charge of, the project seem to inspire Evelyn and she soon became involved in its day-to-day management. She solicited funders in the private sector, helped Sisanda with government paperwork and day-care regulations, managed the financial reporting process, and held an annual day of appreciation and cookout for Sisanda's volunteers at her comfortable home in a middle-class suburb. For Evelyn, this was the first time she had hosted black South Africans at her house as guests rather than as workers.

This volunteer work was clearly important to these middle-class supporters, not only as a form of altruism but as a structured opportunity for the development of social relationships that otherwise were very unlikely to emerge. It also served a powerful function symbolically for these women in terms of helping to perform a kind of 'repentance' and rehabilitate a damaged racial identity that typically cast them as the uncaring and entitled 'white madam'.

Young, middle-class South Africans are another, more racially diverse group of people who seem to find similar benefits in relationship building and identity work through volunteer activities. There are a number of activist NGOs in Cape Town, like the Social Justice Coalition (SJC) and Equal Education, that are driven by young, middle-class men and women from the suburbs but operate in township communities. There are also several national initiatives to inspire young South Africans who have emigrated to return to the country and offer their support and skills through volunteering in social and economic development efforts.

To be sure, these efforts are always shot through with histories of raced, classed and gendered oppression. These volunteers can be naïve and uninformed about the contexts in which they work, and over-estimate the meaning of the relationships they form. They often explain and justify their work as part of a common religious duty or moral imperative, or as an effort to reach a kind of sunny, liberal reconciliation between former antagonists. At their worst, these efforts can become a convenient way for those with continuing racial privilege to trumpet their work 'in the community' and paper over persisting forms of structural violence in which they are implicated.

However, to stop at such a cynical reading of volunteer work across class and colour bars seems insufficient, and it misses the pointed fact that in South Africa, outside of volunteering, there are few opportunities for people across these structural divides to engage with each other directly and positively. Political parties are still largely segregated by race and class, and the work environment often actively reproduces these boundaries rather than challenging them. Although religion is one point of common ground among many South Africans, it is generally only in the context of church volunteer activities that believers from different social groupings get together.

New forms of political subjectivity: better living through volunteer participation

This discussion of the forms, functions and impacts of volunteering has so far focused on individuals, civil-society organizations and the community contexts in which they live and work. There are other stakeholders, however, for whom health volunteer programmes serve important purposes. These include the state, the 'development community' (comprising donor countries, bilateral and multilateral aid programmes, and development professionals), biomedical professionals and academic researchers, and activists. In some cases, volunteers serve an immediate, practical purpose for these stakeholders by performing necessary caring labour or carrying out development initiatives. In other cases, they serve a longer-term agenda having to do with the inculcation of new forms of medical and political subjectivity.

Volunteers, for example, have become a central figure in the state and development community's promotion of 'community-led development', a notion of development that privileges 'grassroots participation' and consultation in political and policy decision making (Lovan et al. 2004). Like the discourse of participation and empowerment in the US that Eliasoph (2011) describes as 'empowerment talk', this notion of community-led development seeks to empower communities to be 'actively' involved in and take 'ownership' of their own social and economic development (see Brown & Green 2015 for a recent discussion of these issues in East Africa).

Though not explicitly framed as a process dependent on volunteers, in South Africa, the spaces for political participation that the government has tried to promote tend to rely on an intermediate layer of CBOs and NGOs to provide the structure and context for what gets rendered as 'consultation' between community and state. In health, this has taken a number of forms. The narrative about Sinethemba that opened this chapter introduced the Multi-Sectoral Action Teams (MSATs) that the Western Cape Province set up in an effort to connect communities, civil society and the state. Nolwazi was a member of her local MSAT and had received funding from the Global Fund via this body. Phumzile also joined the MSAT in his area when he discovered there were funding opportunities connected with participation. He also hoped to encourage the provision of 'male-friendly' STI and HIV services at his local clinic by participating on the committee. The assumption behind the MSAT programme was, of course, that the CBOs and NGOs that participate in them would, in turn, represent the broader communities in which they served, a dubious assumption at best. Nonetheless, it was about the only forum in which people living and working in a community could have the chance of accessing local decision makers in the state.

The local clinic health committees (CHCs) in South Africa are another example of the use of volunteers and NGO/CBO structures as a vehicle for political participation. These CHCs are supposed to be set up for every clinic in the country and are supposed to provide a form of local governance and oversight over health services in their area. Again, they are composed entirely of volunteers who commit to coming to monthly meetings and representing various sectors of their community. In most places, they operate with no budget for meeting expenses and CBO and NGO representation tends to dominate on most CHCs (Padarath & Friedman 2008).

Though often framed as a forum for consultation and engagement with the broader community, these forms of political participation in fact are channelled through layers of ad hoc committees, unelected advisory groups, and weakly supported representative bodies like the MSATs and CHCs. These structures often struggle to get their own volunteers to meetings on time much less represent broad community input. The MSATs themselves were initiated out of a recognition of the failure of an earlier scheme to create Local AIDS Councils and a Provincial AIDS Council. CHCs in most communities in the country are either non-existent or dysfunctional. These 'middle spaces' of political participation have generally not been that effective (Thompson & Tapscott 2010). The state, however, seems to continue to be committed to this particular model of community empowerment and participation.

While the state has sought but struggled to use volunteers to enable political participation, the state has been more successful in making use of volunteer labour to meet the health needs of its population. Even during the Mbeki administration's general neglect of health services for those with HIV/AIDS, NGO- and CBO-sponsored CHWs filled a considerable gap in addressing health needs and taking pressure off of the health system. Recently, there have been moves by the subsequent administration of President Jacob Zuma to 're-engineer' the primary healthcare system and formally integrate CHWs into the Department of Health. Despite real concerns about the costs and feasibility of such a move, there now seems to be an unexpected optimism in many quarters of the state that integrating CHWs into the public service will be an effective way to deal with the long-term health demands of a chronic HIV epidemic. There is also a concern in the background that as CHWs transition in this plan from being community volunteers to something like formal healthcare workers, the powerful unions in the country will organize them, raising the potential costs of CHWs considerably. The state seems to want to get ahead of the curve here and regulate and capture the productive value of volunteer labour as efficiently as possible.

Volunteers, though, not only serve a potentially practical function for the state in terms of direct service provision. They are also figure importantly in the development of what has been referred to as 'therapeutic', 'biological' or 'health' forms of citizenship (Nguyen et al. 2007; Petryna 2002; Porter 2011). This is a form of liberal governmentality in which individuals come to frame their engagements with and claims on the state through a language of biological health, biomedical protocols, and scientific knowledge. In Northern contexts like the US and Europe, these forms of citizenship don't necessarily rely on volunteer labour for their reproduction (though health social movements in the North have been one important vehicle for these forms of biopolitical subjectivity – Brown et al. 2006). In Africa, however, given the weakness of many states, the lack of biomedical services and technology, and low levels of health and scientific literacy, it has often fallen to civil society, and by extension, the volunteer, to be the critical vector for these new forms of political and medical understanding.

In Sinethemba, for example, Nolwazi's volunteers attended regular trainings at the local clinic on infection control, safe sex practices, and ART treatment adherence and were tasked by the clinic nurses with ensuring 'their patients' understood and followed this advice. These volunteers also assisted community members with accessing clinic services and with making applications for disability and other welfare grants that have medical criteria for receiving benefits.

Similarly, Khululeka members often encouraged an elaborate form of self and group discipline around members' adherence to ART. On arrival at their meetings, each member would be required to write their latest CD4 blood count and their next clinic appointment date up on a large sheet of paper on the wall. Those members who didn't have this information were encouraged to pay closer attention to their treatment protocols and progress. Those who were able to maintain high CD4 counts and consistent clinic visits over time were celebrated.

It is conventional perhaps to read these practices as forms of Foucauldrian self-disciplining into particular regimes of knowledge and political governance. In this reading, patients are taught to accept and even embrace the authority of medical knowledge, and by extension, the authority of the state that provides medical intervention. They spend a great deal of time policing their health and health behaviours, ensuring that they are both responsible patients and good citizens. There is indeed a strong element of self-policing and subjugation to scientific and state authority in these accounts. In this sense, they reflect part of the state's broader efforts to frame its public health policies and obligations along narrow, technicist lines.

Activists, however, have also been quite successful in using the form and substance of health citizenship practices to achieve their own political goals. TAC, again, is perhaps most well-known in this respect through its promotion of 'treatment literacy practitioners' (TLPs), lay volunteers, usually HIV positive, who are trained to educate patients with HIV to a relatively advanced level of scientific understanding of ART, including the different classes of antiretroviral drugs (ARVs) and their mechanisms, the form and function of different immune system cells, and the treatment alternatives that are possible when side effects emerge. TAC's argument, largely borne out in its political successes, was that patients with very low levels of formal education can be educated to take their treatment effectively and that this process of education would empower them and help build the political movement for free treatment access.

The SJC has adopted a similar strategy. SJC is a new, relatively small but surprisingly effective NGO that works in informal settlements in Cape Town's townships to address the interrelated issues of access to sanitation and security. People living in these areas have very little access to proper sanitation and are vulnerable to violent crime when they seek out toilet facilities far from their houses. SJC engages with the City of Cape Town to improve the level of services available in these areas and has often found itself disputing the official statistics the City uses to claim its service delivery is at appropriate levels. Rather than asking the City or outside experts to redo these figures, SJC has trained its volunteers to produce regular monitoring reports and self-census data on toilet access, health outcomes and sexual violence in their communities. They have begun producing their own systematic data on these issues, using community volunteers to collect and interpret it on a weekly basis, and have challenged the City to make use of the much more up-to-date information SJC has produced. This effort has both encouraged the community to be more invested in who produces knowledge about their community and forced the state to recognize and address gaps in its service delivery.

In both examples, it is critical to activists' strategy that volunteers, rather than paid staff or outside experts, take on the role of producing and making use of scientific knowledge. Rather than mere consumers of expert knowledge from the state or the academy, community volunteers with SJC produce and then use scientific knowledge, and the authority that it carries with it, to their own political ends. While neither case challenges (but rather reinforces) the authority of scientific knowledge and its use as a tool of governance, it does show that the political effects of this form of governance are not necessarily predictable, nor do they operate in only one direction.

The figure of the volunteer thus proves valuable to a wide range of stakeholders beyond the immediate web of community relations. The state and development community relies on civil-society volunteers to produce the effect of political participation and empowerment (even when it is more illusion than reality). The state relies on volunteers more directly to deliver actual caring labour, labour that some might argue is rightly the responsibility of the state itself and not unpaid volunteers. Volunteers also help to produce new forms of medical and political subjectivity in this context, doing much of the work of training citizens into new forms of medical knowledge and (self) regulation. Finally, activists have attempted to harness the power of these authoritative forms of biomedical knowledge and subjectivity and put them to their own political ends.

Volunteering in global scientific knowledge production

There is another set of actors, often working beyond national borders, for whom health volunteers serve an important purpose – the producers of scientific biomedical and global health knowledge. While states and activists try to mobilize scientific knowledge and its authority to serve a variety of local and national political projects, producers of this knowledge often use volunteers to serve more global scientific, institutional and economic ends.

Perhaps the most familiar intersection between volunteerism and scientific knowledge production is the figure of the clinical trial participant. Much has been written recently on the globalization of clinical trials and the ways in which these global scientific enterprises seek out new volunteer populations and end up creating in some places quite durable local 'trial communities' thick with social relations, meanings and expectations (Nguyen 2011; Petryna 2009; Reynolds 2012; see also Birgitte Bruun's Chapter 4).

South Africa, with its combination of very high HIV burden and well-developed research and medical infrastructure, has been one of the focal points for this globalization of medical experimentation in the context of HIV. Volunteers who have participated in clinical trials for vaccines,

48   *Christopher J. Colvin*

other prevention technologies or treatment regimens can be found in most communities. The relationships that develop out of the performance of these trials do in fact persist in many places, as do the expectations among participants that they will gain some direct benefit from these trials or, if not, that they are at least 'on the map', as Nolwazi said, of those researchers with whom they worked.

Phumzile, for example, volunteered to participate in the first trial of ART provision in the public sector in South Africa. His participation saved his life as he was quite sick and there were no other treatment options for him at the time. His engagement with the researchers and activists involved in the trial led to his involvement in TAC as well as his decision to strike out on his own and start Khululeka. He even ended up reconnecting years later with the visiting French doctor who had initially put him on ART and married her shortly thereafter. Of course, not all volunteers have such enduring or personally rewarding relationships with the producers of scientific knowledge. Many end up like Nolwazi, uncertain about which trials they participated in and their effects, but optimistic that their large binder of consent forms and letters of appreciation might one day translate into something more productive.

The intertwining of volunteers and research is not limited to the lone clinical trial subject, though. Most contemporary trials depend on the input of a wide range of local volunteers, from using CBOs and NGOs to recruit participants and raise awareness, and using CHWs to deliver aspects of the trial intervention, to using volunteer members of Community Advisory Boards (CABs) to gain community access and trust, negotiate consent and disseminate findings.

Trial-based clinical research is far from the only kind of research in which volunteers support and participate. South African communities, especially those hit hardest by HIV/AIDS, are criss-crossed by a wide range of public health, social and behavioural science, and public policy research projects. These projects enlist volunteers to provide data, offer field research assistance and translation, and communicate research findings back to research participants. Birgitte Bruun describes in Chapter 4 a similarly complex landscape of health research volunteering in her examination of the experiences of people in Zambia who volunteer for medical research.

The result has been the development in some places of an ad hoc 'industry' of volunteers and organizations that support and sometimes subsist on these health research projects. Several Khululeka members, for example, worked regularly as local guides for foreign researchers, oftentimes playing both the role of research assistant (by seeking out people to interview) and research participant (by being interviewed themselves). While they were generally paid for this work, researchers typically tried to frame the Khululeka member's input as an extension of their volunteerism for Khululeka. Members were often offered relatively small amounts of money and told it was 'just to cover' their transport or their time. Sometimes researchers paid this money to Khululeka directly, rather than the individual, calling it a 'donation' to the CBO. The proliferation of projects seeking to interview and understand patient perspectives on health and HIV/AIDS even led in some clinics to the emergence of the 'professional research participant' who would show up at a clinic on a regular basis and ask which research projects were on that day and what they provided in exchange for participation.

In the end, what emerges out of this activity of global scientific knowledge production, whether conducted by global for-profit clinical research organizations or local public health or social-science researchers, is a complex process of relationship building and meaning-making that far exceeds the technical intervention. It is a process that produces local institutions and expectations of research support as well as deep personal connections that nonetheless carry within them uncertain trajectories and often conflicting meanings. This process also both produces a wide range of kinds of volunteers and at the same time depends on volunteers – their labour and their moral valence – to achieve their scientific goals.

Going to the field: the moral projects of student volunteers

Finally, the figure of the 'student volunteer' is another familiar and important part of this landscape of health volunteering (see the three chapters in Part III: Hosts & Guests for in-depth case studies of this type of volunteering). While not exclusively foreign, student volunteers come overwhelmingly from Europe and the United States and generally are at some stage in the process of training into a biomedical career. The imperative to not only 'study abroad' but to also volunteer abroad in an NGO or CBO has become widespread, especially in US universities. Many students who hope to go to medical school or on to graduate training in global health believe that they have little chance of professional advancement without this opportunity to volunteer overseas. As a result, thousands of student volunteers arrive in South Africa (and elsewhere around Africa and the rest of the world) every year, often staying for only a month or two. Their contributions to projects are often not planned out until their arrival in country and considerable resources can be spent by local organizations orienting them to programmes and getting them started.

There are often competing agendas as well in terms of how each side understands the purpose of the volunteer's time with the project. Both Sinethemba and Khululeka have had volunteers who have arrived and when given a set of programmatic tasks to accomplish as volunteers, have told local staff that this work did not really fit with what their university required of them. Student volunteering in this sense often took the form of students 'volunteering' to do their own research projects with the local organizations. It is only the most well-organized and confident NGOs that seemed to be able to make effective use of the contributions of these student volunteers.

Most of the local NGO volunteers I have worked with remember the time spent with these foreign student volunteers fondly, despite the disruptions and difficulties they sometimes presented. These volunteers often entered into relationships with NGO, CBO and community members naïvely but also without the difficult social and political baggage that came with engagements with middle-class South Africans. Student volunteers also reported the same positive sense of connection with those with whom they worked. As with the young middle-class activists and white women 'champions' described above, student volunteers and the people they worked with found volunteering to be a useful catalyst for identity work and relationship building across entrenched racial and class divides. Students generally framed their intentions before going 'to the field' in broad humanitarian terms, as part of an altruistic project to 'help' local people (Handler 2013). But when they left, they spoke of their time in terms of what they had learnt, the relationships they had made, and the transformed sense of self that they carried away.

Back home, of course, their experiences also translated into valuable commodities on the career market. Whatever the positive personal relationships that developed, it is these professional development imperatives that ultimately structure and animate volunteerism for these students. Volunteering in this sense is as productive of value for foreign students as it is for local volunteers, a fact that is equally uncomfortable to volunteers on both sides. It is also significant that these students emphasize that their experiences were 'volunteer' experiences, rather than merely internships, or field research projects. The moral valence of volunteering is clearly intertwined for them, and for those they are seeking to convince of their competence and potential, with the technical skills and experiences they may have also gained in the process. This says something not only about the moral project of volunteering itself (see, for example, Wendland, 2012 on the 'moral maps' of clinical tourists in Malawi) but also about how moral valence of volunteering is tied up with the moral projects of both science and education in the North.

Conclusion

Health volunteerism in South Africa since the end of apartheid has served a wide range of purposes for an equally wide range of stakeholders involved in the practice of volunteering. Driven primarily by a need to respond to the HIV epidemic in the absence of an effective government response, health volunteers in South Africa have offered vital care and comfort to those infected and affected by HIV, oftentimes representing the only formal care to which those dying from the disease might have access. This work is underpinned in most volunteers by a strong sense of duty and commitment to sacrifice for the good of their communities.

At the same time, a number of other forces shape profoundly what, how and why they do what they do as volunteers. Poverty is a reality for most health volunteers in the country, a fact that both animates their engagement with volunteer work as a form of career development while also restricting and complicating this agenda. Volunteering is also a richly social practice, one that inevitably brings volunteers into complicated relationship with a range of local social and political actors, alliances and agendas. For many, volunteering also offers an opportunity for identity work and relationship building. These personal projects are of course never complete. They are also complicated by racial, class and gender histories, and they have to contend with a range of 'ambiguities' and precarities in relation to labour, identity and the social that threaten to disrupt them (Prince 2014, 2015). Nonetheless, volunteering does represent for many volunteers a rare and valuable opportunity for fashioning new senses of self and belonging.

For political actors in the state, and the development and activist communities, health volunteers represent an opportunity to both carry out practical agendas for social, economic, political or health intervention as well as promote new forms of political subjectivity and relationship. These initiatives aren't always successful and their effects aren't always predictable. But they nonetheless lay the foundation for the continued production, reproduction and reliance on forms of volunteer labour. Finally, global producers of scientific knowledge also make wide use of and shape profoundly the experiences and expectations of health volunteers in South Africa.

Three further lessons stem this analysis. One is that the South African state, like many states in Africa, remains in ambivalent relationship to civil society and its largely volunteer work force. Foreign and local civil-society actors have long bypassed the state in Africa and in some ways, the South African government is attempting to rein in the proliferation of volunteer programmes and activist energies and put them more coherently to the service of the state. Health volunteers have indeed served a range of practical and legitimating functions for the South African state but they have also complicated its efforts to promote its vision of public health policy, one that is largely technicist, biomedical and professionalized in its orientation. The volunteer here represents for the state a force that needs regulation and some degree of capture by its institutions. At the same time, however, the South Africa government has proven unable or unwilling so far to really support or integrate volunteering into its governance or service delivery in health.

Secondly, if the state doesn't seem to quite know what to do with its volunteers, neither do communities. While health volunteerism has certainly flourished as a result of the HIV epidemic, and played an important part in some of the key political struggles against stigma and for treatment access, it has also unfolded in an organic, fragmented and sometimes chaotic manner. It has been driven by a wide range of needs and agendas and a complicated mix of actors who aren't always in alignment with each other. This state of affairs reflects the urgency of need in many communities as well as the wellspring of energy and commitment that can be tapped. But it makes for a messy process that can have a range of the kind of unintended consequences described here.

Finally, on the part of both the state and civil society, there has been a distinct lack of an ideological framework through which to interpret and shape volunteering. Though HIV is often described as the 'new struggle' that replaced the struggle against apartheid that ended in 1994, it is a struggle that has largely been apolitical, in the sense that the political conflicts that emerged around HIV did not really articulate with broader ideological conflicts within the state or the public sphere. By contrast, CHW work during apartheid was animated and guided by the greater struggle against apartheid, one that drew clear ideological lines and had clear political alternatives on offer. President Mbeki tried to frame his resistance to mainstream AIDS science in similar ideological terms and sought to structure the debate around HIV as one about poverty and neo-colonialism. But he was not successful, and his denialism was largely written off by most people as an aberration of his personality.

The chronic character of the HIV epidemic, and the growing inequalities in health, education and economic opportunity in most communities mean that the need for volunteer labour, and the economic incentives volunteering represents, will not soon disappear. It remains to be seen, however, if the various actors with a stake in health volunteering – communities, patients, healthcare workers, the state, academic researchers and others – will be able to bring some coherence to this enterprise and realize its potential for improving public health. As it stands, these volunteers represent both a vital potential resource to state and community as well as a puzzling, though familiar, problem of how to shape a diverse set of actors with a complex mix of intentions towards instrumental ends.

2

**The Civics
of Urban Malaria
Vector Control**
ANN KELLY
& PROSPER CHAKI

Grassroots
& Breeding Places
in Dar es Salaam

In July 1961, the African Medical and Research Foundation ... wished us to undertake a review of the medical services of Tanganyika. The terms of reference for this assignment were as follows: To examine the present organization of the medical services in Tanganyika, bearing in mind the desirability of close integration of government and the voluntary agencies health services and to recommend ways and means of extending the curative services over the next five years in order to achieve maximum even coverage territorially.

Richard Titmuss, 1964: vii

Architect of post-war British social policy, Richard Titmuss understood state capacity as underwritten by volunteer action. Volunteers actualize imagined communities by nurturing the common good: social-welfare systems, Titmuss argued, should not be judged by what is given to citizens but rather by the opportunities presented for citizens to give to each other.[1] During times of crisis, volunteers act as stopgap and scaffold for society, linking dispersed populations to public goods and it is this prosthetic potential that animates the Health Service Report Titmuss prepared for a newly independent Tanganyika. Drawing from detailed surveys of staff numbers, hospital capacities, epidemiological trends and budget constraints, the report argues that with limited human and financial resources, the state should prioritize local services, mass education, environmental hygiene and preventive care. The temptation to invest in 'specialists from overseas, chromium-plated resources and impressive equipment' betrays a colonial legacy; by harnessing 'the strengths of the community development and self help movement' the

---

[1] Titmuss famously argued of blood donation, 'volunteer ... donor systems represent one practical and concrete demonstration of the fellowship relationships institutionally based in Britain and in the National Health Service' (1997 [1970]: 311). The 'right to give' allowed us to imagine the community of strangers that make up the nation; altruism bound modern publics together.

report envisions 'a health service developing that is not separate and aloof from the life of the nation but an expression and reinforcement of national unity' (1964: 214). Titmuss' proposals for a national health service had considerable political traction (Iliffe 1998). The report's recommendations were recapitulated in the Tanganyika African National Union's (TANU) first five-year development plan (1964–69), which emphasized expanding rural health infrastructure, mass health education and tight links between voluntary agencies, local populations and government (Heggenhougen et al. 1987). But more broadly, the report's underlying commitment to spatial justice achieved through volunteerism resonated with President Julius Nyerere's vision of African Socialism. In the years following independence, Nyerere set in motion a raft of policies aimed at redistributing public resources from urban centres to rural peripheries. Popular participation was the critical instrument of governmental extension: through local initiatives, such as the building of schools and clinics, digging wells, clearing and cultivating of bush, a nation could be created out of a colonial territory (Hunter 2015; Brown & Green 2015). 'The people', Nyerere argued, 'cannot be developed, they could only develop themselves' (Nyerere 1973: 60). That ethos of self-reliance was cultivated through the resettlement of scattered peasant households into development villages (*ujamaa vijijini*) – 'volunteer association[s] of people who decide of their own free will to live together and work together for their common good'.[2] Building upon an associational culture strongly promoted during the colonial period, these new forms of social proximity were intended to foster civic consciousness and administrative legibility through a thoroughgoing re-territorialization of the nation (cf. Hunter 2015; Scott 1998).

The economic and political failures of compulsory villagization notwithstanding, Nyerere's efforts to 'spatialize the state' (Ferguson & Gupta 2002) through grassroots activity has profoundly shaped contemporary Tanzanian civil society (e.g. Jennings 2007; Samoff 1973). Recent anthropological scholarship has illuminated the conceptual freight participation carries in development and global health, the discrepancies between the models of good governance promoted by the World Bank and the World Health Organization (WHO), and how volunteered action is locally understood (e.g. Dill 2009; Green 2010; Marsland 2006). Rather than a population to be reached, these accounts show how the 'grassroots' is performed, and performed differently, through shifting alignments of non-governmental, community-based,

[2] The role of development villages in the socio-economic development of the Nation was refined in 1967, following the initial failure of large-scale collective farms (see Schneider 2004). In his essay, 'Freedom and Development', Nyerere writes: 'Ujamaa villages are intended to be socialist organizations created by the people, and governed by those who live and work in them. They cannot be created from outside, nor governed from outside' (Nyerere 1968 [1973]: 67).

foreign and state actors. As Prince and Brown suggest in the Introduction to this volume, volunteering is an interstitial activity, heavily mediated by organizations often tangential to formal institutions or pre-existing sites of 'community life'.

This chapter draws upon these insights to explore the landscape of participation traversed by a recent malaria-control programme implemented in Dar es Salaam. Designed by a consortium of local, national and international partners, with support from the Bill & Melinda Gates Foundation and the Wellcome Trust, the Urban Malaria Control Program (UMCP) aimed to introduce a comprehensive vector control strategy by integrating the treatment of mosquito breeding grounds into routine municipal services. Between 2004 and 2009, the UMCP operated in fifteen of the city's seventy-three wards – an area of over fifty-six square miles that included more than 600,000 residents. Its implementation involved all administrative levels of the city, but it was mostly at smallest scale of urban governance – the Ten-cell unit (TCU), or cluster of households – that the work of malaria control was carried out. Here, the crucial figure was the community-based resource person (CORP), a volunteer appointed by residential administrators and delegated the task of locating, monitoring and applying larvicide to places where Anopheles gambiae mosquitoes, the primary malaria vector in Dar es Salaam, were likely to breed. In 2010, the financing for these activities were taken over by the Tanzanian Government, while complementary research into programme monitoring and evaluation continued to be funded separately by international funding bodies.

The attempt to make malaria control part and parcel of the city's routine administration, to fold the research project into the city's infrastructure, was the UMCP's answer to the perennial puzzle of public health coverage. While the UMCP was funded as a research project, its goals were pragmatic: 'to establish a model programme for implementation, monitoring, evaluation and research within five years so that a truly effective, stable and locally run UMCP can be maintained in Dar es Salaam' (Dar es Salaam City Council 2004). To that end, the proposal promised 'to harness existing infrastructure within Dar es Salaam' – a delicate balancing act of delegation and oversight that would take years to refine (Chaki et al. 2014). Vector control is resolutely political; all aspects of city's life – its built environment, the circuits along which water and waste circulate, the movements of its permanent and transient inhabitants – are implicated in the feeding habits and reproductive preferences of anophelines. As community residents and non-salaried volunteers, the CORPs promised to link formal and informal, visible and invisible, physical and immaterial aspects of urban life – the kinds of situated connections required to encompass the evolving bionomics of malaria transmission.

The CORPs' efforts to transform Dar es Salaam's alleyways, gardens and edgelands into spaces of intervention provide a privileged vantage on Dar es Salaam's civic topography. Yet, while the CORPs' embodied routines generate the points of contact between residents, local and municipal authorities sought after by the UMCP, their efforts to mediate these political scales also revealed a more disjointed public sphere, one circumscribed by passage and impasse, provisional intersections of people, practices and materials, what AbdouMaliq Simone (2004) describes as the 'processes of conjunction' that sustain urban life. The CORPs' gradual mastery of a dynamic pathogenic landscape entailed negotiating a field of past and present political propinquities beyond the scope of street-level bureaucracy (cf. Lipsky 1979). We take the work of the CORPs, then, as an opportunity to expose the spatial imaginary of the urban volunteer and to elaborate a more granulated – if not unsettled – map of 'grassroots activity' in Dar es Salaam.

The argument will proceed in four sections. The chapter begins by describing the history of urban vector control from the first colonial efforts to build distances between humans and mosquitoes to latter-day applications of 'species sanitation'. What is interesting for our purposes is how, over the century, larval control provided a solution to financially constrained administrations by 'responsibilizing' residents to care for the health of the city (Prince & Brown, Introduction). But more than that, we see how that stewardship – the capacities of volunteers to extend the state – was grounded in a territorial knowhow, a lived awareness of how to activate the collectivities that characterize the political dynamics of Dar es Salaam's back alleys and city streets.

The second section explores the territorial orientation of UMCP's efforts to graft disease control measures to the municipality through the enrolment of the CORPs. 'Participatory mapping' offers an example of how CORPs brought 'informal' and 'formal' resources into strategic alignment to create the kind of situated coverage necessary to uproot Anopheles from the urban terrain.

In the third section we then contextualize that cartographic exercise within the daily experiences of the CORPs, exploring some of the challenges the CORPs faced when negotiating their roles as casual labourers, public servants, community volunteers and research participants. Of particular interest is how the technical demands of larval control take civic shape, and the role of the local labour in formatting the city as a site of anti-malarial intervention.

In the fourth and final section, we review some of the strategies involved in expanding the UMCP across Dar es Salaam. The different ways the experiment has been made to encompass the city provides an opportunity to revisit how the territorial capacities of urban volunteering relate to its civic potential and the challenges these spatial co-ordinates pose when bringing 'community-based' public health projects to scale.

Unearthing public turf: malaria control in Dar es Salaam

From the German zoning ordinances of 1891, mosquitoes have been an organizing force in the political and material development of Dar es Salaam (cf. Mitchell 2002). Initially designed to create separations from 'noxious' soil and native bodies, the tripartite division of settlement into 'European', 'Asian' and 'African' homes provided the basis for more extensive engineering efforts following the discovery of the mosquito's role in transmission (Curtin 1985). Despite the numerous sanitation measures the Imperial Health Commission deployed to prevent the stagnation of water and to eliminate potential breeding grounds across the city, Dar es Salaam posed a troubling topography for public health intervention (Clyde 1967: 23–7). The sheer extent of the flooding, annually transforming streets into rice paddies and settlements into a network of seepages, suggested that minor drainage works would fail to make even the slightest dent in the mosquito population. Under the urging of Robert Koch, the German administration pursued the mass distribution of quinine, focusing on the prophylactic treatment of semi-immune natives employed and living within, or immediately adjacent to, the white quarter. This programme relied heavily on the active support of the administrative authorities and, in particular the police, to inspect and compel asymptomatic natives to take the prerequisite three grams of quinine every ten days.

Despite early optimism, after ten years of outreach and distribution, transmission levels in Dar remained relatively stable.[3] The transient nature of the population, circulating from the city to rural hinterlands and from harbour to the sea, made it impossible to keep track of the infected. More troubling, mounting resistance to frequent blood sampling thwarted efforts at systematic treatment. Eventually, it was concluded that 'anything approaching success can only be anticipated first by increasing staff so that the entire population may be treated and second by introducing a legal compulsion to take quinine', a fiscal cost and political risk that the German Government was not able to bear (Clyde 1967: 42). As Andrew Burton has argued, the failures of colonial policy often had its roots in the 'the assumption that an African's identity was necessarily a tribal one' (2003: 33). To improve the health of Dar, therefore, required a drastic rethinking of the political scope and locus of its publics as anchored in both rural and urban associations.

Directed towards environmental changes, malaria control sought to elicit the emergent civic capacities of the native population and in this regard, experienced some success. In its Annual Report, the British

---

[3] Beginning at the Berlin Evangelical Mission on the north shore of the harbour and radiating from Main Avenue into town, the quininization campaign was so exhaustive that the German Imperial Commission had no 'hesitation in stating that by the end of 1903 Dar-es-Salaam may be regarded a sanatorium of the East African Coast' (British Medical Journal 1902: 809–10).

Consul in German East Africa noted that 'natives do not rebel against means to enforce sanitation but, on the contrary, show a desire to assist and to seek instruction' (British Medical Journal, 1902).

Building on that cooperative spirit, the Colonial Health Commission shifted its tack, introducing legislation which mandated that 'ponds, vessels, tubs, tins, coconut shells and the like should be emptied of water at least once every four days by the owners, and that water-accumulating depressions in the grounds of property-holders be filled or kerosene poured on regularly'. These sanctions and their accompanying penalties (a minimum of one hundred rupees and a maximum of ten days in prison), were extended by a barrage of small-scale and highly-localized interventions – e.g. installing pumps and inverts, clearing larger bodies of water of vegetation, punching holes in cans, releasing of minnows into ponds – carried out by teams of labourers recruited by the District Officer. The elimination of breeding grounds from Dar es Salaam demanded not only manpower, but ultimately, commitment.[4] A public health report submitted to the German Governor, Heinrich Schnee, in 1913 emphasized: 'it does not suffice for officials to carry out this work in a routine manner or as an unpleasant duty which has to be faced only until something better turns up to be done. One must be a little bit of a sportsman in sanitation and a good deal of an enthusiast' (Orenstein 1914, quoted in Clyde 1967: 45). In short, public health was an exercise in civic attention, best approached as a challenge of residential upkeep and not clinical compliance. What was at stake for the German colonial administration and what environmental approaches to malaria control sought to achieve, was a thoroughgoing transformation of the population from disease reservoir to reserve army of civic labour.

As a British Protectorate after World War I, Tanganyika saw this emphasis on civil service applied in earnest. More comprehensive sanctions for the 'suppression of mosquitoes' were introduced and the Royal Army Corps were deployed to construct drains, straighten streams and reinforce embankments in a number of townships.[5] Before the work,

---

[4]   The coordinator of these efforts was Alexander J. Orenstein, an American doctor with entomological training, who had worked with William Gorgas on a highly successful and much touted anti-malaria campaign in the Panama Canal Zone (e.g. Sutter 2007). The weakness of mass quininization, Oreinstein argued, was not that it underestimated the elusiveness of the native population, but rather that it conceptualized the urban environment along racialized lines: Anopheles are as likely to breed in puddles on a golf course as they are in a swamp (Orenstein 1914). While gradually these comprehensive approaches became par for the course of malaria control in Dar, working with the German municipality, Orienstein found 'required a thorough learning away of the cobwebs and red-tape which now render ineffective the work of the best of men' (Clyde 1967: 44). The constraints administrative systems place on locally coordinated initiatives is a leitmotif of latter-day efforts to conceptualize the civic as a ground from which to enact and extend public health.

[5]   The 1925 'Suppression of Mosquitoes' and the 'Extermination of Mosquitoes Ordinance', incorporated into Township Rules from 1935, established that 'the breeding of mosquitoes in any receptacle of any kind whatsoever whether natural or artificial and whether fixed or

public health maintenance was generally undertaken by what was termed 'volunteered labour' – or rather, Africans who could not pay the hut tax (Berg 1965). However, as environmental management became the order of the day, dedicated mosquito finders were added to the municipal budget, the average salary for a 'mosquito finder' ranging from 20 to 30 Shillings (Scott 1963 – about GBP £19–£29 or USD $30–$46 in 2015 values). Malaria auxiliaries, paid at a slightly higher rate, were trained to oversee regional public works and provide support to district level 'malaria assistants', who coordinated local larval control squads in settlements of three thousand inhabitants or more. Dar es Salaam, which had experienced significant growth following the war, was subdivided into sections in order to facilitate the methodological destruction of mosquito larvae. Whereas the provision of public services often fell short in the high-density areas of town, the organization of urban mosquito brigades were a relatively inexpensive way to improve the quality of life for a burgeoning urban African population (Kironde 2007). In the late colonial period, environmental hygiene was one of the areas of responsibility delegated to the ward councils – administrative bodies intended to represent (supervised) native interests to the Municipal Council.[6] Controlling malaria was no longer conducted within a space of quarantine, purification and exclusion under the remit of the police (Foucault 1995: 198–9). With the vector as its focus, reducing transmission was a feature of everyday administration and followed the emerging spatial organization of the state.

By the time Titmuss had undertaken his survey, malaria-control activities and, in particular, staff salaries, absorbed the lion's share of the Ministry of Health's expenditure. However, Titmuss notes, after Tanzania's independence much of the environmental health services were taken up by rural self-help schemes and coordinated by local authorities. The localized nature of larval control rooted in residential maintenance and guided by 'local knowledge' chimed with Nyerere's broader plan for national development (Schneider 2004). This perhaps explains why, in Tanzania, malaria control continued to rely on labour-intensive techniques of 'environmental management' despite a Global

---

(contd) movable in which water whether of a permanent or casual nature is or may be conveyed or contained whether by design or chance and if by design for any purpose whatsoever shall be prevented by such of the measures hereinafter prescribed as may be necessary or such of these measures as may be required by notice in writing by the Sanitary Authority' and failure to comply resulted in similar penalties to those laid out by the Germans in the 1912 'Ordinance for Combating Dangers Arising from the Bites of Mosquitoes', but increased the potential maximum period of imprisonment to 15 days (quoted in Mackay 1937: 53).

6   In contrast to the pre-existing communal associations, dismissed by officials as 'tribal', the councils were modern institutions, vehicles for, as Andrew Burton puts it, 'transforming tribesman into townsmen' (2003). As he demonstrates, these efforts to democratize urban administration were half-hearted and largely unsuccessful, as Councils were given little or no financial or administrative power. Political mobilization would emerge outside of, and ultimately in reaction to, colonial supervision, first in the form of labour unions and ultimately through the Tanganyika African National Union (TANU).

Malaria Eradication Program that emphasized indoor residual spray and aerial dustings of DDT. Well into the 1970s, large-scale larval control activities were a regular feature of urban life and the mosquito brigades a reliable source of employment. A dedicated force of over one hundred people serviced Dar es Salaam, collecting receptacles, fill in holes, spraying marshes, riverbanks, pit latrines and drains within fourteen zones of the city (Bang et al. 1973). These squads moved through urban areas that presented an administrative challenge to the state; indeed, the surveillance of breeding grounds often created the necessary public health justification to clear out unplanned areas and repatriate the unemployed (Lugalla 1997; Burton 2007).

Even as the gap between urban space and administrative capacities widened, anti-larval measures remained highly effective; in 1973, the malaria transmission rate of Dar es Salaam reached its lowest point in a century. However, during the late 1970s and 1980s, under conditions of deepening economic crisis, funds for environmental management quickly evaporated: the National Malaria Control Program was discontinued and chemical treatment of the diseases through pharmaceuticals became de facto the sole anti-malaria intervention available (Yhdego & Majura 1988: 479–80). Under the banner of 'decentralization', local authorities were dismantled and infrastructures progressively fell into disrepair. As the population in Dar exploded, so too, did the density of Anopheles (Kironde 1995).

In recent years, the rise of multi-drug and insecticide resistance has reinvigorated interest in strategies of environmental management with a focus on larval control.[7] Dar es Salaam's long history with these approaches has made it an attractive site for public health intervention and experimentation. Between 1987 and 1996, the Japan International Cooperation Agency (JICA) sponsored an extensive and expensive vector control programme that involved the stereoscopic mapping of Anopheles breeding sites, the distribution of larvicide and the clearing of more than a hundred miles of colonial-era drains. Despite effectively reducing malaria incidence among children, the programme was discontinued due to a 'lack of sustainability': 'it was found that efforts to dry, fill, and drain anopheline mosquito breeding sites would be difficult to sustain without cooperation from local residents in addition to local government efforts' (Takashi et al. 2006: 68).

The UMCP was designed with these recommendations in mind. By integrating larval surveillance and control into routine municipal services, it sought to replicate mid-century approaches and bring breeding grounds

---

[7] The malaria vector is particularly adept at responding to changes in urban ecology. Anopheles gambiae, for instance, have become progressively better at breeding in polluted water. They are also increasingly exophagic, feeding more and more often outdoors (or earlier in the day, before people go indoors), thus evading the two most widespread technology of vector control in most of sub- Saharan Africa: insecticide-treated bed nets and house walls.

under control. But in the absence of official planning and increasing privatization of public resources, the civic landscape is highly fractured. Entire neighbourhoods remain invisible to a government unable to provide basic amenities, and local collectivities empowered by non-governmental development programmes to represent the 'community' are no longer guided by, or oriented towards, state-projects (Mercer and Green 2013). To a considerable degree then, the UMCP's proposal to 'harness infrastructures' required actually bringing them into being – a performative politics largely undertaken by the CORPs.

The UMCP: tackling the Ten-cell unit

A slow-moving stream marks the edge of Jangwani, an unplanned settlement in a central district of Dar es Salaam. Dug by residents, the flow dumps sewage into the Msimbazi Creek, which, during the rainy season, swells, spreading the waste across the settlement. The service provision in Jangwani, while arguably crude in the extreme, is more characteristic of Dar's infrastructure than not. Today, only 25 per cent of the city's residents receive water from the Dar es Salaam Water and Sewerage Authority (DAWASA) while, according to some estimates, a mere 6 per cent are serviced by sewers (UN-Habitat 2009). The vast majority of the population depends upon a thriving private market or on community-based provision, obtaining water from wells or private vendors and relying on pit latrines with poor (if any) drainage.[8] The fragmentation of services spawn a diverse and erratically distributed range of Anopheles habitats, from blocked drains and ditches, to tire tracks and abandoned containers where Anophelese can thrive.

To make any impact on malaria transmission, larval control must be both extensive and intensive, reaching not merely across the city but infiltrating its surfaces at remarkably fine spatial scales. This comprehensive urban intelligence was largely unavailable to the municipality: public officials struggle to keep apace with rapid urban growth and a large part of the city has been built without regard to the existing planning procedures (Kironde 2006; Kombe & Kreibich 2000). A recent UN-Habitat report notes that

> planning in Dar es Salaam has been taking place in a vacuum without following set plans and regulations. Such a situation causes spatial disorder in the city. There is a lack of space for business activity, poor transportation infrastructure, inadequate water and sanitation facilities, and congestion. (UN-Habitat 2009, 9)

---

[8] According to one official in the City Council's Solid Waste Management unit, of the 5,000 tonnes of solid waste generated daily by the city, less than half is removed to a disposal facility – and by removal what is meant is simply that it is transportation to a 'dump' site, almost certainly within the city limits – the rest is left uncollected or abandoned in drains and public spaces (Interviews, 2011).

Delegating the routine work of detecting and treating breeding grounds to community volunteers was intended to knit together that 'spatial disorder'. Initially ninety in all, the CORPs were recruited into the programme by local administrators and given assigned at a rate of 3,000 Tanzanian Shillings (then about USD $2.45 or GBP £1.50) a day – an amount that was offered strictly as compensation and not salary, but we will return to this point below. What was critical for the UMCP was that these individuals found their way into the programme through Street Health and Environmental Sanitation Committees, a volunteer body organized in the 1960s to mobilize casual labour for small-scale hygiene-related tasks such as soap distribution and road sweeping (Chaki et al. 2011). While today the national treasury no longer defrays the cost of the services they provide and their terms of reference are unclear, Street Health Committees, now functioning on a volunteer basis, remain loosely situated within a multi-tiered hierarchy of municipal administration, with the City Council at its apex, three municipal councils, Ilala, Temeke and Kinondoni functioning as administrative intermediaries, and wards, sub-wards or neighbourhoods (mtaa), and TCUs at its base. Dar's decentralized urban governance distinguishes between the coordinating powers of the Council and the responsibility of routine provision, which tends to fall to volunteer mtaa and party-political TCU leaders, who extend makeshift infrastructures by employing local fundis (freelance craftsmen), water vendors and waste collectors, or by enlisting the support of NGOs (Kyessi 2002).[9]

The UMCP's operational framework was designed to cut a path through these layers of governance, extending a municipal vision to the extra-legal workings of urban life (de Soto 2006). Selected by Street Level Chairmen (generally mtaa leaders, but sometimes TCU leaders) and trained by UMCP scientists, the CORPs were placed under the direct supervision of the Ward supervisors who, in turn, provided weekly reports to Municipal Mosquito Control Coordinators (MMCC). The accuracy of those reports was assessed through weekly spot checks of six randomly assigned TCUs – data which the MMCC subsequently presented to the City Mosquito Control Coordinator (CMCC) on a monthly basis. The CMCC, in turn, produced a written narrative of the programme's progress for the City Mosquito Surveillance Officers (CMSO) (Fillinger et al. 2008). This iterative network of reportage – spreadsheets, action points, collection

---

[9] This structure was formalized in 1996 following a National Conference, 'Towards a Shared Vision for Local Government in Tanzania', and sought to empower local councils 'de-linking administrative leaders from former ministries; creating new central-local relations based not on orders but on legislation and negotiations'. The difficulty in untangling the relationship between municipal, city-wide and national authorities in the everyday governance of Dar es Salaam is compounded by the fact that while each municipality is often in control of tax revenues and expenditures, many of the agencies that provide key services – such as the Dar es Salaam Water and Sewerage Authority (DAWASA), or the Tanzania Electric Supply Company (TANESCO) – are accountable only to national Ministries, not to the local authorities.

forms and written feedback – linked informal and formal administrative bodies and, through a bureaucratic performance, engendered both scientific integrity and political legitimacy (Riles 2006). The UMCP's initial challenge was to calibrate this organizational structure to the dynamic topography of malaria transmission. Every morning, beginning at six, CORPs would arrive at their respective Ward Supervisor's office and collect a pile of description forms. Walking out to their assigned area – typically less than 1 km² – searching not only for the active (i.e. wet), but also potential breeding grounds (dry depressions in the soil). Upon identifying a breeding ground, they would describe their characteristics (circumference, depth, plant life, presence or absence of larvae), identify their type according to a twelve-category taxonomy (e.g. puddles, rice fields, swampy area, water storage tanks), and record their position relative to landmarks (e.g. road, coconut tree, vegetable garden).

Although advances in Remote Sensing Technology and Global Positioning Systems made it possible for the scientific team to analyse the position of breeding grounds in relation to the distribution of disease, these digitalized representations bore little relationship to the CORPs 'rigorous searches on foot' (Mukabana 2006: para. 2). At the same time, municipal authorities possessed no map of Dar es Salaam at a sufficiently large scale, or adequately up-to-date, to allow the proper inscription of the breeding grounds that the CORPs were discovering during their walks. In order to produce a new map of the intervention that could mediate between these representations, CORPs were instructed to draw a sketch map of every TCU within their area of responsibility.

These sketch maps, the UMCP managers indicated, should represent every single plot of land in the TCU, and identify for every one of them an owner or occupant. Ascribing plots to specific TCUs and single individuals was not, however, straightforward task. Open areas are often 'shared' between different TCUs. Much of Dar es Salaam, moreover, is a no-man's land, with no easily identifiable (let alone legally entitled) owner. Thus in training the CORPs to produce maps the UMCP stressed that the plot should corresponded to 'that unit that a specific person owns, claims to own, or he/she regularly uses', but clarified that 'when we refer to an 'owner' of a 'plot', this goes beyond just those surveyed plots with legal owners to include river valleys, open fields, swamps, cultivated areas, etc.' Identifying a person responsible for every plot of land was essential not only to locating and monitoring breeding grounds, but in gaining permission to spray larvicide if Anopheles larvae were found to be breeding there (Dongus et al. 2007).

To ensure that they could identify both the boundaries of every TCU and the occupants of every piece of territory in them, CORPs were instructed to take their first tour of their area accompanied by the leader of the relevant TCU, and preferably the leaders of the adjoining areas (or their representatives). 'Explain to the 10-cell unit leaders', the training manual states, 'that unless the boundaries are correctly and mutually agreed upon, mosquitoes will breed in these boundary areas and fly into the 10-cell units'. Disputes about which TCU included a particular plot of land were common. Not only because in some cases open areas were sometimes shared by several TCUs, but, more generally, because 'plot' was not always a relevant category to demarcate territory on the ground. More often than not, the tours taken with TCUs merely served as an initial scoping of the area – one that was continually revised following consultations with residents. Extending these discussions beyond the remit of local leadership were critical. In theory, the CORPs connection to the TCU was intended to bolster community support for larval control activities: a recognizable actor on the public service landscape, the CORPs could more easily negotiate access to private properties or successfully convince residents to inspect their homes and gardens for potential breeding grounds. In practice, the opposite could be the case: the TCU was the fundamental building block of Nyerere's one-party state, its elected leader of the TCU (mjumbe) served both as a party official and as a municipal officer. While they have ceased to play an official role in urban governance, that legacy is still apparent – wajumbe still fly the party flag at their houses – and continue to exert an insidious influence over municipal affairs (Weinstein 2011). Many residents, therefore, regard the TCUs and mtaa as tools of the central government, and look to other participatory forms of resource mobilization, such as volunteer associations or community-based organizations (Kyessi 2005). Without the proper efforts of outreach, the CORPs could be greeted with suspicion and, in many cases, outright hostility. In contrast, those who took care to explain their work to residents directly not only produced more comprehensive maps, but also managed to convince homeowners to regularly inspect drains and toilets and empty their washbasins, reworking edgelands as civic spaces (cf. Lewinson 2007).

When completed, the CORPs' sketch maps were then delivered to the ward office (and later to the Municipal Malaria Control Coordinator's office). With the help of an aerial photograph of the area, the boundaries of TCUs were drawn on satellite-produced images of the city. Sometimes sketch maps would be checked or complemented by members of the UMCP team, especially in areas where the boundaries between different TCUs were unclear. For the fifteen wards encompassed by the UMCP, and particularly for the three wards where breeding grounds were treated weekly with larvicides, malaria control resulted in the production of the most detailed maps of Dar es Salaam produced to date.

But though the UMCP's technical maps hang on the office walls at Dar es Salaam's City Council, these maps do not constitute an abstraction of Dar es Salaam – 'a sequence of point-indexical images, but as the coming-into sight and passing-out-of-sight of variously contoured and textured surfaces' (Ingold 2000: 239). As an administrative space recognizable to the CORPs, the TCU created an anchor for the ever-shifting correspondences between puddles, plots, cisterns and gardens. But it was the CORPs efforts to adjudicate the political logistics of that space, mobilizing local expertise and authority that created the kind of fine-grained coverage upon which the UMCP depended. That capacity, UMCP scientists argue, was down to their status as 'community-based' actors: monthly programme assessments showed that CORPs recruited through mjumbe and mtaa leaders significantly outperformed those recommended by higher order administrators and even those with prior experience with larval control enrolled directly by the UMCP scientific staff (Chaki et al. 2011). As we shall see, the intermediary role also became the source of considerable frustration as the CORPs came to realize the structural limitations of their 'volunteered' participation.

The CORPs as citizen, servant and subject

The designation 'CORP' has a long and multivalent history, as both an instrument of contemporary development practice and an artefact of post-independence iterations of national self-reliance. However, as we suggested above, the CORP is not merely a resource to be deployed, but rather one that must be strategically produced by knitting together distinct residential, non-governmental, municipal and state authorities that collectively constitute Dar's civic administration. A number of the CORPs had worked previously with Community Health Committees, organized on an ad hoc basis through the mtaa, providing advice on how to maintain a clean household and maintain the pit latrines on plots, and thus had some experience moving across these areas of jurisdiction. The UMCP's budget lines and operational protocols extended this system, refocusing broader concerns of environmental hygiene to the task of vector control. Though the success of the UMCP's malaria-control activities was deeply implicated in other informal networks of provision – e.g. garbage collection, sewage systems and water delivery networks – the self-limiting nature of the pilot project circumscribed the role of the CORP as a community-based resource.

While enrolled by grassroots authorities, the CORPs were not community 'volunteers' per se, but also experimental subjects; before being enrolled their informed consent was sought (Fillinger et al. 2008). Their contribution, moreover, was compensated with a 'minimal emolument', held distinct from salary, not merely because of its framing as community development, but also for ethical reasons (see Bruun, Chapter 4). Here, as in all human subject research, fiscal benefits can impugn the integrity of consent and rapidly convert enrolment into coercion. Much recent social scientific work has demonstrated the fragility of the bioethical trope of volunteerism and, further, its lack of empirical traction in contexts such as those in many parts of Africa, where biomedical research offers key sources of both health care and employment (e.g. Geissler 2013; Kelly and Geissler 2011). Indeed, for the vast majority of CORPs, the remuneration they received from the UMCP was the primary source of income – less than the minimum wage, but a slight increase from a typical day's take from petty trading. Arguably, then, the CORPs' volunteered participation reads as simply another example of the contingent forms of disenfranchised labour under advanced capitalism (cf. Rajan 2005).

But even this discrepancy was contained by the pragmatics of the UMCP, which measured the success of its intervention in terms of its efficacy and sustainability. Compensating the CORPs with the 'minimal' 3,000 Shillings ensured that, in the final analysis, the annual cost per person protected by larval control measures compared well with that provided by a long-lasting bed net (Geissbühler et al. 2009). More broadly, the sum indicated that larval control could be effectively conducted by community members with relatively limited education and skills – presumably, the only kinds people that just such an 'emolument' might attract. As a test case, the CORPs work was generalized to make a case for the potential of larval management for sustainable malaria control in cities across Africa. Thus, while their activities were meant to map onto the neighbourhood, the design of the intervention followed more of what Rottenburg has described of AIDS programmes in Tanzania, as 'the archipelago pattern' (2009) – rather than coverage, the UMCP sought to produce spaces of analysis and comparison across different intervention zones.

The inherent ambiguity of the CORP's participation as experimental community-based work was complicated by its technical demands. First and foremost, larval control is exceedingly labour intensive. The sheer physical stamina it takes to locate and spray each and every potential breeding ground across even a few houses meant that on any given day, the CORPs could expect to be 'in the field' for seven hours or more, leaving little time for any other work (Chaki et al. 2011). Moreover, it is repetitive: surveys have to be conducted weekly in order to register any changes in layout and constitution of the neighbourhood, and larvicides must be deposited weekly as well, since they have a limited residual effect. Finally, it can feel futile: a year of rigorous maintenance can be undone by one missed breeding ground – as one CORP explained:

> I have been in the programme for over three years now, yet I have not had leave for even a single day because the programme needs me. Do you think I don't get sick? Do you expect my performance to be the same throughout the year?

That these less-than-ideal employment conditions also came with the greatest degree of responsibility was not lost on the CORPs. In discussions and interviews, the CORPs continually compared their work to that of the Ward Supervisor, who spent relatively little time 'in the field' and yet was paid more and enjoyed the benefits – e.g. security, pension, paid leave, advancement – that a salary entails. The UMCP unwittingly inflamed that sense of imbalance by promoting particularly proficient CORPs to supervisory positions, but without the status of an official public servant.

While regarded as highly capable by the programme staff, the CORPs' structural position in the UMCP as grassroots actors suggested that they were expendable: 'I do not think', one CORPs put it, 'the leaders [UMCP programme administrators] truly value us.'

Beyond its physical demands, larval control requires considerable social capital. As the task of participatory mapping illustrates, traversing public and private areas can be political sensitive, particularly in neighbourhoods as heterogeneous as in Dar es Salaam. More than half of the breeding grounds located by the project were behind fences, access to which, in unplanned areas could be more or less easily (if not delicately) negotiated. It was in the better-off areas, where house ownership was more clearly established and forcefully protected, that a low-skilled and modestly-paid local volunteer was in no position to secure permission to enter private premises without the intermediation of local party-political leaders or, in some cases, of foreign members of the UMCP scientific team. One CORP working in Mikocheni ward (only metres away from the research centre where the UMCP scientific team was based) had the following comment.

Here lives a white man, he keeps snakes and dogs. I have not been able to go in because the security guards had advised me not to, even though I can see from here that there is a swimming pool and tyres.

To counter these situations, CORPs were provided with a UMCP tee-shirt and a letter of introduction from the scientific staff. These trappings of institutional identification served to disassociate the CORPs with both their modest backgrounds and the 'informal' administrative tasks that took place on the level of the ward. By programme design, however, the CORPs' contact with the UMCP technical staff was limited, their training and supervision delegated to ward supervisors.

Ultimately, the CORPs' designation as 'UMCP' underscored the precarity of their position supported by an experimental public health project limited in focus, time and space. The CORPs experienced those limitations in manifold ways, from the time limits on their contracts to the transnational origins of fiduciary compensation. But perhaps the most striking example of the fragile nature of the 'civic' the CORPs were asked to perform inheres in their appointed object of intervention. The majority of mosquitoes in Dar es Salaam are members of the Culex genus, a species that, while highly irritating, do not carry the malaria parasite. The UMCP staff quickly realized that without a significant reduction in the number of these 'nuisance biting' mosquitoes, they would lose community support, leading to further resistance to the CORPs' inspection visits. Thus, in addition to their more intensive vector control activates, the CORPs were asked to monitor and treat habitats, such as latrines, water tanks or soakage pits, that were unlikely to contain Anopheles but could be ideal locations for Culex larvae. Gradually, however, those activities were phased out and replaced with offering households with small bags of larvicide (granules of Bacillus sphaericus) free of charge, so that they treat their domestic containers themselves. The constraints on the UMCP to justify their expenditures to their external funders in terms of malaria control also meant that less money and time could be spent on training communities to recognize breeding grounds and more on soliciting community consent (Dongus et al. 2010).

Social scientific work on the professionalization of volunteering in Africa and, most prominently, the chapters in this volume, suggest that participation in development cannot be reduced to economic motivations. Volunteering offers political and social opportunities, and is a critical site of training and identity making (e.g. Green 2012; Mercer 2002; Prince 2013). These aspects of the CORPs role were underdeveloped as their position as community-agent and mouthpiece was overshadowed by the role of formal municipal authorities in supervising their activities, on the one hand, and the limited public service scope of the experiment, on the other. Furthermore, the distinct roles of employed district officials and volunteer local leaders reflect the assumptions of contemporary development funders that participation is best done through local associations endowed with a significant degree of autonomy. As the lines between state and non-governmental activities are blurred, however, external development agencies and CBOs are seen as both a support and extension of government services (Shivji 2004). The partial overlaps between the UMCP's experimental activities and conventional forms of residence-based environmental hygiene put CORPs in a highly awkward position. Neither able to adequately connect with 'community interests' nor with the global resources suggested by the UMCP, the volunteer, in this instance, seemed to run parallel to, rather than intersect with, the civic life of the street (cf. Lange 2008).

Scaling urban attention

Ultimately, the UMCP was deemed a success. In addition to lowering malaria rates across its area of intervention, it was able to do so relatively cheaply. Thus unlike any number of experiments whose impact on local public health ends with the conclusion of research (cf. Kelly et al. 2010), the Tanzanian Government agreed to fund an expansion of the UMCP across the city. With the UMCP's shift in scale and institutional location, new questions arise as to the roles and responsibilities for larval control and, critically, who will receive payment and of what kind. The fate of the CORPs became a central point in these discussions. As the experiment drew to a close, many of the municipal supervisors felt that using the same personnel would provide the critical baseline knowledge to train the vast number of new recruits needed to scale the programme up to the city's ninety wards. If this was to be the case, then perhaps the city budget should pay for a dedicated full-time task force. Alternatively, recruitment and financing of larval control could be organized on the neighbourhood level, integrating the task of surveillance directly into other networks of maintenance service provision organized by the mtaa. Vector control would then continue to operate through 'tactical governance' – what Ilana Feldman in her study of bureaucratic practices in Gaza as a condition of government that 'focused on coping with current conditions than with long-range planning, took actions based on partial understandings rather than comprehensive analysis, and could count only on limited resources and often tenuous authority as it did so' (Feldman 2008: 18).

However, controlling malaria in a few wards is not the same order of practice as reducing malaria in Dar es Salaam proper. To establish a nationally run programme that attempts to locate all potential breeding grounds may require a more totalizing vision – one that is less tactical and more tactile; extending a more intimate connection with the city streets. In fact, the UMCP itself laid bare some of the difficulties in achieving comprehensive coverage (Chaki et al. 2009), difficulties that would only be compounded with the geographical extension of the area of intervention: hundreds of CORPs would need to be supervised, hundreds of thousands of breeding sites would need to be visited regularly. In the face of such administrative challenges, several researchers who had been involved in the UMCP argued in favour of a more explicit targeting of certain kinds of habitats; a bionomic shift, in other words, that would see the programme focus on those locations with the highest mosquito productivity. Taking this route would imply extending the oversight of scientific experts while reducing the role of the CORPs, at least as it is currently imagined. For while efficient at finding breeding grounds in general, as the intervention becomes more targeted, there are good reasons to professionalize, hiring a fewer number of better-trained and better-paid technicians. Of course, this strategy would entail abandoning the 'civic' appeal of the project and potentially, reduce the reach, resonance and effectiveness of vector control for the city's residents.

For now, the Dar es Salaam City Council remains committed to an exhaustive coverage of the city, relying on the voluntary labour of the CORPs under the supervision of the Municipal Council. A factory for Bacillus thuringiensis israelensis, or Bti (the bacterial larvicide used by the UMCP), newly built in Dar es Salaam by the Cuban Government, and the commitments to make ample use of this product, is another reason why a potentially more-efficient reformulation of the community-based platform of the UMCP is not under consideration. In any event, the politics of larval control are apt to change. One consistent observation of public policy professionals is that 'scaling up' a promising public health project is rarely a matter of 'becoming larger' (Bloom & Ainsworth 2010). Shifts in scale imply changes not only in the number but the type of actors involved, and more critically, in the quality of their relations (Kelly & Lezaun 2013). Expanding the geographical area of application is as much a political as a technical exercise: depending on how Dar es Salaam City Council decides to manage the increasing number of breeding grounds has implications for who will control the process. The widening of the UMCP's territory amplifies the points of intersection between vector behaviour and the multiple 'vacuums' in governance – the infra-dimensions of urban living, the unplanned settlements and the lack of infrastructure, would become highly visible demanding forms of community action, public health and municipal response. The question might then be raised: why go to the effort to locate breeding grounds if the system of water distribution and waste collection does not improve?

Conclusion

> Malaria eradication ... is not a matter of miracles suddenly imposed from without by benevolent international agencies. It can only be achieved from within by building a community health organization.
>
> Richard Titmuss, 1964: 216

Malaria control features in Richard Titmuss' Report as one of the most compelling examples of the sort of health improvement that can only be achieved through volunteer-driven community-based action. Over half a century later, this conviction was still echoed by the UMCP, whose architects insisted that 'communities represent the greatest and least exploited resource available for malaria control in Africa today' (Mukabana et al. 2006, para. 3). Through historical and ethnographic materials, we have sought to illuminate the institutional and socio-political dynamics through which those 'communities' take shape in Dar es Salaam. We have argued that the 'civic', often understood as a cooperative stewardship of community health, is produced at the interstices and disjunctures of residential, state and transnational agencies that execute Dar's central administrative tasks. The contradictory resonances of the CORPs' work – as casual labour, public service and participation in a research process – underscore the ambiguity of this particular enactment of the civic, and raise interesting questions about the territorial and infrastructural dimensions of the urban volunteer (Kelly & Lezaun 2014).

The CORPs' capacity to create links between the official and unofficial, formal and informal aspects of the city's life and administration reveals a complex pattern of interpenetration, and even symbiosis, between these two domains of public action (cf. Hinchliffe et al. 2005). The production of TCU and mtaa maps is in this sense exemplary: though they are produced through 'informal' resources, they have clear (if yet unspecified) uses for the governance of the city. Indeed, much of this fine-grained knowledge about the urban terrain was non-existent or unavailable prior to the development of the UMCP. The CORPs are here the link that binds formal and informal political structures in Dar es Salaam with the goals, modes of operation and sources of funding of foreign stakeholders. In fact, there is an explicit connection between foreign expertise and funding on the one hand, and the production of a body of local knowledge that is key to the administration of the city, on the other, even if at some level the objectives of these two sets of actors (i.e. producing publishable scientific data versus enhancing the capabilities of national or local authorities operating in the city) are difficult to align.

For any system of local administration, and particularly for one limited in its ability to steer a city growing so rapidly and in such an unplanned manner as Dar es Salaam, the allocation of resources for malaria control is a contentious matter. Decisions about which form of intervention is most 'cost effective' are shaped by fluid interpretations of which aspect of the city's material and social fabric is more or less amenable to change – and which type of action is more likely to render the expected results – results that in turn are not measured exclusively in terms of health outputs, but also on the basis of political and administrative success. These judgements are rarely simply local – global institutions, national priorities and local realities conspire to make some forms of malaria control more or less prevalent. The current Tanzanian National Malaria Control Program, for instance, prioritizes the distribution of insecticide-treated bed nets (ITNs). This has partly to do with the recommendations of the WHO (2006) and other international institutions (such as the African Leaders Malaria Alliance (ALMA), or global philanthropic organizations), but also with the fact that the distribution of bed nets does not need to be integrated into the urban planning process, avoids the labour costs of drainage work or regular spraying, and offers a direct, material connection between the national government and the individual household.[10]

The notion of 'Integrated Vector Management' (IVM), with its claim to offer 'a rational decision-making process for the optimal use of resources for vector control' (WHO 2008), begs the question of how limited resources are to be distributed along the range of possible interventions at any particular point in time and in a specific local context.[11] The CORPs volunteered labour, deeply attuned to the material and social realities of Dar es Salaam, reveals some of the civic histories, landscapes and commitments involved in making grassroots political networks coextensive with the always evolving realities of urban breeding grounds, in the process transforming malaria into a matter of civic control and responsibility.

[10] In January 2011, the African Leaders Malaria Alliance presented an award to Jakaya Mrisho Kikwete, President of Tanzania, for his 'exemplary leadership in accelerating and sustaining access to malaria control and treatment commodities', particularly by removing tariffs and taxes on insecticides, nets and drugs (ALMA 2011).

[11] 'Bringing together different types of vector-control interventions is not simply a matter of adding them up. It requires careful consideration of synergies and antagonisms to achieve vector control goals in specific settings. It also requires reconsideration of these combinations over time, as contexts change and needs evolve' (WHO 2008).

PART TWO | Unequal Economies

3

The Purchase of Volunteerism

STÅLE WIG[1]

Uses & Meanings of Money in Lesotho's Development Sector

'We don't do handouts' – expatriate NGO worker

'We need something we can touch' – Mosotho NGO worker

Can there be such a thing as a paid volunteer? The idea of exchanging money for work seems to be at odds with how many naturally think about volunteering. To volunteer is to offer something for free, isn't it? Yet, the position from which a paid volunteer appears as a paradox is itself, I will argue, all but natural. In reality, the lines between voluntary and paid labour can be confusingly blurred and – for the purpose of this chapter – an interesting empirical point of focus. The question of whether one can purchase a volunteer goes to the contested core of what volunteerism should mean, in contemporary Africa and elsewhere. To see how this is so, we need to take a step back.

As with all forms of human life, exchange is influenced by considerations of appropriateness. Since Bohannan's paradigmatic study of spheres of exchange in western Africa (1955), and the dispute between the so-called substantivists and formalists was laid to rest, this general postulation has taken hold among the rare stock of anthropological truisms. Tacit or explicit considerations of proper economic behaviour has been a returning theme of inspiration for the study of African societies – from the Tiv's prohibition on converting metal rods 'down' into lowly subsistence market goods (ibid.), to Basotho farmers who disapprove of the interconversion of livestock and cash (Ferguson 1992) or Nuer conceptions of money as 'sterile' and unable to generate life (Hutchinson 1996; see also Piot 1991). In these works, Africans are described as guarding – or, more seldom, transgressing – moral

[1] I would like to acknowledge helpful comments from Webb Keane, Jane Guyer, Desmond McNeill, Bjørn Hallstein Holte, Jon Rasmus Nyquist, Sean Maliehe, Paul Wenzel Geissler, the editors and two anonymous reviewers. Most of all I am indebted to staff and volunteers in Lesotho for including me in their deliberations.

boundaries of appropriate exchange. Such boundaries around forms of exchange extend well beyond Africa. Ethnographic research shows that even the seemingly unbridled 'market-fundamentalist' exchanges of Western societies are morally embedded and controlled (Miller 2001; Zelizer 1997). This challenges the idea that Western economic rationality is morally detached and calculative – an idea which arguably is still powerful in both academic and non-academic circles (Carrier 1995).

The present chapter draws on this genealogy of interest in anthropology about the kinds of relations that are made and prohibited through different forms of exchange. I explore how the forms of exchange involved in volunteering in contemporary Africa are complicated by the coexistence of different moral rationalities in development encounters, namely those of foreign and native NGO workers in Lesotho. The chapter builds on ethnography of the Lesotho National Federation of Organisations of the Disabled (LNFOD) – a non-governmental umbrella organization for people with disabilities – and its four member organizations operating in the fields of visual impairment, deafness, physical and mental handicap.[2] I explore how the practice of providing cash and meals to volunteers was understood differently by expatriate (expat) and Basotho NGO workers. The former argued that such behaviour undermined the true moral values of volunteerism. Cash transfer to volunteers was possibly a part of the picture, but was peripheral, and in the end also contradictory to volunteering. The latter, on the other hand, held cash and material reward to be both strengthening and vital to volunteerism. It is a case where the stereotypical division that characterized early economic anthropology in Africa is inverted: it is Westerners who consider monetary remuneration of volunteers a threat to morality, while the Africans take them as highly legitimate, seemingly constituting no moral 'problem' at all.

More precisely, I will argue that for the Western expats there was a contradiction between personal material benefit and proper volunteerism. To the extent that cash was at all involved in development transactions – between, say, an NGO secretariat and its volunteers – it ought not to create a material surplus for one of the parties. To produce such a leftover would immediately also produce bad incentives. People would be drawn to pursue their material self-interest. For Western expats, voluntary development efforts were good to the extent that they were chosen 'freely' – due to an altruistic compassion for a generalized other – 'the movement', 'the cause'. Consideration of personal profit was the quintessential candidate for curtailing individuals' freedom to exercise proper internal agency.

For Basotho NGO workers it was only right that volunteers gained materially from their efforts. The flow of money or other material sub-

---

[2] The paper draws on data from my graduate thesis, where LNFOD is one of four 'rights-based' NGOs included (Wig 2013). Six months were spent on ethnographic fieldwork, with participant observation and semi-structured interviews.

Figure 1. In his book *Disabled Village Children*, first published in 1987, health care pioneer David Werner illustrates the difference between 'top-down' and 'bottom-up' approaches in disability projects (2009: 405). Illustration reproduced by permission of The Hesperian Foundation (© The Hesperian Foundation).

stances in development transactions was not seen as endangering the goodness of an engagement, or spoiling the moral value of volunteerism. Material benefits rather enabled a valuable relationship between the volunteering and funding parties. If anyone, it was the volunteers who worked for so little benefit who ought to receive their material due. Material benefit was a legitimate motivating factor. It was when material transactions – say, between an NGO secretariat and its volunteers – failed to grant a material left-over for the worse off that it became an immoral act. If volunteers complained or refused to work when such benefits were withheld, it was considered legitimate protest, not sign of moral bankruptcy. To be personally and materially embedded was not considered a sign that someone was passively subordinated and that their agency was curtailed. Rather, personal and material embeddedness was a condition which provided grounds for agency to be practised.

Drawing on recent calls for studying disjuncture in processes of moral and economic valuations (Geschiere et al. 2007; Guyer 2004; Zigon 2007), the first and second parts of this chapter explore how the parties contested the values of volunteerism overtly and implicitly. On a general level, what I am interested in here is, with Zigon, what 'counts as morality in various social worlds' and the 'processes which this morality comes to matter' (Zigon 2010: 13). The third part of the chapter analyses what I call the morals of the story, and seeks to answer my overarching research question: how were the parties able to reach opposing conclusions? What underpinned their different valuations of volunteerism?

In conclusion I argue that the attention to the dissonances between moralities of expatriates and Basotho NGO workers help tease out tensions which go to the troubled core of volunteerism itself. It illustrates dilemmas which underpin any form of social assistance.

Muted disagreements: 'Even volunteers!' (Expatriate version)

'We don't do handouts', Sandra informed me on my week of fieldwork in LNFOD. Both in their mid-twenties, Sandra and her co-expatriate volunteer, Jane, arrived around the same time that I embarked on field-work. They had recently come to the organization through a Western volunteering agency that specialized in sending young men and women to NGOs in the global South.[3] The agency held a commitment to building 'partnerships' across the world in order to create global bonds of 'mutuality and solidarity', which they considered crucial to reducing poverty. For too long, the expats noted, the traditional development gifts of food, clothes and cash had rendered recipients 'passive' and

---

[3] To protect the anonymity of informants, I do not identify the volunteering agency as other than 'Western'.

'disempowered' objects of charity. Rather, their practice premised on a familiar development maxim: Give a man a fish and you will feed him for today, teach a man to fish and you have fed him for a lifetime. Because, Jane reasoned, 'dishing out food and things like that' was not only short sighted but 'it creates dependency'. It was the opposite of 'best practice', which valorized local knowledge, let the poor identify their own needs and assisted them on their way to becoming independent.

These 'bottom-up' commitments resonated not only with contemporary doctrines of development,[4] but related to a genealogy of ideas within disability activism.[5] With prior experience from working in the disability sector in their home country, the expat volunteers were much aware of how advocates and activists across the globe had for decades demanded that disabled people be treated as autonomous, self-determined individuals who deserve to participate equally in processes affecting their lives (cf. Eide & Ingstad 2011; Ingstad & Whyte 1995; Pfeiffer 1993; Shapiro 2011). The expats' job descriptions operationalized these ideals of development and disability: they were to 'build engagement and meaningful participatory relationships with between LNFOD and disability partner organizations (DPOs)', 'build the capacity of DPO members and LNFOD staff'' 'provide training' to rural areas in voting and human rights', 'facilitate consultative meetings', 'coordinate and collaborate' efforts with their counterparts and, finally, participate in identifying new, local sources of income to contribute to 'the future independence of LNFOD and its DPOs from donor funding'.

Avoiding risky incentives

The expat volunteers were surprisingly frank in describing how dissatisfied they were with how development was practised in the organization. An evening after the Basotho staff had left the office I talked at length with one expat about her experiences so far. She had learnt that the bottom-up approach to development – where the self-determined 'grassroots' ought to identify and realize their own needs and goals – was an official priority for both LNFOD and its Norwegian funding organization. However, she matter-of-factly added, in reality this remained a hollow rhetoric. It was a language that had not 'trickled down'. 'It hasn't filtered through. You're just saying what you think you need to be saying ... what you think is going to get you the funding. "Capacity building, tick. Gender, tick".'

What is more, the expats had quickly learnt that the Basotho NGO

---

[4] Much has been written about contemporary doctrines of development (e.g. Cooke & Kothari 2001; Cornwall & Brock 2005; Grillo & Stirrat 1997; Riley 2009; Watkins et al. 2012). While development practice never simply reflects policy (Mosse 2005), few hold that the stress on these values is inconsequential. The present case supports the observation that contemporary development idioms have far-reaching consequences for everyday development encounters.

[5] Reading up on the history of disability ideas, one gets the sense, as Coleridge argues, that 'the situation of disabled people provides a microcosm of the whole development debate' (Coleridge 1993: 4).

workers did offer what they saw as 'handouts'. Some of the programmes run by the organization entailed NGO employees going to villages to train rural populations in human rights and 'advocacy techniques'. On these visits the expats' Basotho colleagues often emphasized that they needed to provide groups directly with meals and cash. If there was no food or transport money to hand out to villagers who attended training workshops or public gatherings, they could become embarrassed or loudly complain. To an important extent, here the expats were in agreement with their counterparts: in attending events such as workshops or trainings, villagers ought not to suffer economically.[6] As Sandra put it, 'I guess I'm all for providing equal opportunities. Transport for people to get there. That's just reasonable.' Some form of compensation was fair. That is, as long as the transaction was symmetrical. As soon as 'transport reimbursements' or meal provisions created a de facto profit for participants, the matter took a dubious turn. Because, the argument went, when take-home drinks, three-course meals and unrealistically large 'transport reimbursements' were up for grabs at workshops, it created risky incentives to participate for personal benefit. In their current NGO, the expats noted, this was exactly what was happening.

It was indeed widely known that most participants walked to and from the workshop on foot, or shared a cheap taxi, despite receiving transport money. The result was that a neat cash surplus, violating official procedure, found its way to the pockets of the allegedly volunteering workshop participants. While the expats did not consider this as 'a big problem' – at least when recipients were disabled villagers who 'are not earning anything at all' – they agreed that the practice contrasted the altruistic and volunteering spirit that would ideally drive such initiatives. By giving villagers cash surpluses through 'transport reimbursements', Jane noted, 'The only major problem is that sometimes you don't get the right people that you want [to attend workshops]'. More than anyone, the truly 'passionate individuals' would participate free from desires and motivations for short-term material benefits.

For expats there seemed to remain an inherent tension between economic self-interest and virtuous practice. The latter ought to be indifferent to personal material benefit. Participation was 'good' to the extent that it was freely chosen due to an altruistic commitment for a generalized other, 'the movement', 'the cause' – disability and development.

It was not only participants in village workshops (some of whom we encounter again as volunteering 'Branch members' below) who seemed to betray this ideal of altruism and volunteerism. Time and again their salaried Basotho co-workers in the office displayed what the expats called 'the poverty mentality': they scrambled for foreign funding rather than plan the organizations' long-term sustainability; they cared more for

---

[6] Much could be written about the topics and ways in which Basotho and expat workers were in agreement, and identified with each other. My concern in this chapter, however, is their disagreements.

'toeing the line' and keeping their own salaries than to risk challenging management and foreign funders about the problems of their programmes. With time, a gap grew between the expats' ideals of good practice and their consideration of their Basotho counterparts. There existed, Sandra concluded, 'no real altruism. Everything is motivated by something for yourself.'

Expats had some sympathy, however, with how salaried Basotho staff seemed first and foremost concerned with keeping their salaries. 'I want people to be more proactive to have more backbone, but I understand – they are just trying to have a job', one of them noted. However, when it came to the affiliates of the organization who were explicitly described as 'volunteers' – such as project volunteers, board members or members of LNFOD's four member organizations – the personal and profit-oriented motivations were outright deplored. Even volunteers were motivated by personal profit, Sandra lamented, 'yes, even the volunteers!'

In evaluating their co-workers and co-volunteers, the expatriates veered between what Stirrat has identified as the stereotypes of 'development mercenaries' and 'development missionaries'. The former is motivated by self-interest and financial gain, the latter 'by a sense of duty and obligation' to a higher cause (Stirrat 2008: 412).[7]

Self-presentation
Importantly, however, expats did not automatically portray their own efforts as a driven by exclusively altruistic motives, either. They could often resort to self-critique along the same sceptical parameters. For instance, they would point out that in the capital, Maseru, they lived in spacious apartments in an upper-class embassy neighbourhood. Full rent was paid by their Western volunteer agency. Regularly, the agency also visited the apartments to ensure that the organizations' extensive security conditions were met, with guards, gates and access to secure shelters in times of political strife. They were provided a monthly allowance that, according to a brochure, would be routinely set 'based on the cost of living in a particular country'. This cost of living was, however, based on expatriate lifestyles rather than those of local staff and volunteers, and was radically different from the livelihood of ordinary Basotho. On one of the rare occasions I recorded talk about this topic, one expat said it was 'absolutely ridiculous' that they as volunteers made more money than the Basotho employees. On another occasion, the question of salaries provoked embarrassment, as two young interns marvelled with large eyes as an expat revealed, blushingly, how much she earned. As studies have observed, to be 'living well' materially while 'doing good' as

---

[7] To these ideal types Stirrat (2008) adds 'development misfits'. What I find fruitful in Stirrat's contribution is not the demarcation between types, but the identification of cross-cutting values which development personnel, at different points in time, veer between. It would therefore be unhelpful to proceed with tit-for-tat matching his ideal types with the actors presented here. (See also Fechter 2012a; Fechter 2012b; Redfield 2012).

white experts in post-colonial settings of brute inequality, produces some dissonance (Fechter 2012a; Redfield 2012).[8]

Expats pointed out that foreign volunteers like themselves 'can do a lot of damage' by, for example 'taking the jobs of locals'. Indeed, Sandra explained, a whole host of potentially harmful 'selfish interests' were served by the expats' transnational engagement, including their own: voluntary engagement in a foreign country reflected well in their personal careers. They were also serving a 'national interest' by lending moral legitimacy to their home country's foreign policy. Moreover, the individuals in the host organization LNFOD benefitted from the expats' presence. Not only did they bring free labour, but expats had noticed how meetings with ministries or funding organizations tended to swing in LFNOD's benefit when a white person was participating. They were also serving interests of their Basotho co-workers, as the foreigners brought with them new, personal 'fundraising connections' to powerful institutions in both their home country and in the expat community in Lesotho.

'Even volunteers!' (Basotho version)

Like the expats, the Basotho staff and volunteers affiliated with LNFOD and its member organizations had a host of complaints against the development practice of the day. The reasoning behind these grumbles was, however, interestingly different.

Due remuneration
One line of dissatisfaction was articulated by the 'intern volunteers'. These were junior Basotho who worked alongside their senior Basotho staff, but received no regular salary. They had come to LNFOD through government internship programmes. Being either still at the university or recently graduated, interns earned small 'volunteer stipends', ranging from roughly US $50 to $200 a month (GBP £30 to £120). The stipends were financed by Lesotho's Ministry of Gender, Youth, Sports and Recreation, which in turn received financing from the UN and the European Union. One day word came that the ministry would hold back stipends for the next two months. Lithapelo, one of the intern volunteers, was outraged: 'I'm volunteering for them and they don't pay me!? And they want me to go and vote? Ah, never!' he said, and threw his arms out. The indignation was shared among his salaried Basotho co-workers in the office.

Mafoko, a programme worker, lamented more generally that, nowadays, 'Even our volunteers are getting nothing! Not even for transport!' She gave the example of another group of Basotho volunteers: the

---

[8] The parallel between NGO expatriates and medical scientists in expatriate trial communities in contemporary East Africa is striking (see Geissler 2013; Samsky 2011). It calls for systematic comparison (Redfield 2013).

organizations' volunteers in villages, the so-called 'Branch members'. These were disabled women and men who would regularly be called to attend workshops in regional hotels where they received training by the NGO staff in 'advocacy techniques', disability rights, human rights and the like. The aim was that these volunteering Branch members would in the second instance return to their home villages to train and empower other disabled people with their newly acquired knowledge. While there were no formal salaries involved, until some years back, the Branch members had received standardized fares when they came to attend workshops, ranging from around ZAR R100 to R150 ($10 to $16 or £6 to £10). The sums were meant to cover their expenses of transport and food. However, it was no secret that the money far exceeded actual costs of meals and transport. For the disabled village volunteers – who often lived on subsistence farming and seldom engaged in formal wage labour – the cash was a substantial contribution to the household. Recently, however, the practice of giving out these small cash grants to attending village volunteers had become rare. The reason was a policy from LNFOD's donor, which demanded that travel expenses were now to be 'reimbursed' precisely. No longer was the NGO allowed to distribute the fixed and unrealistically high fares for meals and transport. Hence Mafoko's outrage that nowadays, 'even our volunteers are getting nothing!' However, there was a way around the new restriction. Village participants would duly sign or put their fingerprint on a 'reimbursement' paper, stating how much their transportation had cost. However, none of the Basotho staff members hosting the workshop complained when, in the next moment, the crowd put the cash in their pockets and walked back home to their villages with a marginal gain.[9] I met not one NGO worker who was ignorant of this 'public secret' (Geissler 2013). Basotho NGO workers considered the small payment highly legitimate. 'Yes! You'd give her or him double that [of what it would cost to use transport]. *Know* that that person would have walked. You have no control over that. You do what you should.' But, I asked another programme worker, did they not feel tricked? 'No, I don't hold any grudges. People in rural areas who are poor, I understand them [the village volunteers]. I give it as a token of appreciation. It is unlike you. If it was you, then I would hold a grudge. Because they are not like you. I normally put myself in their shoes and say 'what would I do?' It is right to give them something to buy some *moroho* [spinach].'

When I talked with Branch members about what they used the workshop money for, they explained that it would buy vegetables and other necessary household items, such as soap or matches. Accordingly, the NGO workers emphasized, the small cash transactions came to highly legitimate ends. Moreover, the way this gain was achieved – the villagers' efforts to walk home to spend the money on their poor families rather

---

[9] 'Marginal' in the double sense of it being a small gain, and one purposefully made at the margins of development interventions (Guyer 2004: 25–26).

than on relatively comfortable taxis – can be viewed as a form of self-sacrifice, much like what the expats requested.

Overall, it was only right that volunteers received a 'token of appreciation', whether it concerned remunerations for rural Branch members who attended workshops, or the provision of monthly stipends for urban internship volunteers for the work they conducted in the head office. Both groups stood in a materially worse-off position to the NGO staff. At display in this hierarchical patron-client-like relationship was a moral logic of appropriate redistribution (Jordan Smith 2003: 706).

Appropriate payment
This understanding of volunteerism differed radically from that of the expats. For Basotho NGO workers, moral value in volunteerism was not inherently undermined by monetary remuneration. The money that changed hands was not a neutral exchange, an equalling of balances, as implied by the idea of 'reimbursement'. Rather, it can be interpreted more along the lines of a 'rightful share' (Ferguson 2015: chapter 6). Money was considered an apt medium to rightfully share goods and appreciate voluntary efforts. Unlike for expats, leaving recipients with some left-over cash threw neither the giver's nor the receiver's motivations into suspicion. If anyone, it was the volunteers who came from poor backgrounds and worked with nearly no benefit who ought to receive more. They could not afford to volunteer in the sense that the expatriates expected (cf. Redfield, 2012). For them, volunteerism was a legitimate means of survival.

Recall that Branch members, after being trained in workshops, would ideally bring knowledge about democratic participation or human rights back to their rural areas and hold new workshops and public gatherings themselves. When in reality such second-line village activities would very seldom occur, the Basotho NGO workers matter-of-factly explained it with the absence of cash payment. 'They will not work if there is no money!' one exclaimed. The fact that project volunteers would not work – or would work less – without money, was not seen as a sign of the moral bankruptcy. One local NGO worker reasoned that it was only right that volunteers got demotivated when they were not paid. 'They were tired of working without money. They were only given tee shirts, freezer shoes, bags, books, forms, pens, but then they wanted money as well ... No one can work without getting paid.'

If the volunteers were only right in getting disappointed when there was no money, the Basotho staff members on their side expressed embarrassment when they failed to come up with cash. Returning from a village meeting where there was no budget for distributing meals or money, one practitioner sighed and said: 'We become ashamed if we don't have something for them. Gathered together, they were expecting food or transport money.'

In sum, both expats and Basotho NGO affiliates recognized the extraordinary status of volunteers. However, their conclusions differed radically. For the expats, a tension remained between economic interest and good practice in development. In principle, 'paid volunteer' was a contradiction in terms. For Basotho practitioners this entailed no contradiction at all. To provide money, meals or other forms of material benefit to the contributing parties did not spoil the altruistic and volunteering spirit. Rather, material benefit was seen as a legitimate motivating factor for volunteers, as they deserved it for their efforts. The provision of material inducements to poor project volunteers or internship workers participants was also acts of extending rightful appreciation and care to those without formal employment. If there was moral neglect here it was the potential failure of providing material benefits to volunteers. When material benefits were withheld, it provoked outrage.

These different valuations of volunteerism within NGO practice were seldom overtly contested. It was a topic to discuss in a friendly tone with a co-worker, or complain about to an anthropologist. The expats' frustrations about the 'poverty mentality' of Basotho NGO workers, for example, were never uttered directly to their counterparts. The awareness of both parties about how 'transport reimbursements' were quasi cash payments to village participants was never formally reported. Rather, it was knowledge that was actively 'unknown' (Geissler, 2013). Generally, open conflicts rarely occurred in the organization, but simmered mutely. In one instance, however, disagreements took an explicit and turbulent turn.

Disagreements out loud: spoiling the spirit

The day of the African Child is an annual commemoration, initiated by the African Union (AU) in 1991 in memory of the children who were killed in the student-led Soweto protests of 16 June 1976. In Lesotho, it was an occasion for NGOs, sometimes in cooperation with relevant government authorities, to shed public light on a given topic. In 2012 the AU had announced that the day was dedicated to 'The Rights of Children with Disabilities: the duty to protect, respect, promote and fulfil'.[10] For the occasion, Sandra and Jane organized a public event in Maseru's biggest mall. They contacted officials in the Ministry of Health and Social Welfare and a host of other NGOs oriented to working with children with disabilities, such as UNICEF and Autism Lesotho, and formed what they called a 'task team' of event planners. From the early stages on, the expatriate volunteers explained that they tried to 'transfer ownership' of the event to their LNFOD counterparts. While the latter duly performed the tasks assigned to them, they seemed unwilling to take clear charge of the planning process. Thus the expats who had initiated the event were left with in overall command. The expats seemed, however, to enjoy this process of planning. They 'brainstormed' which activities to

[10] See UNICEF's press release, www.un.org/apps/news/story.asp?NewsID=42252 (accessed 30 March 2013).

include in the celebration, created a Facebook page for the event, wrote logistical frameworks ('log frames'), contacted 'partners' such as the mall's supermarket to sponsor the event, and media outlets to cover and promote it. Before long, they carried forward a large logistical operation.

A huge flag sketching out a map of Lesotho would take central stage in the event. It was to be hand printed with coloured paint by hundreds of school children and other 'stakeholders' at the celebration. Hand prints were also collected beforehand, in a series of visits to nearby schools outside Maseru where children would line up to make hand prints. Sandra, Jane and their expatriate acquaintances working in other organizations seemed to share high spirits, as hundreds of small hand prints were made on the flag during the school visits, symbolizing their support for the rights of children with disability. The goal was to make it one thousand hand prints.

The day before the mall celebration, Sandra circulated a detailed run sheet to staff members of LNFOD to make sure that things ran smoothly. It assigned specific tasks, and noted in detail where each individual should be at what time during the event.

The next morning, the foreign and local NGO staff, board members and a few dozen of the general urban upper-middle-class audience that happened to at the Maseru Mall, witnessed the event. It seemed for a period to play out neatly according to the programme. A manuscript Sandra had written was read by LNFOD's chairperson. Politicians spoke warmly about the disability movement and the government's plans to fulfil the rights of children with disabilities. Two groups of deaf children, who had been driven to the capital for the occasion, danced for the audience in traditional Sotho outfits. The charity tune *We are the world* soon flowed from the rented speakers, as media representatives snapped photos of the flag where hundreds of hand prints had been made in support for children with disability, and where now also government officials put their hand print down to show symbolic support. As the celebration ended, however, it was apparent that trouble was growing. Sandra, Jane and some expat friends was packing down the event material. A few metres away, a group of Basotho staff and DPO members stood chatting in Sesotho. A murmur was growing. Had the girls not provided lunch as part of the event? Were there no meals to be served? It turned out that the expats had budgeted food only for the children dancers who had been transported from rural schools to perform, not for parents, extra kin or friends who accompanied them. Neither had they catered for the attending LNFOD staff, board or affiliated volunteers. This was unheard of. 'How can you expect the children to eat yet you have nothing for the parents? Here in Lesotho, if you don't give your visitor some food, you are showing that you don't care', Motlatsi said looking at me straight. 'They seem not to care. They have given children food, but not the parents. And here that is very immoral', another added. As the discussion continued among the Basotho staff, around fifteen of the DPO members and some board members clustered by the mall's food court, which was located right next to where the event had taken place. They stood there waiting for meals to be served, the Basotho staff explained. Thabo, a programme officer, went over to Sandra and informed her that he needed extra cash to buy KFC meals for the people who had showed up. She looked at him in disbelief. Standing a few metres away, I could hear her saying pressingly that this was *not* planned for. Did he not know that they had to report any such extra expenses to those who financed the event? Thabo and Sandra went on to discuss for a minute, before she concluded, apparently frustrated: 'Whatever, it's your call'. She reached for her wallet and handed him the cash. Soon after, the two expats left the mall in what I would later learn was frustration at the blatant show of 'poverty mentality'.

The Basotho counterparts who had taken it upon themselves to buy KFC meals for the participants had a different story. As we sat enjoying our chicken in the food court, they explained how they were surprised that provision of meals had been overlooked. One of the internship volunteers laughingly shared some more details of what had occurred. He recounted that soon after the event he and Jane had brought a shopping cart full of sponsored meals to the group of children dancers, who were waiting on the lawn outside the mall. As they approached the waiting crowd, Jane informed him to his astonishment that meals were 'only for the kids'. There might not be enough for the parents and teachers who had accompanied them. But, she added, it should not be a problem, since this was a 'kids' event' . 'What could I do [in that situation]?' The intern looked amazed. 'You just can't *do* that.' Thus, he parked the shopping cart with meals in front of the crowd, left it there for Jane to deliver the food while he walked hastily back inside the mall. The young man explained that he was so embarrassed that he was simply *unable* to be part of the scene which he imagined would follow. Thabo, the oldest of the NGO workers, added reassuringly that instances like these were 'only misunderstandings'. The expats did not grasp the importance of providing for your guest. But, he assured them, 'they will come around' as time passes.

Speaking of the expats, I noticed that they had not come to collect the meals we had bought for them. Naïvely, I phoned to hear if they were coming to join us. Sandra did not hide her irritation as she picked up: 'No thanks, I'll spend *my own* money on food rather that than the donor's money'. Her indignation left Thabo's prediction that the expats would soon 'come around', seeming overly optimistic. What had occurred, the expats would later argue, was blatant corruption based on selfish motivations. While Sandra had no option but to give the money to Thabo at the mall, she did not like it. Not one bit. She had alerted him sharply that such behaviour would be difficult to account for to the donors. When I explained the reasons their counterparts gave for buying the meals, they emphatically refused; this was '*not* a cultural thing'. The 'cultural explanation' for buying meals for guests 'is an excuse. And the reason

I believe that is because ... it is a work situation. It is not a cultural ceremony. And as far as that is concerned, we didn't even provide food to the PS [Permanent Secretary – the government representative who had attended]!'

Jane added that in the eyes of the general mall audience, 'the scavenging for food ... looked bad, really poor'. They agreed that there had to be put an end to such practice, particularly since LNFOD now increasingly were getting international funds demanding increased accountability. 'It is not sustainable to continually keep providing.' There was need to match 'what we do and what we say', Jane noted. The organization's communication to donors underlined that people with disabilities were just like anyone else, and didn't require any special treatment. 'We say that they don't want donations and don't want handouts, but the reality of the situation is very different.'

The event had damaged the relationship between the expats and Basotho staff in the secretariat. In the eyes of the former, the experience underlined 'how things work here'. It was another proof for the expats that the official development ideals remained hollow rhetoric, a language that had not 'filtered through'. Their diagnosis had thus come full circle. 'There is a lot of that stepping in to be a part of something, and not really contributing for other than for your own personal benefit. It is all purely selfish reasons ... It absolutely disgusts me.' While the virtuous development worker neither existed in the umbrella nor the member organizations, it did not mean that the idea of the passionate volunteer was a full-fledged fiction. Such individuals existed, but continued to be excluded from the movement, Jane explained. 'All these older people that are just sitting in positions where they benefit, they are preventing these younger people that are really passionate ... We are keeping the young vibrant people out. That has to change.' Consequently, 'vibrant' practitioners operated independently of LNFOD and the DPOs. But, Sandra remarked, 'we *know* they are out there. They are out there in the community ... It's quite interesting.'[11]

The morals of the story

We have seen that the practice of providing cash and meals to volunteers was conceptualized differently by expatriate and Basotho NGO workers as, respectively, undermining and extraneous or strengthening and integral to the virtues of volunteerism. How could the two groups reach so different conclusions? What logics underpinned their moral reasoning about volunteerism? In this section I argue that what was self-evidently taken to be the case in the encounters above differed radically, and thus

---

[11] Stirrat proposes that the refrain among Western development professionals to search for 'real people' is widespread (2008: 419). In pointing this out, I emphatically do not suggest that the expats' complaints about LNFOD's leadership problems were baseless.

led to contradicting moral conclusions.[12] The different lines of moral reasoning were propelled by disagreements over two questions: What kind of practice can be converted into material benefits such as money? What promotes individual agency in voluntary practice?

The contested role of materiality
If Basotho volunteers or other affiliates of the disability organization came asking for cash donations from the pockets of the Western expats – as had sometimes happened – they would decline. To do so, one expat explained, would both be 'pretty dangerous' and also 'stupid'. 'It reinforces the idea that I am here and I have got a lot of money to give. That I am the rich and then you can go and ask any time you want money and she will give you money. Genuinely, I don't believe in that … It's devaluing on both ends. I am not being valued as an individual, donating my time, and me as a person, rather than me as somebody who is just giving money. And I am not valuing them by giving money, and not being mindful about the fact that I am disempowering that person by just giving money.'

Material donations were considered 'devaluing', 'disabling' and 'disempowering', and therefore morally lamentable. A more legitimate candidate for a development gift, Jane added, was her personal efforts. 'I'm not here to give money to people; I am here to give resources. You've got to think, you know, the most sustainable way to contribute is giving my time, and me as a resource. Giving money is never gonna solve anything.'

Similarly, Sandra noted how 'our job isn't to provide food. Our job is to provide an advocacy mechanism.' Either way, for expatriates, the proper objects of development assistance were immaterial. Their gifts were not shovels and seeds but their own voluntary time and labour, with training, advice and knowledge. To the extent that materiality was at all involved in development transactions – between, say, development practitioners and their 'target groups', or a secretariat and its volunteers – it ought not to create a material left-over for one of the transacting parties. To produce a surplus would immediately cloak the motivations of both givers and receivers in the dubious shadow of material self-interest.

---

[12] An underlying premise here is that what is taken to exist in the world matters for moral reasoning, in the following sense. An explicated moral conclusion is always preceded by some tacit or overt line of reasoning. Moral conclusions are *about* something – a person, a thing, a relation in some other area of life. Thus, for a line of moral reasoning to reach a conclusion, it must have established a conviction about what that something *is*. Consider the example of a house burning to the ground by the strike of lightning. For a person making a normative judgement about the incident, it makes all the difference in the world whether the fire was caused by sheer accident or intended witchcraft. Or, in our case, whether the provision of money and meals was a case of corrupt exploitation of funds by egoistic actors, or an instance of virtuous care for those worse off. In principle then, moral reasoning is contingent upon what was taken to exist in the world. In this sense, 'is' has everything to do with 'ought' (see Keane 2010).

For expatriates, good development practice, and in particular voluntary efforts, seemed inversely related to materiality. Giving meals and transport money undermined the goodness virtue of volunteerism. More than anything, it seems, hard cash epitomized the danger of mixing moral and economic spheres.[13] An individual's voluntary labour ought not to be converted into money.

Meanwhile, for Basotho NGO workers, the conversion of voluntary work into material benefits, such as money or meals, was not morally prohibited. It did not spoil the spirit of altruism. Rather, material donations enabled a valuable social bond between the worse off and not so worse off.[14] This relationship made little sense – and would indeed become morally dubious – without a material transaction benefitting the poor. If anyone, the Basotho volunteers – who in the first place worked with so little material benefit involved – ought to receive their material due. Material transactions in development, say, between development practitioners and their 'target groups' or between the secretariat and its volunteers, ought to lead to material benefits being distributed to those worse off. When that was not the case, it became a hostile, immoral act. Recall the instance where expats failed to budget for food at the mall. The expat volunteers 'seem not to care' and their actions were 'very immoral', according to the Basotho NGO practitioners. This stood in a curious contrast to the 'lack of caring' for which the expats blamed their counterparts.

In line with the emphasis on how material redistribution was valuable, Basotho practitioners also directed complaints at the broader emphasis on immaterial gifts in contemporary development assistance. A Mosotho manager in a vocational training centre for young people with disabilities voiced a common line of critique when she recollected that in the earlier years, her organization had been more concerned with providing jobs, wheelchairs and other material benefits to the disabled. Increasingly 'empowerment' had become concerned with the spread of knowledge through workshops and public gatherings. She emphasized that spreading knowledge also could empower individuals, but was disappointed that this seemed to be all development interventions were about these days: 'Now we know we have these [human] rights. But we need something that we can touch.' For Basotho practitioners, 'empowerment' entailed not only the transfer of knowledge. The provision of material benefits was an equally natural ingredient in their development efforts. Because, as one programme worker rhetorically asked: 'How can you empower people without giving them the capital?'

---

[13] A range of studies make similar points in other contexts, e.g. Geissler (2011); Hutchinson (1996); Parry and Bloch (1989); Shutt (2012).

[14] The way gifts enable and endure social bonds is a classic topic of anthropology (Malinowski, 1922; Mauss, 1954). Moreover, much Africanist anthropology deals specifically with how money can be experienced as a socially binding gift (Durham, 1995), or even a form of care (Coe, 2011) – rather than a one-off payment.

How to promote agency

What is a proper volunteer? For the expats, it seemed, it entailed acting autonomously and unconstrainedly. In the words of the Oxford English Dictionary entry on 'volunteering', it means to act out of 'one's own free will, impulse, or choice'.[15] Proper voluntary acts were unfettered by the motivations of future short-term cash benefit, and are not prompted by other groups or individuals. Agency ought to stem from the internal, altruistic commitment in the individual person, and not be dependent on others.

To the extent that external NGO workers had a role to play, it was as 'facilitators', coordinating a process whereby the poor would be put in a place to help themselves. Their job descriptions' emphasis on 'facilitation' connotes a sense of neutrality, an indirectness and dis-embeddedness that is not shared by the alternative labels of 'expert advice' or 'aid work'. While the expats' attempt, to 'facilitate sustainability' among the disability organizations inescapably entailed some form of bond; the aspired long-term effects of such connection were the opposite: to make external helpers redundant.[16]

The expatriates operationalized their job descriptions through what they termed a 'facilitation' process. They invited members of LNFOD's four member organizations (DPOs) to meetings to plan their future 'sustainability'. On the surface, the expats remarked, Basotho practitioners applauded these initiatives. But they seemed curiously uninterested in putting 'sustainability' into practice. For instance, after a consultation workshop, a long list of topics had been noted down to ensure that the DPOs would achieve greater independence from its umbrella organization. In the workshop, representatives agreed to meet again to start drafting new terms of agreement – memoranda of understanding (MOUs) – between member organizations and LNFOD, now based on the demands of the 'grassroots'. Afterwards, Sandra sent out emails and letters thanking the DPOs for 'participating vigorously in what was a full and fruitful group consultation', and encouraged them to come up with dates to meet again. In line with the overall objective of independence, now they needed to take charge of the process. To Sandra's frustration, none replied. What is more, they all went to the director's office when she called them, and signed the old recycled MOUs with the umbrella organization on the spot. Sandra was puzzled. Their efforts to promote sustainability did not bear fruits, seemingly 'no matter how much participation and ownership we encourage'. 'Why don't they wanna help themselves?' Jane wondered. There was a peculiar 'lack of commitment to change things' that seemed to be in opposition to expats' notion of good practice. 'You can basically give them the tools and you can coach them through something, but it's

---

[15] www.oed.com/view/Entry/224561?redirectedFrom=voluntary#eid (accessed 23 February 2013). See Redfield (2012) for a similar account.

[16] The expats' valorization of 'sustainability' can be seen as a case of what Gardner terms 'disconnect development' (Gardner et al. 2012).

almost like they want someone else to do it for them even though you have given them all the tools.'

Quite right, the DPO members did seem to take little interest in ensuring that their organizations one day could become 'independent' from foreign funding, in the sense that they would have their bonds of financial distribution cut. On the contrary, many matter-of-factly declared themselves to be dependants of LNFOD, their umbrella organization. LNFOD was termed by many simply as 'the mother'. It was commonly lamented how 'our mother' had deserted her duty of sharing the benefits with its 'children'. One the one hand, this obviously related to the fact that LNFOD literally translates 'Mother of organizations of organizations of people with disabilities' (mamekhatlo oa mekhatlo ea batho ba nang le bokoa). However, beyond direct translation to English, the mobilization of idioms of kinship and motherhood had moral implications. As when Thapeli, an outspoken board member of Lesotho's National Association for the Physically Disabled (LNAPD), loudly asserted in a consultation meeting what LNFOD's role was: 'The role is to capacitate us, to give us what we are lacking! LNFOD has four children ... If we have a problem to report, we go to LNFOD. Remember that it is there because of the DPOs!' He continued, and became more agitated as he spoke. 'The role of LNFOD is to coordinate, empower, to advocate [for] these people that are affiliated to LNFOD. That's the role ... to look for the opportunities where it goes, maybe to have a dollar – or whatever LNFOD can do.'

For Basotho practitioners, to acknowledge their dependence on others was not a 'problem' as it was for the expatriates. When DPO volunteers regularly spent time in the umbrella organization's headquarters, it was not to seek out their own independence from LNFOD, but to make use of the benefits of being connected to it: To collect allowances, borrow the internet to check emails, use Facebook and look for scholarships or workshop opportunities, to ask the foreign volunteers (and not the Basotho staff members) for help to fill out forms and applications for such workshops and scholarships abroad, use the office printer, get envelopes – and so on.

As I increasingly got acquainted with the members of the four disability organizations, I realized that just as material donations was not a 'problem' of autonomy, neither was personal embeddedness and dependence a necessary sign of passive subordination. Rather, relations of hierarchy and dependence were the basis from which moral agency could be practised. In themselves, such relations remained largely unproblematic signals of difference.[17] What challenged morality was not the influence of external groups or individuals, but rather the opposite: to cut off relations, and make individuals or organizations into enclaves, solely responsible for their own prosperity. To build on the example above: as a 'mother', LNFOD ought to provide for its four 'children'. By keeping

---

[17] A range of Africanists make the similar point that being someone, across the continent, often implies *belonging* to someone (e.g. Ferguson 2013; Piot 1991).

resources and benefits for itself, many DPO members complained, the umbrella organization illegitimately mistreated its dependants. As such, it was not the hierarchical dependency relationship itself which was deplored, but the way in which it was managed. To be dependent in this sense is not just to assert that you are unequal. A relation of dependence is also a social obligation linking the worse off to the better off.

Conclusion: 'So what?'

This chapter has described different practices and lines of moral reasoning about volunteerism. Broadly, it is a study of ways of handling the relations between morality, materiality and agency. I began by postulating that human exchange is influenced universally by normative concerns, and went on to show how different meanings of money, meals and volunteerism exist side by side, and at times come into overt contestation.

As noted, a starting point has been that moral reasoning is premised on that which is taken to exist in the world (Keane, 2010). Whether the provision of money and meals was a case of exploitation of funds by egoistic actors, or an instance of virtuous care for the worse off made all the difference when it came to drawing moral conclusions.

It is possible to put the empirical material presented above to the same test: how does the present finding unsettle some of the convictions of what volunteerism, development practice and social assistance can be? And thus, how should our moral judgements and corresponding practices be re-arranged? By way of sketching out some initial answers, I draw attention to three terms which may seem contradictory but, I propose, are fruitful to think through in any quest to improve the conditions of those worse off: paid volunteer, empowering cash and free dependent.

Paid volunteer
Can acts ever be untainted by external dependence, unfettered by personal or material driving forces – pursued, as the Oxford dictionary has it, voluntarily, out of 'one's own free will, impulse, or choice'? Basotho NGO workers seem to encourage a rethinking of the assumptions that underpin such questions. If there is no such thing as 'pure' voluntary behaviour, they seem to ask, so what? If acts are driven by 'external' motivations of personal material benefit, does it necessarily undermine their moral value? What if the moral value of development work and volunteerism was not inherently determined by a person's motivations, but rather the outcomes of a person's actions? What if volunteers were not considered to be radically decoupled from the populations they were set out to assist, but were rather themselves in need of assistance? If this was the case, to provide monetary payment to those who are expected to participate voluntarily could become a less problematic, and even moral move.

All of which is not to suggest bleakly that selfishness is the core human feature, and that one should simply face up to that fact. Rather, the present case encourages refraining from measuring the value of volunteerism by the standard of the 'pure', altruistic gift. A paid volunteer need not be such a contradiction in terms, after all.

The idea that volunteer labour necessarily must be unpaid, does not seem to hold in Lesotho, or indeed in other parts of Africa (Brown & Green 2015; Prince 2015). One could suspect, in any case, that those who insists that proper voluntary acts must be fully uncoupled from material or personal motivations will be often end up disappointed by individuals who are too poor, and too personally embedded, to volunteer in such a 'pure' sense.

Empowering handouts
One of the formal aims of the NGO practitioners in this chapter was to promote empowerment through spreading knowledge and awareness to poor populations. This rhymed poorly with demands by villagers and NGO members for 'something we can touch'. As one asked, 'How can you empower people without giving them the capital?' If empowerment should entail a transfer of power, they seemed to argue, giving material resources was just as apt a component as giving of knowledge.

The NGO practitioners in this chapter seemed to be challenged by the fact that their development projects demanded that they would alleviate material poverty with immaterial means, such as knowledge and awareness building. It is tempting to ask, rhetorically, can such materially disengaged social assistance ever be helpful in materially deprived locations, such as in rural Lesotho? Perhaps it can, as in the case of school education. But rather than mount a critique of contemporary emphasis in development on education and rights training (e.g. Englund, 2006), the current case suggests that we think again about the arguably widespread assumption that there is need to avoid providing material 'handouts' because it promotes dependence, which curtails individual agency and 'disempowers' recipients.[18] An alternative view is that material transfers of meals or money are necessary ingredients in promoting peoples' agency, rather than curtailing it.

Free dependant
A final, related question concerns how to morally evaluate relations of hierarchy and dependence. Anyone seeking to promote empowerment of others is faced with the question, how do I, as an agent, enable others to have agency? Are my efforts not ultimately a hierarchical exercise of my own agency over another, a creation of bonds of patronage and

---

[18] A new line of studies has begun to investigate schemes of cash transfers in government and transnational aid initiatives – from quantitative surveys (Noble & Ntshongwana 2008) and policy-oriented overviews (Hulme et al. 2010) to sustained anthropological reflections on the topic of 'handouts' (Ferguson, 2015).

dependence? Indeed, perhaps no matter how hard one tries, the pure gift between 'partners' – free from material entanglements of hierarchical charity – will end up as currency in systems of patronage (Stirrat & Henkel 1997: 74). If this is the case, again, Basotho NGO workers seem to raise the challenge: so what? To be personally dependent on others does not necessarily have to be a lamentable sign of passivity. For them, not only were hierarchical relations of dependence in themselves largely unproblematic signals of difference, they were preconditions for moral redistribution of wealth. Like the dependent relation a child has to her mother, the relations between the worse and better off signalled not only inferiority, but the obligation of the affluent to help the dependent.

Undoubtedly, material inequality remains a staggering problem to be dealt with in Lesotho and across the continent. But the present case de-familiarizes the assumption that relations of dependence between unequal parties are necessarily morally questionable. To be dependent does not mean being without agency. Rather, as both classic and recent Africanist ethnographic research (e.g. Ferguson 2013), particularly in Southern Africa, have suggested: in this region, in order to achieve social personhood and to exercise agency, one must be interwoven in relations of social dependence. In this sense, it is those who are materially cut off and stand outside webs of dependence that lack power. This perspective contrasts the liberal ideal of autonomy and self-determination that the expatriate NGO workers used as a point of reference to evaluate their Basotho co-workers and volunteers.

The question remains what practical implications follow from the above discussion. The present case suggests, however, that we need to pay close attention to the radically different modes of volunteerism and social assistance as they are being contested and experimented with in contemporary Africa, right before our eyes.

4

Positions & Possibilities in Volunteering for Transnational Medical Research in Lusaka

BIRGITTE BRUUN[1]

Upon completion of a transnational medical research project in Lusaka in 2008, outreach workers received a certificate of participation that stated: 'Your contributions help pave the way for women in your community and all over the world to one day have a safe and effective way of preventing HIV transmission.'[2]

The text invoked a link between a particular kind of contribution and notions of solidarity, if not altruism, that embraced women in one's own community and also women far beyond it.[3] Voluntaristic contributions to the progress of health based on solidarity and altruism are at the very core of medical research ethics, but for people in Lusaka other kinds of hopes and possibilities emerged in relation to such research projects. In a part of the city where small medical research projects had only been implemented sporadically until the early 2000s, when the HIV and AIDS epidemic completely changed the landscape of interventions, lay people who engaged in transnational medical research projects were well aware of the long-term purposes and products of these research projects, but their involvement was often a matter of more immediate concerns, relations and responsibilities in a precarious day-to-day life.

This chapter explores the diversity of positions that lay people in urban Lusaka took up when they volunteered in transnational medical research projects as study subjects, recruiters, peer educators and outreach workers in 2008–2009. The chapter suggests how their volunteering can be understood as a variety of practices that shift with the positions

[1] I am grateful to all my interlocutors in Lusaka who have let me follow their trajectories across the ever-changing landscape of projects, institutions and relations during my doctoral research. I also thank my thesis supervisor, Wenzel Geissler, for his suggestions with regard to distilling the argument in this chapter. All errors remain my own.

[2] The transnational project tested the efficacy of a vaginal gel to protect against HIV transmission. The project was funded, designed and monitored by institutions based in one (better resourced) country and carried out in populations and institutions of several other (less well resourced) countries.

[3] See Prainsack & Buyx (2011) for observations about recent references to solidarity in bioethics.

that people learn to take in relation to the projects. These practices and positions unfold in unequal relations in attempts to open a variety of often vague, ambiguous and fickle connections and possibilities in research projects, which include access to care and the chance to learn something, temporary contributions to livelihoods, and maintaining or adding to status and identity by sharing these possibilities with others, which may again open the way to new connections and possibilities (cf. Prince 2015).

This exploration of different volunteering positions offers an alternative starting point for understanding volunteering in medical research that has otherwise been dominated by two different frames highlighting volunteers' individual motives and wider structural inequalities. Both frames invoke an underlying concern with material rewards as problematic in the way that the voluntaristic altruism assumed to be necessary to freely participate in medical research can be undermined by forms of undue inducement.

Moving from these frames to Lusaka the chapter presents transnational medical research in the context of a wider landscape of interventions in that city, and by ethnographically situating processes of becoming involved in these projects within broader concerns that animate people's lives and livelihood strategies. The subsequent three case stories each describe a different trajectory of engagement in transnational medical research. These case studies illuminate both the diversity of forms that volunteering could take and also highlight the ways in which volunteering opportunities became entangled with quite different aspects of people's lives.

Broadening the debate about individual motives and structural inequalities I highlight how forms of volunteering developed differently among a group of women from the same compound who learnt and took up positions in relation to well resourced transnational research organizations and in relation to their partners, relatives, friends and neighbours. I show how volunteering as a practice unfolded in unequal relations with others – including project staff – characterized by care, responsibility and expectations of mutual moral obligation and how these relations framed volunteers' pragmatic attention to the more or less ambiguous and precarious possibilities in the projects.

The analysis presented in this chapter is based on twelve months of ethnographic fieldwork in Lusaka in 2008–2009 where I studied lay people's engagement in transnational medical research projects.[4] Participant observation was carried out in the catchment areas of three public health clinics south of the city centre, and otherwise mainly in one of the larger

---

[4] Transnational medical research is a growing phenomenon globally. In Sub-Saharan Africa it is often carried out by large organizations employing significant numbers of staff, recruiting volunteers and engaging with state and non-state institutions (Crane 2013; Geissler & Molyneux 2011).

shanty towns in the same area.[5] I visited my main interlocutors regularly and both large and small NGO projects. I joined a local women's group and various church-related and secular events and activities. Living in a local middle-class area located between this shanty town and one of the three clinics, I often had people from the shanty town visiting me, or picking me up, on their way to and from the clinic. I did not carry out any research within the clinic buildings, but I spend quite a lot of time in the clinic areas with volunteers from the Neighbourhood Health Committees. Apart from informal conversations with many different people, I interviewed sixty-five lay people (forty-eight women and seventeen men) engaged in one or more projects and programmes.[6] Of these, thirty-two (twenty-nine women and three men) were or had been engaged in transnational medical research. Of the thirty-two, I followed thirteen women and two men more closely, meeting them weekly, fortnightly or monthly. They were engaged in transnational medical research as study subjects, but also as paid peer educators, recruiters and outreach workers, or as unpaid community representatives, and several of them had been involved in research projects in more than one capacity over the years.

Two common ways of framing volunteering in medical research

Volunteering in medical research is formally framed in a way that sets it apart from volunteering in most other contexts by several sets of international ethical codes of conduct and the need of medical research projects involving humans to comply with ethical reviews.[7] Since the Nuremberg Trials of the Nazi doctors after World War II two premises are often emphasized as fundamental. First, individuals should only take part in medical research after they have been fully informed, and out of their own free will (Council for International Organizations of Medical Sciences 2002: guidelines 4, 5; World Medical Association 2008: items 22, 24).[8] Second, medical research is only legitimate and ethically sound

---

[5] I received permission from the Ministry of Health and the Lusaka District Health Management Team to study research activities in the catchment areas of three public clinics. I received ethical clearance from the London School of Hygiene & Tropical Medicine in the UK, and the Tropical Diseases Research Centre Ethics Review Committee in Ndola, Zambia.

[6] English is the official language of Zambia. Although 'Town Nyanja' and more recently 'Town Bemba' (since people started coming from the Copperbelt cities in the 1990s) are the main languages of daily interaction in Lusaka, many people speak English very well and many English words are routinely used in daily conversation, such as, for example, 'volunteer'. The extracts in this chapter are taken from interviews conducted in English.

[7] With the important exception of studies, usually industry funded, that are outsourced to commercial contract research organizations (Petryna 2005).

[8] The Council for International Organizations of Medical Sciences is an international, non-governmental, non-profit organization established jointly by WHO and UNESCO in 1949, representing many of the biomedical disciplines, national academies of sciences and medical research councils. Among other programmes the organization coordinates the

if it benefits science and society (Council for International Organizations 2002: guideline 1; World Medical Association 2008: item 7). The combination of these two premises foregrounds a moral ideal of people volunteering as study subjects in medical research because they wish to contribute to knowledge that could lead to better health for others in the future. This ideal of altruism in medical research has been upheld in spite of – or possibly because of – the eventful history of ethical standards for medical research (e.g. Jonsen 1998; Rothman 2003)[9] and it may figure in study subjects' reflections on their volunteering in medical research (e.g. in Scandinavia and the UK, see Hoeyer 2003; Morris & Bàlmer 2006; Svendsen & Koch 2011).

In Lusaka, however, a common assumption among both research project staff and others was that people volunteered in transnational medical research projects because they received money and free health care. It is, indeed, a general practice across the world to pay, compensate or reimburse study subjects for the risks and inconveniences of enrolling. Depending on the study topic, the research phase, and the particular examinations involved, study subjects may be offered cash, free medical check-ups, free health care and access to the new therapy once it has been proved and approved. It is in connection with this practice that scholars and practitioners debate how to avoid 'undue inducement' (Council for International Organizations Sciences 2002: guidelines 4,7; World Medical Association 2008: items 22, 24). Undue inducement refers to payment or other benefits that may encourage people to take part in research against their better judgement, or without properly considering the risks of joining (cf. Emanuel et al. 2005).

Guidelines that highlight an ideal of altruism and debates about undue inducement frame volunteering in medical research as a matter of individual motives. Moreover, such motives may be located in a continuum between pure altruism and volunteering as self-interest that may 'pollute' altruism. The polarity of this continuum, famously expressed, for example, in Titmuss' case for blood donation by unpaid volunteers rather than paid donors (Titmuss 1971) is an almost inescapable legacy in Western thought on volunteering (Haski-Leventhal 2009), but it is misleading (Pinker 2006). Building upon other ethnographic work that has shown that altruism and an interest in gains often co-exists in volunteering (e.g. Mittermaier 2014), I will show how motives for

---

(contd) development of international bioethical standards. The World Medical Association (WMA) is an international organization representing physicians founded in 1947. The WMA provides ethical guidance to physicians in a number of different areas.

9   Since their wider institutionalization after World War II, the history of codes of conduct for medical research involving humans has been closely tied to high-profile scandals in the USA regarding uninformed and exploited study subjects (e.g. Beecher 1966; Katz (1972); Reverby 2009); to challenges posed by technological and commercial innovations of the pharmaceutical industry (Petryna 2005; Rajan 2006); and to the trend towards globalization of medical research, whereby issues of inequalities between researchers and the researched has become re-actualized (Angell 1997; Nuffield Council 2002, 2005).

volunteering in research projects emerge and shift over time together with different forms of engagement.

A second major observation in debates about volunteering in medical research points to the structural inequalities behind the fact that it is often – but not exclusively – the comparatively poorer or less privileged that join medical research as (healthy) study subjects (Epstein 2007: 42; Stones & McMillan 2010), or people who try to make an extra income (Ondrusek 2010; Zink 2001). With the rapid expansion of medical research since the 1990s, whereby medical research is increasingly often carried out by technologically advanced and well resourced transnational research organizations in locations where many people cannot afford basic health care (Petryna 2006, 2009), undue inducement becomes an even more pertinent issue. Spectres of structural coercion (Fisher 2013) or exploitation based on structural inequalities emerge that are made possible by the confluence of neo-liberal policies and pharmaceutical markets (Rajan 2005, 2007).

Critique along these lines has mainly been directed at industry funded medical research in less privileged settings, but concerns about inequalities are valid whether research is funded by 'Big Pharma' and carried out on populations in the global South for the benefit of rich consumers with lifestyle problems, or funded by state donors and philanthropists to benefit members of the same poor populations that the research enrols (cf. Geissler 2013)

Study subjects in the global South may, indeed, be seen as exploited in both a direct and a structural sense by transnational medical research. While not wishing to downplay the pertinent ethical and political issues that come with this acknowledgement, I maintain that ethnographic curiosity should not end with this assertion. In Lusaka it is indeed people from the poorer compounds who volunteer in medical research projects, but rather than understanding their volunteering in terms of individual motives or structural inequalities I ask how engagement in transnational medical research figures in the lives of people who live at the unfortunate ends of multiple, criss-crossing inequalities that produce profound uncertainty.

In this chapter I propose an alternative frame for understanding volunteering in transnational medical research projects by suggesting how it is an unfolding practice learnt in unequal, but often caring relations, where people in a context of limited and contingent opportunities try out more or less vague possibilities in transnational medical research projects that may stretch well beyond the particular purpose and time-frame of individual research projects. With its focus on different forms of volunteering by people living in the same compound under similar conditions, the chapter also illuminates how the practice of volunteering as a multi-faceted possibility is unevenly learnt and taken up.

The project landscape in a Lusaka compound

Most of my interlocutors lived in one of the compounds south of the central business district of Lusaka. A common term throughout the southern African region, a 'compound' originally referred to a designated African housing area within a colonial settlement. Today, earlier racial divisions have become socio-economic divisions (Hansen 1997) and a compound in Lusaka refers to all so-called 'high-density' low-income areas that are often unauthorized squatters' settlements.

At the time of my fieldwork the compound that I worked in had a population of approximately 70,000 people who shared water from about fifty wells and water taps, and who had limited access to legal electricity and no access to sewerage. In the compounds, many people depended on relatives for food and housing. Wage labour had become increasingly rare since the 1970s and many struggled along in the informal sector. Many tried to make a living from small-scale trading, known as 'business' (see also Hansen 2008), and day labour or 'piecework', including doing laundry, cleaning floors, transporting goods on wheelbarrows and repairing various items. A privileged few made some earnings by sub-letting houses or rooms. Sufficient food was at times an issue for some, while rent and school fees were always an issue for many, and the future was insecure and highly contingent for most people in the compounds.

Education was often seen as the key to social mobility as it had been during the later years of colonial rule and in the decade following independence in 1964. Although the link between education and wage labour had become very uncertain many years ago, many people still strove in many ways to continue their education in the hope that it would open new possibilities – provided that they also had the right connections. Education was very costly, however, so another path to new opportunities for many people was to volunteer in churches, public clinics or NGOs implementing various health and social development projects.

Arriving together with the structural adjustment programmes of the 1980s and 1990s many international NGOs began working in Zambia, both through churches and by supporting the establishment of national and local NGOs. Since 1994, people have had the opportunity to volunteer in the government clinics as members of Neighbourhood Health Committees. Church, state and NGOs were often connected in complex and shifting webs of project collaboration, funding flows and divisions of tasks. Church groups, for example, took turns cleaning the public clinics, clinics and churches hosted a diverse range of NGO sponsored activities, and NGOs supported the government in delivering various services. It was quite difficult to obtain an overview of this web of connections and most people did not make the effort.

Recently, medical research organizations have been added to this landscape of project opportunities. Until the late 1990s the scope and reach of medical research was very limited in Lusaka, but with the massive international attention to the HIV pandemic there was a leap in both the scale and the complexity of studies as transnational medical research organizations, largely funded by American and British state and philanthropic donors as well as the EU, settled in Lusaka.[10]

Looking at the project infrastructure and organization of transnational medical research projects it was not always easy to distinguish between them and other kinds of project activities in health and social development, particularly because their practices and organizational form in many ways mirrored those of NGOs, churches and government organizations. Due to the influence of an entrepreneurial former District Health Manager trained in the USA, many research activities, rather than in the University Teaching Hospital, took place in the district clinics that already ran many health programmes and campaigns involving volunteers. Individual foreign researchers also sometimes worked from the clinics, rather than from the hospital. Other research organizations established specialized and temporary research clinics in the compounds, similar to the few NGO facilities that were operating on and off from there.

The research organizations and their projects were often known among Lusaka's residents by their acronyms, just like many NGOs and their programmes. Some of the research organizations actively moved into the NGO space by linking up with local or international NGOs that offered various income-generating activities, or creating their own support groups. A few large well-funded research organizations expanded their mandate to assist the Zambian Government with capacity development and in the delivery of a range of health services, including HIV testing and distribution of antiretroviral drugs (ARVs).[11] The research staff travelled in large, new vehicles with logos, just like the staff of NGOs, government offices and large international organizations. The occasional foreign doctor or visitor from abroad to these organizations would bear witness to international connections and the promise of resources, just as foreign visitors to the NGOs, the clinics and the churches might do.

The vast majority of research projects dealt with HIV, AIDS and related conditions, just like many of the development agency/NGO/Government campaigns that reached the compounds and the clinics near them. Depending on the set up of the studies, research organizations engage lay people as study subjects, peer educators, outreach workers, recruiters, research assistants, or community advisory board members. In the

---

[10] Within the catchment areas of the three clinics that I had permission to work in I found completed and ongoing research projects run by: CIDRZ and ZEHRP that are two research organizations/NGOs each attached to an American university and mainly funded by American federal institutions and philanthropists; two research projects/groups, ZAMBART and TROPGAN, attached to British Universities and mainly funded by the British state; an EDCTP research project funded by the EU; and several projects by individual foreign researchers. I only came across one commercially driven medical research project, but it closed down before it had really started.

[11] ARVs are antiretroviral drugs to treat AIDS.

following I will present three case stories to illuminate volunteering in transnational medical research in Lusaka as a differentiated practice that offers a variety of positions and possibilities.

Learning and being cared for

Tabita, whose relatives had managed to pay her school fees until she completed grade nine, lived with her mother, three sisters, two brothers, an uncle and a cousin in a three roomed house in the compound. She was 19 years old, and had recently had a baby, when her grandmother, Auntie Loveness, encouraged her to go to the local clinic and join a project. Auntie Loveness was an 'outreach worker' for the project, so it was her job to recruit study subjects, but she was also deeply concerned with Tabita and her friends' situation: *'The young girls are a problem here. They get married too young, before they know anything. When they realize, it is too late'*. She had encouraged Tabita to join, and had also gone to the homes of Tabita's friends, one by one.

Tabita and her friends went to the district clinic and joined the crowd of women waiting to get called into one of the new buildings in the clinic compound. Her grandmother had told her that this was a project for young women if they wanted to learn more about 'lifestyle' and 'how to keep oneself' that are local English expressions for issues relating to a moral complex of norms for womanhood, sex, relationships and health. Tabita soon realized that there would be an HIV test. She and most other women who had come for the project feared the HIV test very much. Some left when they realized that there would be a test, and others left after they had their blood drawn, but before they received the results from the clinic lab. Tabita and her friends, however, stayed. They were reassured by the staff that *'they would still be friends'* and that they would be taken care of if they were positive. This was important in the context of the socially isolating stigma that occurred if a positive HIV test became known (see also Bond 2010). They learnt that they were enrolling in a study to test a vaginal gel to prevent HIV transmission and they went through the informed consent procedure.

During the following eighteen months they came to the clinic twice every month for physical check-ups, tests and new stocks of gel and condoms, and for meetings where they learnt about women's bodies, sex, diseases and how to protect themselves. If they fell ill they could come for free examination and treatment. Every time they came for their scheduled appointments at the clinic they got a meal, a soda, and a small amount of cash as transport reimbursement, which would be enough for mealie meal, vegetables and cooking oil for a meal for about six persons. If the young women missed an appointment they would be visited at home by a project car. These home visits to draw a blood sample would sometimes lead to ambivalence about being in the project, because the combination of cars, blood, money, doctors and foreigners was easily associated with rumours circulating about Satanists sucking blood and selling it abroad to enrich themselves.[12] Still, they trusted the staff because of the way the staff interacted with them and in spite of the fact that they did not meet the same staff members every time they attended the clinic.

The young women did not talk about the products they were testing, nor the possible uses of it if it turned out to be effective, unless I asked. Instead, the young women emphasized how they appreciated the new knowledge they got about their bodies, sex, diseases and ways of protecting themselves. They appreciated this knowledge both as specific knowledge that was relevant for them, but they also seemed to appreciate just learning something. They often referred to the staff as 'teaching' them. Tabita's friend Lukonde spoke very enthusiastically about all the things they had learnt, so I was surprised when I heard that she had in fact not been enrolled in the project, because her husband had not allowed it (with reference to Satanism). Still, she knew a lot and had enjoyed learning from her friends who had told her what they had learnt in the project.

Another aspect of engagement that the young women talked a lot about was the way they felt cared for in the project. The way their initial fear of the HIV test was handled by the project staff transformed the intense discomfort associated with the HIV test into this feeling of being cared for by the project and the project staff – although they did not meet the same staff every time they came to the clinic. This experience deepened with time. Tabita's cousin, Linda, for example, became pregnant during the study and although she had to stop applying the gel, she was still called for monthly check-ups and not expelled or frowned at in the project, as young women might have been at school, at the public clinic, in church or at home.

Apart from being encouraged to join the project, another circumstance that conditioned the young women's engagement was that there was not much else for them to do. Nothing much was happening and many felt both spatially and temporally stuck in the compound (cf. Hansen 2005), where most – many of them already mothers – were 'being kept', meaning that they depended on their relatives or husbands for food and housing,

---

[12] For the research organization the money was explicitly *not* categorized as payment for participation, but as transport reimbursement. For many people in the compounds, however, the money was regarded as payment for blood (see also Geissler 2012). This image was quite powerful and had a long history of encounters between foreigners and locals behind it (Musambachime 1988; White 1993b). Reacting to public accusations of Satanism a few years earlier, in 2005 the Government banned an otherwise very successful Brazilian Pentecostal church all over Southern Africa, The Universal Church of the Kingdom of God, from operating in Zambia (Reuters 2005). The church had built a giant cathedral at the Southern Roundabout in 2003, and people in the nearby compound told me stories of buckets of human blood behind the altar of the church. The same church had been barred by the Government in 1998 because of alleged Satanist practices, a decision that was ruled against by the Zambian High Court (Freston 2005, 61).

without being able to contribute much to their own or others' upkeep. Earlier, following another of Auntie Loveness' suggestions, a few of them had been involved in catering and hair-dressing courses run by an NGO, but not all the teachers had been 'serious' and the hair-dressing course fell apart. Two of the young women sold small amounts of groundnuts, soap or biscuits from home, and one was in a savings club with a few of her relatives, mainly for buying second hand clothes when it was her turn to get the savings. The young women were dependants, and their future would also depend much on others. A few of them had ideas of what they might be doing, such as opening a salon, or getting a job in the SPAR supermarket, but such opportunities would most certainly only materialize if others helped them along. None of them had any concrete plans (cf. Johnson-Hanks 2005), and they expected that others would decide for them what would be possible.

In this context the project appeared a promising opening. Initially, someone they knew, respected and trusted had informed them about the possibility and encouraged them to go. They had the curiosity and enough time on their hands, in spite of household chores (Hansen 2005) to try it out. The young women came with no particular expectations of the project apart from learning about 'lifestyle'. Once they queued at the clinic they were first confronted with the HIV test and then with the realization that they would have to give blood at regular intervals. Still, they wanted to be part of the project so much that they completed enrolment in spite of its discomforts, and at least one young woman lied about her age to fit into the inclusion criteria of the project. This was less a process of rational weighing of risks versus benefits (cf. Leach & Fairhead 2011) or of giving something voluntarily for the good of others, than a matter of waiting and seeing with regard to a 'something bigger' that was vague and ambiguous at first. 'Something bigger' is not a local term, but one I have coined to capture the way many people assumed that there was more to a particular staff, activity or facility than met their eyes.

As they learnt of the purpose of the project, the young women came to understand very well that they had become part of a research project to test a new product, and they talked about being in the 'condom arm' or the 'gel arm' of the study. Thus, their stance towards the project was not a variant of the so-called 'therapeutic misconception', whereby people mistake research procedures for individualized health care (Appelbaum et al. 1987; Kimmelman 2007). The research element was, however, just not very relevant for them.

The young women did not speak of themselves as study subjects with certain rights or entitlements, nor as volunteers. Instead, they enacted a position much like project beneficiaries, enjoying their inclusion into a well resourced 'something bigger'. The young women emphasized how they appreciated being taught and how they felt cared for in the project. This had to do with the way they had been recruited by Auntie Loveness who cared for them; with the respectful way that staff addressed them; and with the material benefits that the project offered. Still, even though I am sure the cash that the young women received as transport reimbursement made a difference to them, this did not figure very much in their accounts of engagement. Likewise, their appreciation of the free medicines appeared to relate as much to the fact that they had access to someone resourceful who would care for them until they were well as it related to the fact that the drugs were free. Their stories were about the way they came to feel included or secured by 'something bigger' in a way that offset their fears of the HIV test and of Satanism. For the young women, volunteering in a medical research project was a way of becoming attached to a powerful organization in the landscape of 'projects' around them (see also Prince 2015).

As they became familiar with the routines of the study they seemed to accept and be grateful for what they received without expecting more or different interactions. In many ways, they engaged – also with me – as young dependent women should behave in relation to authority, also drawing from a position in relations where young 'kept' people can have rightful expectations about being provided for by someone more resourceful (cf. Mogensen 2000 on young women's possibilities for appealing to others' responsibility).

Engaging in the medical research project much like beneficiaries did not mean that the young women were passive recipients of advice, medicine and care. On the contrary, they actively learnt how to be in the project by coming to the clinic at the time of recruitment, by keeping their appointments at the clinic, by assessing whether to actually apply the gels and the condoms before sex, and by managing and resisting relatives' and neighbours' suspicions about Satanism. After the project had ended they missed being attached to the project. As dependent young women they were not actively looking for new projects, but they expected 'to be called' by Auntie Loveness again as soon as the next project would start, which they had heard would be soon. By being in a medical research project, they had learnt how to be in such projects in a way that would make it easier for them to join the next one.

Lack of interest in the research aspect of the projects was a recurring observation among lay people engaging in medical research in Lusaka, but not all related to the projects from a position as recipients or beneficiaries. Rose, whom I will introduce in the next section, for example, explicitly presented herself as a volunteer.

Precarious piecework

Some years before she became involved in a medical research project, Rose, 36 years old, had become active in a community school in the compound. The school had been founded quite recently by Rose's neighbour, whose cousin already worked in an international NGO that would channel resources to education. Working as a volunteer in the school she heard about 'a training' by the same international NGO on home-based care of people suffering from AIDS, which she joined. Because she was also in a women's group that was run by a very active volunteer at the district clinic, she and the others in the group were informed about various opportunities there. Rose, for example, had been called to be an enumerator in a survey of the compound, and she had also joined a training course on infant health monitoring. She had a bicycle and a Traditional Birth Attendant kit in her bedroom from a training that she once participated in. She had begun a course on 'psychosocial' (local expression for psychosocial counselling of orphans and people taking an HIV test), but had not been able to complete it because the international NGO that was supposed to pay for the 'practicals' that took place with a national NGO had not been able to make the necessary funds materialize yet. Even though the training ended years ago, she still talked about the 'practicals' as if they might happen – keeping the possibility open.

Through a contact at the district clinic, Rose learnt about an opportunity to recruit couples for couples' counselling and HIV testing, by an organization that she only knew by its acronym. She was trained and became an 'INA', which was spelled out on her certificate as 'Influence Network Agent' for a period of three months. She was assigned a geographical area from where she was supposed to recruit couples, but she recruited her friends wherever she went, instructed them to say that they lived in 'her' area, and enjoyed the ZMK 20,000 that she earned per couple that actually showed up for testing.[13] During her work for the organization she became curious about what the couples that she recruited actually learnt about HIV. She also wanted to learn, but her husband who had been seriously ill and very weak from tuberculosis for more than five years, refused to go. He accused the organization of Satanism.[14] Instead, she borrowed her neighbour's husband, whom she had recruited earlier for the couple counselling, and they went together to a series of information sessions about how to 'live positively'. She very much appreciated the way staff addressed and encouraged her and other people who came to the sessions as *persons*. She related how staff told them:

> How we should stay positive … yes, and the difference between positive people and negative people. When you are positive you should believe in it, and you should just be as you are, and don't take it 'oooh, aah, now I am finished'. You are still a person, you can even live years and years. In the research clinic they encourage you more than where they test you. They know others have already counselled you to be tested, so at the research clinic they encourage you.

---

[13] In 2009 ZMK 20,000 was approximately equivalent to GBP £3.20 or USD $5. For comparison, 25 kg of mealie meal for cooking *nshima*, the staple food, was K65,000 in April 2009, which was up K20,000 from two months earlier.

[14] It sometimes seemed that a reference to Satanism was a legitimate way of avoiding an HIV test.

Rose learnt that the organization maintained a cohort of HIV discordant couples for future testing of vaccines and other studies. Rose would have liked to join, but since she had come with her neighbour's husband, they had to discontinue when they were asked to enrol in the programme as a couple.

Rose lived in a very small two-roomed house with her husband and their seven children. He used to have a part-time job in a manufacturing company, but since he became ill and got fired, she had worried a lot about how to make ends meet. After years of illness, her husband had finally accepted an HIV test (after reading a leaflet from the research organization that Rose had left on the table for him to find) and, taking ARVs, he was now much better. He sold bananas in one of the big markets, but this income was unstable, so they also got by with the very unpredictable 'incentives', such as lunches, a bit of cash, or a sack of mealie meal that Rose received for her project piecework and through sharing with relatives and neighbours. Rose also crocheted bags from used plastic bags which she sold to a woman who sold them on to a white woman for export, and she sometimes did the laundry for better-off people in the nearby township.

Rose spoke of herself as a volunteer, and she had received a 'Special Recognition Certificate' on International Volunteer Day by an international NGO. For Rose, volunteering seemed mainly to be about work and she wanted to be rewarded for her efforts: 'See', she said wryly one day when I met her at the clinic, 'I brought my big purse today, but I only got 20,000' for ten days of walking around the compound to enumerate people, toilets and taps for a census. She had expected K50,000, and she made her dissatisfaction very clear, but she was not in a position to demand more. To gain access to new piecemeal opportunities, she depended on other volunteers who were better connected to projects and project staff.

Rose's piecework in the township and at the clinic brought her various and irregular material benefits, but just as importantly it brought new possibilities for a diversity of knowledge and contacts. Drawing from this experience, her mode of engaging specifically in medical research resembled that of piecework. At first, it brought her a temporary income and later, when she saw the opportunity to learn more about positive living, which was of deep concern to her, she took it up by borrowing her neighbour's husband until the opportunity closed again, because he was not her real husband.

Rose practised volunteering in medical research with evolving hopes of possibilities or openings that were inherently material and immaterial intertwined, like her contact with the research organization that fed into processes of learning and knowing in her marriage. Being more experienced than Tabita and her friends, she had the knowledge and ability to pursue these openings as they emerged. Still, although Rose was very active, hardworking and entrepreneurial, there were limits as to which positions she could take up in relation to the research organization.

The reasons were structural, such as formal inclusion and exclusion criteria of the studies, and limits to how long someone could work as a recruiter, but also social. She did not have personal relations with staff in the research organization like the very few volunteers who were able to find temporary work with them. Auntie Loveness was one of the few.

'Having a heart for the community'

Auntie Loveness, Tabita's grandmother who was in her mid-50s, was an experienced volunteer in the Neighbourhood Health Committee at the clinic where she was based as the elected representative of people in her 'zone' of the compound. She was active in the Parent Teacher Association of her grandchildren's school, and more sporadically active in a local religious NGO. She was a widow of a high-ranking civil servant, once stationed abroad, and she took care of seven orphaned grandchildren at home in the compound, apart from the many other people who counted on her for all kinds of support and advice. In return she received gestures of gratitude and respect – material and immaterial – that she often passed on, and she was often elected and re-elected to represent the part of the compound that she lived in when government bodies and NGOs invited for community meetings. She talked about 'having a heart for the community', a common expression about people who were active as volunteers at the clinic, in church or in NGOs. She was very well connected, and was often away on workshops and seminars that she heard about from her contacts.

The combination of her experience, skills and connections at the clinic had made it possible for her to obtain a temporary contract[15] as an outreach worker in a research organization where one of her primary tasks was to recruit and retain study subjects for a particular study. She had made sure to recruit her granddaughter, Tabita, and her friends as some of the first study subjects as a way to take care of them and share the possibilities that the project offered. Moreover, she participated in weekly meetings with the professional project staff, organized community meetings and often just passed through the new project buildings in the old public clinic compound to greet project staff and colleagues. Fluent in English, she used many acronyms and scientific terms for various aspects of research procedures, and the specific language that comes with intervention projects in her accounts of her work, such as 'screening', 'retention', 'informed consent form', 'stigma and discrimination', 'sensitize', 'the community', and 'the field'. After the project had ended she waited for the next study to start. She was in regular contact with staff at the research organization and one day as we were sitting in her relatives' sunken plush chairs she told me

---

[15] The salary was about ZMK 1 million (£160 or $260 in 2015), a little less than a junior nurse.

there is this lady who came ... from Canada. She has offered a scholarship for a two week advocacy training in Canada. We have been asked
to write why we want to go there. Everybody wrote, Angela and me,
we went to write. They will pick two outreach workers and two CAB
[members of the trial Community Advisory Board] ... Me and Angela
were supposed to go to Brazil in 2006 to represent the outreach workers
but the boss called us and said 'Sorry, we are taking this lady here, who
is HIV positive'. She is also an outreach worker, but it was our turn. Mr
Musole already went to Tanzania, then it was supposed to be me and
Angela, but the boss picked the person she wanted. This time – instead
of picking us, she asks us to write something first. She comes and asks
everyone to write. She can't pick. Although she knows that they have
been successful in their studies because of us, not because of those
with degrees! The researchers have just opened a very big cancer clinic
at UTH [University Teaching Hospital], they will need people to work
there, they could at least squeeze people in there, in the kitchen or in
the offices, but they can't. But some of the Zambians are very greedy,
they will put their relatives. I complained to the DHMT [District Health
Management Team, a government body] that at least they should give
us a job, because we are the old people, Angela, Mr Musole and me,
we opened the study with them and they should show us appreciation.

Auntie Loveness' remark gives a glimpse of even more possibilities
that volunteering can offer, such as travels and wage labour, but also how
transient they are (cf. Prince 2013). As for Tabita and Rose, volunteering
for Auntie Loveness was deeply entangled in unequal relations where
different forms of care and responsibility, but also merit and recognition,
entitlements and obligations, competition, envy and ways of trying to
influence things were involved. She was very conscious about her position
in the research organization, her position in relation to other volunteers,
what she had given, and what she felt that she had earned and should
be entitled to. She had seniority, experience and connections to offer,
which was otherwise solid currency in many other local contexts, but
she worried that this would not be sufficient in relation to the workings
of the research organization. I helped her organize her CV to submit with
the writing for the advocacy course in Canada, and it mainly consisted
of a long list of courses, seminars and workshops over the years, but
no employment since the late 1980s. Her paid job with the research
organization had been time-limited. It ended with the particular project
to which she had been attached, and at the time of our conversation there
were rumours that the next study would pay outreach workers based on
performance (number and retention of recruited) instead of a monthly
salary. She was not pleased with this prospect and she was uncertain
about her future relation to the organization.

Auntie Loveness was acutely aware of the temporary nature of her
attachment to the research project and she worked to prolong it by being

attentive to her personal relations to staff in the organization, thereby trying to turn her temporary employment into a sustained form of mutual obligation and thus a kind of career (cf. Swidler & Watkins 2009). A few volunteers were very skilled in working to stabilize or secure their relation to research agencies by juggling positions and relations characterized by varying degrees of obligation. Knowing the temporalities of interventions and being good at judging organizational set-ups (many people guessed and often misjudged) was a useful skill often based on previous experience in organizational work. Understanding relations, projects and organizations made some volunteers able to stay abreast with any changes in the landscape of interventions, for which they could then try to position themselves. Still, such possibilities were very few and fickle.

Positions and possibilities in volunteering for medical research

In Chapter 1, Christopher Colvin describes the diversity of forms and uses of volunteer caregiving in South Africa. In this chapter, Tabita, Rose and Auntie Loveness' trajectories of engagement show how volunteering in transnational medical research may also take different forms, even among women who to some extent share the same conditions of being relatively poor and marginalized.

Tabita and her friends engaged in a transnational medical research project, or 'something bigger', from a position not unlike beneficiaries in a health or development project. They enjoyed learning something (including the more tacit learning about how to be in projects) and being cared for. Their engagement was limited both in terms of time and stakes as beneficiaries, but they were ready to be called for the next project.

Rose first volunteered in a research project as a recruiter to make an extra income as a kind of piecework. Her engagement changed character when she learnt more about what the project was about, and she tried to become more closely attached to the large and well resourced organization that could support her and her ill husband not only in terms of treatment, but also in terms of offering a space where they could share their predicament with others in the same difficult situation. Her relation to the organization, however, stayed fleeting because she did not succeed in convincing her husband to join the research project. For her, volunteering continued to be a matter of piecework with the unstable possibilities and connections that this position offered.

Making sure to share possibilities and connections with people for whom she felt responsible, Auntie Loveness' case highlights how temporary employment in a research project as part of a long trajectory of volunteering may merge with a broader identity as someone with 'a heart for the community'. For her, volunteering and working for the research organization was indeed a matter of making a livelihood, but it was also very much a matter of maintaining her ability to care well for others and to act out her own patron-like position by sharing possibilities. For this reason the temporary and transient nature of possibilities in research projects was of even more consequence for her than it was for Tabita and Rose. Her identity as someone in a position to give and to share was at stake.

Before concluding, I will draw out four observations about volunteering based on the three cases. The first observation is about the particularities of volunteering in a medical research project compared to other kinds of health and social development projects. Common to Tabita, Rose and Auntie Loveness was that they all knew, or soon came to know, that they were part of medical research projects to produce new knowledge. There were, of course, some fundamental differences between engaging in transnational medical research projects and most other interventions, particularly for study subjects. Among these was the informed consent procedure that is crucial in research ethics and that has been intensely debated in the ethnographic literature (e.g. Gikonyo et al. 2008; Harper 2007; Molyneux et al. 2004; Mulder et al. 2000). Similar to what this literature often observes, my interlocutors were not too occupied with the procedure and did not bring it up unless I asked. Signing the paper was not the moment of deciding to join or not, but rather another more or less familiar step in exploring what would come next in the relation to the organization (cf. Whyte 2011: 35). A less-examined difference was the discipline required in following research procedures at home (taking pills, applying gels, etc.) and in keeping appointments at the clinic. This discipline was sometimes troublesome, but people found different ways of managing these routines, including not following them – at least not all the time. Once enrolled, the required discipline did not seem decisive for people's engagement in the projects. Discipline and not applying the products on trial was linked to yet another difference that has been unevenly addressed in the literature, namely the corporeal aspects of engagement. A few of the people who had had the opportunity to enrol in studies, but who chose to decline, referred to concern with the medicines' unknown effects on their body and health, and a few of the women expressed unease with the risk of having their private parts examined by a male doctor. The giving of blood samples and receiving money for them, however, was a recurring concern, closely associated with popular images of Satanists. These images were similar to older concerns with the occult extraction of blood by witches and foreigners for sinister purposes (Musambachime 1988; White 1993a) that are also known elsewhere in contemporary Africa (Geissler 2005), and that can be interpreted as concern with extraction by people in more powerful positions. In Lusaka these images are so commonly encountered that a director of district health remarked that any new research or health programme would be suspected of being Satanic (Bond & Shanaube 2005). Many of my interlocutors, however, did not express lasting concern with this aspect of engagement or any of the other differences between research projects and other health and development projects. Instead, they were engaged by the possibilities that the medical research projects – or any project – might bring along.

Second, transnational medical research projects are indeed very similar to other kinds of projects and interventions in terms of material, organizational and operational aspects and it was these aspects of the projects that were relevant for study subjects and temporary employees. It was not only a matter of the cash that people received in transport reimbursement and the free health care, but indeed also the possibility to learn something, to share what was learnt, to care for others, and to feel cared for in the project, as well as the satisfaction in being acknowledged for one's expertise and seniority on an uncertain path towards new possibilities in the projects and for the future.

Third, the position from where diverse possibilities in projects could be shared with others was an important aspect of volunteering. Turning common parlance on its head, Rose and Auntie Loveness referred to themselves as volunteers in connection with the medical research projects, although they were often in (temporary) paid positions. Some of them were among those who received the certificate pictured earlier. Others, like Tabita and her friends who would usually be referred to as volunteers, engaged more like beneficiaries enjoying care than as study subjects contributing their bodies to the scientific research. Tabita and her friends were not yet very experienced with projects, but people who referred to themselves as volunteers usually had previous experience in project work at the district clinic or with NGOs and knew the language that came with such projects. In this particular context, 'volunteering' invoked a more specific, although fuzzy field of meanings emerging between the morally and socially rewarding practice of making ones labour available for free, expecting material reward proportional to ones labour, temporal duration and hopes of extension.

The final observation is that the notion of volunteering to contribute to improved health in the future did not appear very prominent for my interlocutors in Lusaka. Study subjects did not necessarily think of themselves as doing good. Instead, as mentioned above, they took up a position as beneficiaries. People who had been attached to research projects for a longer period of time or even lucky enough to be temporarily employed in them, however, sometimes referred to their work as doing good by contributing to making new knowledge. One of the most-experienced outreach workers in the project that Tabita was part of, who had worked with several other research projects over the years, even scolded the study subjects that they did not understand research when they threw the microbicide applicators in the pit instead of using them as instructed. This was not a common position, however, and most of the employed 'volunteers' were more occupied by how their position could be applied to share the possibilities that came out of being in the project that were not directly related to the scientific purpose of the projects.

Conclusion

This chapter began by presenting two common entry points to understanding volunteering in transnational medical research as a matter of individual motive or of structural inequalities. It is, indeed, possible to discuss engagement in medical research in terms of individual motives and to explore degrees and extents of solidarity, altruism and self-interest, however defined. Still, this seems an ill-fitting approach to understanding what volunteering is about in Lusaka. A focus on motives for volunteering, whether ideal or supposedly real, derails an understanding of volunteering in medical research in Lusaka as a practice where possibilities are forged and shared in unequal relations. Besides, volunteering is not only about what people might gain, but also about what people might learn, the processes they might undergo and how they may change during their involvement (Haski-Leventhal 2009: 293).

Exploring volunteering as a practice it becomes possible to see how volunteering in transnational medical research takes many forms in Lusaka. It draws from and melts into other forms and positions of engagement such as being a beneficiary or an employee. Volunteering merges with these other forms of engagement in the context of the profound insecurity and contingency that saturate day-to-day life in the compounds where a stable income is rare.

Volunteering is indeed a matter of making livelihoods, but livelihoods in the widest, social sense. People who are able to maintain the discipline that is demanded for volunteering in medical research are rarely the most destitute, so volunteering is not about livelihoods as survival, but more about an attempt at broad-spectrum insurance against uncertainty intertwined with engagement in the web of obligations that comes with everyday ongoing relations. Volunteering in medical research projects – as in many other kinds of projects – presents a possibility to be cared for and to care for others, not in an abstract altruist way, but very concretely in terms of sharing knowledge, material benefits, contacts and project openings with one's family, friends and neighbours. Such possibilities mix and traverse the material and the immaterial and they are often mediated in webs of unequal relations.

Looking at unequal relations on a larger scale, there should be no doubt that volunteering in medical research in Lusaka is predicated upon global structural inequalities – the same inequalities that have spurred the proliferation of health and social development interventions in Africa since the 1980s, thereby opening new possibilities for incorporation (see also Prince 2015). This chapter has offered ethnographic insight into ways medical research projects may be seen as yet another ambiguous possibility for incorporation in a context of marginalization on many scales (cf. Ferguson 2013). Volunteering in transnational medical research projects in Lusaka is a pragmatic search for unspecified possibility in 'something bigger' for oneself and the people one cares for, including new connections and openings that might outlast time-limited projects in a wider landscape of fickle possibilities in interventions. Along the way relations, positions and futures are at stake. As such, volunteering in medical research in Lusaka is better understood with reference to the wider literature on volunteering and voluntary work as an emerging and precarious form of practice in Africa than as a matter of altruism and undue inducement in medical research ethics or of structural inequalities.

PART THREE Hosts & Guests

5

Doing Good
While They Can

International Volunteers,
Development & Politics
in Early Independence
Tanzania

MICHAEL JENNINGS

Introduction

As the winds of change moved across Sub-Saharan Africa in the late 1950s and early 1960s, leading to the first wave of independence from former colonial masters, the breeze blew in a new wave of Europeans and (for the first time in substantial numbers) North Americans. These were not missionaries, nor were they administrative officials (although both of these did continue to follow the migratory patterns established from the mid-nineteenth century that increased engagement of Europe with Sub-Saharan Africa). They were a newly emerging set of actors, ones that would become an increasingly important part of the non-African presence in Africa: development workers. Some were professionals, salaries paid by the Bretton Woods institutions that were beginning to make their presence more fully felt in Africa, by now ex-colonial masters, or paid by the rising non-governmental sector. But many of this new breed of development worker were volunteers, motivated by feelings of solidarity and new understandings of global connectedness, wishing to 'do their bit' to help others, and hoping to experience new adventures and experiences.

Yet these international volunteers, drawn especially (but not exclusively) from North America, Europe and Australia, remain largely invisible in the archival sources, whether official, or those of the NGOs that supported them. They are (infrequently) referred to, mostly in passing, or else in the context of a problem that has emerged. While it is not possible to count the numbers involved with any exactitude, the silence imposed upon them by their absence in the archive belies their real and growing presence.

In 1962, an American NGO, Operation Crossroads Africa (OCA), proposed to the then Tanganyikan government that it send a team of volunteers to the country to assist work on a school construction project in Dar es Salaam. OCA would pay for the transport and upkeep of the (pre-University) volunteers, and requested from the Ministry of Education in Tanganyika accommodation for the volunteers, a lorry and driver, skilled technicians to advise on construction, and the building materials. In essence, this was to have been an early forerunner of the 'gap-year' experience that has become so common for pre-university school leavers in the UK in recent years: an experience designed to expand the horizons of those taking part through participation in relatively simple (if still worthwhile) projects, and to meet and engage with people from another culture. Indeed, the experience aspect, more so than the development, appears to have been the central motivation for the organization. Their proposal noted that they 'desire very much to have African students to live, work and travel with the American students'.[1] The response of the Ministry of Education was guarded:

> If the Crossroaders could genuinely do a useful job of work here [the Minister] would welcome the possibility but if they are likely to be more of a nuisance than they are worth then he would not wish to encourage them.[2]

The school was already, the Ministry felt, receiving a good deal of support from other organizations, at the expense of schemes in (harder to reach and less comfortable to stay in) remoter, rural parts of the country. The offer of 'assistance' was not pursued.

For the critics of the volunteering model, especially perhaps the commercial gap-year model of sending untrained young men and women lacking expert skills, this is a typical story, and one that has been replicated in the decades since (see, for example, Wendland et al., in Chapter 7). Indeed, what might make this story unusual is the government turning down an offer of what essentially was unskilled labour – something not in short supply in the country, then as now. OCA was offering its volunteers an opportunity to enrich their lives: whether that experience would also make a tangible difference to those they were purportedly 'helping' was a very different question.

But if OCA represented a particular form of development tourism, it was not the whole story of volunteering in that country. Its historical pedigree stretched back to the mid-nineteenth century and the arrival of missionary organizations, and would stretch on to the current day. It comprised secular, as well as religious, organizations and individuals. As a body its scale expanded significantly, particularly after independence. This chapter focuses, however, on a particular period: the early independence decades in Tanzania.[3] This was a time when the notion of

---

[1] OCA to Ministry of Education (MoE), p.1. 16 January 1962. Tanzania National Archives (TNA) 301 EDG/24.
[2] Note by MoE staff on the back of the file. TNA 301 EDG/24.
[3] Tanganyika will be used when writing specifically about the colonial period. Otherwise the term Tanzania will be used. Tanzania was formed by the post-independence union of Tanganyika and Zanzibar in 1964.

development was being transformed, when new types of development worker were beginning to emerge and become professionalized, and a time when Tanzania was particularly important within growing international development debates. In the 1960s and 1970s, Tanzania became the poster-child for a particular type of development, one that emphasized a development model based upon ideals of equality, cooperative endeavour and social justice. For many development workers, teachers, agriculturalists, health care professionals, etc. (volunteer or otherwise) who specifically chose Tanzania, it was the philosophy of *ujamaa* and the perceived character of its chief architect, first President Julius Nyerere, that attracted them. While, by the 1970s, those ideals were increasingly compromised by the reality of the imposition of the official state-development policy (Jennings 2003), the rhetoric continued to appeal to a generation with expanded global horizons, disillusioned with society in the global North, and looking to create utopias in the newly independent countries of Sub-Saharan Africa. The allegiances and objectives of these volunteers (as well as the professional development workers, academics, and others drawn to the country) were shaped not by imperial design and aspiration, but by a sense of participation in new arguments and discourses about global development, efforts to address poverty, and what appears in hindsight as Panglossian faith in the ability to construct worlds anew. 'Development' was not a new lexicon within Sub-Saharan Africa, but the first decade of independence did create new possibilities of how individuals could 'make a difference' and play their part in addressing some of the fundamental global challenges of the day.

Much of the contemporary critique of volunteering – a critique that has grown stronger with the advent of 'gap-year volunteering-tourism' – has focused on the gap between the benefit to the individual volunteer and that for the community in which they are based – in other words, on the extent to which volunteering presents a real impact or legacy – and the possible burdens created for the hosting organization/community. Certainly one can see elements of such criticisms through an historical exploration of volunteering in Tanzania in the early independence period: irrelevant skills or learning applied in the new contexts in which volunteers were based; the inherent instability of relying on people with short-term contracts, or who can leave at will; conflicting motivations for the work being done.

However, what is often missed out in the critique of the volunteering experience and impact – whether they champion the importance of 'solidarity, reciprocity, mutual trust, belonging and empowerment' (Leigh et al. 2011: xx), or criticize the perpetuation and maintenance of 'simplistic binaries of "us and them"' (Simpson 2004: 90) – is the political. Where politics does appear, it is more frequently linked to the politics of globalization, neoliberalism and neo-colonialism (Lewis 2005; Lyons et al. 2012; Vodopivec & Jaffe 2011; Smith & Laurie 2011; Devereux 2008; Wendland et al., Chapter 7 this volume). Volunteering is typically understood in terms of its relational aspects between the global South and the global North. This chapter suggests that there are other ways to think about both the politics of the volunteer (not volunteer*ing*, note), in particular through thinking about the internal relational aspects of development in which volunteers were engaged in Tanzania itself, at a time when that development was itself incredibly political and politicized.

One of the problems of the archive is that international 'volunteers' are not always described using that term. This chapter identifies as volunteers those who conformed to the conventional definitions of the term: individuals working in the country through active choice to participate (not through contractual, legal or other obligation); working not for financial reward, albeit mostly receiving subsistence and sometimes small reimbursements for expenses; and undertaking work defined (loosely) as being for the benefit for the common good (Leigh et al. 2011: 3–4). Thus the volunteers described in this chapter did receive benefits, in the sense that travel costs, vehicles, small allowances, etc. were provided. But those financial rewards were very small, and their motivations, as much as we can tell, were driven by a sense of altruism.

Volunteers in Tanzania in this period were more than individuals committed to helping small schemes function and flourish. By their very presence, they came to constitute (wittingly or unwittingly, and often the latter) a development *resource* in themselves, to be used, misused, manipulated and fought over as much as capital or physical resources. Volunteers could be ammunition, or tools, in struggles over the control of the political and material resource that was 'the project'. They could play this role, as we will see, as protagonists in that struggle, or sometimes as victims. It was particularly at the local level, where the impact and presence of volunteers was felt more, and where individuals mattered more in terms of the scale of the resource-base they constituted, where the politics of volunteering, and the importance of internal, multi-relational aspects, was most keenly felt. This chapter explores the ways in which those tensions and those struggles played out, and through this the political role of volunteers that resulted from the internal and localized relational dimensions of being a volunteer. It does so through a focus on international (i.e. non-Tanzanian) volunteers.

An obvious immediate critique of this focus is that it ignores local Tanzanian volunteers, who were far more numerous than international volunteers and engaged in patterns of negotiated hierarchies and access that were as political as those of their foreign counterparts. International NGOs made use of Tanzanian volunteers, as did the government, missionary organizations and other actors in the country's development project. Tanzanian volunteers similarly have to be read into the archive, the mass of their work unnoticed (less so, perhaps, than for international volunteers). This remains an important and necessary narrative to tease out (as Emma Hunter (2015) does in her work on volunteerism in colonial and post-colonial Tanzania). However, international volunteers presented a particular, and different, challenge (and opportunity) to the state, to the owners of a particular development scheme, and to external funding agencies, which created particular sets of relational dynamics. Tanzanian volunteers were also political and politicized, but perhaps in different ways, their status as colonial subject or Tanzanian citizen creating different constellations of power dynamics and challenges.

Volunteers in Tanzania in the 1960s and 1970s

The first international volunteers in what was then Tanganyika, as in Africa more widely, were those attached to the various missionary organizations that began to spread out in earnest from the littoral during the nineteenth century. Alongside the traditional missionary societies, volunteer service organizations began to spring up, often linked to universities, offering opportunities for lay volunteering within overseas missions. In the USA, the Student Volunteer Movement for Foreign Missions was created in 1886, establishing itself in all major US and Canadian universities by the late 1890s, and setting up as the Student Volunteer Missionary Union in the UK. By the 1920s, it had sent some 20,000 volunteers to work in Christian missions across the world, 13,000 from the North American branches (Harder 1980: 141–3). In places like Tanganyika, with the colonial government effectively contracting out almost all primary school education, large parts of health service provision (Jennings 2013), and other forms of training to the missionary organizations, these mission-based volunteers were undertaking tremendous amounts of development and welfare activity.

Throughout the colonial period in Tanganyika, then, much of the local development and welfare activity was not only undertaken by, but relied upon, volunteers. Most were linked to missionaries, but wives of colonial officials and administrators, often denied a formal role to play in colonial society, also volunteered: setting up women's groups, running small programmes designed to educate and inform on European ideas of hygiene, motherhood, participating in relief operations. Come independence, the landscape of expatriate staff working on development and welfare projects and schemes expanded significantly. During the 1960s and 1970s Tanzania exerted a peculiarly powerful magnetic force on citizens of the global North, who flocked to the country attracted by its radical development philosophy of *ujamaa*. The emerging NGO sector saw in Tanzania an ideal opportunity to put its ideals into practice, as did volunteer workers, supported by these new NGOs and by counterparts based back in the home countries.

Many of the new development projects run by the state, or established by communities on a self-help basis and funded by the also new-to-the-scene international NGOs relied upon international volunteers for their running.

A brief snapshot of activity gives an impression of the scale and types of activity in which such volunteers were engaged. Two British volunteers, supported by Voluntary Service Overseas (VSO), were assisting in the running of a famine relief programme in Singida in 1962, a programme that was supporting up to half a million people at its peak.[4] During the 1960s, the Ruvuma Development Association (RDA), a pioneering cooperative settlement scheme in southern Tanzania (see Jennings 2002), was led by a volunteer who was recruited directly by the settlement founders. Short-term volunteers, working in the villages of the scheme, were provided by Volunteer Teachers for Africa, American Friends Service Committee (AFSC), the Swiss Volunteer Corps, and VSO (Ibbott 1969/70). A summary of the types of activity undertaken by US Peace Corps volunteers in one region, Mbeya, during the early 1960s, included:

1. Construction of village feeder roads and bridges;
2. Construction and painting of additional and present buildings at the schools;
3. Reorganization of school and town libraries;
4. Assistance at teacher refresher courses;
5. Organization and supervising of sports clinics and sporting instruction;
6. Scoring of African music for permanence and for use in the schools; and
7. Surveys of social conditions, etc. in connection with the village settlement schemes, just to mention a few.[5]

The Mbeya Regional Office, having solicited districts for schemes to which Peace Corps volunteers could be attached, returned to the organization with a wish list, including construction of buildings such as dispensaries, classrooms, teachers' quarters and community centres; infrastructure projects such as construction of wells and bridges; and surveying for new settlement schemes.[6] An AFSC-supported volunteer was employed by the government Village Settlement Commission at Kabuku village settlement in 1966, reporting on progress, helping recruit and manage the settlers, and sending detailed reports back to the Commission. Another volunteer, P. Unwin, had been sent by the Village Settlement Commission, from his initial placement at Mlale settlement, to Kabuku in order to survey progress and the economic viability of the programme earlier that year.[7] In 1968, Oxfam provided £700 a year for two

---

4   Minutes of Central Region Regional Development Committee meeting, Appendix A, 17 September 1962. TNA 320 CD5/3/1.

5   John Hohl, Associate Director Peace Corps, Southern Area Office, Mbeya, to Regional Commissioner Mbeya, 25 June 1965. TNA 465 D3/2.

6   Administrative Secretary, Mbozi District Council to Regional Commissioner, 9 July 1965; Administrative Secretary, Mbeya District Council, to Regional Commissioner, 15 July 1965. TNA 465 D3/2.

7   A. T. Vawter to Village Settlement Commission, 29 December 1966; Chief Planning Officer to P. Unwin, 10 June 1966. TNA 515 KBK/D/4.

years to support a volunteer working on a well construction programme with a basic allowance and to provide him with a vehicle.[8] At a rural training centre in Buhemba, the New Zealand Missionary Society was paying the expenses of a qualified agriculturalist and a financial advisor to the scheme in the early 1970s,[9] while Oxfam supported a British VSO volunteer mechanic.[10] In 1971, despite a wave of nationalizations of private (church-run) hospitals, these hospitals and clinics still provided almost a quarter of the country's doctors.[11] Without such volunteers, Tanzania's health care services would have collapsed.

That volunteers were deemed to be inherently political, not necessarily by intention, but certainly by their presence, is clear from government efforts to seek to impose controls over the sector. It had two key concerns: first to ensure that as many jobs as possible should be done by Tanzanian nationals; and second to avoid external assistance becoming external imposition of priorities and objectives. Volunteers were not the sole target of such concerns, but they were included as potentially problematic. In 1966, the Principal Secretary of the Ministry of Community Development warned of the dangers of foreign actors engaged in development projects:

> One of the jeopardies is that so many of the outsiders who are anxious to help are not interested in our Tanzanian program, but they are bent on introducing their own program which is pre-concocted and preconceived before they arrived in Tanzania. These outside intrusions upset our ideas of joint planning and action.[12]

Indeed, such were government fears over the possibility that volunteers working on development projects might 'upset' government plans that in 1964 it proposed the establishment of a national organization to which all foreign volunteers would belong:

> In this way it is believed that international understanding and harmony may be achieved among all volunteers in the United Republic for their own benefit and the benefit of this country which they have volunteered to serve.[13]

The plan came to nothing, but it illustrates very well the dangers volunteers were perceived as presenting, alongside the benefits they brought.

Nevertheless, volunteers were welcomed, provided they accepted the limitations the government sought to impose. But where expatriate

---

[8] Oxfam field director to CDTF, 31 May 1968. Oxfam Archive (OxA) TAN 6.

[9] Director, Buhemba Rurual Training Centre, 'Assessment of Progress and Prospects', 14 April 1972. Christian Aid Archives (CAA) CA2/A/27/2.

[10] Oxfam correspondence, 9 April 1972. OxA Tan 44.

[11] World Bank, 'Tanzania: Population, Health and Nutrition Sector Review, 1988', Report No. 7495. TNA reports: 61.

[12] Principal Secretary, Ministry of Community Development, 'Rural Development in Tanzania', 1966. TNA 40 CD/CONFE.

[13] Principal Secretary (Establishments) to all Permanent Secretaries, Heads of Independent Departments and Regional Commissioners. 24 July 1964. TNA 198 DS/1 v.II.

influence was (from the perspective of the state) too dominant, or where the running of the scheme deviated from the official vision, relationships deteriorated. This was the case at the Bigwa Institute of Social Work, a residential training college set up and run by Unitas-Africa, a lay Dutch Catholic order, in central Tanzania. All senior positions were held by Dutch volunteers, including the headmistress. It offered a scholarship for thirty poor young women to be trained in topics such as 'home economics, simple poultry keeping and other agriculture, health education and handicrafts', with most graduates entering government employment after the three year course as community development workers in villages.[14]

Despite receiving support from external funding agencies, the focus of the course was challenged over its relevance, and the institute for the dominance of the expatriate staff. An early visit by Oxfam, in 1970s, created some doubts as to the value of the training:

> I would have wanted to see a more comprehensive section on agriculture and horticulture, and much less on social case work, economics, etc. ... There is surely a risk that trainees, taking this three year course straight after leaving school will 'grow away' from the conditions of rural life, and will see the course not as training for a practical skill, in fairly tough conditions, but as a continuation of 'education'. ... it is too theoretical, and too much a transplant from Western concepts and methods of social case work.[15]

A report from a second Oxfam visit two years later confirmed this initial impression: 'The girls are being educated to too high a standard, their living conditions were too smart, and I had the feeling they were trying to produce well-mannered young ladies'.[16]

In part, Oxfam suggested the problem lay with the 'expatriate stranglehold'[17] on the project. There was only one Tanzanian teacher, with plans for a Tanzanian Principal waiting the completion of the candidate's training in Holland (not in Tanzania, continuing the theme of transplanting a model perhaps less suited to local experiences). The expatriate presence certainly caused hostilities between local and expatriate volunteer staff. A plot in 1972 by a newly arrived Tanzanian teacher to oust the Dutch principal (the teacher reportedly told the students to 'refuse everything the [Dutch expatriate teachers] say; say that they scold you for pigs, that they beat you, that they give you pig feed'[18]) ended with the plotter and four co-conspirators removed from the institute by security police. But the domination and leadership of the Institute by expatriate volunteers was an increasing anomaly in Tanzania, as well as in the ethos of volunteerism

---

[14] Application for a Grant, Unitas Africa, 5 January 1970; Oxfam field director, Supplementary Report on Tanzania, April 1970. OxA TAN 47.

[15] Oxfam field director to Oxfam head office, 31 January 1970. OxA TAN 47.

[16] Report on a visit to Bigwa, Oxfam field director, 14 April 1972. OxA TAN 47.

[17] Ibid.

[18] Dr Nijkamp to Oxfam field director, 26 February 1973. OxA TAN 47.

(which was supposed not to replace Tanzanian labour and expertise, but to fill gaps where necessary).

The tensions over expatriate dominance were not only internal, but increasingly marked in relations between the Institute and government. Dutch volunteers were aware of the precariousness of their position, and the perception of them in government circles. A visiting consultant reported on a conversation with the headmistress and teachers at the end of 1973:

> I was struck by their commitment to Ujamaa policy and eagerness to assist it through their teaching, and by their commitment in general in what is evidently a tricky political situation. The headmistress herself said that it seemed highly likely that the Tanzanian [government] would take over the operation of the [Institute] within the foreseeable future. The teachers there, perhaps with a scepticism that the [government] would do as good a job as they, respond by teaching harder and faster and to more pupils, in their eagerness to do good while they can.[19]

Relations at the local level, with the Regional Commissioner, were reported to be 'excellent', those with central government were more strained.[20] The headmistress objected to both the methods and scale of government allocation of all the places. Government had decided the Institute could take more students than it wanted to, and was determined that it, not the Institute, should select those for training.

The sense that Europeans were seeking to dictate what should be done underlay, the consultant believed, the ill-feeling on the part of the government:

> whether an all European staff can really be the best people to know (with all the will in the world) the needs of an African country; and whether this is largely a cause of what may be the hostile relations with the [government].[21]

It was not the principle of volunteering that was under attack, but the impression that it operated outside the orbit of the state, pursuing an independent direction that was at odds with that of the government's official narrative of development. With a state determined to maintain full control over all development activity, any potential challenge generated tensions. In 1975, Oxfam drew a close to their support for the scheme, writing:

> I feel it is best for these Dutch ladies to hand over the work to local people as my own visit confirmed ... views that the end product of the

---

[19] Veronica-Jane Birley, 'The Bigwa Institute for Social Work, Morogoro', p.1. 1974. OxA TAN 47.

[20] Ibid., p.1.

[21] Ibid., p.2.

courses was well-mannered young ladies and not people equipped to make a contribution in the rural areas.[22]

But volunteers were not political solely because of the challenge they could present to central government policies and development planning processes. They were also political because they constituted a development resource, a resource that could be used by parties to further their own interests. This was felt particularly at the local level, where the presence of the volunteer had a much larger impact; and where tensions over precisely what the project was intended to achieve loomed much larger in relations between project 'owners' and the volunteers attached to them.

The politics of volunteering: the Kilango Production and Training Centre and Community Education for Development

We can see the interplay of local politics and conflicts over the 'meaning' of a particular development scheme through two case studies from the 1970s: the Kilango Production and Training Centre (KPTC)[23]; and the Community Education for Development scheme. In both cases, conflicts within the projects over the role of the project and the volunteers within them ended with the departure of the volunteer.

In the early 1970s, the Roman Catholic Bishop in northern Tanzania established a rural training centre on 450 acres of land granted to it by the government. It sought the services of a volunteer, a Protestant missionary from Australia, to run the project. Kevin Trenowden, who had been working at another rural training centre elsewhere in the country, was recruited and his role supported by his home church for five years to set up the KPTC. The key aims, as outlined in the 1974 grant application to Oxfam, were: to produce food and generate an income from agricultural production on the land (and thus make the scheme sustainable); 'to train local people in agriculture [and] nutrition'; 'to train Extension Officers in agriculture / Nutrition [*sic*] ... to follow-up ex-students' projects'; and 'to establish a Small Scale Industries Centre'.[24] The diocese wrote in the funding application:

> the project is attempting to have something to say on the whole problem of human stimulation and dignity which are essential pre-requisites to development activity and accomplishment. We believe that the church [*sic*] should put its seal of approval on healthy development

---

[22] Oxfam field director to Oxfam head office, 11 July 1975. OxA TAN 47.

[23] Given the sensitivities and accusations surrounding this scheme, and the fact that some of the participants are still working in Tanzania, the training centre at the heart of this project and key personnel involved have been given pseudonyms.

[24] Application for a Grant, 11 October 1974. OxA TAN 81.

politics, and this is a practical attempt to do so ... In particular we want to produce, teach, employ, impart skills, give dignity and honour to people as they improve their own life-style. [25]

Alongside Trenowden, a Dutch-funded volunteer was to establish local training needs to be served by the centre[26], and (from 1976) Caroline Williams was to work in the dairy, with local schools and women's groups. By the end of the first six months of the operation of the project, in mid-1975, forty acres of land had been cleared, sisal grown on the land had been sold and the profits used to help pay for the expansion of the project, the local Tanzania African National Union (TANU) branch was participating in the selection of trainees, and the President himself had paid a visit to the scheme in August of that year.[27] By mid-1977, Trenowden reported that the hatchery had produced over 40,000 chickens; the small-industries workshop had completed the manufacture of five incubators capable of hatching 1,000 eggs, to be sent to Zanzibar; and the construction of a new workshop had been completed. The dairy and goat production units were functioning well, and the farm was growing sunflowers, maize, beans and soya beans among other crops. A new volunteer had recently joined, responsible for teaching design and innovation to students at the centre, and they were looking to hire someone to take on community development work, due to arrive towards the end of the year.[28]

Yet within months of that report, Trenowden had been forced out of the country: renewal of his work permit had been refused and he was accused of being a CIA spy. According to Trenowden, the Bishop himself had conspired with the other expatriate volunteers to have him removed from the project. The Bishop, Trenowden alleged, saw the project as an income-generating endeavour for the diocese, not a community-focused 'development' scheme.[29] In a letter sent to all KPTC foreign funding agencies, Trenowden accused the Bishop and his Secretary of ordering the regional immigration official to deny the renewal of his work permit, of spreading the rumour that he was working for the CIA, and of making allegations over the misuse of project money.[30] Trenowden and his family were ordered to leave the country immediately.

Trenowden's version of events was contested by the Bishop, who denied, absolutely and angrily to the Oxfam field director, that he or anyone in the diocese had conspired in this way. Expatriate volunteers

---

[25] Ibid.

[26] Oxfam Project summary, 'Kilango Production and Training Centre', 3 April 1975. OxA TAN 81.

[27] Report on KPTC, Oxfam, September 1975; Oxfam to Kevin Trenowden, 30 December 1975. OxA TAN 81.

[28] KPTC Half Yearly Report, to Oxfam, Kevin Trenowden, August 1977.

[29] Oxfam head office to Oxfam field director, November 1977. OxA TAN 81. Trenowden gave his side of events in a phone call to Oxfam's UK head office, asking the NGO to request the British High Commission in Tanzania raise the issue with the Tanzanian government.

[30] Trenowden, circular letter to KPTC funding agencies, 29 November 1977. Oxfam did not believe either of the allegations, and no evidence of misuse of funds came to light.

involved on the project also rejected the conspiracy narrative, suggesting instead that relationships had broken down between Trenowden and others working on the project and within the diocesan administration (highlighting another important aspect of international volunteering – relationships between international volunteers, which could serve to support or undermine the viability and smooth running of a scheme).[31] One incident in particular was seen as critical in determining Trenowden's fate. When local ruling-party officials came to the KPTC to organize a visit by the Prime Minister, and Second Vice-President, Rashidi Kawawa, Trenowden reportedly 'told them to go away [as] he was busy ploughing'. His 'curt and high-handed manner'[32] had caused offence to the local administration, and the Bishop believed 'the Kawawa incident was enough to get Kevin chucked out … local TANU officials were very angry over this'. The Oxfam field officer concluded that 'the lack of tact in the extreme' underlay the crisis, commenting: 'As I am sure you appreciate one has to be tactful, put-up with things one does not like silently, etc. if one is to work in someone else's country'.[33] The place of the volunteer was not to cause offence or to offer forthright opinion, but to be a good, compliant and above-all respectful guest.

Whether the whole explanation for the events of late 1977 lend themselves more to conspiracy or personal antagonisms (or somewhere in the middle), what loomed large behind it all was the project, and the relation of all the key partners to that project and the resource (economic and political) that it represented. For the diocese, the project was something that could support its wish to engage in development, but also income-generating activities and enhance its local prestige and power within the region (as the focus on production of crops for sale, and the 'selling' of its services suggests); for local officials it represented a means to draw the attention of central government, to be able to use the existence of the KPTC to demonstrate regional officials were pro-actively engaging with the government's drive for development; for central government it was a site which could be used to show state policy was effective and achieving results; for the international volunteers, their own priorities determined their view of what the project should be doing (and what it should not). Trenowden, as project manager, was operating amidst this constellation of interests and the power interests this generated.

In this instance, it is the power dynamics that operate at the local level that are the most significant. As the Oxfam field director noted, the district in which the project was based 'is renowned as being a political hot-bed where many have been hurt before'.[34] Although this was meant as a comment upon the local administrative sphere, the politics of power and prestige of the diocese was also significant. The KPTC was a

---

[31] Oxfam field director to Oxfam head office, 10 January 1978. OxA TAN 81.
[32] Oxfam field director to Oxfam head office, 21 December 1977. OxA TAN 81.
[33] Oxfam field director to Oxfam head office, 10 January 1978. OxA TAN 81.
[34] Oxfam field director to Oxfam head office, 21 December 1977. OxA TAN 81.

development project to external funding agencies such as Oxfam (which is why they continued to support the scheme despite events in 1977), and to Trenowden and the other volunteers who had signed up for this scheme. But 'the project' was of much more significance to the local actors (diocesan and local government officials) under whose jurisdiction it operated.

Trenowden's accusations that the KPTC had become primarily a scheme designed to generate income for the diocese may have been over-stated (certainly Oxfam continued to see the wider community benefits of the project). Nonetheless, Oxfam was concerned that 'the Diocese might possibly begin to look upon Kilango as a source of revenue for its own purposes'.[35] Training, community development and other community-focused activities were conspicuously absent from the record of project achievements in the final report before Trenowden's departure.[36] Caroline Williams, the volunteer brought in to manage the dairy scheme, and to work on community outreach activities, certainly had doubts that community development work was a priority (although she blamed Trenowden himself, and reported that communications between her and Kevin were 'bad'). An Oxfam assessment in May 1977 noted:

> The original raison d'être for the commercial farm was to finance [community development] / Training for the surrounding people. This has been held up partly due to [community development] problems (lack of staff) and lack of funds at Kilanga (in particular the rock bottom sisal prices have meant Kilanga would lose money if it cleared sisal). I am pushing continuously for the local training, but meanwhile Kevin is becoming increasingly involved in training of another sort.[37]

The scheme, it appears, was now more focused on providing training for large-scale government agricultural schemes, rather than local farmers' needs.[38]

The diocese also appears to have been concerned that the buildings of the centre should reflect the prestige of the institution of the church. The Oxfam field director noted:

> It looks basically very good indeed, but I am extremely concerned at the somewhat lavish buildings that the Bishop has insisted be built – including running water, flush loos, electricity, etc. ... the Bishop insisted saying that the Diocese has set standards that people expect and look up to and so must be continued.[39]

The project was, for the Bishop and senior diocesan officials, not just a scheme to alleviate poverty, but a powerful and highly visible symbol

[35] East Africa field director to Oxfam head office, 10 December 1975. OxA TAN 81.

[36] KPTC Half Yearly Report, to Oxfam, Kevin Trenowden, August 1977. OxA TAN 81.

[37] Oxfam field director to Oxfam head office, 27 May 1977. OxA TAN 81.

[38] Ibid.

[39] Oxfam field director, Safari Report on visit to KPTC, 14–15 July 1977. OxA TAN 81.

of the power of the Church, and its active role within Tanzania. It was to function as a highly visible beacon of modernity. For without such visibility, how could a project generate political resources that could be utilized within the local setting?

Local and national politicians also had a stake in the direction the project was now taking. The President of Zanzibar had personally requested support from KPTC in the setting up of chicken hatcheries and banana plantations on the islands. The centre was also helping establish a major state-owned hatchery in Shinyanga.[40] With such a stake, Trenowden's statement in his final progress report can only have caused alarm:

> we who know Kilanga realise that we are probably missing the mark by a very large extent. We know that our efforts and effects in terms of Human Development as understood by the Christian Church and by President Nyerere are not very impressive, and it is a frightening possibility that we are moving further and further away from the people. Therefore we seriously request our donours [*sic*] and all readers of this report who are able to pray and / or work with us to the end we may move closer and closer towards fulfilling our goals in the field of Human Development.[41]

Such a challenge to the project could not be tolerated, for the project was serving multiple masters and multiple purposes (some of which, but not necessarily all, tallied with the original stated objectives as sent out to external funding agencies, and to which volunteers attached to the scheme had signed up to support). The resource of the project, in the way it was being carried out, was under attack, and in November 1977, the source of that attack was ruthlessly removed.

The collapse in personal relationships that reached crisis point in late 1977 was not the real reason for the expulsion of Trenowden. It was the existential threat to 'the project' he presented that was so feared. As a critical resource within a low-income country, and especially at the local level with more limited access to capital than the central state, a development project is a resource that can be used for actual development (as would be commonly understood, in the sense of seeking to alleviate poverty), or for other, perhaps unrelated reasons. As a result, the development project is a kind of performance, consisting of a number of 'expected' elements (project proposal, clearly stated outlines, certain types of activity, certain types of personnel, etc.). Provided the performance, or construction, of that project resembles what is expected from donors, governments and others with a vested interest, what actually occurs may (but equally well, may *not*) do what it claims to be doing. In other words, the 'development project' may be a quite separate thing from the actual development that does – or does not – occur (Ferguson 1994). A project exists because it

---

[40] Oxfam field director to Oxfam head office, 27 May 1977. OxA TAN 81.
[41] KPTC Half Yearly Report, to Oxfam, Kevin Trenowden, August 1977. OxA TAN 81.

has the form of the project – the official paper and financial trail – and the actors play their role in accordance with what is expected.

Wendland et al. (Chapter 7) use Rottenburg's (2009) idea of public stagecraft in a similar way, considering the ways health volunteering serve to legitimize both the institutions of northern biomedical practice, and the forms of humanitarian engagement that occur as a result. The performance, or public stagecraft, legitimizes, justifies, and provides cover for interventions and approaches, as well as silencing and rendering invisible structural relations of power and vested interests in particular modes of operation or specific interventions.

Within this 'performance' at Kilanga, the presence of Trenowden was critical to the success of the fiction, if Oxfam's cautionary assessment is correct. A project requires a project manager, and the presence of Trenowden, the reports that could be sent from him to the funding organization, his role as official representative of the project, enabled the diocese to access resources that would have been otherwise denied it.

The events surrounding Trenowden's departure from the KPTC illustrate the ways in which politics (whether internal project politics, within the wider local setting or even at the national level) swirl around the volunteer, turning them into (mostly unwitting, often unknowing) actors in struggles within local government and other centres of power (in this case, the church). Possessing power by virtue of their professional status as development actors, with connections to external funding agencies (Trenowden was able to shape the initial response of external funding agencies, for example by encouraging them to raise protests through formal diplomatic channels), nonetheless, the particular dynamics of power in play at the local level was insufficient for one without local connections to overcome resistance and opposition.

Given the prominence of church-based development in Tanzania (reflecting the long-held dominance of faith-based organizations in development and welfare in the country, and in the broader East African region), tensions between volunteers and religious leaders over the direction of projects was a common theme. Tensions, if not the acrimony, similar to those found in Kilanga, also fed into the eventual collapse of an adult education project, Community Education for Development (CED) run under the auspices of the Catholic Diocese of Musoma.

Two volunteers, Sister Jane Vella and Sister Drew Rosario, started working for the Diocese of Musoma in 1974, working with families who had attended courses run by the Catholic Makoko Family Centre. Working through individual parishes, they set up and ran seminars designed to raise 'community awareness and unity'.[42] The CED project envisaged a substantial expansion of activities in Makongoro division (within the boundaries of Diocese of Musoma), working with communities in 'an approach to adult learning which will help villagers to make their own

---

[42] 'Community Education for Development, 1977–1981, project funding application, 1976. OxA TAN 56b.

decisions and motivate them to implement the decisions made'.[43] It would 'encourage the villagers to cooperate in formulating development plans for themselves, provide funds for the projects and also labour'.

In the initial application proposal, the local District Development Director was quoted as supporting the initiative: 'There is a vacuum between the (Regional) office and the villages. Too much is superimposed. The villagers are told what to do, not why'. The project was a response to this: 'The Community Education for Development programme aims at consolidating the energies of the community so that major development projects can be better undertaken by the people themselves'.[44] Despite the language of community empowerment and self help, the objective of the project was to better align community efforts with those of the state to better support the implementation of official state development policy. As the application stated: 'The programme aims at facilitating the implementation of the Party and Government plans in Makongoro Division'.[45]

The project was supported by two Tanzanian organizations, the Institute of Adult Education and the Community Development Trust Fund, as well as the Canadian volunteer-sending organization Canadian University Service Overseas (CUSO), and Oxfam who made grants worth £44,283, worth around £333,000 ($535,000) in 2015.[46] The project ran into trouble almost immediately, with one of the two volunteers deciding to leave. The departure threatened to derail the project before even it had started. It was likely to lead to 'significant changes' to the programme, requiring the external funding organizations to rethink their commitments. The best hope was that a replacement could be found quickly, but in the meantime, relying on the work of the remaining volunteer, Sister Drew, meant at best 'the pace is likely to be much slower'.[47] Over the next year, Sister Drew's commitment to the programme, and willingness to undertake the work, appeared to be on the wane.[48] By April 1978 the project had collapsed amidst allegations that a diocesan official had been siphoning off of CUSO funds, Sister Drew reported that the Mara administration had made it clear that she was no longer welcome in the region (echoing Trenowden's experience),[49] and Oxfam cancelled its remaining grants, noting 'project personnel have now left and there is no staff to take over the programme'.[50]

---

[43] 'Project Description', part of papers accompanying project funding application, September 1976. OxA TAN 56b.

[44] Application before committee, 20 October 1976. OxA TAN 56b.

[45] 'Project Description', part of papers accompanying project funding application. September 1976. OxA TAN 56b.

[46] 'Project Description', part of papers accompanying project funding application. September 1976. OxA TAN 56b.

[47] Oxfam head office to Oxfam field director, 9 December 1976. OxA TAN 56b.

[48] Oxfam field officer to Oxfam head office, 10 May 1977; Oxfam field officer to Oxfam head office, 6 January 1978. OxA TAN 56b.

[49] Oxfam field director to Oxfam head office, 11 April 1978.

[50] Note on file. OxA TAN 56b.

At first glance, the failure of CED rested upon the weakening effect of the departure of one of the volunteers. Oxfam, initially, felt a sense of what feels like betrayal, the field director writing:

I too have just heard of Jane's exit – which to put it mildly, is rather upsetting. But I don't think she realises how upsetting she has been, nor what a bad impression she has created by leaving the programme just as the grant is approved, nor how close she came to deceit (she must have had her departure in mind while negotiating the programme)'[51]

The reliance upon volunteers, who could withdraw their labour as and when they chose, created an inherent fragility and instability in the types of small-scale schemes in which they were mostly engaged. For example, the departure of the VSO-provided doctor at Mlilo Hospital in the mid-1980s meant no operations could be undertaken, and its operating theatre was left unused.[52] At Bulongwa Lutheran Hospital, the departure of the voluntary doctor (the decision taken, it was speculated, by her sending agency) had dire implications for maternal and child health services in the district.[53] The future of CED, resting upon a single volunteer, who was apparently becoming ever more disillusioned with the work, and the uncovering of financial impropriety in the use of the funds, was the last straw. A programme that might have survived a permanent, salaried and local staff failed when staffed by volunteers who could leave, or be asked to leave more easily.

While such an analysis may speak to some of the critiques of voluntary action in development (whether voluntary organizations, or individuals), it does not tell the whole story of the CED programme. Underpinning personnel problems was a dispute between the diocese and volunteers over the scope of the programme, and local fears over the political nature of the programme.

Sister Jane's decision to leave appears to have reflected a growing sense of disillusionment with the direction encouraged by the diocese and parish priests. Certainly Sister Drew expressed concern from mid-1977, saying 'she no longer feels that the Diocese is the umbrella under which she should work'.[54] At the heart of the issue was a conflict between Drew and Jane, and the religious leadership in the diocese over the target of community education initiatives. From the start, there had been 'a lot of opposition among the workers of the Diocese to this educational approach':

The most crucial limitation has been the programme confinement to largely Christian groups – in particular the Makoko [the family

---

[51] Oxfam field director to Oxfam head office, 29 December 1976. OxA TAN 56b.

[52] Christian Aid report on Milo Water Project, no date but probably 1986: 12. CAA CA5-A-365

[53] Anna Pettersson (Administrator, Bulongwa Lutheran Hospital) to Sally Meachim (Christian Aid), 7 September 1985; Sally Meachim, Memorandum on Visit to ELCT South Central Diocese, 13/14 November 1986, 8 December 1986. CAA CA5-A-365.

[54] Oxfam field director to Oxfam head office, 10 May 1977. OxA TAN 56b.

centre run by the diocese] families. The team themselves have been aware of this and wanted to break out and deal more with the whole communities, but their success has been limited because of: (a) Opposition within the Diocese to working outside Parish / Makoko Groups ... (b) The team depends upon invitations from groups in the villages. Their umbrella is the Diocese and therefore invitations have mainly been through the parishes.[55]

Drew, in particular, had 'always felt the pressure from the priests to confine the work to Christians'.[56]

Oxfam's funding was always contingent upon expanding the programme beyond members of the Catholic Church in the diocese.[57] While the diocesan officials in charge of negotiations with the NGO were willing to endorse this in principle, with a view to securing funding, in practice they were much less willing. This was a project designed for a particular set of families within the community, and the diocese wished resources to be confined to those families. In the negotiations, it is clear that the volunteers running the programme were the main source of attraction to the funding agency, a political and human resource manipulated in order to secure capital resources. If Trenowden was part protagonist in his own unhappy experience, Sisters Jane and Drew appear to have been victims of an internal struggle over the project and its future direction.

The political nature of the programme, the stated intention of supporting state-led development planning notwithstanding, was noted (indeed welcomed) by Oxfam. The field director wrote of the scheme and Sister Drew:

> it is a highly political organisation and work that is involved (teaching people not to put up with bad village government), and Drew is very politically aware. She has chosen Oxfam from a number of potential contributors because she believes we share her outlook and convictions and approach.[58]

Her efforts to run the programme under the auspices of the district administration, rather than the diocese, were rebuffed, and she was asked to leave the region. The local administration may not have been complicit in the collapse of the programme (as it appears to have been in the case of the KPTC), but it was no doubt relieved that it would no longer have to work with someone whose political views and intentions for the programme were so different and (from their perspective) radical to their own.

In the case of CED the site of battle was between the project itself (and those associated with it) and the officials of the diocese and the parish

---

[55] 'Community Education for Development, 1977–1981, project funding application. 1976. OxA TAN 56b.

[56] Oxfam field director to Oxfam head office, 10 May 1977. OxA TAN 56b.

[57] Oxfam field director to Oxfam head office, 10 May 1977. OxA TAN 56b.

[58] Oxfam field director to Oxfam head office, 11 January 1977. OxA TAN 56b.

priests, without whose engagement the programme could not effectively function. In another project run by the Mennonite church, volunteers became part of an internal turf-war between factions within the church. An American Mennonite missionary, Leroy Petersheim, wanted to establish an unofficial (i.e. outside official government plans) *ujamaa* village at Tarana, close to Musoma town. The plans to create an establishment run on communal lines was supported by the younger members within the church. It was, however, facing resistance from 'Church elders' who regarded the cooperative nature of the venture 'with some suspicion'.[59] Two Mennonite volunteers were brought in in 1970 to act as scheme advisors and to live in the newly established settlement, hoping that they could help overcome resistance to the scheme and see it thrive.[60] This time, it was the project that left the orbit of the mission, rather than the volunteers being forced to leave. In 1970, the government took over the running and administration of the incipient *ujamaa* village, with both volunteers staying on and committed to establishing the settlement as a viable community by the end of their two-year placement.[61]

In this instance, the volunteers formed a key part of the 'resource' portfolio of the project. Without their commitment, it appears unlikely that the scheme would have survived. Their key contribution, from the perspective of the founder of the scheme, Petersheim, was their commitment to the ideals of the settlement – cooperative living and production. In an effort to break deadlock within the church, to undermine the potential for blocking held by the Church elders, the two volunteers were not providing neutral technical advice to the scheme, but (whether they intended this or not) partisan support for the champions of *ujamaa* ideals within the Musoma Mennonite church, over more conservative elements who regarded the official state philosophy, and its place within a church-run scheme, with scepticism and suspicion. By ensuring the advisors to the scheme were so drawn to its underlying ideals, they were able to maintain that ideological commitment, and thus allow the scheme to be absorbed by the state when it sought to more pro-actively promote *ujamaa* villagization across the country.

Conclusion

The experience of volunteering for many of those sent out to the country, then as now, was largely free from the extremes of such politicking as found in the KPTC and CED schemes, and their role in internal struggles for power within an institution were generally less overt than in the Mennonite case. But that does not mean volunteers were not political and politicized. Their very presence, and the sets of local, national and

[59] Oxfam field director to Oxfam head office, 28 February 1969. OxA TAN 30.
[60] Oxfam field director, Report of Tanzanian Tour, June 1970. OxA TAN 30.
[61] Oxfam field director, Project Progress Report, 24 January 1971. OxA TAN 30.

international relations that they constituted created dynamics that could readily feed into local tensions, political struggles and power dynamics about which the volunteers might be unaware. Volunteers were a resource not just because of the skills or expertise that they brought, to be used as part of the inputs in any particular scheme: they were part of the performance of development, in which the project is the act through which capital and other types of resource are accessed and distributed, control over which bestowed considerable power to those able to direct the distribution and define the project objectives. By means of an example, the desire by a community to dig a well to provide clean, accessible water does not in itself bring the money, equipment and expertise necessary to reach that objective. But framing a community desire into a defined 'project', using the language and physical and less tangible objects that make up a 'project' (an application for funding, clearly demarcated boundaries and objectives, the use of an expert to validate the scheme, etc.), does mobilize those resources. The siting of wells, just as the siting of roads and bridges (whose farms does it pass near and who has better access to markets?) are not neutral, they reflect particular interests; shaping private desires as community goods, to be met through a 'project', can ensure that these interests benefit. The volunteer, as much as a 'project application', the evaluation process, etc., was a hallmark of the project, what made it such and therefore made continued access to resources possible.

Sullivan in Chapter 6 shows how medical volunteers in Tanzania were seen in just such as way – as a potential resource beyond the immediate task for which they had come. They were a means for gaining a fee from the sending organization, and a resource to be mobilized for potential future contributions of equipment. They were both the project itself, making use of their skills – albeit, as Sullivan notes, a set of skills not necessarily of appropriate or needed level – and their expertise in their actual role, and a means to mobilize additional resources through their performance of volunteering.

Seeking to move beyond seeing development as something one agency does to another, it is more correct to see it as a process of negotiation. Here, we can borrow from Achille Mbembe's notion of conviviality (2001). For Mbembe, conviviality described the way in which the post-colonial state exercised its '*commandement*', a series of bargains between the political elite and citizens for access to and use of power (Edmondson 2007). Looking at development through its relational aspects, it becomes less a site of conflict (although conflict certainly occurred, as this chapter has shown) than of co-dependency and negotiation over how 'the project' is to be defined, implemented and evaluated. Each aspect of the 'project' is subject to such negotiation, whether it be the project description, a grant application, the personnel attached to the project, or the money attached to it. Each constituent borrows the appropriate language from the other in order to overtly demonstrate common ground, while practice may see multiple objectives playing out, competing and conflicting. The site of development is thus subject to multiple sometimes competing, sometimes complementary claims.

The volunteer becomes a part of this negotiation, their role and presence appropriated and used to establish control over the particular development process to which they are linked. For the funding and sending agencies, the volunteer may represent the 'professional' nature of the project, as well as a sense of ownership (a way to address the principal–agent dynamic). For the owner of the development 'site', the volunteer may represent an additional resource in terms of human capital, may become a mechanism for demonstrating to the funding agency the success of the project, and a means to gain access to further resources. For the state in whose jurisdiction the volunteer is based, volunteers present yet another set of relational aspects that require mediating: a means of gaining global recognition of the needs and policies of that state, a potential point around which opposition to the state policy can coalesce, or a cheap means to access certain skills and types of expertise.

As a result, volunteers became the fulcrum around which conflicts over development turned, especially at the local level between competing interests; and in doing so volunteering was politicized (whether intended or not, and whether recognized by the individual or not). The projects to which volunteers were attached could have multiple uses, some of which were official parts of the project structure and narrative; others were not, and could conflict with the official narrative. Thus controlling volunteers was a means to control the resources to which they were linked.

The Tanzania government in the 1960s and 1970s was defined almost entirely by its development vision: its policies, its effort to control that policy and limit the space of independent action, its relations to external agencies and powers, its internal politics of repression and suppression, were all justified through recourse to the discourse of development. In such a highly charged political atmosphere, where development was not just a technical matter, but coursed through the lifeblood of the state, volunteers could never be anything other than political. Wittingly in some cases, but often unwittingly, volunteers were engaged in this performance of development, a performance whose script they only partially knew, and a performance whose final ending was still being contested and re-written as they carried out their day-to-day work.

6

Hosting Gazes

NOELLE SULLIVAN[1]

Clinical Volunteer Tourism
& Hospital Hospitality
in Tanzania

On a Tuesday morning in July 2011, at Kiunga District Hospital (KDH)[2] in northern Tanzania, two doctors sat in the congested anteroom of the facility's humble major operating theatre, discussing the file of a pre-operative patient. Three Tanzanian nurses busied themselves between the anteroom and the operating theatre, cleaning surfaces or checking equipment in preparation for surgery. In one corner of the room, three *wazungu*[3] volunteers in scrubs sat on a broken cot, sharing cell phone images with each other, lingering in hopes of observing a procedure. I was in another corner, compiling a list of medical equipment lacking in the theatre. The hospital matron intended to share this list with the volunteer placement organizations (VPOs)[4] that brought these, and dozens more, volunteers to the hospital each year, in hopes that VPOs would ask their clients to donate some of the listed equipment upon arrival.

These activities were interrupted when three additional foreign volunteers walked tentatively in. 'Can we observe the surgery?' one asked. They were pre-medical students from the United Kingdom. One of the Tanzanian physicians, Dr Kapiga, whom I had known since 2008, looked at me and asked in Swahili, 'What did they say?' I relayed the request to him. 'Do they have any medical skills?' he followed. 'No,' I replied, 'they haven't started medical school yet.' 'Do any of these *wazungu* have any medical training at all?' he inquired. 'Yes,' I responded, 'the ones wearing scrubs have completed their first year of medical school.'

[1] Thanks to the participants in this research, to the Program of African Studies and the Office of International Program Development at Northwestern University, and to feedback from Claire Wendland, Amanda Logan, Peter Locke, Riley Smith, Helen Tilley, Betsey Brada and Susan Erikson.
[2] Names of all hospitals and individuals within this chapter have been changed or obscured to protect participating institutions and individuals.
[3] *Mzungu* (pl. *wazungu*) is the Swahili word for 'white person' or 'European'.
[4] Among VPOs there is a tremendous amount of variation. Some are large businesses that make volunteering arrangements in low-income countries all over the world. Others are non-profit organizations or very small businesses offering a small number of placements in one or two fields.

Dr Kapiga looked thoughtful, then asked me a question that echoed my own concerns with situations such as this, which by 2011 had become frequent at the hospital: 'Would it be permitted for random guests[5] to enter, and watch or do any surgical procedure they wanted where you live?'

The scenario of foreign volunteers entering the surgical theatre at KDH is a relatively recent phenomenon, first initiated in 2007. During eleven months of ethnographic research on a different topic there in 2008, I counted no more than thirty such volunteers. Yet from September 2012 to September 2013, KDH hosted about 100 volunteers, the majority arriving between June and August. If seeing *wazungu* at the hospital in 2007 was rare, today their presence in Arusha, not only within clinics, but also throughout orphanages, schools, churches, and NGO offices, is routine. What was less common was Dr Kapiga's question – one of the rare occasions when a Tanzanian health professional verbally expressed to me a concern about the appropriateness of foreign volunteers in the hospital.

Volunteers come to health facilities in Tanzania to observe or experience in a variety of ways, from gazing upon the intricacies and intimacies of the human body and biomedical intervention, to experiencing a health system different from their own. Amidst all of this 'experiencing', most volunteers also hope to find opportunities where they, as individuals, might make a difference in the lives of patients or the quality of healthcare provision. Yet, contrary to what is often assumed, foreign volunteers are tremendously expensive to clinics. Hosting volunteers requires that hospital staff – already inundated with biomedical and administrative duties amidst inadequate resources – take on added burdens of translating, orienting, teaching, supervising, and managing volunteers who bring added congestion to already-crowded health facilities. Staff receive no additional compensation for doing so.

This chapter emerges from an ongoing project on clinical volunteering in northern Tanzania, where I have conducted ethnographic research since 2008. While my interest in clinical volunteering began in that year, I have been exploring this phenomenon in greater depth over four field seasons since 2011.[6] In what follows, I present a preliminary analysis, based on hundreds of hours of participant observation, field notes from meetings among hospital staff and between administrators and volunteers, and qualitative interviews with eighteen foreign volunteers and five Tanzanian health professionals in Arusha.[7] The opening vignette

[5] The Swahili word for 'guest', '*mgeni*', is also the word for 'stranger'.
[6] I conducted participant observation for one month each in 2011 and 2013. Field seasons in 2014 and 2015 were two months each, in which interviews were conducted with Tanzanians and foreign volunteers, first at the two health facilities outlined here and later at an additional four hosting health facilities in Arusha region. The majority of the arguments outlined here are based on an analysis of the data from 2011–2014, although the data from 2015 is consistent with this analysis.
[7] With two exceptions, all interviews with Tanzanians were in Swahili. Interviews with

– one that, minus Dr Kapiga's comment, I have observed dozens of times, now across six health facilities – brings up an important set of questions, which this chapter aims to explore. Why, if tourists are sometimes sitting around waiting for procedures to begin, and doctors are concerned about visitors crowding their departments, does clinical volunteering persist? What hopes, values or expectations punctuate these interactions? What can paying attention to these motivations and values tell us?

This chapter's main argument is that attention to the motivations and values of *both* volunteers *and* their health professional hosts can make visible important structural inequalities and societal norms of both host and home country. These inequalities, and the discourses that surround them, are insufficiently explored in existing literatures on clinical volunteering and volunteer tourism more broadly. Understanding the desires that bring foreign volunteers from largely high-income countries and health professionals from low-income countries together[8] – and how those desires inform interaction – carries important implications for ways both volunteering and global biomedicine are theorized (Wendland 2012). Such an analysis draws attention to wider structural and cultural concerns that impact both groups, and how each navigates their worlds.

For foreign volunteers, motivations for travels abroad are tied to expectations of access in order to learn, give, and experience. These desires are inextricable from larger values within biomedicine and global health that expect aspiring students to demonstrate altruism and 'experience' prior to acceptance into health professions programmes. Such pre-health prerequisites beyond academic performance convert 'altruism' and 'experience' into moral commodities for prospective students to consume; 'low-resource' countries provide ample places where that consumption might take place.

Meanwhile, hospital administrations and staff members in Tanzania operate based on a different set of logics and desires. These relate closely, I argue, to three major factors: (i) values Tanzanians associate with hospitality, (ii) a lack of investment in either the ideas or needs of the very health professionals who are charged with providing (and bolstering) care within fragile health systems, and (iii) persistent hopes that volunteers might somehow become a gateway to envisioned institutional,

(contd) volunteers were all conducted in English. In the field season of 2015, my research team was able to secure interviews with an additional twenty-seven foreign volunteers, and over fifty Tanzanian healthcare workers. It should be noted that similar silences, omissions and hospitable phrases marked these interviews with Tanzanians in 2015 as those observed in prior field seasons.

8   In some sense this is a false dichotomy, particularly as clinical volunteering abroad continues to expand. While the vast majority of foreign clinical volunteers in Tanzania come from high-income countries, increasingly international volunteers are also originating from other countries in Africa, the Middle East and Asia. However, given the inequalities that underpin foreign clinical volunteering in Tanzania, and the origins of most volunteers, the distinction of movement trends from high-income to low-income countries continues to have salience.

professional and personal futures that are not easily available otherwise (see also Green 2014). How the interactions of clinical volunteering unfold is intimately connected to the different desires and logics that individuals have in relationship to his or her other, and to the socio-political worlds in which they engage. These engagements are also coupled with the wider structural constraints that each face, both within Tanzania, and beyond.

The ambiguous 'clinical volunteer' in Tanzania

Movements of foreigners to Africa to work in biomedicine are not new. Indeed, first missionaries, and later colonial administrations, brought health professionals to Africa as part of evangelistic and imperialistic endeavours.[9] From the post-colonial period to present, the flow of foreign medical professionals in Africa has continued and expanded, through mission hospital placements, short-term contracts and, by the late 1960s, the introduction of international medical electives (IMEs) for students (see Jennings, Chapter 5). However, since the late 1990s, the burgeoning of global health education programmes throughout North America and, to a lesser extent, Europe, has incited a remarkable increase in consumer demand for 'global health experiences', medical/nursing internships, and clinical volunteering opportunities abroad, particularly in what are called 'resource-poor' countries (Brada 2011; Drain et al. 2007). By 2010, two thirds of all North American medical students had completed an IME before graduation (Huish 2012). Meanwhile, pre-health professions students and adult non-medical professionals are increasingly engaging in the practice. In Arusha, pre-health professions students outnumber students with clinical training significantly.[10]

The expansion of interest in global health and service learning has made it difficult to separate 'volunteering' from formal clinical electives and short-term medical brigades. From pre-health students with negligible clinical skills to health professions students nearly qualified, virtually all refer to themselves as 'volunteers'.[11] The vast majority arrive through a VPO. Indeed, the few health professions students I met who thought of themselves as 'students on elective' told me their peers quickly re-socialized them to adopt the label of 'volunteer'.[12] Many VPOs offer split

---

[9] The linkage between foreigners, biomedicine and colonialism is not unique to the African continent. See for instance Arnold 1994; Street 2014.

[10] Neither the Tanzanian government nor other statistical entities record the number of foreign volunteers (clinical or otherwise) in the country. However, in my research within six main health facilities that host clinical volunteers in Arusha region, overall I estimate the pre-health students to outnumber the health professions students by at least two to one.

[11] Hanson et al. (2011) note that few IMEs are formally part of comprehensive global health programmes, thus those students wanting to participate in IMEs often do so in haphazard ways. Choosing a placement through a VPO, which does not generally require curricular or contextual preparation, is a popular avenue for completing an IME.

[12] While it is beyond the scope of this chapter, foreign interviewees expressed considerable

placements: mornings volunteering in hospital, afternoons in orphanages, weekends on projects in Maasai villages. 'Volunteer' as a category subsumes a wide variety of practices. For the purposes of this chapter, I define clinical volunteers as those individuals who do placements in health facilities abroad for short-term periods of between one week and four months, regardless of motivation. In Tanzania, the majority of foreign clinical volunteers are female, between the ages of sixteen and forty years; this is consistent with international volunteering more broadly (Mostafanezhad 2013a). Most are students. While volunteers come from a variety of countries, the largest contingents in Tanzania originate from the United Kingdom, the United States and Scandinavian countries. Placement periods range from one week to four months, but the majority of volunteers stay two to six weeks.

Celebrations and critiques of clinical and international volunteering

Debates about the benefits or pitfalls of volunteer tourism are largely divided between those that highlight its merits or potential, and those critical of the entire industry and its commodification of inequality. For scholars with a positive view, volunteer tourism offers an alternative and potentially beneficial form of cross-cultural engagement and mutual learning (Wearing 2001; Wearing & Ponting 2009). In these depictions, international volunteering promotes cross-cultural communication, fosters transnational connections and begets more culturally sensitive global citizens (Wearing 2001). One study demonstrates that volunteers, NGO facilitators, and host community members alike felt a sense of intimacy in their encounters with one another, and saw this as a key positive feature of volunteer tourism (Conran 2011). Despite a dearth of studies exploring host communities' perspectives, some suggest that host communities appreciate volunteers, their resources, and the opportunities they present for knowledge exchange (DeCamp et al. 2014; Green et al. 2009).

In the medical literature, IMEs have long been celebrated for their benefits to prospective physicians and the health systems in their home countries. Exposure to global health experiences in resource-poor settings arguably creates more competent future doctors, with improved diagnostic capabilities and a better understanding of the nuances of culture (Drain et al. 2007). Some optimistic views hold that IMEs may have a positive benefit for medicine as a practice overall (O'Neil 2006). In the era of 'global health', the variety of popular and academic celebrations of clinical volunteering, and international service learning more generally, curtail important critical discussions that might serve to address significant concerns about a far-from-homogenous set of practices (see Wendland et al. in Chapter 7).

On the ground, the perceived effects of short-term volunteer projects are extremely variable (Green et al. 2009). Several concerns have emerged about the logics and practices that make up clinical volunteering. Given that volunteers lack training in healthcare provision in resource-poor settings, familiarity with social and cultural contexts, and skills in local languages, the appropriateness and efficacy of volunteer services is questionable (Berry 2014; Conran 2011; Hanson et al. 2011; Mostafanezhad 2013a; Simpson 2004). Some scholars express concern about an underlying logic of volunteering: the notion that some care (regardless of quality or appropriateness) is better than no care at all (Berry 2014; Simpson 2004; Shah & Wu 2008). McLennan highlights the dangers of medical voluntourism:

> Medical voluntourists can and do make a difference in some communities and in some patients' lives. However, while medical voluntourism is often perceived to be simply helpful, simply egotistical and/ or harmless, voluntourists can also unknowingly harm those they have come to help. Naivety, a lack of preparation, inadequate training and experience, and poor resources and misunderstandings do not just limit the work done by many medical voluntourists, they can also lead to physical, psychological and emotional harm. (McLennan 2014: 175)

Thus, for scholars critical of clinical volunteering, the ultimate effects of these journeys for purported beneficiaries require further scrutiny.

In addition to these concerns, volunteers can create challenges for hosting governments, taxing scarce resources in order to 'do good'. Some hosting communities and organizations are worried that presence of volunteers may cause disinvestment in existing health systems because volunteers are available 'for free' (see Berry 2014; Garland 2012; Green et al. 2009; McLennan 2014). In addition, the presence of volunteers may remind hosts of the structural inequalities that inform who gets to travel, and who does not (Brada 2011; Garland 2012; Mostafanezhad 2013a; Wendland 2012). Moreover, lacking sufficient background education and training, volunteers may understand structural inequalities such as poverty as mere differences in culture, simplifying global political dynamics in problematic ways (Garland 2012; Shah & Wu 2008; Simpson 2004; Swan 2012).

Notably, existing studies focus either on the perspectives and motivations of volunteers, or on hosting communities' opinions of or perceived benefits from volunteers. In short, within the current literature it appears that volunteers have motivations or (problematic/celebrated) perspectives, while recipient communities or individuals merely have opinions of volunteers. Rarely is the political utility of the category 'volunteer' explored, despite the fact that the term entails a wide variety of practices (but see Becker 2015; Jennings, this volume, Chapter 5). Very few existing studies address precisely why hosting communities or organizations participate – let alone why they participate in the ways that they do (but see Berry 2014; Ezra 2013). Yet, I argue, motivations are the basis upon which these distant others become entangled as they do. Motivations, whether those of the volunteers or those of their hosts, reflect not only differing values and desires, but also unearth the various structural constraints and discourses that inform how each attempts to attain aspired-to futures – and, indeed, what futures seem (un)attainable and how.

There are important scholarly precedents that attest to the analytical potential of attention to desires and aspirations. Drawing inspiration from Gilles Deleuze, Biehl & Locke emphasize the productivity of considering individuals' efforts at 'becoming', and the hopes that punctuate how people engage with the world and its structural inequities (2010). Swidler & Watkins demonstrate the indirect effects of donor sustainability and 'empowerment' discourses on local subjectivities, altering the aspirations of local actors in significant ways that have important implications for current aid discourses and practices (2009). The authors reveal how local groups 'used their ingenuity to satisfy the expectations of donors while pursuing their own agendas' (*ibid.*: 1187); locals participate, but they have differing interests in doing so (see also Tsing 2005). Significantly, Maia Green argues that Tanzanians' participation in formal development organizations or practices is not necessarily due to a desire to develop the country, but rather is often seen as a means to expand one's individual networks or resources in order to 'develop' one's own life (2014; see also Becker 2015).

Within clinical volunteering interactions, both Tanzanian healthcare professionals and foreign volunteers collaborate based on divergent expectations or aspirations. Tanzanian hosts engage foreign volunteers based on cultural values of hospitality, and on imagined institutional, professional or even personal futures. For the majority of foreign pre-health volunteers, the opportunity to observe (and perhaps participate in) healthcare in 'low-resource' countries is a means of demonstrating the experience and altruism that educational and medical systems in the global North find attractive (see Colvin in Chapter 1). For health professions students, it presents an opportunity to test one's competencies by practicing 'real medicine' abroad (often with minimal or no supervision) in a place where the scale of suffering and the dearth of resources mean any effort to help is depicted as morally sacrosanct, regardless of actual impacts (see Wendland et al. in Chapter 7).

Below, I provide a brief outline of the Tanzanian health sector. After describing the two hospitals depicted in this chapter, I explore three key themes that are important to clinical volunteering practices in Tanzania: hope and hospitality, gazes in clinical volunteering, and altruism. Ultimately, these themes and the motivations that attend them make visible structural inequalities and global politics in both home and host countries. These political factors underpin many of the ethical concerns characteristic of critiques of clinical volunteering, international volunteer tourism and global health more broadly.

Biomedical scarcity and tied aid in Tanzania

The proliferation of demands for global health experiences and clinical volunteering are mapped onto longer histories of biomedical scarcity, in which health sectors in the global South grappled with promises for 'development' that no government could adequately provide either during colonialism or after it.[13] In the wake of structural adjustment programmes imposed by the World Bank and the International Monetary Fund during the 1980s, Tanzania, like many other countries, was forced to decentralize and semi-privatize its health sector. As a result, the number of actors in global health expanded significantly in the 1990s and 2000s, with a mushrooming of NGOs and foundations joining the existing bilateral and multilateral agencies traditionally involved in international public health. Since 2000, a plethora of highly targeted global health initiatives, primarily addressing HIV/AIDS, malaria, reproductive health and business logics, have emerged.

Currently, main sources of financial support to the health sector in Tanzania come from the federal government, patient user fees, insurance reimbursements, and NGOs implementing donor-funded programmes. Federal government and NGO funding is primarily tied to budgets. Annual financial inputs from the federal government are regularly delayed by several months, and often less funding is provided than is requested at the local level. In 2000, the Tanzanian government instituted patient user fees for health services within government facilities, with each facility able to use those fees to support local services. Although patient fees are beyond the means of poorer Tanzanians to pay, they are still inadequate to maintain, let alone improve, health services at these institutions. Meanwhile, of the few Tanzanians who possess health insurance, reimbursements rarely cover the cost of providing care to patients. In Tanzania, there is a pervasive popular impression that those who pay cash for health services receive better care than those who have insurance.

While donor-sponsored NGO programmes are generally well funded, distribution tends to be highly restrictive. NGOs have narrow interests (HIV/AIDS, malaria, etc.); the overwhelming majority of external funding is tied to those priorities. As a result, some departments receive infusions

---

[13] There is a rich body of literature on the history of biomedical health services in East Africa. For information on the gaps between policy and practice, and the longer history of shortages and their effects on health professionals and institutions, see Beck 1970; Bech et al. 2013; Iliffe 1998; Prince 2014.

of targeted funds, becoming 'enclaves' of biotechnical and bureaucratic resources (Ferguson 2006). Others within the same facility are chronically underfunded, understaffed and under-resourced (Sullivan 2012). At health facilities in Tanzania, these recent shifts have had important practical effects that directly relate to the attractiveness of hosting volunteers.

Hospital hosts

For each volunteer, the hosting hospital receives a fee, which varies between USD $100 and US$150 (GBP £60–£100) depending on the host institution's contract with the VPO. This flat fee applies regardless of the volunteer's length of stay. Unlike NGO programmes or donor initiatives operating in the hospital, the fees that clinical tourists pay in order to volunteer are flexible. This private, untied source of funding can be used for administrators' own institutional and professional priorities. The more volunteers hosted, the more flexible funds available to the hosting facility.

The two hospitals depicted in this chapter are located within Arusha Region, in northern Tanzania. Placements in this region are highly desirable sites for volunteer tourism generally, because the region is a gateway to some of the most popular tourist sites in the country. Arusha is a launching point for safaris on the northern circuit (Serengeti, Ngorongoro, Tarangire and Manyara), a short distance to the foot of Mount Kilimanjaro, and close to a major airport with regular flights to Zanzibar for tropical vacations.

The first facility, Kiunga District Hospital (KDH), is located approximately sixteen kilometres (ten miles) east of Arusha town – a government hospital serving a largely agrarian populace of 130,000. It consists of 150 patient beds, and is the main referral hospital for the health centres and dispensaries in the district. KDH began hosting volunteers in 2007, receiving US$100 (£60) per guest. In 2012, KDH increased the fee to US$150 (£100). Since 2008, the number of VPOs and foreign programmes arranging volunteer placements at KDH has increased significantly, with approximately fifteen organizations arranging placements at KDH by 2014.[14] Volunteer fees have been used to repair or update infrastructure: covering pitted cement flooring with new tiles, replacing crumbling ceilings, converting existing rooms to new uses, buying out-of-stock drugs or, in 2014 as discussed below, contributing in part to a new covered walkway. Accustomed to catering their funding proposals to the donors' and NGOs priorities, the prospect of increasing access to untied funds is attractive.

The second facility, St. Anne's Hospital (SAH) is an urban missionary health facility located in Arusha town, and has approximately 100 beds.

---

[14] It should be noted that in 2014, several organizations beyond formal volunteer placement organizations were seeking volunteer placements at KDH. These included VPOs that were registered specifically to an American university, safari companies and orphan foundations expanding placements beyond orphanages to health facilities.

The catchment area includes approximately 500,000 people. In 2014, in addition to the four main VPOs that place volunteers at the site, the facility hosts a small selection of students on direct placements through partnerships with universities in Europe and North America. The US$100 fee that each volunteer pays is, according to the Medical Officer In Charge in 2014, used to replace any of the equipment (gloves, face masks, soap, etc.) that the volunteers use during the placement. While it is unlikely that equipment used by volunteers would add up to this sum, the ways that volunteer fees are employed at SAH remain somewhat ambiguous.[15] Overall, however, while volunteer fees are sufficient to address small improvements at each hospital, they are inadequate to support the wider institutional futures that hospital administrators envision. Given the lack of additional remuneration provided to those health professionals who opt to work closely with volunteers, what motivates understaffed and overworked hospital personnel to take on the burden of teaching, supervising, translating and hosting volunteers?

Hope and hospitality

To hospital staff, clinical tourists are not only volunteers; they are also, always, '*wageni*' – guests/strangers. Values of hospitality have a long history in Tanzania, and are not limited to the health sector. At least since the sixteenth century, hospitality was an important societal value that went beyond patron-client relationships (Fourshey 2012). Being hospitable to both strangers and familiar guests was a moral expectation that itself facilitated societal development. Significantly, in 1983, Tanzania's president Julius Nyerere gave a speech drawing on an ancestral heritage of hospitality: 'To have visitors is a special honour, and to treat a visitor well and hospitably is an act of good manners. When visitors come to Tanzania, it is an honour to this country, and they should leave with a good opinion of our land' (Nyerere 1983: 2, cited in Fourshey 2012: 26). Furthermore, the popular Swahili proverb '*mgeni njoo, mwenyeji apone*' (come guest/stranger, so that the host can heal) suggests that hosting guests can be beneficial, allowing the host not only good health, but also prosperity. In south-western Tanzania, 'outsiders potentially brought originality in perspectives, technologies, and approaches, which could lead to innovations to invigorate and restore the host(s)' (Fourshey 2012: 32).

---

[15] I asked three different administrators at SAH how volunteer fees were used; all directed me to inquire with the Medical Officer In Charge (MOI). The MOI's response is not necessarily indicative of misuse of funds, however. As MOI, he is the chief administrator, but he also works as the head doctor of a department – completing rounds, treating patients and doing surgeries. It is just as likely his lack of detail indicates insufficient time (or interest) to go into detail on the financial allocations of his hospital with a foreign researcher.

The generalized value of hospitality extended to the ways that local Tanzanian healthcare workers interacted with foreign volunteers. At KDH and SAH, hospital staff often describe the benefits of hosting volunteers in similar ways; the interaction itself is seen as valuable (see also Colvin in Chapter 1). As a result, when asking dozens of health workers across both hospitals about their ideas or concerns relating to the foreign volunteers at the health facility, the prevalent responses were 'a guest/stranger is a blessing' (*mgeni ni baraka*), 'volunteers are just fine' (*mavoluntea ni wazuri tu*), or 'if a guest arrives, it is happiness' (*mgeni akifika ni raha*). Formal interviews and casual conversations rarely reflected the challenges that volunteering might pose for the health facility or its staff, although those struggles were visible when observing volunteer–staff interactions.

The role of hospitality in clinical volunteerism was best articulated to me by a nurse on break at SAH in August 2014, who shared her thoughts on volunteers thus: 'Here we are poor, but even poor, as my guest you will eat. If I have eaten all my food [at the time you arrive], I will at least buy you a soda. But this is not easy for the *wazungu*. They will see you, then continue eating and reading their magazine.' Going beyond the mainly positive responses of her counterparts, this nurse implied that Tanzanians were extraordinarily generous hosts, and would even endure considerable hardships in order to be hospitable. However, she also voiced concerns about the generosity of the volunteers she hosted. Being generous was 'not easy for the *wazungu*', either within the hospital, or more generally in interactions beyond it.

While good hospitality towards guests is a value in its own right, many hospital administrators and staff hoped that the relationship with volunteers could be extended and strengthened after the latter departed. Tanzanian understandings of who foreign volunteers actually *are* is important here. In a recent study of volunteer tourists conducted in a village in Arusha region, Ezra describes the lack of a local term to equate to 'volunteer tourist'. Among community members, the term that people used was generally '*wafadhili*' – sponsors (Ezra 2013). Many locals saw volunteer tourism organizations as a pathway to increased wealth, and several of Ezra's respondents hoped to establish volunteer organizations for this very reason. The study further notes that the 'prevailing notion to most members of the host community is that the non-black volunteer tourists volunteer because they have an excess to [sic] material wealth' (Ezra 2013: 91). Overall, there is a long history in Tanzania of associating foreign volunteers with the potential of access to resources otherwise unavailable (see Green 2014; Jennings, this volume Chapter 5).

Among Tanzanian health professionals, there was no *expectation* of reciprocity, but they spoke often of hopes that volunteers would see their needs and fundraise or donate. This differs significantly from neighbouring Uganda, where development programmes' avoidance of material donations are locally perceived as 'a failure to recognize the obligations of patronage' (Scherz, 2014: 125). In Tanzanian health facilities, as well as beyond them, the assumption of patronage is not expected, but merely wished for – institutionally and personally. At the hospitals, rumours abounded that some staff had found volunteers to sponsor them through additional training, or to pay children's school fees. Several staff members received private gifts from departing volunteers with whom they had established a relationship: white coats, pen lights, stethoscopes, pocket reference books, watches and antibacterial hand gel. It was not uncommon to see Tanzanian staff wearing these gifts within the workplace, although I know of no staff members who managed to remain in long-term contact with any of the volunteers they hosted, and no one seemed to know which staff members had managed to secure a sponsor from among their volunteer guests. Yet the possibility existed that one of these guests might help the individual staff members to achieve their personal or professional goals, and the receipt of such personal gifts from departing volunteers was always appreciated. Desiring to be both good hosts and to nurture potential volunteer benefactors, Tanzanian hospital administrators and (at least some) staff accommodated volunteers, their gazes, and their expectations. It is to the volunteer gaze I now turn.

Gazes in clinical volunteering

On the surface, clinical volunteering is mainly about experiencing unfamiliar medical and social cultures, while 'making a difference'. From volunteer testimonials on VPO websites and travel blogs, to formal interviews with an anthropologist, clinical volunteers highlight aspects of seeing when narrating their experience. 'Seeing' has been an important feature in both social studies of biomedicine and tourism studies. Here, the notion of 'the gaze' has become a central feature in how scholars think through (and debate) the politics of encounter. Claire Wendland (2012) employs the term 'clinical tourism' to refer to the journeys of health professions students and practitioners on short-term placements in other countries. Drawing on Urry (2002) and Foucault (1975), she argues that 'clinical tourism' highlights how the tourist gaze and the clinical gaze intersect through these encounters.[16]

Clinical volunteers' expectations of their journeys both prior to departure, and at least upon their initial arrival, are closely related to their motivations for going to clinical settings abroad to begin with: that the experience will build their resume or help them in the selection process for educational programmes back home, and that they will be able to see and experience (and perhaps intervene within) a different medical system

---

[16] Many scholars have departed significantly from Foucault's original analysis of 'the gaze' in biomedicine. Given the improvisational nature of biomedicine in low-resourced places (see Livingston 2012; Wendland 2010), Alice Street (2014) demonstrates that hospitals in Papua New Guinea are sites where a variety of actors (patients, health professionals, politicians) engage in 'visibility work' in order to incite affect and therefore compel others to act on their behalf.

and country. Said Thomas, a pre-medical student interviewee from the United States in July 2014, 'I've never been to Africa, and I thought it would be a good experience; and on top of that, you volunteer so you're helping people and it doesn't look too bad on your resume; so I figured it's a win all the way around.' In Tanzania, clinical volunteers hope to be placed in health facilities that will make these engagements possible. As shown below, they expect that the overburdened and under-resourced hospital environment will provide opportunities for them to be able to not only *see* but also potentially *do*.

Accessing gazes

For volunteers at both hospitals, opportunities to observe – whether through tourist or medical gaze, or both – became an important aspect of their experience, and largely an expectation given what they paid the VPO for the placement.[17] Said one British male pre-medical student in a meeting of volunteers with hospital administrators at KDH in August 2014: 'There is such a wealth of choice [in VPOs]. Once you've paid you know you're going to get [access].' KDH did not disappoint. An American pre-medical student placed at KDH, Kara, described in an interview in August, 2014:

> The cool thing about the operating theatre, especially the major, is that the doctors really explain what they're doing if you ask questions. And so, they all speak very good English, and they are very willing to teach. Dr M always tells us it is our right as a student to be in the operating theatre and asking questions.

Here, a Tanzanian doctor purportedly asserts the volunteers' access as their right, as foreign students, to engage in the clinical gaze. Another pre-medical British student, Beth, described one such instance:

> There was the two doctors performing the surgery, the anaesthesiologist ... and then there were five volunteers; and we're all posted by the window. And then they were like 'oh come have a look at this', and literally we were all crowded around this patient looking at this hernia. And he was like 'here is the hole where the hernia is, and this is where it is ruptured.' And he was like 'oh can you see', and he was like pulling this lady open, so we could see. We were so close around this lady.

[17] Fees for VPO placements in Tanzania are very expensive. They cover accommodation, some food, and the placement itself. Depending on the VPO, these placements can cost between hundreds and over a thousand US dollars per week. All volunteer interviewees from 2014 and 2015 knew that some of the fees went to the placement site, but very few were aware of how little (US$100–150, or £60–£100) the hosting institution actually received. When asked if they knew about payments to the placement site, some interviewees became curious about the distributions of the funds they paid; others were not. However, the volunteers nearly universally felt that the fees that they paid should provide them with unfettered access, meaningful coordination, and good supervision, regardless of their awareness of fee distributions to the hosting facility.

As a foreign pre-medical volunteer, Beth was thus able to take on a clinical gaze, facilitated by Tanzanian doctors who were willing to provide her with the opportunity to do so. The involvements of volunteers in the hospital were not limited to merely seeing, however. It was common for guests – even those with no medical skills – to participate in some procedures as well. Said Thomas:

> Well, generally, there are no hard fast rules, so generally I'm technically not allowed to do much other than like blood pressures here and there; but um, if you – if you work with the doctors there long enough, they'll allow you to do other things; like I've done up casts, slabs, I was the non-sterile assistant for an appendectomy.

From setting bones to assisting in surgeries to delivering babies, some volunteers felt comfortable doing procedures for which they were not qualified at home. Anya, a global health undergraduate from the United States, found these involvements troubling, stating: 'A lymphoma, like my friend assisted in cutting some things out. Just like cutting the mass out. But it sort of bothers me because he wasn't even CPR [cardiopulmonary resuscitation] certified and he's doing surgery.'[18]

Observing pre-health volunteers' enthusiasm for hands-on work, the reactions of health professions students in the middle or near the end of their education was mixed. Some advanced health professions students found the conduct of pre-health volunteers shocking. One Hungarian medical student felt that the pre-health volunteers had 'loads of enthusiasm,' but that their interventions were unethical 'because they don't know any better because they haven't seen it any other way. They don't have anything to compare this experience to.'[19] She tended to avoid the pre-health volunteers when possible, feeling that it was not her role to correct them. Others with similar concerns tended to avoid the 'hands-on' departments like maternity and major surgery, and attend ward rounds instead, where they could learn about tropical medicine and local diagnostics.

By contrast, other volunteers with clinical experience 'coached' pre-health volunteers to do hands-on procedures. Training volunteer peers to deliver babies was commonplace. One British second-year midwife student described how she instructed an American male pre-medical student how to deliver a baby: 'before we even thought about getting that volunteer a delivery, I explained to him how you deliver a baby and what happens in the delivery ... so that once the time came he was fully prepared to do that'.[20] This midwifery student's two years of training, observation and close supervision during her training in the UK was subsumed into a fifteen minute explanation to a fellow volunteer, who delivered his first baby that very afternoon. While there were Tanzanian midwives in the building at the time, it is unclear whether or not they

[18] Interview, 24 July 24 2014.
[19] Interview, 11 August 2015.
[20] Interview, 24 July 2015.

were aware of what was happening, or of the lack of skills of the male volunteer who undertook the delivery.

While all medical students eventually learn on live patients (see Gawande 2002), this kind of opportunity is rarely granted to pre-medical students at home, due to the policies protecting patient rights. Indeed, some volunteers had tried at home to observe procedures before coming to Tanzania. Thomas explained: 'Because it's really hard to see surgeries in the States. You have to get a lot of clearances. You have to – or at least for me anyway – I had to get a lot of clearances. You have to know somebody that's doing the surgeries.' Unprecedented access made the experience all the more rewarding for the volunteers. Being invited to undertake the medical gaze in this situation was an important highlight, and volunteers exchanged such experiences with one other regularly.

While not all Tanzanian health professionals were so indulgent, both hospitals had some staff willing to work with volunteers. From teaching the volunteers to set bones, to allowing them to hold and weigh newborns, accommodating Tanzanian staff worked to find ways to involve students, observing through time what stimulated their interest, and inviting those kinds of involvements with future volunteers. As stated above, if feelings of intimacy were important to host communities in Conran's study (2011), in clinical volunteering, providing *access* to biomedically intimate procedures and activities was a means of fostering intimacy between volunteers and their Tanzanian hosts. Volunteers tended to stay close to those Tanzanian staff members who would teach them or allow them to participate, as I explore below.

Hospitable teaching at SAH

It is 10:30 am on the 5 August, 2014. I am observing ward rounds in the surgical department of SAH. The ward is small, with eight beds, aligned head to foot, two per row with narrow walkways in between so that patients, relatives and hospital staff can pass between the beds. As the building is inadequate to provide for the number of patients, overflow beds are in the hallways, making movement difficult. Within the male surgical ward, eight volunteers surround the ward doctor, who is also the Medical Officer In Charge (MOI) for the hospital and explains each case to the visitors. The head surgical ward nurse, Mr James, efficiently squeezes between volunteers to place patient files on the beds and make notes on further procedures. The doctor gestures to the German nursing student, 'Come, examine this abdomen' ... The nurse squeezes past the crowd of volunteers and palpates the abdomen, as the patient winces. 'There's a mass here!' the doctor says, moving the nurse's hands. 'Can you feel it?' For the next case – a Maasai child with third degree burns on his abdomen and severe malnutrition – the doctor explains typical Maasai diets, gendered divisions of labour and food allocation challenges.

When volunteers are present, the scene depicted above is a daily occurrence during ward rounds at SAH, particularly in the surgical and paediatric departments where doctors and some support staff are particularly receptive to volunteers. Here, both cultural and medical specificity are infused into the doctor's engagements with volunteers. Teaching within the context of SAH allowed for the convergence of both clinical and tourist gaze. In an interview, Mr James told me, 'I like to teach them. But there are those [hospital personnel] here, they don't want to teach because they have no time. So I am loved [by the volunteers] because I participate and teach. The volunteers like people who will teach and speak to them in English. Those that will not, the volunteers flee them. Yet I teach them and I lose my time.' At both SAH and KDH, particular workers learnt how to accommodate volunteers' hopes to learn and experience by catering to their expectations to the extent they understood them, without, Mr James reminded me, additional remuneration. For those personnel who enjoyed interacting with the foreigners, such encounters provided a variety of other pleasures, from demonstrating their expertise (particularly given their low-resource environment) to learning from volunteers about medical practices abroad, to the joys of sharing meals or potentially establishing longer-term personal connections that might help the Tanzanians in the future, institutionally, professionally or personally.

Restricting gazes: inhospitable hosts and managing 'bad guests'
As hospital staff members were reticent to say negative things about volunteering, dissatisfaction, where it existed, was often expressed through action. Ignoring or limiting volunteer involvement was the most common means of expressing disapproval. I have observed this countless times at KDH since 2008, and on several occasions at five other health facilities in Arusha between 2014 and 2015. It also came up in numerous conversations with volunteers. Most often, hostilities towards volunteers were subtle. Asked about her counterparts' problematic experiences at KDH and SAH, a British pre-medical student interviewee described:

> The doctors just won't talk to the volunteers. They'll just communicate in Swahili to themselves and won't say anything in English, even if the volunteers are asking questions, the doctors ... just ignore them sometimes ... At [St. Anne's], they definitely don't get as much involvement [as at KDH]; they don't get as much learning to be done. Apparently there is one nurse there that hates volunteers. And she just doesn't have time for people, and that's just not what you want for a placement, you know you want people that want you there and want to teach you ... People do night shifts [at SAH] 'cause they're not welcome during the day.

What the volunteers wanted, I learnt, was teachers such as the MOI mentioned above. While he challenged the volunteers boisterously during ward rounds, they often spoke after rounds about how much they appreciated the time and attention he gave them, and how much he challenged them.

However, in 2013, dissatisfaction with some volunteer conduct incited a formal response. At least three hosting health facilities in Arusha region independently began limiting access of pre-medical volunteers. Most of these restrictive policies centred on restricting gazes, and maternity and surgical departments of the hospitals were the primary foci. One government hospital stopped hosting pre-health students entirely. In late 2013, both SAH and KDH adopted separate policies to restrict pre-medical students from labour wards and major operating theatres, due in large part to previous experiences with 'bad volunteers'.

Pre-health volunteers' interests in observing births made Tanzanian health professionals particularly uncomfortable. Said an administrator at SAH: 'They should not just stare at that mother in wonder. They should not just *look!*' An administrator at KDH interviewed in August 2014 felt that pre-health students' interest in observing births constituted an inappropriate tourist gaze:

> We saw that many people come like those who want to be tourists. Eh? And tourism doesn't happen on the body of a human. Tourism is done with animals and other things which are *not living things.* Now we see when they come many want to go into the theatre, want to go in the labour ward, these *are cases* which we cannot permit. In the beginning they entered and went [to these areas of the hospital] but now we have decided to change because we don't see the reason. We don't see the reason a person who is *pre-medical* wants to go into the labour ward to see a woman give birth. (translated from Swahili, words spoken in English are italicized)

Tanzanians rejecting intrusions of pre-health volunteers into the operating theatre and labour ward were largely expressing objections to students without medical training viewing the naked bodies of patients without their consent. This was a biomedical intimacy they felt was unwarranted.

Yet in practice these policies were challenging to uphold, as demonstrated in the case of the male pre-medical student at KDH delivering babies. I learnt that some volunteers who were restricted access at KDH would show up during the night shift at maternity because, as the shift is short-staffed, they could deliver babies unassisted. As the Matron of SAH outlined to me in 2014, when the volunteers arrive in their white coats or scrubs,[21] it is often difficult for the staff to discern their degree of

---

[21] White coats or scrubs are part of the required attire by the VPO. Indeed, some prominent VPOs actually provide white jackets with the VPO logo emblazoned upon them to all of their volunteers, whether secondary school students or seasoned professionals. This is not universal, however. Another VPO produces an identification badge for each of its volunteers that outlines their area of medical study and what year they have completed. The former practice, however, introduces significant ambiguity into volunteering practice, as several junior nurses or clinicians may feel unable to ask about the qualifications of a volunteer wearing scrubs or a physician's jacket.

training. Meanwhile, despite official hospital policy, many staff members invite pre-medical students into both departments, regardless of their training level. No pre-health volunteers I encountered in 2014 or 2015 were refused access to the major operating theatre at KDH unless there were too many volunteers already present. Pre-medical volunteers who were prohibited from maternity often waited a couple of days and then went, or gained entry through a volunteer who had permission. The sheer volume of volunteers at the facilities made keeping track of who had what training difficult for the Tanzanian staff. At SAH in 2014, restrictions were easier to uphold with Mr James coordinating volunteers. However, by 2015, his role had shifted, and volunteers moved freely between the departments with little supervision.

Nurturing altruism amidst decline

While most volunteers cite their professional and personal motivations for clinical volunteering as primary motivators, nearly all of them also speak of a desire to 'help' or 'make a difference' in their placement site. The presumption of being able to help, promised to them by their VPO, is often undermined in practice, however (Brada 2011; Swan 2012). Mostafanezhad refers to the 'popular humanitarian gaze' characteristic of volunteer tourism, where seeing suffering provided space for 'the transformative power of the individual' as a source of meaningful help, through 'promises of authentic and intimate encounters with humanitarianism through a volunteer holiday' (2013a: 114). Volunteers in Tanzania regularly expressed desires to help in terms of providing their own labour, rather than financial or other forms of assistance. In other words, notions of 'giving back' were thought of in terms of offering 'something of themselves' (Handler 2013). American pre-medical volunteer Lucy described, 'I feel like I was expecting more of a shortage of – not just like knowledge, but kind of a shortage of knowledgeable professionals and that, almost, I guess it's very arrogant, but I guess that I could catch up quickly and be able to help a lot'.[22] The desires to see, do and help are specifically linked to values of global health and medicine more broadly, which emphasize professionalism, self-discovery and altruism. Due to their payment for the placement, the expectation to assist became a kind of commodity that some volunteers expected to consume. Yet Tanzanians valued a very different form of 'help' than did the volunteers.

'Help' and its others

Tanzanian hospital staff's definitions of 'helpful volunteers' were often framed in terms of assistance with mundane tasks, such as counting

[22] Interview, 23 July 2014.

out pills, cleaning floors, changing bed sheets, taking dirty linen to the laundry and preparing surgical gauze. When volunteers took on such tasks, Tanzanian personnel had additional time for patient care, documentation, or sometimes a much-needed break. Along with this kind of assistance was always the hope that volunteers would want to make a financial contribution to the hospital, or might purchase equipment while on placement. Asked how the volunteers help the hospital, the MOI of SAH responded:

> They help in dressings and also making gauzes, which we use then for theatre. And they assist in operations, some of them, from second year, third year, fourth year … Some are useful, and some, of course, are here to learn. Those that are helpful are doing the dressings.

Rarely were volunteers without clinical skills seen as potentially helpful in specialized tasks. These guests were not valued for the skilled labour they could provide, contrary to Lucy's hope prior to arrival.

Volunteers' donations of small equipment brought from their home countries were often appreciated. However, the possibility of donations also carried a potential burden for hosting hospitals. During an interview, the Matron at SAH described that many volunteers arrive with expired drugs and equipment from home. Gesturing to a large box on her office floor full of expired donated equipment, she said: 'Why bring us things that have already been damaged?' In addition, the matrons at both SAH and KDH had experiences with volunteers asking for lists of needed supplies that were never delivered. SAH's matron stated:

> I take a lot of time to prepare [the list] but then never hear from them again. One I talked to a long time about building a ramp [to the outpatient's department]. I got a quote for the volunteer and sent it by email, but she never responded. If any volunteer asks now for a quote I am scared because I pay for that quote and then it eats the fruits of the hospital.

On a wider scale, in 2015, I encountered a hospital that housed four enormous metal shipping containers of equipment and expired drugs from the United States. An administrator complained that the equipment within – such as heated maternity delivery beds – was completely inappropriate to Tanzanian infrastructure. She not only had to find a way to pay staff to unload the containers, but also had to pay the government to have the contents properly removed, in compliance with national policies for safe medical equipment disposal. The amount of money to ship those containers to Tanzania would have provided a significant infusion of much-needed flexible funds, but instead the hospital carried the burdens of good intentions from afar. All hospitals appreciated financial donations, or donations of new equipment that was appropriate to the infrastructure. They hoped that future prospective benefactors would actually ask them what it was that they needed, and put their efforts in those directions instead.

Hovering and declining helpers
For many clinical tourists, aspirations to 'help' floundered in the face of the structural challenges of their placement hospital. When asked why she wanted to come to Tanzania as a clinical volunteer, Lucy responded, 'I wanted to get a feel for the place, or a place I guess. And I think a medical experience was good too, that was a big thing. And then, I mean, to help. Which is really cliché. But, to try and help people.' Given that the shortages at KDH were more related to infrastructure and equipment than labour, it was difficult for volunteers to find spaces in which to be 'useful'. Lucy later elaborated, 'There's so many people [volunteers] that it's not really necessary.' Even for volunteers with skills this was a challenge. Said one British midwife to me in July 2014, 'we want to help, but we don't know what they want us to do. We're white, we're in scrubs, we're just hovering.'

Anya, who had been on a comparatively long placement at KDH, found it difficult to watch her peers struggle with the limits of their ability to help:

> When Natalie and Brian and them came, they were like, really gung ho about everything. It was nice but then I [pause] … it kind of sucked to watch them, like, decline. Yeah. 'Cause they were so into helping everything and then they realized they couldn't because that was just, like, the way things were.

Combining their lack of impact on their hosting hospitals with their desires to have tourist experiences in Tanzania enhanced Anya's difficulties with the placement. She described her desire to avoid becoming a 'voluntour', saying:

> I feel like it's hard not to be when you're, like, you know, you come but you're not certified, and you try to help but you can't really, and you're kinda just there and the hospital doesn't really know what to do with you, and then you go on safari. So it's hard to kind of not be one.

Anya's statements were echoed by many of her peers. Volunteers dealt with these conundrums in a variety of ways. Some restricted their involvement to observation or participation that they felt was justified based on (or despite) their training. Others spent less time at the hospital and more time exploring the country. Still others found a way to be meaningful in the hospital by taking up a call of the KDH matron, who was particularly clever in her ability to cater to desires to help while suggesting means of making that help most useful to the hospital's needs, as an excerpt from my field notes illustrates.

'Medicine is the same; infrastructure is different':
creating opportunities to help
It is July 2013, and the Matron of KDH has asked me to accompany her on another tour with newly arrived clinical volunteers. When I arrive

at her office in the female ward, four volunteers emerge. 'You will see a lot of things here', the matron tells them. 'But everywhere, medicine is the same. It is the infrastructure that is different.' ... 'Also, you must provide us with feedback. Written. There is no use for you to be here without providing us with that feedback. I will present it to our staff. So we can improve. We can learn from each other,' she offers. As we leave to start the tour, the matron tells them about the covered walkway the hospital is building, funded in part by volunteer fees and in part by other private benefactors. Now, they do not have enough money to complete the project. 'It is not good. Mothers get rained on when they are going to the operating theatre to have caesarean sections. Perhaps you will talk to your friends and maybe you would like to help to finish it,' she tells them.

Volunteers who donated cash to infrastructure were rare at KDH. The staff prioritized the construction of the walkway in 2008, but only by 2014 had they cobbled together enough funds to start the project. Matron asked me to go around to the dozens of volunteers at KDH from June through August 2014 to ask for assistance in funding the walkway. While all said they would like to, only one volunteer contributed. As of mid-August, 2014, walkway construction had ceased, awaiting additional sponsors. Suspicions of corruption were an oft-cited concern of volunteers, who preferred to donate their own time and labour, or equipment they brought with them instead. Monetary donations were not seen as contributions of 'something of themselves', and volunteers rarely remained incountry long enough to observe how their money was spent.[23] However, each summer I have conducted research at KDH, at least one group of volunteers has taken the Matron to the city to purchase small medical equipment, so that they knew where their money went. This equipment was always appreciated, and made an impact not only on capacity at the facility, but also on the morale of the health professionals there.

Yet for those volunteers at KDH between 2013 and 2014, Matron's encouragement for feedback became very important. This prerogative to observe and provide feedback changed the ways that volunteers interacted at the hospital. Unlike SAH, where volunteers often felt helpless in the face of challenges they encountered, at KDH these became inputs that they could compile into a feedback report; thus, volunteers – even pre-health students – began to see themselves as learners and teachers simultaneously. The Matron's call allowed them to find a way to find meaning in their role as 'volunteer'. Some volunteers erected

---

[23] Some volunteers cited to the hospital staff their status as students and that they were unable to afford monetary contributions to the hospital beyond the volunteer fee, due to what they had paid the VPO for the experience, often paid for via student loans or with contributions from family members. This never sat so well with the Tanzanian staff, who often listened as their volunteer colleagues described to them adventures such as safaris, trips to Zanzibar, or hiking to the top of Mt. Kilimanjaro – excursions that are rare undertakings by average Tanzanian health professionals, let alone their patients.

lists in the maternity ward of rules of proper hygiene or managing the various stages of labour. Similar laminated placards could be found in the paediatrics ward and laboratory, all in English. Subsequent volunteers expressed to me frustrations that despite former volunteers' efforts, things had not changed much. However, they still compiled feedback, often collaboratively, to give to various staff members or directly to the matron.

Hospital staff's solicitation of feedback therefore became a means for volunteers to meet their aspirations of being of some use. Some staff members even asked for personal feedback from volunteers. Departing pre-medical volunteer Kara said:

> If we'd had more time, we'd probably like to talk to the doctors – like Dr E. came to us today and he said 'maybe tomorrow we can have a talk about my work and what I can do better', and we're like 'oh, this is our last day; you know we'd love to but there's no time to do that'.

Here, knowing that her departure was near, a physician asks a pre-health student volunteer for feedback on the quality of the care he provided. It was not clear to me whether the physicians approaching volunteers in this way felt that this feedback would be helpful, or whether it was an attempt at fostering future relationships. However, such requests for feedback – personally or institutionally – were common. Kara's statement about her inability to provide feedback due to her pending departure indicated another divergence in how volunteers and Tanzanians thought about their encounters. Upon leaving, the majority of volunteers interviewed planned on maintaining contact with other volunteers and perhaps their host families, but rarely with the hospital or its staff. Tanzanians, by contrast, hoped to foster such connections.

A future for hosting gazes

'We want to make a network, a networking between the hospital and you people' the head administrator of KDH told a group of new British volunteers in his office on 1 August 2014. In this meeting, the administrator shared a new strategy of the hospital administration to facilitate volunteer access to the hospital, circumventing the VPOs. Realizing that several of these students would be linked to hospitals in the UK, he hoped the volunteers could become what he called 'an ambassador of this hospital to England', encouraging aspiring volunteers to contact the hospital administrators directly to make transport, accommodation, hospital placement and even safari arrangements. He elaborated on the possibilities he saw:

> When you go back to England you can just introduce our hospital to your hospital there where you are working. Most of the people, especially the surgeons, the senior doctors, they would like to do their

holidays, they would come to Tanzania and would like to do a safari, but would like to practice maybe for one or two weeks. Maybe they would want to do some orthopaedic surgeries here. Most of them, they come with their instruments already. That's what we want, to make that relationship.

Orthopaedic surgery was one of the major strategic imperatives the hospital hoped to develop. Marketing the hospital as a site to host volunteer gazes, the administrator hoped the meeting would establish the long-term networks that might make an orthopaedic surgery future possible. As of 2015, this institutional vision continues, but the hospital is no closer to achieving it than previously.

International clinical volunteers do not generally go abroad to assist with the 'big-picture' institutional or professional aspirations of their hosts. Volunteers undertake these journeys for professional and personal aspirations – to use the experience as a stepping stone to a coveted educational programme or job, to become more culturally competent, to have an adventure and 'know a place' other than home, and often, to try to 'help' with 'something of themselves'. For Tanzanian health professionals, interacting with volunteers is tied closely to values of hospitality, and hopes for institutional, professional or personal futures that are not easily accessed without wider networks (Green 2014). In the meantime, being a good host is a source of pleasure and pride in its own right. The values of hospitality largely silence the hardships that volunteers bring to Tanzanian hosts; at least, vocal opposition is rare. Several Tanzanian health professionals found ways to be unwelcoming when they felt the burdens of hosting were too great, mostly through action rather than words. Future studies should consider how local hospitality values, and perceptions of *who* volunteers are or what future resources they may have available, may impact hosting communities' interests in providing critical feedback. The meaning of hospitality for clinical volunteering is context-specific, and deserves further attention.

Motivations as an analytic can make visible aspects of global health and global inequality that receive insufficient attention in academic literatures and volunteering rhetorics. Here, I outline two. First, attention to the desires of Tanzanians makes clear the possibilities and limitations of engagement for health professionals and institutions in low-income countries. State and donors' narrow health priorities limit the ability of health professionals to advocate for the capacities and services they prioritize. The ability or willingness of foreign volunteers to assist hosting facilities achieve their aspired-to institutional futures is limited at best. Nor are such volunteers particularly helpful in the daily grind of health service provision amidst inadequate resources, despite best intentions. The stakes of limiting health professionals' creative engagement with health futures to narrow donor priorities and inadequate state budgets are high. The 2014 Ebola outbreak in western Africa demonstrated not only the importance of strong primary care systems, but also the risks of narrowly targeted donor programmes that claim to 'save lives' without supporting the wider social services on which those lives depend. Unveiling the impacts of such restrictive funding puts responsibility back onto the donors to align with efforts to prioritize high quality primary healthcare delivery over narrow targets. Donors, governments, NGOs, VPOs, and other organizations involved in 'global health' would do well to actively engage in the ideas and aspirations of the people already there, doing the work.

Second, attention to the desires of volunteers sheds light on the ways that aspiring health professionals are internalizing the popular discourses and narratives of global health, international medicine and humanitarianism. The notion that a foreign volunteer can – based on his or her own talents – single-handedly 'make a difference' (all while improving a resume!) commodifies individualized altruism while silencing wider political conversations about global markets and inequalities, aid industry cultures, or the kinds of people and institutions that merit investment. The implied adage 'any help is better than no help at all' suggests that no one is actually doing anything in countries receiving foreign volunteers. That Tanzanian hosting health professionals are too polite or hospitable to criticize does not negate their daily efforts towards better institutional, professional and personal futures. As wider consequences of the celebratory rhetorics of international medical volunteering are covered elsewhere in this volume (see Wendland et al. in Chapter 7), in closing, I wish to hone in on one type of implicated institution. By valuing 'volunteering' and 'altruism' in their prospective applicants, universities in high-income countries are complicit in the (often unwittingly) unethical engagements that occur within international clinical volunteering. Instead, these educational institutions should foster wider conversations about the complex and messy ethics and inequalities that make up clinical volunteering abroad, and what might be done to address them. To do so would require a very different narrative within home institutions sending students to volunteer abroad. Beyond conversations around ethics, institutions might adopt a new adage: efforts to 'make a difference' should always begin by asking communities what differences they actually hope for, and what resources they need to attain it.

7

**Beneath
the Spin**

Moral Complexity
& Rhetorical Simplicity
in 'Global Health'
Volunteering

CLAIRE WENDLAND,
SUSAN L. ERIKSON
& NOELLE SULLIVAN

Two smiling young white men in sunglasses, proudly displaying tee-shirts with the logo of their medical school, beamed from the cover photo of the alumni magazine. Behind them a wooden sign beginning with an all-capitals 'CONGRATULATIONS' announced that at 5,895 metres this was the highest point in Tanzania, Kilimanjaro's Uhuru Peak. The cover story's title: 'STUDENTS TAKE THE COLLEGE OF HUMAN MEDICINE TO NEW HEIGHTS'.

As the story made clear, those 'new heights' represented the many volunteer opportunities taken up by medical students. The two men featured on the cover were the central illustration. Having just finished their first year of medical school, they 'spent much of the summer caring for people in remote villages of Tanzania, where medical professionals seldom are seen. With little supervision from physicians, they travelled village to village caring for patients suffering from malaria, HIV, chronic pain and other illnesses' (Michigan State University 2012: 3). The students were as enthusiastic about their experience as the reporter seemed to be. One of them was quoted as follows:

> Just being thrust into a situation like that made all of the classes we took that first year very real ... You learn quickly that way, because you don't have a choice ... I don't think I could have done anything that would have recharged my batteries more ... It was incredibly rejuvenating and reinforced my choice to go into medicine, to see the impact you have on people. You're helping them, and they're incredibly grateful for that. [*ibid.*: 3]

This celebration of clinical volunteer experience in an African context is one among many. Contemporary US and Canadian medical schools recruit students with the prospects of 'global health electives', and foreground global health institutes and programmes in pitches for donor support.[1] Academic medical centres design and promote such service-

---

[1] While African electives and volunteer opportunities are also popular among European

learning electives as means to 'capture' student idealism (Smith & Weaver 2006). African sites are not the only places where global health electives, programmes, and volunteer opportunities are situated, but they are among the most popular – popular enough to have been characterized by one observer as part of a new scramble for Africa (Crane, 2013).[2]

It is not just medical students who enthusiastically take up volunteer opportunities. Northerners of many ages, creeds, areas and levels of expertise engage in health volunteering: midwives, nurses, doctors, public health students and practitioners, Peace Corps volunteers, pharmaceutical industry personnel involved in corporate social responsibility projects, undergraduates lecturing on hygiene and handing out mosquito nets, engineers repairing broken medical equipment and running new water and sewer piping to clinics.[3] Inundated with images of disease, trauma and indecent poverty, Europeans and North Americans often experience a powerful urge to help. Stunning international disparities in death, debility, vulnerability to disease and access to health care lend additional motivating force. People with medical or nursing training – already highly action-oriented – may be especially driven to intervene in bodily suffering.

But there is more to the picture. Health volunteering by expatriates in Africa today is tightly bound up with a larger assemblage of 'global health' practices and rhetorics. Inasmuch as any numbers are available at all, it appears that the surge in short-term volunteer experiences correlates closely with a sharp escalation in philanthropic and public funding since the turn of the millennium, and with the institutional elaboration of global health centres and programmes that accompanied that escalation (Cohen 2006; Crane 2010).[4] In this chapter, we argue that the celebrations and silences surrounding short-term medical volunteering obscure the

---

(contd) students, and not uncommonly taken up by students from Asia, Latin America and elsewhere in Africa, they are usually self-arranged rather than sponsored by the students' home medical schools. In part for this reason, estimating the scale of such electives for students outside North America is difficult.

[2] Crane's characterization primarily referred to the carving out of territories for global health research in Africa by North American universities. In practice, however, universities' service-learning projects, clinical electives, and other short-term opportunities that blur the borders between education and volunteering often build on the social and logistical foundations of research centres.

[3] We use the term 'Northern' to describe these volunteers self-consciously and with an awareness of its serious limitations. For an analysis of alternatives see Shakow & Irwin 2000; see also the user-friendly discussion by Silver at www.npr.org/sections/goatsandsoda/2015/01/04/372684438/if-you-shouldnt-call-it-the-third-world-what-should-you-call-it (accessed 15 August 2015).

[4] In the USA, the number of university programmes in global health more than quadrupled just between 2003 and 2009. The proportion of US and Canadian medical students with some sort of health volunteer experience overseas has also increased more than fourfold in the last two decades. As noted above, the scale of the phenomenon for students from other parts of the world is more difficult to estimate. See Merson & Page (2009) for a useful discussion of this expansion and some of its implications.

roles that volunteer programmes (and volunteers) play in larger political and moral economies. In obscuring these entanglements and in flattening a heterogeneous range of activities, these rhetorics make it difficult to assess the actual costs and benefits of global health volunteering, and hinder our ability to learn from – or even to identify – successes and failures.

To consider the rhetorical practices that attend health volunteering in Africa, and to think about their implications for understanding the phenomenon, we might begin with a mental experiment. Let us transpose the young men on the cover of the alumni magazine with a hypothetical pair of their African counterparts. Around the world, first-year medical students are studying the 'basic sciences' of medicine: biochemistry, physiology, anatomy, etc. Typically, they see no patients during that year. So let us imagine two such students, in this case medical students from Muhimbili University in Dar es Salaam, who take the summer after their first year of school to travel in the remote rural towns of northern Michigan where physicians are rarely seen, providing medical care for patients with diabetes, atherosclerosis, chronic obstructive pulmonary disease, the sequelae of substance abuse, and the other common disorders of rural poverty – with little supervision, and with rudimentary (if any) knowledge of English.

Would the students' summer adventure still merit publication on the cover of a magazine distributed to well-heeled physicians around the country? Or would it be something to be hushed up – perhaps even a prompt to disciplinary or legal action against the participants? To be acceptable and ethical, would this Michigan experience require greater degrees of clinical skills and experience, linguistic or cultural fluency, a commitment to stay in the long term, or perhaps close collaboration with a local physician? What conditions make the actual Americans' volunteer adventure in Tanzania appear laudable to many, when the hypothetical Tanzanians' stint in the USA appears alarming?

The authors bring diverse experiences to bear on the issue of health volunteering in Africa. One of us (Wendland) has herself been a medical volunteer on the continent off and on for years, including a few months as a medical student and later more extended periods as a specialist in obstetrics and gynaecology. Another (Erikson) spent two years in African schools, hospitals and well-baby clinics as a Peace Corps volunteer. All of us have conducted long-term field research in African clinical settings, in Malawi (Wendland), Sierra Leone (Erikson), and Tanzania (Sullivan). All of us have spoken at length with African colleagues who work with volunteers routinely. All of us have regularly encountered Northern volunteers in settings ranging from 'bush' clinics to mosquito-net distribution projects to peri-urban research programmes to central referral hospitals. One of us (Sullivan) has interviewed dozens of expatriate students and volunteers working in health facilities in Africa, as well as dozens of the local clinical staff that host them. We have seen wildly varying levels of preparation, ability, motivation, commitment, caution and humility brought to the table by the health volunteers – from inexperienced students to highly skilled specialists – who work in African settings. We intend no blanket condemnation of health volunteering in Africa. We are, in many respects, a part of the phenomenon. Our task in this chapter is instead to interrogate the rhetoric of celebrations and silences that currently attends it. Health volunteering by expatriates in Africa is remarkably heterogeneous. It is rife with tensions, frictions, moral ambiguities, ethical and social conundrums. Volunteers' motivations are variable, multiple and often only half-acknowledged (Philpott 2010). In our experience, individual motivations for volunteering run the gamut from self-interested resume building to outright acts of domination to compelling acts of generosity and even love. What motivates someone to volunteer initially can break down or transform on the ground. Programme structures too are variable, and often remarkably ad hoc; some of them are 'programmes' in name only, with minimal structure to guide volunteers. Volunteers are too frequently dropped off and left to fend for themselves. Some programmes, and some volunteers, do great good. Some do real harm. Mostly, helping and harming are entangled. In this chapter we ask: given the complexity and variety of volunteer work, which stories about it get told, which ones might get told but do not, and what are the consequences? What do our African colleagues have to say about health volunteering in the institutions where they work, and to whom do (and don't) they say it? When these volunteer opportunities are celebrated, in what terms? When they are critiqued, on what grounds? What concerns might be raised but are not? What conversations are prematurely foreclosed by these practices of celebration and silence?

A gush of celebration

Proponents sometimes characterize health volunteer work as a return to a medical past of old-fashioned values, reconnecting the individual volunteer to the moral foundations of medicine and 'renewing the dignity of our calling' (Shaywitz & Ausiello 2002: 357; see Wendland 2012). The language used by the student doctor quoted in the alumni magazine to describe his African volunteer stint – rejuvenating, reinforcing, recharging – is commonplace in personal narratives and popular-press stories of health volunteering that feature the chance to provide 'real medicine' to grateful patients. Indeed, the most optimistic proponents of health volunteering suggest that it has the potential to transform medicine more broadly (O'Neil, 2006).

Volunteering is represented widely as an expression of altruistic impulses. In academic medicine in the North, students and faculty sometimes also understand it as a way to cement those impulses early in a student's medical training before cynicism and burnout set in – a form of moral training. For would-be medics, volunteering clearly has what Colvin (in Chapter 1) calls 'moral magnetism', the rare and compelling power to reshape the self. Brada (2011) showed that for expatriates in an HIV/AIDS clinic in Botswana, for instance, the opportunity to witness African suffering and to act upon it personally was seen as a stage in one's moral career. That opportunity might even extend beyond the individual volunteer. In the words of a medical student, '[t]he educational benefit of understanding the plight of those in the developing world helps develop one's own moral capacities. The stories and presentations one can later give might also develop the moral imagination of peers' (DeCamp 2007: 22).

This rhetoric of moral uplift features prominently in the marketing of opportunities by for-profit, governmental and NGO-run volunteer placement programmes, where it appears alongside more instrumental claims. Organizations' websites emphasize the professional utility of volunteer placements in African health facilities, many claiming that these experiences increase one's competitiveness for professional school admissions or other career opportunities (but cf. Fischer 2013). They also promise personal transformation through giving, experiencing, or worthy action, a theme echoed in the testimonials from former volunteers featured on many sites. These volunteer narratives operate as a sort of affective marketing technique. Past volunteers entice prospective ones by celebrating opportunities to have a transformative experience, to be more 'hands-on' rather than restricted to observing, to have a real impact while learning important professional skills. As a returned volunteer testifies on the Voluntary Service Overseas (VSO) website's front page, 'Not only did I make a real difference, I also developed professionally'. The VSO slogan: 'Be the difference. Be the volunteer'.[5]

Congratulatory rhetoric is not limited to individuals, nor to students. Volunteerism also redounds to the credit of institutions such as universities, corporations, and even governments. Pfizer's Global Health Fellows – half at the time of this writing working in African nations – are employees of the pharmaceutical company who volunteer through its corporate social responsibility programme for three- to six-month stints to 'improve health services for people in greatest need in developing and emerging markets.' As Pfizer puts it, the programme 'leverag[es] the full range of the company's resources – people, medicines, expertise and funding – to broaden access to medicines and strengthen health care delivery for underserved people around the world'.[6] Well

---

[5] Both quotations are taken from the Voluntary Service Overseas website, www.vso.org.uk [accessed 18 September 2014] (now www.vsointernational.org).

[6] See www.pfizer.com/files/philanthropy/Global_Health_Fellows_factsheet.pdf and www.pfizer.com/responsibility/global_health/global_health [both accessed 14 September 2014]. This example raises another issue: Pfizer's volunteers, like those in the Peace Corps and many other medium- or longer-term global health programmes, are paid a salary (or stipend) while abroad. Meanwhile, non-payment of African health workers is not uncommon. We

publicized, it is Pfizer's major corporate philanthropy endeavour.

Political analysts see global health volunteerism, sometimes accompanied by other activities intended to promote health in African contexts, as an important arm of diplomatic soft power; it has been a central element of Cuban diplomacy for decades (Andaya 2009; Huish 2009). Soft-power justifications underwrote the development of the United States Peace Corps, the United Kingdom's International Citizen Service (ICS) programme and many similar groups. They now support the new US Global Health Service Corps, in which doctors, nurses, midwives and other trained medical professionals spend a year's service in one of three African nations. A key principle behind the Global Health Service Corps, like the Peace Corps, is that individual citizens volunteering abroad put a good face on the entire nation, and thus 'represent one of the best avenues Americans can pursue to improve relations with the rest of the world' (Rieffel & Zalud 2006: 1). Individual action is co-opted as means to public, foreign policy ends.

A steady drip of critique

While justifications for Northern health volunteering in Africa may refer to national or international-level concerns, critiques raised in the popular press and the medical literature focus largely on the actions of individuals rather than the *systems* of volunteering. The most common concern about health volunteering raised within academic medicine is the danger of practising beyond the limits of one's competence. Volunteers may make diagnoses with little knowledge of pathophysiology, dispense medications with only a rudimentary understanding of their risks and benefits, or perform procedures for which they have not been trained.[7] This concern is raised most commonly for – and sometimes by – students, but it is not exclusive to trainees (Banatvala & Doyal 1998; Shah & Wu 2008). Wall and colleagues (2006), for example, have critiqued gynaecologists' 'fistula tourism' to the Horn of Africa. Genitourinary fistula in wealthy countries is extremely rare. Gynaecological surgeons, who may never have seen a fistula, travel to Africa to 'try their hands at fistula repair,

---

[contd] are aware that many Sierra Leonean health professionals were not paid during the Ebola outbreak, and that Malawian nurses and doctors have worked unpaid during periods of government retrenchment. The asymmetries of wage labour, when workers are unpaid and volunteers are paid, are silenced by the adjective 'voluntary'.

[7] The opportunity to exceed one's knowledge is part of the appeal of African health work for some volunteers. For instance, one of us knew a family physician who boasted of travelling among maternity clinics in southern Africa handling complex obstetrics cases and performing a number of symphisiotomies. Symphisiotomy involves cutting through the cartilage anchoring the pubic bones together at the front of the body. While it can be useful for certain forms of obstructed labour when caesarean section is unavailable, it has serious complications and is very rarely performed even by highly experienced African clinicians for that reason.

thereafter returning home well stocked with clinical tales with which to amaze their colleagues, but leaving a medical legacy of dubious value behind them in the places where their surgical sightseeing took place' (*ibid.*: 560). Because the first repair is the most likely to heal acceptably, the damage done by inexperienced surgeons may mean the difference between a successful repair and a woman's lifelong incontinence. As the authors note, such damage represents 'a darker side to these sorts of activity which are rarely remarked upon in either the popular press or in medical journals' (*ibid.*: 560).

While concerns about volunteers acting beyond the scope of their training are by far the most common, a few other infractions on the part of individual volunteers also occasionally appear in medical scholarship and popular accounts. Expatriate medical workers may bumble into cultural *faux-pas*, failing to understand the language, context and culture of those to whom they are providing medical treatment. They may fail to understand local disease patterns and resource availability, and so misdiagnose patients or refer them to treatments that do not actually exist. In general, these individual-level critiques of African health volunteerism are about the skills, knowledge bases and accountability of volunteers. The proposed solutions typically involve better pre-departure volunteer training and improved on-site supervision, sometimes combined with ethical pledges or codes of conduct to be reinforced by peers (DeCamp et al. 2013).

Slightly broader critiques of institutions and projects do sometimes appear in the medical literature (see e.g. Crump & Sugarman 2008), although they are rare. Here we note three. One is an observation that volunteer programmes may divert local personnel away from necessary clinical work, as when trained nurses and medical assistants get corralled into being translators for volunteers. The second is a concern that volunteer programmes typically fail to nurture local medical talent at the sites where they operate. The third is that many programmes do not provide for long-term follow-up of patients treated. These critiques are important. However, they are still relatively narrow.

Broader consideration of the social and cultural impact of volunteerism in global health, when published at all, almost always appears in social-science or humanities scholarship rather than that of medicine. (For an exception, see Bezruchka 2000). Both Bezruchka (2000) and Lewis (2007) argue that medical volunteerism in poor nations may promote the spread of a pathogenic technology-oriented form of medicine that opens markets and creates desires for pharmaceuticals and procedures while undermining actual public health. Other authors express concern about the effects of volunteer programmes on national staff: that volunteers may become objects of envy or resentment, that different institutional treatment of expatriate and national workers instantiates hierarchies of more- and less-valued humans (Fassin 2007), and that the obvious inequities that allow African clinics and hospitals to become spaces of 'global health' activities can erode African professionals' senses of efficacy and competence (Brada 2011).[8] These kinds of concerns and observations rarely (if ever) appear in the literature of academic medicine, or in the testimonials produced by and for volunteers.

Rarely do we find acknowledgement of the larger cultural discourses and structural relations of power that make medical volunteering in Africa possible, and that such volunteering reinforces. Yet the issues at stake are substantial. In the absence of a larger critical discourse and active work to resolve inequities, health volunteering can occupy a problematic place in the global moral economy of health care. Volunteer programmes run the risk of (i) reinforcing a neo-liberal model in which market forces or philanthropists deliver short-term 'solutions' to problems of poverty, (ii) encoding power differentials along pre-existing lines of wealth and of race, and (iii) locating accountability – for timely, ethical, and competent care – in the homelands of the volunteers, not in the places where recipients of medical aid actually live.[9] Could volunteer programmes reverse these troubling trends, rather than reinforce them? If so, what would – or what do – those programmes look like?

Silencing practices

The narrow range of critique found in the medical literature on health volunteering in Africa fits within a longstanding pattern of individual-izing in medical work and scholarship. This pattern has long been critiqued, by anthropologists and others, for its depoliticizing effects (Lock 2001; Scheper-Hughes 1990). Both overt and more subtle forms of silencing, among Africans and non-Africans involved in health volunteer programmes, also limit the breadth of critical analysis. Silencing of critical perspectives is a widespread practice in medicine, as a recent paper in *Academic Medicine* contends; the authors note that rigid professional hierarchies, intense competition for funding, and the power of peer review all play roles in suppressing critical views, in part by encouraging self-censorship (Dankoski et al. 2014). These and other factors work to limit critical analysis of health volunteer programmes

---

[8] Wendland (2012) has noted, however, that Malawian doctors who encounter volunteers sometimes consider *themselves* to be the better clinicians – better at physical examination, more flexible, better able to see the big picture of disease and community health. Erikson has noted too that the presence of volunteers can be understood by Sierra Leoneans as a sign of deep regard, or love. We return to this point below.

[9] Volunteers in Africa may be held accountable for practicing acceptable medicine only by the institutions in their place of origin, leaving African spaces where volunteering takes places as a 'living laboratory' (Tilley 2011) where any kind of medicine can be practised. Even substandard care is presumed to be better than whatever medicine is already there, a presumption often summed up as 'something is better than nothing'. We are concerned that this is a double misunderstanding: healing practices (including biomedical ones) already available in African spaces are usually *not* 'nothing'; and even when they are scarce, 'something' is not always better.

too, as a few examples of overt and more subtle forms of silencing will show.

Two of us encountered unusual difficulties during an attempt to publish an opinion piece examining structural inequities typical of most global health outreach programmes run through academic medical centres in the USA and Canada. The argument in short: it is relatively easy for North American medical or nursing students to do a clinical elective in Tanzania, Sierra Leone or Malawi (or other African nations). It is extremely difficult for Tanzanian, Sierra Leonean or Malawian medical students to arrange clinical electives in Canada or the USA. Cost is only one barrier. Students may have to take and pass various board exams, they may have to arrange for private liability insurance, they may have to pay full tuition to the host medical school, they may find attaining a visa difficult or impossible. These practices act as a sort of one-way valve for medical students, making a torrent from West to East, North to South, and a trickle in the opposite direction.[10]

Our opinion piece made the rounds at several medical journals and was finally accepted after many rounds of peer reviews and revisions. What happened next, however, was a form of silencing we had never previously encountered. When a new incoming editor took over at the journal, just before the publication date, our 'accepted' paper suddenly became unacceptable. The editor cut our already short piece by two thirds, provided a new title, and removed every critical reference to North American institutional practices (the entire point of the piece) in a radical editorial surgery justified, in the editor's words, by making the piece 'safe' and 'a good read'.' We pulled the manuscript rather than agree to these drastic alterations. In its place, the editorial team published an uncritical article that did not go through peer review – a piece that could easily be mistaken for a blog post. It was written by a medical student who had just returned from a global elective and who waxed lyrical about how valuable the experience was to *her* education. Our article was later published after considerable pushback and editorial board intervention, but we as anthropologists found the route to publication a fascinating window on the formidable investments that multiple institutions (medical schools, medical publishing houses, national healthcare systems) make to keep volunteerism in the realm of moral good. Volunteerism is not just uncritiqued, but uncritique-able.

Political forces also shape the discussion of health volunteerism in Africa. At a panel on health and politics in an academic conference, two US political officials with distinguished diplomatic careers presented papers on the role of African health efforts – including volunteer programmes – in state diplomacy. Audience members asked about the health costs of aggressive US patent protections, and of continued US pressures on African governments to shrink civil sectors and the effects

---

[10] The flow goes in the opposite direction after trainees are fully qualified specialists.

of that shrinkage on basic epidemiological surveillance and public primary health care. The officials explained that global health served as a 'bipartisan oasis': a rare arena in which political opponents from right and left could agree on what to do.[11] Raising such questions would have introduced dissent into this oasis of cooperation, and so these issues – and others, such as support for safe abortion – were sidelined in favour of efforts like development of the Global Health Service Corps.

Self-silencing in a context of funding competition is likely another factor in the suppression of critical perspectives. All three authors have heard academic social scientists, humanities scholars and medical professionals afraid to voice questions about global health activities lest they affect their job security, jeopardize potential funding streams or alienate colleagues and supervisors. Each of us has one or more times been asked to give a professional presentation and warned explicitly by our hosts that 'this isn't the audience' for a critical perspective on global health. Typically the audience for which critical perspectives are deemed unacceptable is one of health or pre-health students or medical professionals. Interestingly, in our experience and that of colleagues, these audiences are in fact quite open to discussion of the complexities of global health efforts. Sometimes, they are hungry for it. Why, then, are they to be protected from critical analysis?

In the USA, 'global health' is awash in funds. Corporate and philanthropic interests are at a high-water mark even as funding for other kinds of work runs dry. Much of this funding goes to research, it is true, but some goes to volunteer or educational opportunities. Sometimes the lines between volunteering, education and research are blurred in practice. For instance, US university funding or academic requirements for electives abroad may require that students not merely observe, but also 'do something', whether clinically or through participation in research.[12] Even self-funded volunteer work can be seen as a way to get a foot in the door of an international health career. The instrumental stakes are high for medical students, academic medicine faculty, medical anthropologists, medical historians and politicians to agree that medical

---

[11] Erikson notes that this characterization is conspicuously untrue. During her early career work in Washington, DC, working at the US Agency for International Development (USAID) and with US State Department and Congress officials, she regularly bore witness to fevered battles between respective proponents of market versus welfare ideologies in international development and foreign policy decision-making processes.

[12] Sullivan's interviews with dozens of foreign clinical volunteers in Tanzania have indicated that British health professions students are often given strict instructions to restrict themselves to observation, due to the lack of liability coverage for students who may make a medical error while abroad. Meanwhile, students from other countries, and the USA in particular, are often encouraged to 'get involved'. In 2015, a first-year medical student in the USA applied to his institution for funding to support him as a research assistant on Sullivan's qualitative project in Tanzania. All of his applications were denied, with the explanation that doing qualitative research was insufficiently 'hands on'. He would only be provided with support if he agreed to immunize children or do some other procedures for which he had had theoretical training, but minimal clinical experience.

volunteering is simply a 'good thing' – even a moral imperative. To raise questions about the institutions that support health volunteer efforts is to risk accusations of protecting turf, squashing idealistic impulses, callously ignoring the plight of the poor and suffering, or even being negligent. In the words of our journal editor, such critiques are neither 'safe,' nor 'a good read'.

African professionals with critical perspectives may also engage in self-silencing to avoid putting possible funding streams at risk, as Sullivan's work (in Chapter 6) makes clear. Her colleagues in Tanzania in a district hospital that hosts many European and North American volunteers sometimes grumbled privately about the burdens involved – of translating, of explaining local disease patterns over and over again to people who stayed a few weeks and then never came again, of coping with visitors' ignorance or entitlement. Sullivan believes that proud local traditions of hospitality are part of what keeps these professionals from complaining to the programme administrators, but only part. The Tanzanians also expressed hopes that one or more short-term volunteers would eventually develop lasting ties to the hospital, and become long-term personal, professional, or institutional benefactors.[13] In a context in which donor funding is tightly tied to specific interests (Sullivan 2012), and public funding inadequate to support the healthcare needs of the wider community, even a slim possibility of additional 'untied' funds is not worth jeopardizing.

Finally, self-silencing on the part of volunteers themselves plays a role. Privately, health volunteers in Africa frequently express disappointment that there is little for them to do, that they are not very helpful. In some cases they are limited by inadequate (or no) language abilities. In others, especially for pre-medical or pre-nursing volunteers, it is their lack of clinical training that leaves them with nothing to do. Wendland has encountered specialists frustrated by the dearth of human or material resources they deem necessary to do their work, to the extent that some have cut short their intended volunteer stints. Sometimes there are simply too many volunteers at a single site. As Sullivan found in Tanzania, volunteers often experience themselves to be 'just taking up space' or unable to 'make a difference'. But when they talk to friends and family members at home they typically conceal these disappointments; their social networks often helped fund their trip to volunteer, and the volunteers do not want their supporters to think it was all for naught. The inflated rhetoric used to sell volunteer stints as opportunities for heroic activity makes experiences of boredom, bumbling, and uselessness all the more deflating.

[13] Maia Green (2014) makes a similar point about the motivations of Tanzanians to engage with development projects more broadly. Personal association with funded development initiatives in Tanzania is a means through which people aim to expand their social networks and access resources relevant to personal plans to build lives for themselves.

What interests are served by celebration and silence?

These various practices of silence have instructive parallels with those described by people who study transnational research in Africa. Johanna Crane (2010), who studies the activities of US universities and research institutes in Uganda, perceptively notes that the very field of global health research *requires* the inequalities it ostensibly addresses. To avoid the uncomfortable spectre of neo-colonialism, academic institutions make such inequalities disappear with a rhetoric that celebrates partnership and collaboration – for instance, in institutional contexts such as legal memoranda of understanding, or in conferences like those sponsored by the Consortium of Universities for Global Health.

In global health interventions more broadly, rhetorical strategies – including silencing – are often employed to render these engagements 'ethical'; they are particularly notable in transnational medical research conducted in Africa (Kingori 2013). To be constituted as ethically acceptable under international codes of research conduct, medical research requires participants to be free agents, not swayed in any way to participate in clinical trials. As in the educational initiatives described by Crane, in medical research, a language of participation, partnership and collaboration implies equality. Geissler (2013) recently described the practices of 'unknowing' required to produce this imagined equality in a transnational East African research centre rife with severe and obvious economic inequalities. 'Unknowing' takes work: much has to be silenced to keep as 'public secrets' the stark differences in material wellbeing that everyone knows exist. Geissler showed that some routine actions that acknowledge inequalities never got reported anywhere – such as the continued clinical care that doctors and nurses on the research team provided for trial partici- pants after they had left the studies. Other acknowledgements got reported in 'field logs' but erased from 'data', and yet others were renamed in language that effaced the reality – such as when payments to trial participants were called 'transport allowances', even when participants were travelling on foot.

Medical volunteering in Africa arguably pushes this paradox even further, in that it is typically justified *explicitly* through difference – a difference in material and bodily wellbeing that demands a compassionate response. In that respect, medical volunteering explicitly encodes a material and knowledge differential between the expert subject who acts, and the suffering object of that action (Butt 2002). As Holte (in Chapter 8) shows for the wealthy Kenyan youths who spend time in a poor community near their school, volunteering can be understood as the responsible, compassionate response to privilege even as it reinforces that privilege. However, *power* differentials must at the same time be effaced, denied, or 'un-known' to avoid the appearance of neo-colonialism – or worse, in the case of some forms of health volunteering, of exploitation of the unwitting by the untrained.

These examples from medical research and from university 'partnership' projects suggest that institutional interests may be served by rhetorical strategies that conceal inequalities. But what interests, or whose, are at stake in the patterns of speech and silence that attend expatriate health volunteering in contemporary Africa? We suggest that three institutions are bolstered by uncritical celebration of 'global health' volunteering: the state (or rather, some states), the medical marketplace and academic medicine.

Legitimizing state power

Granting legitimacy to the state is the overt aim of promoting global health volunteering as a form of diplomatic soft power. This kind of legitimation has a long history. In a previous era, the depiction of biomedical care as an urgent humanitarian need was used to justify colonial conquest (Greene et al. 2013). Images of African suffering, African diseases and European nurses and doctors were part of the symbolic scaffolding on which the project of colonization was built: colonization was necessary to bring the benefits of modern medicine to people imagined as non-modern, backward, sick and needy.[14] The similarities in images and imaginations can be striking. The old regimes of tropical medicine in Africa explicitly registered hierarchy and dependence as justifications, however, while the proponents of the new era of global health outreach take pains to distinguish our own ventures from those of an era in which medicine became a means of domination and a reinforcement of inequality. As Geissler (2013) has pointed out, this distancing frees us from connotations of colonial hegemony – and also from the implication of ongoing responsibility or lasting commitment. Silence about the costs and the ethical ambiguities of health volunteering helps to minimize uncomfortable echoes of colonialism, even while state-sponsored health volunteer programmes allow wealthier states to be seen 'doing something' about global health.

'Travelling' biomedicalization

In his perceptive work on the larger phenomenon of humanitarian medical science, Richard Rottenburg (2009) raises another possibility:

---

[14] The pattern is hardly unique to Africa, of course. The presumed beneficent effect of biomedicine was used to prop up imperial ambitions in many places (see e.g. Arnold 1994; Street 2014). Anderson (2003) has argued that 'tropical medicine' in fact helped to construct a global whiteness that supported the dominion of some nations over others while surpassing any individual nationality.

that science, politics and capital interests are entwined in contemporary medical humanitarianism. Rottenburg contends that humanitarian medicine can be a form of public experiment, justified by the rhetoric of emergency, and staged as a dramatic and benevolent intervention. Humanitarian medicine expanded rapidly in a post-Cold-War, post-structural-adjustment era in which prevailing ideologies ensured that the '[b]ypassing of national governments in development cooperation changed from being an illicit act to being a sign of concern for the poor' (Rottenburg 2009: 428). If that bypassing served market interests, so much the better. Medical humanitarianism is not innocent: it comes with a bias towards technologies – devices, diagnostics and treatments – capable of catalysing market value but not always of improving health outcomes, especially for poor people the world over (Dumit 2012; Rajan 2012).

Global health volunteering is not innocent either. It supports – or even renders as a moral imperative – the export of a model of commercially driven care that has had dire consequences for impoverished and marginalized people in many parts of the world, rich and poor (Elliott 2010; Pfeiffer & Chapman 2015). Uncritical praise of health volunteering in Africa legitimates more than just the state. It also legitimates the global political-economic structures and commercial interests of Northern high-technology medicine. Promoted as 'magic bullet' solutions in the absence of access to good quality healthcare access, many of these high-tech innovations are so costly that either they remain out of reach or their purchase renders other basic care impossible. They also distract from conversations about improvements to overall healthcare delivery, including the roles that non-allopathic modes of healing might play, both at home and abroad.

Staging a global moral economy of medicine

Volunteer work could, at least in theory, call into question the moral legitimacy of medicine as practised in the wealthiest nations of the world. The offhand invocation of 'real medicine' to describe health volunteering is one suggestive piece of evidence. An organization that recruits medical volunteers, primarily for African and Asian postings, is called 'The Real Medicine Foundation'. It is not uncommon for us to hear medical colleagues refer to the one or two weeks a year they spend in Ethiopia, or Ghana or Malawi, as their chance to practice 'real medicine'.[15] The language of return is also striking. As we noted above, those who call

---

[15] A parallel will strike some anthropologists: while nearly all in our profession will stoutly defend domestic anthropology done in European, US or Canadian urban centres as legitimate and important, there lingers a sense that *real* anthropology is best done far away, preferably somewhere 'muddy and malarial', in a non-European language. The prestige structures of the profession reinforce that sense. See Mwenda Ntarangwi's probing discussion of this phenomenon in *Reversed Gaze* (2010: chapter 2). Thanks to Hayder Al-Mohammed for articulating this parallel in discussion.

for global health volunteering often invoke images of regeneration, renewal, recapturing, return to old-fashioned values, even (re-)awakening Hippocrates. This kind of language implies something questionable about the present, and volunteering in Africa as one way to get back to a desired or imagined past in which medicine was a morally worthy endeavour and an unquestioned good.

In the USA, a historical shift in academic medicine's care for the destitute left both a legitimation crisis and a teaching predicament in its wake. The surge in 'global health' in US academic medical centres began just as their role in providing health care for the domestic poor ebbed. For decades prior, students and residents had learnt their skills on the destitute. Faculty would then bill the state for the services provided – even if faculty were not physically present for any of it – and the health centre would be seen to be serving the public good, while not eating the full cost of the medical care. (In the USA, government-funded health care is generally limited to the poor, the elderly and military veterans.) Belated enforcement of existing regulations in the 1990s, along with other changes in state and federal funding, meant that these practices ended in most teaching hospitals. If the state was to pay for health care, a fully credentialed physician needed to provide it. Because clinical faculty time is more lucratively spent providing care to people with good insurance, academic health centres were in a financial bind. Many teaching hospitals no longer opened their doors to legions of poor patients, and students and residents had to look elsewhere to gain experience. One of the 'elsewheres' looked to was poor countries overseas, where a faculty member or two could take many trainees with little supervision and little regulatory oversight.[16] Lest this line of argument sound like a conspiracy theory, we quote the article mentioned above that discusses how clinical electives in poor countries help in 'capturing student idealism':

> AHCs' [academic health centres'] social and historic mission to provide care to indigent and underserved populations is being severely challenged by the financial burdens facing them in this time of increased competition, managed care, and declining resources. This situation has the potential to further reduce students' opportunities to learn how to provide care for these populations, and to negatively affect their idealism. AHCs need to encourage and support innovative curricula that can help address these issues in a cost effective way. (Smith & Weaver 2006: 533)

The innovative and cost-effective approach these authors championed was to take first-year medical students with no clinical skills overseas (in this case to a very poor Central American nation) for three weeks, where they rotated through village clinics, took night call for emergencies

---

[16] Sullivan notes here that free clinics for the urban homeless, staffed by medical students with one or two volunteer faculty physicians and typically not billing for care, may serve similar functions.

and dispensed medications in clinic pharmacies. In later iterations of the programme, faculty added a one-week historical, cultural and language orientation after returning students requested it.

This particular version of global health volunteering reads as an offshoring of compassion: 'capturing idealism' in an export processing zone, as it were, someplace where it can be done cheaply. (If it works for clothing, why not for idealism?) To consider it *not just ethical but laudable* requires habits of uncritical celebration.

The costs of silence: exploring heterogeneous volunteer experiences

We have described a pattern of high-toned moral celebration that attends expatriate volunteer work in African health, and another pattern in which certain kinds of structural and cultural – but not individual – critiques are silenced. Felicitas Becker (2015) argues that attention to the ambiguities of volunteering helps to delegitimize the dominant 'donor speak' that surrounds it, a language that is never a transparent description of African realities. Delving into what these rhetorical patterns reveal and what they conceal allows us to position volunteers in larger stories and longer histories (see also Jennings in Chapter 5), and at the same time to understand the extraordinary heterogeneity of contemporary global health volunteering.

A powerful flattening occurs when a three-week excursion by someone unskilled and ill-supervised (such as the one in Tanzania we described in our opening case) is celebrated in the same terms as a multi-year commitment by a fully trained and experienced clinician. These patterns of celebration and silence reshape a deeply uneven set of volunteer and humanitarian practices into a monolithic phenomenon, and they depoliticize that phenomenon. The cost of this flattening is thus substantial. The editors of this volume contend that volunteering can be thought of as a political form: people work together in the service of a greater good, perhaps even a common good. Silencing depoliticizes. It drives the questions and fears of participants in medical volunteering underground, converting to personal shame, regret or anger what might have been important political analysis about what actually works to promote health sovereignty and sustainability, rather than to perpetuate a charity model in which healthcare always depends on outsiders.

Each of the authors has seen health volunteer programmes that we believe really work. In Malawi, we think of a research and clinical-care programme that focuses on paediatric malaria, and a community-based orphan care project. Both are long-term programmes in which locally urgent problems drive the clinical agenda. While each uses expatriate volunteers to a limited extent, each has a majority Malawian staff. In each, Malawian and expatriate personnel are true colleagues who share the risks and rewards of work (including opportunities for professional growth), and the difficult conversations about equity and succession happen even though they are uncomfortable. In Sierra Leone, we think of a programme begun by a surgeon formerly with Médicins Sans Frontières, one that trains rural Sierra Leonean community health officers in basic essential surgical techniques – or a midwifery-led maternal care clinic with birth outcomes that would be stellar anywhere in the world. In Tanzania, we think of a collaborative programme for children with congenital clubfoot. A Tanzanian trade school for adolescents with disabilities operates a clubfoot clinic, casting children serially over a period of months. Germans supported relevant infrastructure and capacity building in a local Tanzanian hospital. During two weeks each year German and Tanzanian health professionals work side by side to conduct necessary surgeries for the dozens of children for whom casts are not enough. Both the Tanzanian medical personnel and the local trade school ensure adequate rehabilitation and follow-up for the patients. Each of these programmes treats the desires of volunteers as subordinate to the needs of African patients and the imperative of nurturing African capacity.

Healing endeavours always also entail the capacity for harm. Silencing particular stories and analyses obscures this duality. Iatrogenic damage is not caused only by individual volunteers who overstep their surgical competence or the extent of their pharmaceutical knowledge. It is also caused by volunteer projects that draw scarce medical personnel into roles as translators and supervisors, and by those projects that reserve the important decision making for those holding the purse strings, and in so doing undermine local health infrastructure.

If developing local capacity matters, so does work to support local leadership and the development of health sovereignty. Here the situation described by Sullivan (in Chapter 6), in which Tanzanian staff wait ... and wait ... for volunteers to fund a covered walkway so that they can transport patients safely to the surgical theatre, uncomfortably echoes larger patterns. Malawi's plan to initiate a nation-wide antiretroviral drug programme was held up for years while the crucial donors (who provide more than half the health sector's budget) debated whether and when it should be funded. Longstanding patterns of waiting on donors or volunteers can have devastating effects. In March 2014 staff from Sierra Leone's Ministry of Health and Sanitation met with officials from several non-government and multilateral organizations to organize a response to the growing number of Ebola cases in the country. The lines of decision making were not clear, as the ministry officials who fought for immediate quarantine measures were countered by those who wanted to wait for direction from international bodies. By the time WHO declared Ebola a global health emergency in August of 2014, hundreds of Sierra Leoneans had died – including many doctors and nurses.

Support what works

The programmes that work typically expect volunteers to commit, to return again and again, to stay involved for the long haul. The norm in some humanitarian volunteer organizations, like the professional norm in international public health, is skewed more towards mobility: volunteers are to rotate through country after country without developing firm attachments to any particular locale or people. As Redfield (2012) has noted, this mobility works against solidarity. In contrast, the programmes we describe here as 'working' prize the stickiness and messiness of local attachment. In typical circumstances, length and depth of engagement matter. Learning the language, living the life of one's local peers, taking public transport and eating local food, these matter. The African who praises a volunteer for being 'more like a missionary than an expert' is referring to this kind of engagement, as is the Malawian doctor who relishes opportunities to 'work together as one to overcome difficulty' with people of different cultural backgrounds and medical training histories.

Long-term engagement is one important measure of an effective volunteer programme. When the risks are greatest, however, simply showing up also matters. Erikson notes that colleagues and friends in Sierra Leone often refer to international engagement, including work by expatriate volunteers, as a form of love. Love is an important social category in Sierra Leone (see e.g. Bolten 2012). In a region where child fosterage is widespread, sending one's children is an act of respect and regard for another's wellbeing. During the war, one Sierra Leonean told Erikson, other nations were unwilling to 'send their children' to volunteer, a socially significant marker of global ostracism. 'The world did not love us. No one came. We were abandoned.' In the early months of the recent West African Ebola outbreak, that abandonment happened again as volunteers fled, leaving their West African colleagues behind to face patients and dangers alone. These are tragic examples of volunteerism as a 'dialectic between lives to be saved and lives to be risked' (Fassin 2007: 500). In the Ebola case, however, this abandonment was not the end of the story. After the virus decimated an already small pool of Sierra Leonean physicians and nurses in 2014, volunteers from all over the world stepped in as first responders to help manage the health emergency. Global volunteers in this case helped Sierra Leoneans save lives.

An ethical tension here needs to be part of the larger conversation on health volunteering. When volunteers' *presence* keeps indigenous organization from taking root, when it keeps African health systems from African self-determination, it is harmful. When volunteers' *absence* signifies an abandonment, a lack of love, that too can be devastating. At their best, health volunteer programmes combine long-term commitment and short-term shared risks (and rewards), invest more in the messiness of human relationships than in the fantasy of magic bullets, and remain open to revision. Sometimes volunteering is the wrong answer, and it is never the whole answer. There are no guarantees that it works.

At the very least, asking 'what works' is an important way to initiate necessary conversations about the moral and economic complexities of health volunteering. What works for whom, assessed on what basis, over what duration? Those questions are long overdue. The rhetorical simplicity of celebration and silence we have described deprives people who work in the spaces of African 'global health,' both expatriates and locals, of the ability to learn from mistakes, from history, and from one another. When every African health volunteer stint is depicted as a hero holiday and every African health volunteer programme a testament to institutional beneficence, critical conversations are not possible. The costs of this rhetoric – to patients, to local expertise, to political analysis and to health sovereignty – are steep.

PART FOUR Moral Journeys

8

A Third Mode of Engagement with the Excluded Other

Student Volunteers from an Elite Boarding School in Kenya

BJØRN HALLSTEIN HOLTE[1]

This chapter presents an ethnographic account[2] of students from an elite school in Kenya who volunteer at a Bible Club for street children and children from poor families. Volunteering is often cast as requiring the construction of a different other and for the students who feature in this chapter, volunteering at the Bible Club is precisely an encounter with the excluded other of their school, 'the people outside the gates'. The ethnographic account and analysis in this chapter concerns how volunteering as a mode of engagement with the excluded other feeds into the formation of the students who volunteer as privileged subjects and their relation to the public outside the school compound. The ethnographic account shows how the students give what they call 'love' and assume 'responsibilities' towards the children who attend the Bible Club, treating them as members of a public in which they do not themselves take part as equals. Based on personal relationships and senses of responsibility across different ethnic backgrounds (with which the students are generally not concerned) and vast socio-economic differences (with which they are), this new public thus emerges around something akin to what James Ferguson (2013: 232–3) calls '*social* inequality'. *Social* inequality, for Ferguson, is inequality that is lived and experienced within personal and moral relationships as opposed to inequality that is not conceived of in relation to the mutual obligations of a society. The analysis in this

[1]   I am grateful to the students, teachers and workers at the boarding school and to the children and staff at the street children's project for welcoming me. I would also like to thank P. Wenzel Geissler and Ståle Wig for useful comments to drafts that eventually became this chapter.
[2]   I conducted fieldwork at the school from January to July 2012 and participated on several trips to the Bible Club. The ethnographic account in this chapter is based on field notes that I wrote as soon as possible after the trips, when I returned to my house in the afternoons, as well as photos from the Street Children's Project and the Bible Club. I also conducted semi-structured interviews with twenty-five students who had volunteered at the Bible Club during the fieldwork. Some interviews were conducted immediately after the trips, while others were conducted at other times during the week. I took notes during the interviews and transcribed the interviews from these notes, but I did not record them.

chapter shows how volunteering instils senses of personal relationships and responsibilities across socio-economic inequalities in some of the students who volunteer, rendering the inequalities social in part.

Most of the social-science literature on volunteers in Africa has been concerned with international volunteers in elite positions, European and North American students on gap years, and young Africans without work who seek a professional identity or minor material advantages through volunteering. In concerning young Africans from privileged backgrounds who volunteer, this chapter introduces a new type of volunteer. This also entails a shift from situating volunteerism mainly in relation to global socio-economic inequalities towards situating it in relation to inequalities that are internal to contemporary African societies.

My analysis is inspired by the anthropological literature on gated communities, which approaches them as a spatial expression of socio-economic inequalities. Important ethnographies in the genre portray the retreat of privileged families to gated and often guarded peri-urban enclaves in Los Angeles (Davis 1992), São Paulo (Caldeira 1996, 2000), San Antonio and New York (Low 2001, 2003), and in Johannesburg (Murray 2004, 2011). A core argument in these ethnographies is that gated communities separate privileged families from less privileged ones and at the same time facilitate the continued employment of low-paid domestic workers by privileged families; that gated communities facilitate the exclusion of the less privileged as peril and their inclusion as workers – two modes of engagement that coexist in considerable friction. In the first two sections of this chapter, I address how these two modes of engagement apply to the international boarding school that features in this chapter. I then progress to the ethnographic account from the Bible Club and an analysis of volunteering as a third mode of engagement between the people of the inside and the people of the outside of the school compound.

The inside and the outside

The international boarding school that features in this chapter is situated on a large, rural estate in the Kenyan highlands. It is a Christian school, although some of the students have other faiths.[3] Since it opened in the early 1930s, it has been a domain of privilege – educating children of European descent in the colonial era and increasingly children of Indian descent and the children of the black African elite as the post-colonial era progressed. During my fieldwork, the majority of students were black Africans. Fifty-nine per cent of parents' addresses listed in the school's student files were in the East African capitals Nairobi, Kampala or Dar es Salaam. Most of the addresses were in the more prestigious suburbs, and

---

[3]   The Muslim minority of students was overrepresented amongst those who participated on the trips to the Bible Club on which the ethnographic account in this chapter is based.

over half of the parents were listed as 'businessmen' or as professionals of some sort. The majority of teachers are white Europeans employed on one- or two-year expatriate contracts, with a minority of Kenyans and nationals of other parts of the former British Empire. Parents generally expect students to attend universities abroad and to have successful careers in business, public service or politics, and many of the students share these ambitions.

In contrast to the teachers and students at the international boarding school, most of the population outside the school compound is sustained through small-scale agriculture and simple day jobs. Where members of a family are employed – such as the 200 unskilled and semi-skilled workers employed by the school – their wages amount to a fraction of the school fees at the international boarding school[4] and workers who have families often also keep a *shamba* (vegetable garden) to supplement their wages. Some own land near the school, but others live in rented accommodation and use land availed by the school or have their own land and their family elsewhere.

Labour arrangements like these have historical continuities that can be traced back to the early colonial era in Kenya (see Kanogo 1987; Stamp 1986). In the colonial era, land ownership in this part of Kenya was reserved for settlers of European descent. Black African workers and their families often conducted small-scale farming on the margins of farms owned by white Europeans and in the nearby forests. However, all the farms in the area near the school were sold to African owners in the 1960s and 1970s and many of the farms have since been subdivided into smaller plots that, today, are farmed for subsistence and that often also function as rural homes of families that extend to the Kenyan cities or abroad.

A trading centre has been built near the main road and the school over roughly the same time span. A family of Indian descent ran a general store in the area during the latter half of the colonial era, but resettled in the mid-1960s. Black African families have since acquired plots, built houses and invested in businesses here. Today, the trading centre is comprised of a number of brick houses and about fifty small shops: *agrovets* that carry seeds and simple farming equipment, general stores, beauty salons, workshops, soup kitchens and pubs. The centre houses some of the unskilled and semi-skilled workers employed by the school, who also contribute a significant portion of the revenue of these local businesses. The business cycle, shop owners told me, peaks after the pay-days at the school and is at its lowest during the school holiday when many workers leave for their home areas.[5]

---

[4] During my fieldwork, the annual tuition and boarding fees for a college student (years 12 and 13) were over KSh. 1,500,000 (approximately equivalent to GBP £12,000 or USD $19,000 in 2015), comparable to the monthly wage of approximately KSh. 10,000 (£79, $126) earned by unskilled workers employed by the school and the daily rate of KSh. 200 (£1.60, $2.50) of unskilled day labourers in the area.

[5] The low season has less to do with students and teachers leaving the school. Procurement for the school is managed through contracts with individual businessmen and businesswomen

The area that surrounds the school and the trading centre is multi-ethnic and it was an epicentre of violence and destruction after the national elections in 1992, 1997 and 2007. Many people were killed, orphaned, widowed or left landless by the post-election violence and a number of families have resettled more or less permanently to the trading centre. Living near the trading centre, some of the refugees told me, was safer than living in the hinterlands, and the opportunities for wage labour to compensate for income lost on *shambas* that had been destroyed was better. Since 1992, when an aerial survey was done, the number of houses in the trading centre have increased manifold.

An electric fence was put up to protect the school from the violence that followed the 2007 elections. While the school compound had not been fully enclosed since the 1960s, when a barbed wire fence that was erected during the Mau Mau Emergency was removed, entry is now restricted at a guarded metal gate at all times. Guards patrol the perimeter of the electric fence with dogs at night, and departures from the school compound are restricted after dark. Students are not permitted to leave without accompaniment of parents or teachers, but neither do they wish to. A group of college-girls who were talking about escaping from the school one Saturday afternoon during my fieldwork concluded that it would be to no avail: '[the trading centre] isn't even a town. It's more like a village.' In interviews with me, some of the students expressed concern that they were 'spoiled brats' who were out of touch with their surroundings, but students more typically experienced the school as an island of calm and safety in an area that is otherwise 'traditional', backward and dangerous. Because their families' incomes suffice for international branded clothing and expensive hairstyles, and because they have access to international fashions through travel, the internet and satellite TV, the students are visibly different from their rural neighbours.[6] When they venture outside the school compound, they attract unwanted attention from beggars who try their luck for a few shillings and children who shout 'Howareyou! Howareyou!' On the roads, overloaded *matatus* (public minibus services) drive carelessly, drunk drivers cause accidents and a number of car hijackings have taken place near the school at night: for the students, the roads, too, are spaces of danger to be navigated only in chartered buses or private cars with seatbelts on and always to be avoided after dark. Students and teachers do not travel by *matatu* or other public means of transportation in Kenya, except as adventures that often also become the

---

[(contd)] as suppliers rather than through the trading centre, though some of the suppliers live there. While some of the teachers buy agricultural produce from traders in the trading centre, most do not. Instead, teachers shop at an urban supermarket about an hour by car from the school and trade harvests from vegetable gardens by their houses within the school compound amongst themselves.

[6] Lila Abu-Lughod (1993, 2004) and Charles Hirschkind (2001, 2006) both address how such media figures differently in the formation of subjects from different socio-economic backgrounds in Egypt. A systematic analysis would find similar patterns of difference between the privileged and the poor, and between rural and urban residents, in Kenya.

subject of jokes and conversation. Until recently, a few teachers stayed in houses outside the school compound, but break-ins and robberies have made most relocate to houses on the inside of the compound. This has contributed further to the separation of the school from its surroundings.

However, the school has retained integration with other international schools in Kenya through sports, teams shifting between the schools every weekend, and with the suburban upper-middle-class residences where most parents stay. From the inside, the school is thus experienced as part of a 'patchwork geography' that is composed of 'zones of civility joined by fragile corridors of safety in environments otherwise presumed to be, literally, out of control' (Comaroff & Comaroff 2006: 35). In the next section, I show how this privileged life within the school compound is lived in relation to the 'people outside the gates' both as peril and as workers before I turn to volunteering as a third mode of engagement with the less privileged.

Three modes of engagement

The three modes of engagement between the inside and the outside of the school compound work through distinctive practices that I outline briefly in this section of the chapter. The first mode, the exclusion of less privileged others from privileged domains, is fundamental to the constitution of hierarchical societies (Stallybrass & White 1986). The separation of privileged children from members of less privileged social groups has been shown to have been important in colonial schools for European children (Kennedy 1996: 117–46; Stoler 2002: 112–39; Summers 2011) as well as in the British public schools (Gathorne-Hardy 1977; Wakeford 1969). The school that features in this chapter has direct continuities with both traditions, but separation has taken various forms through the colonial and post-colonial eras. In the 1930s and 1940s, during the colonial era and as more land was gradually appended to the school estate, the African workers' houses were gradually moved further from the main school buildings and down a slope facing away from the school. The workers were thus rendered invisible: out of sight from the school buildings and mentioned neither in reports from governmental inspections nor in early yearbooks. After the declaration of the Mau Mau Emergency in the early 1950s, security measures such as the erection of a barbed wire fence and armed patrols were introduced. Repealed in the aftermath of national independence and the first change of headmaster in the school's history in the mid-1960s, such security measures have gradually been reintroduced since the 1990s. Currently, the demarcation of the inside and the outside of the school as two domains is managed through their spatial separation by security practices along the fences and at the gate: the guards, dogs and restrictions on entering and leaving mentioned above. Among students and teachers at the school, circulating stories about violent crime and discourses on 'traditions' and 'African culture' work to legitimize the segregation in a similar way to what Teresa Caldeira (2000) calls 'talk of crime'. Talk of crime is a discursive practice that creates essentialized and caricatured categories of people as either good or bad in response to crime, violence and fear. In gated communities, such discursive practices produce images of the outside as diametrically opposed to the inside and thus work to legitimize the separation of the inside and the outside as two distinct domains.

The second mode of engagement, the partial inclusion of low-paid workers into the privileged domain, is managed through such practices as signing contracts, paying wages, and recording workers' presence with a fingerprint scanner at the gate of the school compound. Writing of São Paulo, Caldeira (1996: 310) notes that 'the intensive use of domestic labor is a continuation of an old pattern, although in recent years some relationships of labor have been altered, and this work has become more professional'. Attempts to control workers and domestic servants have caused tensions since the early colonial era in Kenya (Anderson 2000, 2010; Kanogo 1987; Stoler 1989). While I have not been able to reconstruct this part of the school's history in great detail, also here the relationship to workers has been professionalized. In administrative terms, the school has become a large organization and its estates and human resources are now managed from specialized administrative positions. Some services have been outsourced to an international security company that employs and rotates the guards, and new technologies, such as the fingerprint scanner mentioned above, have been introduced.

The third mode of engagement, volunteering, is the main subject of this chapter. I will show how volunteering challenges the forces of separation between the inside and the outside of the school compound that is implied by the first mode of engagement. It also challenges the order whereby the people of the inside are privileged and prioritized over the people of the outside, a basis of the second mode of engagement. Through volunteering, the students come to see the children who attend the Bible Club, people of the outside, as differentiated individuals similar to themselves rather than as an undifferentiated group of different others. At the same time, the ethnographic account shows how volunteering makes the socio-economic inequalities between the students and the children directly visible (see also Holden 1997; Nenga 2011). Responding to this, and echoing their mainly white Christian teachers, some students drew on morally laden notions of 'love' and 'responsibility' to make sense of their experiences and encounters at the Bible Club. Towards the end of this chapter, I address how volunteering at the Bible Club thus reflects and reinforces the pre-existing inequalities between the students and the children who attend it.

In the curriculum and extra-curricular programme of the school, volunteering is conceptualized variously as 'service' and as 'charity'. Service is any unpaid work that students record in their logs to meet the requirements of the 'Building Leaders' programme or the 'President's Award Scheme' in which many students participate.[7] Service may be undertaken within the school compound or as activities that take students outside the school, such as volunteering at the Bible Club. It is a mandatory activity, but students can choose between several different activities to fulfil these requirements. Charity is a more elusive concept, though most of the students whom I interviewed tended to understand it as activities undertaken to benefit the 'people outside the gate' or people who are 'in need of help'. The students may understand volunteering at the Bible Club as charity if it is not logged as service for Building Leaders or the President's Award, and as both charity and service when it is logged. However, some students suggested that an activity could not be charity if it was logged as service because they see charity as a selfless activity and the service logs as a reflection of self-interest. Others emphasized that they found volunteering more rewarding when they did not record it in their service logs or when fulfilling their service requirements was not the main reason why they were doing it. Overall, the students' understanding of charity as disinterested giving is in line with both Christian and Islamic traditions as well as contemporary Western understandings of volunteering (cf. Benthall 2012; Wig, Chapter 3, this volume). Because they are the terms in which volunteering is conceptualized within the school, the distinction between service and charity is important as a backdrop for my analysis, which follows after the ethnographic account below.

Planning

At the school, an open meeting is held in one of the classrooms just after lunch almost every Friday. All students from year nine to year thirteen (thirteen to nineteen years old, approximately 250 students in total) are welcome, but attendance varies from two to fifteen students. The hour after lunch is a time of the day that students dispose themselves, and most spend this time relaxing in the dormitories, catching up on work or socializing with friends. At the meeting, one or two teachers give some information about the Street Children's Project, the Bible Club and about the specifics of this week's trip for student volunteers. Most students already know about the Street Children's Project, which was started by teachers at the school and has received donations from school fundraisers. It provides uniforms and lunches for poor children to attend local schools as well as accommodation for a few children and their poor single

---

[7] Building Leaders is a training programme developed at the school that comprises weekly seminars or lectures on practical skills such as managing time or giving critique, as well as mandatory unpaid work as 'service'. The President's Award in Kenya is related to the Duke of Edinburgh Award and is awarded to youth who have undertaken expeditions, volunteered as 'service', and learned certain skills to required standards.

mothers. Most of the students, however, associate the project primarily with the Bible Club where small groups of students hold lessons about the Bible almost every Saturday morning during terms. The students' participation is voluntary and planned on a weekly basis, and while some students return to the project almost every week, others attend trips only once in a while.

If there are students at the meeting who have not volunteered at the project before, a brief outline of the schedule is given. The teachers explain that the time at the project is split between two activities – the first half is set aside for playing with the children, and the second half for Bible studies in the classrooms. The teachers tell the students what Bible story will be in focus for the Bible studies session, that the students are free to present the story in a creative manner if they wish, and they show what materials will be available to the students that week. During the first term of my fieldwork, the stories were all on Jesus' miracles and materials varied from ideas for activities to equipment for simple crafts. The teachers also explain that the activities are intended to make the children think through the Bible story to better understand how it relates to them.

All the students at the meeting sign up, writing their names on a sheet that is passed around, and they are told to prepare for teaching during the Bible studies session. Usually, the teachers make an effort at splitting the students into three groups, corresponding to three age groups for the children at the project, and at distributing Kiswahili language speakers evenly between these groups. This is a concern because many children at the project do not speak English and many students have limited if any knowledge of Kiswahili (the *lingua franca* of Kenya) and, for that matter, of vernacular languages. The students are dismissed after about twenty minutes and sometimes get together in their groups to plan ahead, but more usually they split up for what is left of their midday break.

Leaving the inside

The students meet at 9:15 a.m. on Saturday morning and are taken to the project in a purpose-built Toyota Land Cruiser or HiAce minivan. Both vehicles are painted bright white with the school logo stretching the full height on both sides. The accompanying teacher sits in front and makes sure that everybody wears their seatbelts before the vehicle departs. The vehicle leaves the school compound through the main gate, and the drive takes about a quarter of an hour. Some of the drivers live along the way or send their children to less expensive private schools, as many Kenyans in paid employment do, and they point out their houses and their children's schools to the teachers. The school buildings are small compared to those of the international boarding school of the teacher and students and, like government schools, these schools rarely have computer facilities or libraries. The fees charged usually amount to about one twentieth of the fees at the international boarding school, though this is not mentioned.

The students are usually quiet, some listening to music on their iPods or reading books brought from school, others stare blankly through the windows. The first part of the drive is on decidedly rural roads – donkey carts and livestock mingling on the road with the occasional tractor, lorry, *matatu* or saloon car passing by. The gently rolling hills surrounding them are scattered with *shamba*s, unpainted brick houses, a sawmill and a bottled water plant. After less than ten minutes, a minor town becomes visible from a hilltop. The south-eastern outskirts of the town are densely scattered with recent brick houses, but nearer the town centre the buildings are older and painted. On Saturday mornings, this part of town is bustling with activity as vendors and customers flock to the roadside. All kinds of consumer items are sold along the road: used clothing, pirated DVDs and local agricultural produce. The road is tarmacked, but in poor condition.

Past the town centre, on a road that was being repaired for the better part of my fieldwork, the vehicle turns left by the gate on the far end of the Street Children's Project's brick wall. The black metal gate is of the kind that is produced locally and inscribed with the Bible reference 'Matt. 25:40'.[8] The car stops for a while, for there is no guard at the gate and the children open it themselves when they hear the vehicle. From inside the vehicle, some of the students engage with the children – waving and smiling through the windows – while others are still concerned with their music or books when the vehicle comes to a halt under a large tree. This tree is at the centre of activity at the project, where project workers are busy by the kitchen, the roofed eating terrace and the temporary classrooms of corrugated metal.

When the vehicle has come to a stop, the students take some time to leave some clothing, their books and all electronics in the vehicle before they open the door and disembark. Because it keeps the students separate from the outside and allows them to carry many of the comforts from inside the school compound, the vehicle functions as an enclosed extension of the compound. In this sense, it is only when the students disembark from the vehicle at the project site and meet the children that they leave 'the inside' for 'the outside'.

Playing and teaching

Having disembarked from the vehicle, the students stand together in front of it and those of the children who have aborted their playing stand a few metres away gazing at them. The children are younger than the students and most are smaller in stature. Many of them wear clothing that is torn and

---

[8] Matthew 25:40: 'The King will reply, "Truly I tell you, whatever you did for one of the least of these brothers and sisters of mine, you did for me".'

some are barefoot. The students remain standing in front of the car for some time, looking at each other or the children as if unsure what to do. Most of the students wear jeans and dark blue polo shirts stitched with the school logo. The girls typically have straightened hair or hair extensions. Those of the students who have visited the project before are quicker to greet the children, shaking their hands or exchanging brief phrases in Kiswahili. As more students do this, the children also get braver until the youngest ones, a few years old, finally walk up to the last remaining students for their attention, pulling their trousers or hands if they have to. Among the students, the girls usually entertain all the youngest children, holding some and taking extra care to include others, but otherwise the games tend to be split into single-gendered groups, the boys playing football on the sloped field after they have moved the grazing sheep, and the girls skipping rope or playing other games. The students sometimes initiate this, the children following them, and sometimes the accompanying teacher or the project staff engages them by distributing balls, skipping ropes and other simple toys. Only on one of the trips that I attended did the teacher take an active part in the games as they had got going.

During the time spent playing, it is usually rather the students who organize games. One of the male students who participated on several trips often arranged boys in line to take penalty kicks. Although he does speak Kiswahili well, also this student interacted with the children mainly through gestures rather than speech. Similarly, a female student gently pushed one of the older boys aside and smiled to one of the younger girls who then took his place while we were swinging a skipping rope together. These examples show that when students intervene in games to ensure the inclusion of younger and shyer children, it is usually through gestures rather than spoken words. The children, in turn, accept the students' authority and abide by it. While some are rowdy when playing with other children, most are respectful to the students. To the children, the students may seem like the international volunteers who occasionally stay in a guesthouse at the project and who also play with them from time to time.

After an hour of playing, the children are called by the project staff to line up for *uji*, a thick, nutritious porridge made from fermented flours and water. For many children, this is the first and sometimes only meal that day. The students do not line up and are not offered *uji*, but some join the children at the eating terrace while they eat. Others stay together in small groups a short distance away. In my ensuing interviews, a few of the students suggested that staying with the children when they eat strengthened the personal bonds formed between children and students. Some spoke of this as a matter of personal engagement, seeing students who do not accompany children to the eating terrace as less concerned with the children than those who do. Another student emphasized that she would have liked to sit with the children for their meal, but that she found it difficult to engage with them because she only spoke English. She had chosen to stay with the other students, away from the children.

After the meal, students and children proceed to the classrooms – small rooms of corrugated metal with concrete floors that smell drily of dust, the walls covered by posters with English phrases and illustrations, information on dental hygiene, work from earlier Saturday Bible Clubs and other decorations. Each classroom has a small blackboard and they are furnished with locally made wooden desks, benches and chairs. There are shelves with a few donated books, writing utensils, chalk and other equipment in all the rooms. The children sit down and most of the students remain standing. The students are responsible for the lessons, while the accompanying teacher walks between classrooms, watching the lessons from the doorways and sometimes taking photos that are used for a variety of purposes within the school. Most of the photos that are eventually used in presentations in school assemblies or on posters that are hung up within the school are of students holding, helping or otherwise engaging with the children. They always have the students in focus.

In the older age groups, where children may be up to ten years old, the first focus of the lesson is the Bible story. On one occasion, the students acted Jesus turning water into wine while one of them read the story aloud, reading each sentence first in English and then in Kiswahili. The translation from English to Kiswahili had not been prepared, but was helped along by comments from a project worker who was standing in the doorway. On other trips, however, the story was simply read aloud in English and the children were taught a 'memory verse' in English. The memory verse is a Bible verse that is related to the story in question and emphasized as key to remembering it. It is read aloud by a student and sometimes written on the board, and then recited by the children until it assumes a rhythm in their collective voice. Recitation is a mode of teaching that is common in Kenyan schools, but is rarely used in the international school that the students attend. It is also often criticized in national media and popular discourse for making students too dependent on authorities and unable to think for themselves. In individual interviews after the trips, several students similarly expressed doubt as to whether the children understand and remember memory verses, or whether they only hear, remember and repeat them as rhythms. The students nevertheless take on this mode of teaching because it demands less of those who do not have mutual languages with the children and who have problems communicating effectively. Simultaneously, it contributes to highlighting the differences between the students as teachers and the children as learners.

'Jesus provides what we need'

On another trip to the Bible Club, the lesson provided by the students was titled 'Jesus provides what we need'. The students read and acted out the miracle of the five loaves and two fish wherein Jesus feeds a large crowd of people with very little food. Involving the children as the crowd to be fed, the students acted the story out several times. Instructions and explanations were given in Kiswahili by one of the girls who also narrated the story. When the students, as Jesus' disciples, distributed imaginary food to the children as the crowd, the children eagerly held out their hands and many shrieked with joy and laughed when students acted out the distribution of food. The students took care to touch each child's hand, giving each imaginary food on every round of distribution.

The memory verse was from John 6:35: 'I am the bread of life'. After the last enactment of the story, it was read out by one of the students and recited by the children collectively three times. It was then to be recited individually by each child. On this occasion, one of the students had brought sweets and the students gave each child a sweet for their recitations until, finally, everyone had done so. There were about fifteen children in the room. The first few stood up and recited the verse loudly, clearly and in full. Some of the boys shouted it as loudly as they could. The last few, on the other hand, were helped along by the students and hardly muttered the words. Each was rewarded with a sweet.

After the recitations, the students supervised the children colouring and making small paper boxes on which they were supposed to write their 'needs'. As it had been explained on the Friday afternoon meeting, this would help the children relate to the story about Jesus providing what people need. The instructions, however, got skewed as they were translated into Kiswahili, and most of the children simply coloured the boxes and had students help to assemble them. A few drew their needs – or what they liked, as one of the Kiswahili-speakers among the students remarked – on the outside of the boxes: one a fish, another a named friend. The students complimented these choices, but did not encourage use of the activity for further reflection by asking the children *why* they drew what they drew.

In general, talk between students and children lost out because the students were kept very busy helping the children with the boxes and because many shared no languages. It was impossible for most of the students to converse with the children, even if they wanted to. On this occasion and many others, I heard students wondering among themselves why the children draw what they draw. The students were interpreting their drawings, discussing them with each other. This, however, was rather a matter of trying to understand the children than of trying to encourage them to reflect on the Bible stories. Generally, the students did not volunteer because they had pedagogic goals or to share a Christian message, but rather because they wanted to get to know the children. When I asked one of the younger students who also speaks Kiswahili how being with the children while they are drawing contributed to this, she replied by providing two examples:

Like if a kid colours everything black, you know he's in a really dark place. And there is this little girl who is so careful to always colour within the lines [on copies from colouring books]. She's really neat. And when I asked her about it, she told me that she just wants it to look pretty.

After they had made the boxes, the children and the students all left the classroom. One boy held his box up in front of one of the students and crushed it on his way out. He then ran out, laughing wildly. Another boy came up to the student who had brought sweets and begged her for more on his way out. He did not get any, but the student later told me that this had forced her to question whether the children appreciated the 'time and love' that she was giving them. Like other misunderstandings described in this ethnographic account, the student's disappointment may be understood as a result of how the children, the students and the teachers think differently about the Bible Club (an issue that Noelle Sullivan discusses in Chapter 6 in relation to encounters between medical students and hospital staff). While the teachers who introduce the project every Friday emphasize the Christian outreach and talked to me about how this allowed students to meet and learn about life as it is lived outside the school compound, most of the students whom I interviewed were much more concerned with getting to know the children. While some of the children do get to know individual students, my impression is that they rather come for the food, the fun of playing with each other and with the students more generally.

Listening

Once outside the classrooms, a few of the students get back to playing with the children as before, while the others gather near the kitchen. The project workers, local women employed by the project and a few youths who have themselves been helped by the project, serve tea and coffee for the students and the accompanying teacher. Only occasionally do a few of the students have any. While not accepting tea or food prepared by the hosts would be considered offensive in most Kenyan households, this is not observed at the project. The project workers are used to receiving international volunteers who do not share this mode of expression, and the students are generally associated with urban elites that are considered by many Kenyans to be out of touch with 'African culture'. For the project workers, encounters with student volunteers at the Bible Club contribute to confirming this.

By the kitchen, the students rather chat with the project manager who is also a teacher at their school. She tells the students about the children's personal stories: some are orphaned, some look much less than their age because under-nutrition has stunted their physical development, and others have walked for more than an hour to get to the project. These are stories that the children do not articulate themselves, and they emphasize how vulnerable the children at the project and other children are to lack of care. In important ways, the stories serve the opposite function of Caldeira's (2000) 'talk of crime' in showing how the children and members of their families are led into petty crime, prostitution and drugs by their desperate situations. I asked most of the students whom I interviewed whether they thought of the children at the Bible Club as different from or as similar to themselves, and all but one told me that the children were much like themselves. They attributed specific differences to the children's social context with phrases such as, 'if I lived like them, I'd be stealing, too'.

Returning to the inside

Before leaving, the students gather by the vehicle and count over the things they have brought to the project to make sure that nothing is left behind. While their personal possessions have been left inside the vehicle, they have made use of colouring pencils and other stationary that has been brought from the school. This needs to be brought back. When the students and all the boxes with equipment are inside the vehicle, most of the students look through the windows and wave to the children as the vehicle departs – engaging with them in a way that many did not when they arrived. Through the activities at the Bible Club – playing, interpreting drawings and listening to stories – the students have begun to see the children as individuals differentiated from each other instead of as an undifferentiated group. For first-time volunteers, only a few children may stand out, but students who have volunteered at the Bible Club a few times may know many by name.

The students are quiet during the drive back to school, and most of the students reflect on their experiences at the Bible Club. 'Arriving at the project made me happy because the children are so innocent and happy, but hearing their stories made me sad', one of the younger students told me in an interview shortly after her first trip to volunteer. This tension, between enjoying the time spent with the children and being troubled by their stories, ran through most of the interviews. Some regretted not being able to do more for the children, such as one student who told me in detail about a barefoot girl with a wound on her heel that she had been unable to care for.

With one exception, all the students told me that the children were much like themselves and many dwelt on the arbitrariness of the distribution of wealth and the effects it had on the children's lives. Many spoke of the project as a haven where the children can be 'normal kids' and emphasized the need for children to be dependent upon others in stable relationships. Many of the students who kept returning to the project understood their role at the project as providing 'stability', 'time' and 'love' for the children. One of the younger students said that she volunteered because 'I want them to feel like they're loved and like they still matter'. The students who had volunteered at the Bible Club a few times told me that their initial motivation for volunteering had been to satisfy their curiosity or simply to leave the school compound for a while. Other students told me that they had volunteered to fulfil requirements for service. Many emphasized that their motivation had gradually changed to doing 'something good for others' or that, as they got to know individual children, they felt that regular attendance was important not to 'let the children down'. As they formed personal relationships with the children, in other words, a change took place from understanding volunteering at the Bible Club as an activity that would accommodate their own needs and desires to understanding volunteering in terms of personal relationships and a sense of responsibility towards the children. Volunteering thus gradually reconfigured some students' experience of the people of the inside as privileged and prioritized over the people of the outside, the basis of the second mode of engagement with the people outside the gate. One of the boys who frequently volunteered at the Bible Club told me in our interview that volunteering provided him with a 'different perspective': 'When I am at school, everything is always about me. At the project, it's more about the children.'

Forming ethical subjects and a public

When I interviewed students about their trips to volunteer at the Bible Club, they talked about themselves as being responsible and loving. This is a stark contrast to the talk of themselves as spoiled brats that some of the same students engaged in at other times, as mentioned above. Generally, the students who volunteered at the Bible Club shared a sense that it was a morally good thing to do. Some also condemned those of their co-students who did not volunteer. One of the older students who had volunteered at the Bible Club several times came up to me one Saturday, a few hours after she had returned from the Bible Club, and said:

> When I asked my housemates to come along [to the Bible Club] today, they just laughed and said that when they get rich they will donate a lot of money to street children. You see – that's what my friends are like.

When she draws on the notion of 'being the kind of person who volunteers' (Holden 1997: 128), the student addresses how volunteering reflects the ethical selves of those who volunteer as well as those who do not. Echoing what other students who volunteered at the Bible Club told me in interviews, her remark suggests that volunteering is morally better than donating money. It is a different kind of action that reflects a different kind of self, but also one that contributes to the formation of this self as an ethical subject. Unlike the giving of monetary donations, volunteering as the giving of 'time' and 'love' instils the students with dispositions that form them as ethical subjects. In other words, volunteering can be understood as a 'mode of subjectivation' (Faubion 2001, 2011) that contributes to the formation of students as subjects who are disposed for ethical action as well as a moral action or ethical end in itself (see also Fleischer, 2011).

While some of the students who volunteered regularly told me that they also volunteered at similar projects with their parents, they all emphasized that volunteering had changed them in important ways. The reflections cited in the previous section can be taken to indicate that the students feel that volunteering at the Bible Club turns them into loving subjects who understand and act on the street children's deficits by giving of their own time and love. As loving subjects, the students are concerned about the wellbeing of the street children, very real others. These concerns are based in certain affective intensities that were articulated as the sadness that some of the students felt when they heard the children's stories and the desperate desire some expressed to do more than they were already doing. These intensities motivate further volunteering and thus reflect the formation of the students as ethical subjects, subjects who are disposed for ethical action.

However, these dispositions and the subjects they are part of must be understood in relation to the highly unequal socio-economic context in which they figure. Based on ethnography from France and Italy, Didier Fassin (2005) and Andrea Muehlebach (2011) show how dispositions for compassion work to integrate publics that are fundamentally unequal, where the wellbeing of some depend on the dispositions of others. At the Bible Club, too, students' dispositions are formed in relation to the street children as objects for their love and responsibilities. Like compassion, the students' dispositions for love and responsibility reflect and reinforce inequalities between the students and the children that originate beyond the Bible Club and that are evident already when the students arrive in buses after the children have walked there, some of them barefoot. That the students are offered tea and coffee, rather than *uji* like the children, and that the students teach and the children are taught, underline the same inequalities. Engaging with the children at the Bible Club, the students retain privileged roles but ensure a specific form of equality between the children when they organize games to ensure the participation of the youngest children, and give each child imaginary food or a sweet for reciting the memory verse. In this way, the students engage with the children as members of a public towards which they have responsibilities but in which they do not themselves take part as equals. Volunteering, in short, affirms the students' privilege and instils them with dispositions for loving and responsible exercise of it.

9

Undoing Apartheid Legacies?

Volunteering as Repentance & Politics by Other Means

THOMAS G. KIRSCH

For political commentators, South Africa's general elections in May 2014 were a watershed event in this country's more recent past because, about twenty years after the introduction of a non-racial democracy, members of the first generation born after the end of apartheid were among those voting. Mass media speculated about how South African political culture might be transformed under the growing influence of the so-called 'born-free generation' which has no personal recollections of the apartheid era and which grew up at a time when neo-liberal policies were gaining momentum in South Africa. This generation can be said to be 'born free' not only in terms of being able to lead a politically liberated life, but also, figuratively speaking, with regard to the emergence of new forms of subjectivity created by neo-liberal ways of 'governing through freedom' (Rose 1999; see also Lacey & Ilcan 2006) that incite action and stress individual autonomy, self-responsibility and the necessity to employ one's own volition (see also Murphy & Throop 2010).

The latter point becomes evident when we look at the special importance given to volunteering in post-apartheid South Africa. For example, in his speech on the occasion of the Youth Day celebrations in June 2008, then President Thabo Mbeki expressed the view that 'the nation expects the youth of today to follow in the footsteps of the 1976 youth and become agents of change, this time in the continuing struggle to achieve the goal of a better life for all our people'.[1] While the young people involved in the Soweto uprising of 16 June 1976 had been campaigning against the apartheid regime, Mbeki was calling on the current generation to fight poverty, unemployment, crime and drugs. Further, and most important for the present chapter, he placed the emphasis on volunteering and morality: 'The good role models among us ... must be those who work with the community, who help the poor, who volunteer to help improve their neighbourhoods ... and those who respect the values of Ubuntu and good moral conduct.'[2]

---

[1] www.thepresidency.gov.za/pebble.asp?relid=3328andt=79; accessed 16 August 2014.

[2] *Ubuntu* is a Bantu term that has gained prominence in the context of South African debates

Volunteerism is widely promoted in South Africa as a means to promote community and nation building, social welfare and post-apartheid 'development'.[3] There is evidence of a rich and varied history of grassroots voluntary activities in South Africa, most particularly in the anti-apartheid struggle.[4] We also find a vivid interest in volunteering among present-day South Africans. According to the latest statistical data compiled in the *Volunteer Activities Survey*, over a million South Africans spent nearly 400 million hours on volunteer work in the twelve months up to June 2010.[5] More than half of them engage in volunteer work on an individual basis, and about one third through an organization, for the most part NGOs and religious institutions. Similarly, a study published in 2006 'demonstrates that in contemporary South Africa, service programmes are growing in range and number, fostered by the policy framework that has been put in place in the new democracy since 1994' (Perold et al. 2006: 6). The main sectors of this volunteer engagement are 'health, social development, education, environment, construction and agriculture sectors' (*ibid.*).[6]

Although Mbeki praised the volunteer engagement of the young, not all of these volunteers belong to the 'born-free generation'. There exists a substantial number who have lived through the apartheid era and thus have vivid, though often also haunting memories of their personal entanglement in the predicaments of the apartheid system. By examining case studies of volunteers in the field of non-state crime prevention in contemporary South Africa, I show in this chapter how biographical self-reflexivity by these volunteers shapes the rationale, practical modalities and social orientation of their volunteer engagement.[7] More particularly, at the empirical core of this chapter are the autobiographical narratives of four South Africans, all of whom attribute their motives for volunteering to the wish to compensate symbolically and practically for what they describe as their personal wrongdoings in the past.[8] In that

---

[(contd)] concerning the need for an 'African renaissance'. It has been described as a philosophy of life promoting humaneness, compassion, mutual respect and solidarity (for critical perspectives, see Coertze 2001; Marx 2002).

[3]   Another area where volunteers recently played an important role was Jacob Zuma's political mobilization of ANC members prior to the elections in May 2014 that was framed as a re-launching of the 'volunteer brigades' (cf. Lodge 2004).

[4]   For example, the role of women as volunteers in the anti-apartheid struggle is discussed in Kimble & Unterhalter (1982) and McClintock (1991).

[5]   Statistics South Africa, Pretoria, 2010; available at www.statssa.gov.za/publications/ P02113/P021132010.pdf; accessed 19 November 2015.

[6]   For example, a well-known organization which relies heavily on the input of volunteers is *Treatment Action Campaign*, which promotes access to HIV medicine in South Africa (see, for example, Heywood 2009; Robins 2006).

[7]   Fieldwork in South Africa, especially in Eastern Cape Province, was conducted between 2003 and 2008 and was supported financially by the German Research Foundation. The data presented in this chapter were collected through narrative interviews, informal conversations and prolonged periods of participant observation.

[8]   I would like to stress that the following analysis of biographical interviews is not meant to imply that there is a causal, one-dimensional relationship between a person's experiences

way, volunteering reflects a deliberate moral choice (see also Mattingly 2012) and the wish to express repentance for one's past failures, a wish that has a strong influence on how the volunteers engage with others in the present.

The case studies I have chosen to examine are those of an ex-soldier in the apartheid-era military who nowadays engages as a volunteer in his neighbourhood's Community Policing Forum; a former member of a township gang who after the end of apartheid started to work voluntarily in a non-governmental programme to prevent youth at risk from becoming entangled in criminal networks; an ex-prisoner who was sentenced for killing an alleged informant of the apartheid regime and who after his release from prison began to give talks in anti-crime awareness campaigns; and a woman who for several years worked as a volunteer in non-governmental anti-violence programmes and who portrays her past life as a housewife as being characterized by 'inexcusable political naïvety'. The life histories of these volunteers differ from each other in many significant regards. Two of them had been classified as 'white' in the racist political policy of the apartheid era, and they say that they have actively collaborated with or at least passively endorsed the oppression exerted during that time. The other two had been classified as 'black', which, broadly speaking, at that time almost automatically put them into the structural position of belonging to those who had to suffer most under apartheid. However, as I demonstrate below, according to the latter two volunteers' own views of their life histories, membership in a criminal gang and involvement in a collective act of violent self-justice, though to some extent representing indirect and unintentional side effects of the apartheid regime, actively contributed to the injustices of that era in problematic ways.

Despite marked differences between them, the cases studies have in common the fact that they thematize connections between volunteer activities and the volunteers' (political) pasts. By focusing on how these connections are made, the analytical focus on volunteering is widened. It takes into account the fact that volunteering emerges out of specific biographies, themselves embedded in specific socio-political histories and historical terrains, and that – as a consequence – the volunteers' quest for the 'good' not only seeks to repair *current* wrongs, but sometimes also to right *past* ones. In other words, and with reference to the emerging anthropological interest in volunteerism (see, for example, Fechner 2012; Holden 1997; Mittermaier 2014; Mostafanezhad 2013b; Parreñas 2012), this chapter complements the dominant synchronic approach to volunteer work using a diachronic perspective in order to explore the ways in which the volunteers' (re)interpretations of the past have a bearing on their present-day attempts to become 'moral citizens' and to create a better society.

(contd) in the past and this person's being-in-the-world in the present. Instead, I am interested here in the narrative construction of the past as told and made meaningful in the present.

I suggest that this perspective allows important insights into volunteer activities in post-conflict societies such as South Africa, mainly because it allows us to determine how self-reflexive (re-)interpretations of the volunteers' (political) pasts have an influence on what it is in particular that the latter are seeking to achieve through their volunteering. As regards the case studies that follow, I argue that, in different ways and with different results, my interlocutors engaged in social engineering in order to undo what they perceived to be legacies of apartheid.[9] In that sense, their volunteering can be said to constitute politics by other means, even if some of them claim to be politically neutral. For the actors involved, apartheid was such an ubiquitous phenomenon that almost each and every aspect of their biographies can be narratively linked to it. Thus examining how connections between volunteering and the volunteers' (political) pasts are made enables us to catch sight not only of the diversity of local perceptions of the apartheid era, but also of how the past is being employed to act upon the present and the future by means of the volunteers' endeavours in social engineering.

This chapter also differs from previous research on volunteerism in that it discusses a specific area of voluntary activities that has long been neglected by studies of this topic, namely non-state crime prevention. In doing so, the chapter brings together two fields of research that are normally treated separately. On the one hand, the familiar association of volunteering with 'social welfare' and the 'common good' seems to suggest that certain sub-disciplines can claim exceptional competences in dealing with this subject matter, such as public health, medical anthropology, social work and the anthropology of development and humanitarianism. On the other hand, as regards volunteer activities in non-state crime prevention, the voluntary dimension of these practices usually remains implicit in notions like 'self-justice' or 'community policing'. What is more, and as is well-known from social-science studies of and media reports on 'self-defence units' and 'neighbourhood watch groups', volunteerism in the field of safety and security does not always lend itself to unreserved ethical approval, to say the least. Due to intolerance and violent exclusivism, many of these groups are under suspicion of belonging to what Simone Chambers and Jeffrey Kopstein (2001) have called 'bad civil society'. The title of a chapter by Sabelo Ndlovu-Gatsheni and Gwinyayi Dzinesa (2008) succinctly captures this ambiguity of volunteerism in the field of security: 'One man's volunteer is another man's mercenary'. In line with what Ruth Prince and Hannah Brown have noted in the introduction to this volume, volunteering in the

---

[9]   Due to lack of space, I am not in the position to present many details on my interlocutors' biographies and the specific crime-preventive activities they were engaged in as volunteers. Instead, the analysis of the case studies will mainly concentrate on how my interlocutors construed narrative connections between their efforts in social engineering in the present (or recent past) and their respective lives during apartheid times, most particularly on the rationales underlying these efforts.

context of non-state crime prevention therefore tends to be controversial and to create social tensions of its own.

Taken together, as I will show in what follows, looking at volunteering in the context of non-state crime prevention promises to shed light not only on an influential form of volunteer activity in South Africa, but also on challenges to post-apartheid nation building that concern the contested issue of reconciliation and the moralization of citizenship in this country.

Non-state crime prevention in South Africa

Given the commonly held assumption in political theory that the state has a monopoly on the legitimate use of violence, the empirical object of study of the present chapter, namely 'volunteerism in non-state crime prevention', requires some explanation. After all, looked at from this point of view, measures undertaken to prevent, control and sanction crime are the rights and duties of representatives of the state, while ordinary citizens are the reference objects of these measures.

In this section, I will first use recent insights from the field of political anthropology to question this ideal-typical model and outline a concept of 'the state' as an assemblage that is practised through a combination of state and non-state units. Second, I will sketch the developments that led to the increasing involvement of citizens in the prevention and control of crime in post-apartheid South Africa. I discuss these two points in order to sketch out some of the dominant coordinates within which volunteers in this field, whose life histories are explored below, find themselves navigating (Vigh 2009).

Crime prevention in fragmented systems of authority

Generally speaking, if we concur with the perception widely held among legal and political anthropologists that the concept of 'crime' is always and necessarily co-produced with the antithetical concept of 'law' and that, in turn – in contrast to 'custom', 'rules' or 'norms' – the latter presupposes the existence of political entities in the form of 'states', then the notion of 'non-state crime prevention' reflects a concern with a state-based category *outside* the institutional framework of state agencies.

Of course, the idea of a clear-cut separation between 'state' and 'non-state' has recently been challenged as regards the African continent following the recognition that the 'notion that Africa was ever composed of sovereign states classically defined as having a monopoly on force in the territory within their boundaries is false' (Herbst, 1996–97: 122). Decentralization and fragmented systems of authority are salient features of the African colonial and post-colonial scene, and 'the state' is thus better regarded as a plural assemblage that is practised through a combination of state and non-state units.

Concerning the topic of this chapter, therefore, it can be noted that 'non-state crime prevention' not only exemplifies the aforementioned concept of 'the state' as a plural assemblage, but also takes the peculiar form of an internally convoluted configuration whereby 'the state' is implicitly, yet also inextricably, folded into its opposite (that is, 'non-state') through use of the concept of 'crime' on both sides.

State and non-state crime prevention in South Africa

Self-justice, vigilantism and the state-endorsed involvement of private individuals in acts of policing and crime prevention have always been marked features in South African history. Given the country's divided society, different types of groups have engaged in the prevention and control of crime, in doing so disciplining and suppressing other people while frequently also being an expression of the struggle for autonomy and self-assertion in face of domination by oppressive social groupings and/or state agencies. In general, their activities have been framed in racial, ethnic, territorial or political terms; they have come into existence among both dominant *and* subaltern sections of society, and they have been legitimized in a variety of ways.

Some of these groups among white sections of the population have considered themselves to be a rightful adjunct to the activities of state agencies (Etherington 1988; Murray 1989). For example, such groups came into existence in the context of 'rape scares', that is, as an allegedly pre-emptive measure against the threat of white women being raped by black men. This threat was instrumentalized by white men in order to control white women by instilling fear, presenting themselves as protectors and, in doing so, promoting female domesticity (Martens, 2002). By contrast, certain sections of the South African black population engaged in vigilantism as part of the anti-apartheid struggle. Here, self-justice was a strategy to resist state power by establishing an alternative judicial system and silencing (purported) collaborators. Finally, in the history of South Africa, a large number of such groups took recourse to self-justice for the simple reason that there was no alternative to it. In the early 1990s, 80 per cent of all police stations were located in the neighbourhoods of the white population, who, however, represented just 10 per cent of the overall population (Mufamadi 1994: 4). In the areas officially allocated to black and 'coloured' populations, by contrast, police forces were hardly seen – and when they were seen, their actions regularly involved indiscriminate killings, humiliations and gross human rights violations (Brogden & Shearing 1993; Proudlock 1999).

This overview makes it clear that non-state policing and non-state crime prevention have long been systematic constituents of the South African socio-political environment. In this setting, what was at stake were the interrelated questions of the legitimacy of the state, the legitimacy of means and ends in instituting and asserting law, and the legitimacy of the actors involved in the prevention and control of crime. Groups of various backgrounds all claimed to establish, maintain or re-establish social order. But how in particular this social order was envisaged and how it should actually be accomplished was controversial. Among other things, this was because the different groups – the vigilante groups, self-defence units, gangs, neighbourhood watch groups and community courts – had widely diverging understandings of the relationship between 'common good' and 'private benefit'. What was deemed desirable and legitimate by some was often seen as undesirable and illegitimate by others. In addition, the boundaries between the different types of social groupings were blurred, so that what appeared, for instance, to be a 'neighbourhood watch group' at one point in time and from one perspective, at another time and from another perspective was indistinguishable from a 'criminal gang' (see also Kirsch & Grätz 2010).

Against the backdrop of these complexities, the first post-apartheid government saw itself confronted with a series of challenges: a deeply divided society, citizens who mistrusted each other, and public perceptions that the rate of crime was increasing drastically. It had to build on a state apparatus whose legitimacy had become highly questionable during the apartheid years, and it had to face the existence of a variety of more or less informal groupings that engaged in whatever they defined as 'crime prevention' and 'crime control'.

Given this strained situation, post-apartheid governments in South Africa have devised and implemented policies aimed at consolidating police accountability (see also Hornberger 2011; Marks 2005), while also enhancing the effectiveness of policing and of the prevention of crime. An important part of these policies is the creation of interfaces between the police and local 'communities' as represented by volunteers, namely Community Policing Forums (CPFs). Being based on an organizational model that has been instituted in several countries worldwide, the establishment of CPFs in South Africa has been acclaimed for representing a shift from 'authoritarian' and 're-active' to more 'democratic' and 'pro-active' policing (cf. Davis et al. 2003), and thus for expressing and being a catalyst for post-apartheid transformations (Kirsch 2010).

Besides such links between police reform and political self-legitimation, there is no doubt that the increasing formalization and institutionalization of the involvement of private individuals in acts of policing and crime prevention also needs to be seen as an effect of neo-liberal policies that endorse public–private partnerships and the outsourcing of what have previously been the functions of state agencies. Yet, what is regularly overlooked and what is central to the present chapter is that this development not only entails a shift from the public to the private sector, but also the increased official acceptance of volunteerism in the prevention of crime.

As I came to learn during my fieldwork in South Africa, this also finds expression in the fact that nowadays there exists a great multitude of non-governmental organizations (NGOs), non-profit companies, social clubs, faith-based organizations and associations of different sorts that, in one way or another, are seeking to contribute to crime prevention. Some of these organizations are professional, highly formalized, single-purpose bodies, such as Business Against Crime South Africa (BACSA), which describes itself as 'a non-profit Company, with a Section 18A status (i.e. donor funds are tax deductible by the donor organization) ... [that] was established by business in 1996 in response to a request from then President Nelson Mandela who invited business to join hands with Government in the fight against crime. It is a special purpose vehicle, with the sole mandate to engage and give support to Government on crime-related matters'.[10] Other organizations, such as certain boxing and soccer clubs in Mdantsane township in Eastern Cape Province, have included 'crime prevention' as a part-time add-on to their usual portfolio of activities. Still others represent more or less informal associations of people sharing a particular profession who have decided to do something against crime and violence. In the area of my research, Taxis Against Crime and Hawkers Against Crime were two groupings of this kind. While the latter pursued the crime-preventive surveillance of streets where informal traders were active, the former aimed at increasing the security in spaces which for a long time were considered to be among the most dangerous in South Africa's urban settings: taxi ranks. Last but not least, there exist a large number of charities and NGOs whose main objective is social work and social welfare, but which also try to make a contribution to crime prevention by, for example, taking care of street children or facilitating the social rehabilitation of offenders. What these groups have in common is, first, that they have been established on the independent initiative of non-state actors, and secondly, that they usually rely completely or at least to a substantial extent on work input by volunteers.

Volunteering against crime

In order to assess what is entailed in volunteerism in the field of non-state crime prevention, it is worthwhile to begin with a basic question. Imagine for the moment what the world would look like if every member of a given community were a volunteer in the same field of activities. In this scenario, would it be apposite and in any way meaningful to use the term 'volunteer'? There are good reasons to doubt it would, for the most part because volunteering is a relative notion not only with regard to the relationship between the 'donor' and the 'recipient' of the volunteering, but also with a view to the fact that volunteerism indicates a certain over-fulfilment of what would normally be expected from a member of the respective community.

---

[10] www.bac.org.za; accessed on 16 August 2013.

To grasp the latter point more fully, let us compare volunteering with two types of action orientation that were first outlined in a classic work in legal anthropology, Bronislaw Malinowski's *Crime and Custom in Savage Society* (1926). Searching for an answer to the question why people in the non-western world, so-called 'natives', obey rules, Malinowski criticized the then prevalent idea that their lives are characterized by a deep and instinctive 'reverence for tradition and custom (that leads to) an automatic submission to their biddings' (*ibid.*: 10). By contrast, he stressed that these people's observance of the rules of law are 'at best partial, conditional and subject to evasions' (*ibid.*: 15) because, according to Malinowski, rule compliance is an effect of 'mutual dependence, and realized in the equivalent arrangement of reciprocal services' (*ibid.*: 55). Law therefore ensures 'a type of co-operation which is based on mutual concessions and sacrifices for a common good' (*ibid.*: 64). Compare this to how volunteering is ideal-typically described: when engaging in volunteerism, the individual deliberately puts aside his or her self-interestedness and acts freely to the benefit of others which, in the final analysis, contributes to the interest of the common good.

We therefore find a continuum of action orientations. At the one extreme, an individual's actions are conceptualized as being devoid of free will and to be nothing but the blind fulfilment of social expectations and prescriptions; here individual interests are conceived to be identical with social interests. In the middle of the spectrum, individuals are said to strive for a balance between self-fulfilment and their fulfilment of social obligations. At the other end of the continuum, self-interestedness is eschewed, the emphasis being placed on the individual's voluntary – that is, non-prescribed – commitment in actively responding to social concerns.

I address the conceptualization of volunteering in more detail in the next section in order to develop a framework for the analysis of biographical interviews with South African volunteers. At this point it suffices to note that the notion of the 'volunteer', first, generally relies on the categorical distinction between 'the individual' and 'wider social realms', and second, presumes that certain individuals show relatively more engagement to the benefit of (some section of) this wider social realm than they are socially obliged to do, and more than would normally be expected of them. The combination of these two aspects, plus the fact, outlined above, that volunteers in non-state crime prevention make use of the state-based category of 'crime', provide a first indication of why this form of volunteering is so often perceived to be thoroughly ambivalent on the side of the (purported) recipients of volunteer activities.

Volunteering as gift-giving
'Volunteerism' is a controversial and elastic term which 'embraces a vast array of quite disparate activities' (Wilson 2000: 233). Broadly speaking, it usually refers to work that is performed without monetary reward. As such, social scientists have considered volunteering to be part of a

general cluster of helping activities, *pro*-active rather than *re*-active, a pro-social activity that is positively valued by the recipients. The term 'volunteering' is consequently often used in conjunction with terms like 'caring', 'helping', 'charity', 'altruism' and 'beneficence'. The complexities involved are partly due to the fact that the meaning and the socio-political role of 'volunteering' have changed over time. In some European countries, for example, historical processes first involved a transformation of volunteerism from religious 'charity' to secular 'altruism', then – with the advent of the welfare state – there was a relative decline in volunteerism, followed more recently by the mainstreaming of volunteerism into neo-liberal public policy (see Cunningham & Innes 1998). Also, we can observe a great diversity in how people perceive voluntary work. In the United States, for instance, where volunteerism in the form of civic associations has always played a greater role than in Europe, members of conservative Christian churches, according to sociologist John Wilson, 'think of volunteer work in terms of sacrifice [while] liberals think of it in terms of self-improvement' (2000: 219).

Given this background, anthropologists, geographers, political scientists and sociologists have studied *who* volunteers are, for example, in terms of age, gender and class, and individuals' motivations for volunteering (e.g. Maes 2012; Watts 2002). Others examine the political, economic and social contexts that influence volunteering activities (e.g. Erickson 2011; Smith & Laurie 2011), as well as the role of volunteerism in public health, service delivery and development aid (e.g. Boesten et al. 2011; McWha 2011).

It is the issue of motivation which has given rise to the most controversial debates about volunteerism, with some scholars subscribing to rational choice theories and others to theories of altruism influenced by Emile Durkheim's dictum that 'Altruism is not … an agreeable ornament to social life, but it will forever be its fundamental basis' (1993: 228). According to Daniel Bar-Tal, social scientists who focus on the motivational aspect of altruism tend to agree that 'altruistic behaviour (a) must benefit another person, (b) must be performed voluntarily, (c) must be performed intentionally, (d) the benefit must be the goal by itself, and (e) must be performed without expecting any external reward' (1986: 5).

However, as we all know, there is no free gift (see also Derrida 1992; Douglas 1990: vii). Gift-giving, according to Marcel Mauss, is 'apparently free and disinterested but nevertheless constrained' (2002: 4). As a consequence, for Mauss, the gesture of voluntarily giving a present is 'only a polite fiction, formalism, and social deceit, [while] really there is obligation and economic self-interest' (*ibid.*). Similarly, volunteering is an ambiguous form of social interaction. It functions, I argue, analogously to what Maurice Godelier has written about gift-giving, which, he states, '*decreases* the distance between the protagonists because it is a form of sharing, and … *increases* the distance between them because one is now indebted to the other' (2002: 12; italics added; see also Holden 1997).

In order to determine why and how volunteering increases the distance between social actors, it is important to recall that 'reciprocity' consists of three elements, namely the obligation to give, the obligation to receive and the obligation to reciprocate. According to sociologist Alvin Gouldner, 'volunteering', by contrast, is the 'giving of aid ... to those who cannot reciprocate it' (1973: 274). What he terms the 'norm of beneficence', 'calls upon men to aid others ... solely in terms of a need imputed to the potential recipient' (*ibid*.: 266). But this also implies that '[t]he donor gives because of what the recipient *is*, not because of what he does. The recipient self that seeks something for nothing is therefore powerless to modify the conditions of his existence' (*ibid*.: 270; italics added). Gouldner concludes: 'In other words, the price of unconditional help is the helplessness and unconditional dependence of the recipient on the donor' (*ibid*.: 271). It is in the latter sense that volunteering represents a powerful way of constructing social asymmetries between 'active' and 'passive' subjects.

Volunteering as repenting

When looking at 'volunteering' as a form of 'gift-giving', as we have done in the previous section, the focus usually lies on a synchronic structural form, such as the simultaneity of decreasing and increasing the distance between social actors. However, another picture emerges once we take into account the (real or imaginary) *earlier* relationships between the 'donors' and 'recipients' of a particular social configuration involving volunteering. Such a diachronic perspective is especially revealing in the analysis of post-conflict societies such as South Africa, because volunteer activities in these societies often function as a means to make up practically and/or symbolically for the inequalities, injustices and atrocities of the past. In other words, for those who held (or are believed to have held) privileged positions in the past, engaging in voluntary activities for the benefit of previously disadvantaged sections of society promises to *decrease* their distance from the latter because, as noted above, volunteering is a professedly *pro*-social and *pro*-active mode of interaction.

As I demonstrate below using the example of four case studies from my fieldwork in South Africa, becoming active in this regard is felt to be necessary by this kind of volunteer because of what they consider to have been morally ambiguous aberrations in their biographies during the apartheid era. In this context, voluntary commitment to the active promotion of the common good in post-apartheid South Africa allows them publicly to symbolize and practically enact the achievement of a reformed self that renounces previous wrongdoings, thus using volunteering 'as a means to fashion particular kinds of identity' (Prince & Brown, in the Introduction to this volume). In doing so, volunteering represents a self-legitimizing strategy for attaining and publicly performing moral integrity and integration into the newly (re-)forming society.

Yet, as will also become clear, this integration-seeking motion into the wider society through voluntary activities is not a single event but something that has to be re-enacted time and again by the volunteers because of the fact, discussed above, that volunteering simultaneously decreases and increases the distance between social actors. In other words, the volunteers' deliberate attempts to decrease the social distance that is perceived to be a legacy of the apartheid era as an unintended (and usually unacknowledged) consequence goes along with a certain increase in social distance in the present that is due to the structural asymmetries implied in volunteering.

I argue that my interlocutors are seeking to suspend this social distance from the recipients of their volunteering by expressly distancing themselves from their apartheid biographies and presenting themselves as reformed selves capable of making constructive contributions to post-apartheid sociality. By repetitively and performatively 'making a break with the past', to adopt a phrase from the anthropology of Pentecostal Christianity (Meyer 1998), volunteering therefore takes the form of active repentance, that is, of a publicly performed demonstration of one's readiness to make atonement for one's previous, self-professed misdemeanours. (For an analysis of how volunteering can serve the rehabilitation of stigmatized identities in the context of HIV/AIDS in South Africa, see Colvin in Chapter 1).

Volunteering as politics by other means: four case studies

I have already noted that the growing importance of volunteerism in present-day South Africa is macrostructurally connected to the increasing purchase of neo-liberal policies that promote 'self-help and the "responsibilization" of citizens in the maintenance of their own welfare in a context of state diminution and retreat' (Goldstein 2010: 498). But volunteerism also prompts important questions with a view to local interpretations of how people's volunteer engagement relates to the political, as well as to past, present and future forms of sociality. As we will see in what follows, when talking about and self-reflexively making sense of their volunteering in conversation with me, volunteers exhibited an astonishingly broad range of perspectives in describing this relationship.

Volunteering as a politics of new beginnings
Rob was a white ex-soldier who, after he quit the army in the mid-1990s, started to voluntarily engage in the CPFs of Trenton, the municipal area of Eastern Cape Province in which I conducted part of my fieldwork.[11]

---

[11] The names of my interlocutors, of the volunteer organizations mentioned in this chapter as well as of most of the areas where I did my fieldwork, have been changed to keep them anonymous.

For him, the command-driven and hierarchically organized institution of the South African army, his previous employer, stood paradigmatically for what he considered to have been a distinctive apartheid way of doing politics. In his view, 'apartheid's key to success' basically relied on the majority's readiness to accommodate, acquiesce and remain politically passive. In retrospect, the momentous move to become a professional military person, if only to remain in the rank of a common soldier throughout his working life, to Rob appears to have been the last decision made of his own free will, because the army 'was all about obedience and about forgetting who you really are'.

There were moments during our interview when Rob self-critically alluded to the violence he had inflicted on others while serving in the apartheid army, for example, when recounting how he and his comrades set alight the wigs of black sex workers they had seized on the streets at gunpoint. At large, however, the topic he predominantly dwelt on was that entering the military for him meant embarking on what in subsequent years he experienced as a life largely out of his control and in utter passivity.

By contrast, listening to how Rob depicts his role as a volunteer in the CPF, which involved patrolling the streets, engaging in local crime-preventive measures and low-key crime awareness campaigns as well as serving as an interface between the police and residents of the neighbourhood, it is striking how much emphasis is put on the active-mindedness characterizing his social engagement: 'I do whatever I can. Sometimes I leave early in the morning. Then I just walk around and chat with the people I meet on the street, making sure that everyone in Trenton knows me. This is so important! ... It does not look like a patrol, but people ought to know that I'm around'. Thus, while Rob associates his life as a soldier during the apartheid era with his segregated and passive withdrawal from the social world, he presents volunteering in post-apartheid crime prevention as a way of pro-actively socializing with people and engaging in what Hannah Arendt in a different context has called *vita activa*. According to Arendt, one of the central features of action is 'freedom', understood less as the ability to make choices between options than as the capacity to begin anew: 'To act, in its most general sense, means to take an initiative, to begin ... to set something in motion ... It is in the nature of beginning that something new is started which cannot be expected from whatever may have happened before' (Arendt 1958: 177–8).

When seen in this light, Rob's active enthusiasm in volunteering appears as a quest for an everyday politics of new beginnings. Acting as a volunteer for him means leaving behind what he pejoratively describes as a politics of prescribed roles and expectations. It also requires a readiness for the unexpected:

> It is funny but life has become more risky. You understand what I mean!? I was a soldier and I was used to being confronted with dange-

rous situations. But nowadays, when I go for a stroll and approach people I have never met before, ... I sometimes feel like an adventurer entering unknown territory. Going straight up to someone you don't know, trying to win this person over for what we are seeking to achieve, that's the risk I am talking about. Who knows! Many things can happen, good or bad.

Rob's account of how he turned to volunteering has certain features in common with conversion narratives as known from the religious realm. It is the narration of a momentous personal transformation, not from a sinful to a divinely ordained life, but from 'asocial passivity' to 'social pro-activeness'. Further, the way he describes his personal transformation has analogies with how the wider socio-political transition following the end of apartheid is commonly talked about in present-day South Africa. In both narrations, we find an appreciative emphasis on 'new beginnings' and the commitment to the idea of a desegregated sociality. Through such implicit narrative resonances, Rob's biography becomes embedded in the context of overriding societal visions of what has been called an 'African renaissance', in so doing endowing his life with social significance beyond the purely personal. At the same time, volunteerism is depicted as a privileged means to accomplish these visions. The publicity and conspicuousness of Rob's volunteering should therefore not only be interpreted as a crime-prevention strategy that indicates his 'preparedness' (cf. Collier & Lakoff 2008) and serves surveillance purposes, but also as an attempt to establish a social role model for others.

Volunteering as anti-politics
Strikingly different from this idea of volunteering as a politics of new beginnings is the approach of a female white volunteer that makes a sharp distinction between volunteering and politics of all sorts. Talking about her wedded life in the late 1980s, Ann recounted: 'We should not forget that life was different then. I was a very domestic person. That's how I thought it ought to be ... My husband went to work, and I was taking care of the children and the household. Of course, both of us were active in church, trying to help wherever we could. Otherwise we were just an average couple.' The way she described her family life reflects a widespread gendered division of labour in the apartheid era, mentioned above, whereby white women were kept at a distance from black men.

However, when her husband became unemployed in the late 1990s, Ann took up a part-time job to support the family. This new situation led to an increase in her mobility, as a consequence of which she came to realize that she had previously been embarrassingly ignorant about the social and economic problems faced by other (black) sections of society: 'You have been to Duncan Village [an overcrowded and largely poverty-stricken area of the city of East London, Eastern Cape Province], so you know what I am talking about. But for many years, I had no idea. There was simply no reason to go there ... Then, one day, I was shocked when Peter [a colleague] gave a lift to some person from the company who lived there, and I was sitting in the car ... I felt ashamed, but it also got me thinking and made a big change in how I was looking at things.'

Following this incident, Ann started to act periodically as a volunteer in different NGOs in the field of social work and social welfare. The work of these organizations also aimed at crime prevention through, for example, campaigns against (domestic) violence and the care of street children. Yet, several months before I came to know her, she had abandoned this social engagement due to what she described as feelings of frustration. Interestingly, both her motivation in engaging in volunteering and her decision some years later to give it up again have to do with Ann's critical view of 'politics'. According to her, the sudden and direct exposure to overcrowding and poverty she had experienced during her initial visit to Duncan Village made it impossible for her to continue turning a blind eye to the fact that post-apartheid politicians had failed to produce socio-economic equality, dignity and justice among *all* sections of the South African population. What is more, Ann came to see political strategizing and power-wielding as the root cause of this failure and, most importantly, volunteerism as the antidote.

From Ann's point of view, volunteering should ideally be a politics-free practice devoted solely to the promotion of social welfare to the benefit of what she considers to represent members of 'humanity' (cf. Feldman & Ticktin 2010). Of course, 'the refusal of political positioning not only has political effects, it is also a political strategy' (Redfield, 2010a: 56). Introducing the term 'anti-politics machine' to describe this strategy, James Ferguson has forcefully demonstrated that the development apparatus is 'depoliticizing everything it touches, everywhere whisking political realities out of sight, all the while performing, almost unnoticed, its own pre-eminently political operation of expanding bureaucratic state power' (1994: xv). In more recent years, this insight has fruitfully been applied in various anthropological fields of study, such as political anthropology (Fisher 1997), medical anthropology (Harper & Parker 2014; Prince 2012b) and the anthropology of humanitarianism (Ticktin 2011). Yet, as Peter Redfield cautions, confining oneself to simply dismissing the claim to political 'neutrality' as fiction and camouflage would miss the point and (re)produce nothing but ethnographic truisms. He suggests that, '[i]nstead of denying self-interest ... neutrality expresses it through an attempt to restrict or alter the terms of engagement. By expressing a desire to stand apart, the would-be neutral asserts independence, and by implication the capacity to maintain or form an alternative connection' (Redfield 2010a: 56).

The latter observation throws light upon Ann's understanding of volunteering as a politics-free practice. Her volunteering certainly widened the world for her. In contrast to her previous life, which she describes as having been confined mainly to the domestic realm and church circles, her years as a volunteer were characterized by increased social mobility. In turn, associating 'volunteering' with a programmatic commitment to 'humanism' – that is, to 'discourses and practices that constitute subjects first of all as human beings' (Malkki 2010: 59) – rendered it possible for her to overcome to some extent the segregational legacies of the apartheid era. At the same time, however, Ann tended to keep a certain distance from both her co-volunteers and those who benefitted her volunteer work. This was because she felt it necessary to watch out constantly and critically for other people's attempts to politicize volunteer activities. Thus, in seeming contradiction to the pro-social mindset that motivated Ann's volunteering, her fundamental aversion to politics – in her understanding of this notion as 'power-wielding' and 'potentially amoral strategizing' – made her, figuratively speaking, stand apart socially. Eventually, when she became aware that ANC politics had come to play a crucial, albeit largely unacknowledged role in certain institutional contexts of her volunteer work, she decided to quit. Most particularly, she felt personally betrayed when the NGO she was working in as a volunteer in the early 2000s started to downplay the statistical occurrence of violence and criminal incidents in the wider region, in doing so complying with an unofficial policy by representatives of the local ANC branch (which at that time suffered a political legitimation crisis due to the high crime rates).

Volunteering as the domestication of the public sphere
Khwezi grew up in the township of Mdantsane in what was practically a female-headed household because he hardly saw his father, who had migrated to Western Cape Province many years ago. He remembers that his mother used to host relatives from rural areas in her home, a small-sized 'matchbox house' (cf. Ginsburg 1996) of the type commonly used by middle-class residents in this township:

> I enjoyed socializing with relatives from the villages, many of whom I had not known before. But we had a serious problem with space … I had to sleep underneath the table; my younger brother, who was much smaller than me, was lying on top of it; most of the others were sleeping on the floor. When you woke up in the middle of the night with an urge to go to the toilet, one had to be very careful not to step on someone's head.

It was only after his Xhosa initiation ceremony, followed by a time of isolation in an initiation hut which was situated in a scrubby wasteland, that Khwezi briefly experienced a less crowded housing situation.

His stay in the initiation hut was also the moment when Khwezi's contacts with petty criminals intensified.

> Normally, nobody dares to come close to the *ibhoma* [isiXhosa term for 'initiation hut'] because it's a dangerous place for everyone apart from

the newly circumcised. But some of my friends, who knew that I and two other initiates were staying there, didn't mind at all. One night, they paid us a visit and asked us to help them and to store some things for them, a DVD player, a suitcase, some plastic bags and other stuff. We helped them. We didn't talk about it, but it was clear to all of us that these things had not been paid for with their own money, if you know what I mean.

Having returned to normal life, Khwezi kept in touch with these 'friends' and was gradually integrated into a social network of adolescents who were hanging around together, supported each other and occasionally got involved in petty criminal activities.

In hindsight, Khwezi still wonders how smoothly he had made the transition to becoming a member of what to outsiders must have had the appearance of a gang, even if it lacked a name and some of the typical gang structures. The activities of this group concentrated on a specific area of the township, and since the members of the group had a sense of ownership over this area, they were both feared and asked for protection by local residents. In other words, the group which Khwezi had joined during the apartheid era was characterized by an ambiguous group identity, oscillating between 'criminal gang' and 'neighbourhood watch group', as described above.

In conversation with me and others, Khwezi made no pretence that the activities of this group had involved a sometimes violently enforced distinction between members and non-members, physical violence being exerted within and outside the group, as well as criminal activities such as muggings and robberies. When talking about it so many years later, all of this caused him feelings of guilt, yet – no different than Rob, the ex-soldier – he never went into details regarding the wrongdoings he had committed. When asked for details, he stated in no uncertain terms that the ghosts of the past should be left behind. At the same time, it repeatedly struck me in our conversations how much emphasis he put on the strong sense of community which, he said, at that time prevailed in his peer group and which was so different from his mother's emotional indifference:

> I do not think that my mother really cared for us. Sure, she had her own matters to deal with. My father was away for the most of the year. He had no choice, because that's how the system worked. But I sometimes got the impression that my mother didn't even notice when I was staying out during night time. It was different with my sisters, yes, and my younger brothers also had to ask for permission ... but I was left to my own devices.

By contrast, when reflecting on his time as a gang member, he often spoke in high terms of the group's code of conduct and mutual expectations of trustworthiness and reliability:

It wasn't always easy for new kids to get used to it. They had to tell us whom they met and what they were doing, no matter what it was. But don't dare to lie to us! If you want to be cared for, you need to be worthwhile to be cared for. It's a give and take ... and if one of them was trying to cheat on us, we made sure that this would not happen again.

Mutual support among the members of the gang was rooted in enforced accountability, mutual surveillance and physical sanctions in the case of non-compliance. Nonetheless, for Khwezi, this code of conduct aroused feelings of being part of a close-knit and protective in-group of like-minded people. In our conversations, he even spoke about a 'homely feeling', which his actual home was lacking due to the absence of his father and to what he perceived to be his mother's lack of interest.

There is a certain irony in the fact that Khwezi's experience as a gang member during the apartheid era, though recounted in retrospect with a slightly nostalgic undertone, in post-apartheid South Africa served as a blueprint for what he envisaged to be the ideals and objectives of his voluntary activities in non-state crime prevention, which he started in the late 1990s. Since he regarded dysfunctional families such as his own to be the main cause of asocial behaviour and criminal activities by adolescents, Khwezi felt that the non-governmental voluntary organizations he was involved in should seek to establish 'surrogate families' for youth at risk, not in the literal sense of the word 'family', but in the figurative sense of a protective and caring form of sociality which would allow young men to develop respect for others as well as to prevent them from becoming entangled in criminal networks. Awakening their interest for sporting activities, like boxing or soccer, was his preferred and primary means to this end.

In this way, Khwezi not only projected an idealized and overall quite romantic view of domestic relationships into the wider social sphere, he also self-identified as a person for whom involvement in a gang represents both a legacy of the past *and* a lesson for the future. As a legacy of the past, Khwezi's time as a gang member was actually the raison d'être for his commitment as a volunteer in non-state crime prevention. But as we have seen, he simultaneously depicted this time as a distinct way of life that provides social stability for adolescents, even if it might be to others' detriment. For the latter reason, Khwezi claimed an autobiographically deduced expertise for himself in how to win over dangerous and endangered young people to conciliatory and domesticated forms of sociality.

Volunteering as a plea for making rational choices
What left a lasting impression on me when I first met Ntando in the backroom of an office building close to Mdantsane's main shopping area was the extraordinarily circumspect manner in which he responded to

my questions. A sturdy, middle-aged man, there was a certain shyness and cautiousness to him which stood in sharp contrast to the contents of what he told me.

The interview had been arranged by a member of a CPF in Mdantsane township with which Ntando had cooperated on several occasions. It took me a while to realize that the relative brevity of our encounter and the silent periods characterizing it replicated something of Ntando's accustomed role in public events addressing crime prevention, such as awareness campaigns for school children. During events like these, Ntando made his appearance as a person who years ago had been imprisoned because of his previous involvement in a sudden outburst of violence leading to the death of an alleged informant (*impimpi*) of the apartheid regime. On most occasions, Ntando was not expected to say a lot. Instead, his physical presence during these events was for the most part of a symbolic nature, accompanied by a simple message: 'Do not let yourself get carried away on the spur of the moment. Do not mindlessly imitate your friends. Think twice. Otherwise, you will end up like me.'

My interview with Ntando followed a similar pattern. We did not talk for long, nor did we deal with many different issues; I will therefore restrict myself to the main topic of our conversation. Skipping all information about his personal background and briefly elucidating the events leading to the murder of the alleged informant, Ntando emphasized that, for him, killing this person was *not* a political act. Instead, he described himself as an angry young man, who at that time was willing to let out his frustration on more or less anyone who happened to be around. One day, when he incidentally overheard that some of his neighbours were gathering in order to teach someone suspected of having contacts with the apartheid security apparatus a lesson, he spontaneously decided to join them. What followed was an emotionally charged eruption of deadly violence which, in retrospect, he said he would love to undo – if only it were possible.

Ntando's participation in crime-prevention campaigns as a volunteer can be interpreted as a means to publicly enact repentance for his past wrongdoings. His view and experience of the apartheid era culminated in a burdening image of affect-driven effervescence and inconsiderate group behaviour. As a consequence, the primary message he was trying to convey to people following his post-apartheid release from prison was that they should abstain from impulsive behaviour, act in a deliberate manner and plan ahead, and that they should constantly monitor and reflect their social surroundings and their own conduct in it. In this way, Ntando's approach to volunteering in crime prevention was hallmarked by advocacy of rational contemplation. Building on his self-characterization as a person who had been easily susceptible in the past, it represented a plea for self-awareness and self-control as the foundation of a peaceful post-apartheid society.

Conclusion

In his widely acclaimed study of the Truth and Reconciliation Commission (TRC) in post-apartheid South Africa, Richard Wilson points out that 'the amnesty hearings were a theatricalization of the power of the new state, which compelled representatives of the former order to confess ... Perpetrators were compelled to speak within the confines of a new language of human rights, and in so doing to recognize the new government's power to admonish and to punish' (Wilson 2001: 20). What is more, according to Wilson, the TRC functioned as a 'truth-making machine' (*ibid.*: 33) through which the diversity and complexity of individual memories and histories of apartheid oppression were synthesized – and thus, reduced – to a moralizing narrative.

On the face of it, the phenomenon explored in this chapter shares several features with this account. First, in 'making a break with the apartheid past' when talking about their motivations for volunteering, volunteers presented themselves as having achieved the reformed self of a 'moral citizen' that renounces previous failures and/or wrongdoings. Engagement in volunteerism thus served as a self-legitimizing platform for stressing moral integrity and becoming (re)integrated into post-apartheid sociality. However, in contrast to the TRC amnesty hearings, this was not enacted in a singled-out 'confession' but took the form of the volunteers' continuous enactment of 'repentance'.

Second, comparable with the TRC's use of a language of human rights, my interlocutors gave expression to their reformed selves as volunteers by employing the language of the common good. Yet, as distinct from the TRC hearings, this meant not only revealing and renouncing previous wrongdoings, but also demonstrating that one had learnt one's lesson by actively engaging in politics by other means – even if, as in Ann's case, it took the form of social engineering on the basis of a professedly anti-political stance.

In the case studies examined above, we thus find a double-edged constellation. On the one hand, volunteers in crime prevention emphasize the need to do things differently in post-apartheid South Africa than how they used to be done under apartheid. On the other hand, the ability to do this is depicted as depending on one's personal experiences during the apartheid era. Rob presents his pro-social active-mindedness as a CPF volunteer as an intentional counter to the passivity and submissiveness that characterized his time as a soldier. Ann's autobiographical narrative delineates a movement from a life immersed in tacitly politicized domesticity to volunteer activities for the promotion of a non-political 'common good' in the public realm. Khwezi aims at transposing certain qualities of sociality from the milieu of his former township gang into the post-apartheid public sphere in order to make the latter more 'homely' for youth at risk. Last but not least, Ntando wants his biography as an ex-prisoner to act as a forceful reminder to others that post-apartheid social engineering should, literally speaking, be well thought out.

The fact that volunteers in non-state crime prevention are not compelled to volunteer but act out of their own will begs the question of what triggers their motivation to volunteer. In this chapter, I have focused on autobiographical forms of explanation, in doing so complementing the synchronic approach to volunteer work with a diachronic perspective. I have shown how the rationale, practical modalities and social orientation of volunteering are shaped by the volunteers' own (re)interpretations of their life histories under apartheid. This allows us to catch a glimpse of the diverse, multi-faceted and partly unexpected ways in which apartheid is remembered by those who played a role in it, thus disentangling simplified historical accounts of apartheid. It also enables us to discern how volunteerism in non-state crime prevention in present-day South Africa is different from apartheid, an antidote to it, yet at the same time a counterintuitive product of it.

Epilogue

Ebola &
the Vulnerable
Volunteer
PETER REDFIELD

The contemporary world order leans heavily on volunteers. If often overlooked in sweeping discussions of capital flows and geopolitics, actual relations between people and places involve both material and imagined forms of voluntary action. Indeed, upon inspection, the figure of the volunteer appears increasingly vital to global governance and exchange. As this volume demonstrates, voluntary labour and associated sentiment play a particularly prominent role in Sub-Saharan Africa. Both national and international efforts to foster public health and economic development have repeatedly sought to inspire altruism and a sense of social solidarity as a means to mobilization. In the aftermath of European empire the voluntary actor could thus appear an heir to the anti-colonial nationalist and the earnest missionary alike, mediating strikingly disparate political visions, forms of expertise and conceptions of community. As a consequence it has grown hard to imagine social change without some appeal to civil society, as premised on national or global citizenship.

The case studies assembled in this volume underscore tensions running through this world of voluntary action. First and foremost, the degree to which individuals can separate labour from livelihood reveals stark inequalities between their economic positions, part of a larger fault line that limits efforts to promote solidarity across social divides. Simply put, who can afford to volunteer? The reality of unequal economies hits home whenever altruism stretches beyond a momentary gesture, and the 'spirit of volunteerism' clashes with material necessity as well as self-interest. From development projects in Lesotho to clinical trials in Zambia, moral sensibilities and social obligations mix uneasily, returning repeatedly to questions of payment. On top of economic inequality, the often fragmentary and unstable associations that connect non-profit ventures with political organization fail to gel into unified endeavour. Thus efforts to encourage community engagement in response to health threats such as HIV/AIDS or malaria encounter the problem of defining and stabilizing a shared conception of public good. Shifting focus to the exchanges and encounters engendered by voluntary action reveals other spheres of inequality, along with their political and economic constraints. Thus international volunteers played a role even in Tanzania's initial effort to achieve self-sufficiency in addition to independence. More recent efforts by clinical volunteers to 'make a difference' in resource-poor hospitals can ignore costs as well as benefits, even as they overshadow other discussion of the very inequities that make them possible. The moral projects that inspire volunteers do so precisely because they hold out a promise of self-improvement or redemption. This prospect of reclaiming moral responsibility resonates widely, motivating individuals to cross not just international borders but also internal divides in settings such as Kenya or South Africa. Thus matters of personal virtue and global governance conjoin uncomfortably in the figure of the volunteer. The result offers as many questions as answers, a testimony to what the editors fittingly distil as the 'complexities, ambiguities and political importance of voluntary involvements in Africa' (Introduction).

Here I offer a final case for this collection, addressing the medical humanitarian response to the recent Ebola crisis. Unlike the other chapters, it features an emergency context, both in the medical sense of fierce urgency and immediate need, and in the political sense of a condition that exceeds ordinary legal and bureaucratic conventions. If anything, this exceptional case only proves the general rule. Core themes of the volume resonate strongly throughout the Ebola response: the recurring spectre of economic inequality, the continuing question of how volunteer action relates to a public good, the twin problems of moral responsibility and the intersection of voluntary action with global governance. Moreover, the case raises additional, uncomfortable stakes with regard to vulnerability and security, along with the limits of individual and national sacrifice.

In international aid settings volunteers may expect to demonstrate a degree of solidarity with those they try to assist, and even share some of the burdens or discomforts they might experience. Thus virtue – along with insight – can accrue to those who live closely and humbly within a given community, and fall away for those who distance themselves. Rarely, however, do even intrepid aid workers expect any sacrifice on their part to include their own lives. When facing emergency conditions this limit to giving grows painfully visible. As a number of observers have noted, a core discomfort for humanitarian action lies in the inequities it lays bare and cannot escape. Didier Fassin (2012: 223–42) makes the point most forcefully when he underscores the fundamental inequality that distinguishes between those who might venture into risk and those who remain actively subject to it, separating the sacred lives of foreign expatriates from the expendable ones of national staff. At a critical moment of crisis and evacuation some climb on a plane and others do not, their very existence weighed by a passport.

The recent Ebola outbreak in West Africa offered a dramatic elaboration of this general principle of inequality, alongside variations on the theme of volunteer vulnerability. Below I offer a brief sketch of that experience, as seen over the shoulder of the organization Médecins Sans Frontières (Doctors Without Borders, or MSF).[1] Although unplanned, this choice of example is both predictable and revealing. Without actively setting out to do so, MSF became the *de facto* lead agency for the outbreak – an independent NGO transformed into the quasi-official voice of a global health crisis. Long used to controversial stands and a range of medical disasters, the group nonetheless found itself newly overwhelmed. The episode inspired a fresh round of soul-searching in and beyond the organization, as well as a veritable industry of innovation and commentary, now entangling this author as well.

An exceptional disease

Before turning to volunteers and their vulnerability, let me first underscore the specificity of the disease and MSF's relation to it. From the perspective of medical humanitarianism, Ebola has long appeared a relatively exotic problem – deadly and disturbingly unknown, but also thankfully rare and usually quite restricted in geographic scope. Compared to common concerns like malaria or HIV/AIDS, it had previously affected only a handful of people, and only in episodic flashes. Unlike cholera, which appears with depressing regularity around the world among displaced people, it seldom featured in the global humanitarian portfolio.[2] Rather, to follow a useful distinction made by Andrew Lakoff (2010), Ebola fell into the purview of global health security, a complex of experts and institutions devoted to monitoring and preparing for potential threats such as avian influenza, severe acute respiratory syndrome (SARS) and West Nile virus. Concerned primarily with protecting national populations in wealthy countries from external threats, this security regime clearly foresaw the deadly potential of the Ebola virus. It did not, however, prepare particularly well for the outbreak that actually materialized (Lachenal 2014).

[1] For current information on MSF see the international site www.msf.org and the USA site www.doctorswithoutborders.org. See also the Ebola blog page at http://blogs.msf.org/en/staff/blogs/msf-ebola-blog. For recent profiles of the organization see Redfield (2013b) and Fox (2014). For background on Ebola from the perspective of anthropology and associated disciplines see the series of posts on the blogsites Somatosphere *Ebola fieldnotes* – http://somatosphere.net/series/ebola-fieldnotes, *Cultural Anthropology* – www.culanth.org/fieldsights/585-ebola-in-perspective and (on a more applied note) the Ebola Response Platform – www.ebola-anthropology.net. Also see issue number 5 of the journal *Limn*, edited by Andrew Lakoff, Stephen J. Collier & Christopher Kelty – http://limn.it/issue/05 (all accessed 4 December 2015).

[2] Even in the low year of 2013 MSF treated 27,900 patients with that condition, many times the total number who had ever experienced Ebola in the past and still more than official numbers for the 2014 outbreak. See www.cdc.gov/vhf/ebola/outbreaks/2014-west-africa/cumulative-cases-graphs.html (accessed 4 December 2015).

If hardly focused on biosecurity or emerging diseases, MSF had nonetheless developed a measure of familiarity with Ebola. The virus appeared in just the sort of places where humanitarians frequently found themselves: largely rural landscapes in countries like Democratic Republic of Congo, Sudan and Uganda. This was MSF's home turf so to speak, as much or more than any other medical entity. After responding to a series of small African outbreaks over the last two decades, the group could even claim a certain expertise with the disease alongside WHO and the US Centers for Disease Control (CDC). It is important to note that in MSF's case this expertise derived from internal initiative, and not any formal mandate. It remained an independent NGO, largely fuelled by voluntary commitment and private donations. Thus by the turn of the millennium the group had developed a kit for Ebola, as well as a set of protocols. At an organizational level, at least, it felt equipped to respond.The disease itself remained unsettling, however, hovering at the very edge of medical capacity. Intervention focused on setting up a quarantined treatment unit in an effort to arrest the outbreak and safeguard the surrounding population, a goal that previous Ebola responses ultimately achieved. For actual existing patients who arrived at one of these units, however, the treatment on offer proved distressingly minimal. Medical staff endeavoured to provide basic supportive care (rehydrating, maintaining oxygen status and blood pressure, treating any complicating infections), and essentially hoped that the patient would recover. They had little more technique to offer, and limited time or means to do much else. Ebola is a relatively fast and deadly affliction. Although reported death rates vary by viral strain and treatment context, they often fall above 50 per cent and can run as high as 90 per cent.[3] If not especially infectious as far as viruses go, the manner in which Ebola disrupts a host body – multiplying rapidly as the patient declines and increasingly oozing out in bodily fluids – places caregivers at particular risk. Both tending to an afflicted person and treating a corpse become hazardous acts. Indeed, care itself becomes a primary vector of transmission. As a consequence Ebola eats through the very bonds of human compassion, infecting those who offer assistance: relatives, mourners and health care professionals.

Due to this heightened risk of transmission, medical personnel themselves feel acutely vulnerable. They don an elaborate second skin of protective equipment before attending to Ebola patients. Once done with a shift they then shed this shell again, laboriously adhering to strict protocols and nervously hoping to avoid exposure. Commentators often note how the outfit resembles a space suit, and similarly signals a primary need for self-preservation. Seeking to seal themselves from the hostile environment of their patients, caregivers effectively become other-worldly figures, frightening as well as frightened. As widely reported earlier in this exceptional West African outbreak, Ebola teams can incite

---

[3] www.cdc.gov/vhf/ebola/outbreaks/history/chronology.html (accessed 4 December 2015).

suspicion and arouse resistance. The appearance of ghostly aliens who keep patients at arm's length, spraying everything with disinfectant, and then hurriedly spirit them away to a distant location where they often die does little to inspire confidence. Staff from several organizations, including MSF, found their vehicles pelted with rocks, and members of a Guinean education team were murdered.[4]

Such extreme distrust and violence becomes less surprising in light of the longer history of the disease. Earlier responses to outbreaks likewise provoked a swirl of rumours, active mistrust and attempted flight by patients.[5] They also inspired misgivings and soul-searching on the part of caregivers. A report from a 2001 workshop on the theme of 'Justice and MSF Operational Choices' addressed the Ugandan outbreak of the previous year at some length. It noted that while MSF had been invited to help on the basis of its clinic experience to reduce hospital infections, which had killed thirty-two hospital workers, the very practice of accumulating patients together might have had the opposite effect, not only saving few lives but potentially amplifying the disease through care. At best, one expert estimated that clinical care increased survival by about 5 per cent. Even the group's desire to reduce stigma around the disease had encountered an unexpected obstacle in overexposure, as 'we felt that the world-wide publicity probably made things look worse'. The report's assessment of the intervention closed on a gloomy note, wondering how to explain to the local population why MSF had chosen address Ebola and not another health problem: 'Working on the wards you didn't feel like you had made much of a difference for a patient. Most died anyway. But the 5% improvement on admitted cases does not measure the intervention and its consequences on the economic and social costs.'[6]

Similar concerns continued to surface when discussing subsequent responses to Ebola and other viral haemorrhagic fevers. If not saving that many lives, then what did MSF's response achieve? Did the supportive care at least have palliative effects, easing suffering and allowing patients to die with dignity? At an annual meeting of MSF-France in 2005, debate surfaced about recent treatment of Marburg virus (a close relative of Ebola) in Angola. As recounted in the section's internal newsletter:

> The highly lethal nature of this viral hemorrhagic fever meant that the teams had to work wearing special protective clothing, similar to those worn by cosmonauts. In the town of Uige, MSF set up an isolation and treatment center for patients, which led one volunteer to comment: 'We're asking them to come here and throw themselves straight into the

4   www.cnn.com/2014/09/19/health/ebola-guinea-killing (accessed 4 December 2015).

5   Hewlett & Hewlett (2008: 56–7). See also www.washingtonpost.com/news/morning-mix/wp/2014/09/19/why-the-brutal-murder-of-eight-ebola-workers-may-hint-at-more-violence-to-come (accessed 4 December 2015).

6   MSF-Holland. Justice and MSF Operational Choices. Report of discussion held in Soesterberg, Netherlands in June 2001: 25–7.

grave.' A member of the audience described that we were reduced to 'health police', while another expressed regret concerning the remote, paranoiac attitude of the majority of caregivers, increasing the gap that already exists between doctor and patient.

Most ultimately agreed that the brutality of the operation was regrettable, and concluded that in future anthropologists and psychologists should be involved to a greater degree in such circumstances, since caregivers' actions consist here in particular of supporting the patients and their loved ones through the dying process.[7]

In later operations MSF would attempt to recognize to some degree the humanity of its patients. A 2008 edition of MSF guidelines calls for efforts to demystify Ebola treatment centres by allowing people to see inside them, as well as providing survivors and relatives of the deceased with a 'solidarity kit' to compensate them for items destroyed for fear of contamination.[8] None of this, however, proved sufficient for the current outbreak.

When the virus unexpectedly appeared in West Africa, humanity soon took a backseat to security.[9] As the disease escaped initial containment, panic began to set in. Protocols, kits and hasty attempts at quarantine could not substitute for incapacity, poor judgement and early inaction. In some settings (Senegal, Democratic Republic of Congo and – to great relief – Nigeria), public health efforts managed to smother local outbreaks, erasing them from the headlines. In others, however, disaster only grew. After initial eruption in Guinea, the patchwork, aid-based circulatory system of medical care in Liberia and Sierra Leone dissolved before the onslaught, itself endangering a much broader pool of patients.[10]

From the outset, MSF was working on the frontlines. The organization's own news briefs, initially measured and business-like, began to express alarm by the end of March, recognizing the geographic dispersal of cases was unprecedented, and then, when hope of containment failed, pronounced it out of control by mid-June.[11] The updates grew

---

[7] MSF *Messages* 138 (November 2005): 14.

[8] Filovirus Haemorrhagic Fever Guideline by Esther Sterk, MD, Médecins Sans Frontières, 2008; see especially: 27, 121. Available at www.medbox.org/ebola-guidelines/filovirus-haemorrhagic-fever-guideline/preview (accessed 4 December 2015).

[9] See Raphael Frankfurter The Danger in Losing Sight of Ebola Victims' Humanity, *The Atlantic*, 22 August 2014, available at www.theatlantic.com/health/archive/2014/08/the-danger-in-losing-sight-of-ebola-victims-humanity/378945 (accessed 4 December 2015).

[10] www.doctorswithoutborders.org/article/sierra-leone-msf-suspends-emergency-pediatric-and-maternal-services-gondama (accessed 4 December 2015).

[11] www.msf.org/article/guinea-mobilisation-against-unprecedented-ebola-epidemic, see also www.doctorswithoutborders.org/news-stories/field-news/msf-remains-vigilant-ebola-outbreak-continues-guinea-and-liberia, and www.businessweek.com/articles/2014-11-13/ebola-doctors-without-borders-shows-how-to-manage-a-plague. For a timeline of events see www.cnn.com/interactive/2014/11/health/ebola-outbreak-timeline and for an analysis see the contributions in *Limn* 5: Ebola's Ecologies – available at http://limn.it/issue/05 (all accessed 4 December 2015).

increasingly shrill as the summer wore on and conditions deteriorated. In early September, feeling overwhelmed, the group took the extraordinary step of calling for military support (though not forced quarantine). In a speech to the UN, MSF's international president Dr Joanne Liu accused member states of joining a 'global coalition of inaction' and challenged those that had invested in biosecurity to deploy their resources to stem to the epidemic.[12]

Who, after all, was in charge? This core concern of security thinking grew increasingly unclear in the absence of effective national health care.[13] Although WHO had global authority, its mission historically emphasized planning and policy rather than direct action; even the agency's Epidemic and Pandemic Alert and Response programme promised 'support' to member states in the African region rather than overt leadership.[14] The CDC was ultimately an arm of a particular national government, however large and influential it might be. Although MSF might have been playing a leading role, it remained an NGO staffed primarily by volunteers and sought no official coordinating status.[15] As the crisis continued through the rest of the year, rival security and humanitarian impulses animating global health directly collided over Ebola. When a handful of international volunteers themselves became sick, their return home for treatment sparked a resurgence of nationalist concerns about borders and quarantines. While no expense might be spared in seeking to care for these lives, the moral heroes of humanitarian medicine had become a potential threat.[16]

[12] www.msf.org/article/global-bio-disaster-response-urgently-needed-ebola-fight and www.msf.org/article/msf-international-president-united-nations-special-briefing-ebola (both accessed 4 December 2015).

[13] For an analysis of the Liberian health care system see Sharon Abramowitz, 'How the Liberian Health Sector Became a Vector for Ebola' in *Cultural Anthropology*'s Fieldsights series: www.culanth.org/fieldsights/598-how-the-liberian-health-sector-became-a-vector-for-ebola (accessed 4 December 2015).

[14] www.afro.who.int/en/clusters-a-programmes/dpc/epidemic-a-pandemic-alert-and-response.html. As noted in several news reports, WHO had also suffered budget cuts: www.washingtonpost.com/sf/national/2014/10/04/how-ebola-sped-out-of-control and www.nytimes.com/2014/09/04/world/africa/cuts-at-who-hurt-response-to-ebola-crisis.html (all accessed 4 December 2015).

[15] www.msf.org/article/ebola-msf-should-not-replace-governmental-responsibilities. See also www.nature.com/news/ebola-outbreak-thrusts-msf-into-new-roles-1.17690 (both accessed 4 December 2015).

[16] See Adia Benton Race and the Immuno-logics of Ebola Response in West Africa that *Somatosphere* posted 19 September 2014 http://somatosphere.net/2014/09/race-and-the-immuno-logics-of-ebola-response-in-west-africa.html on the differential national/racial valuation of lives. As of 2 December, the *New York Times* reported twenty cases of Ebola treatment outside of Africa, five of which ended in death (an effective mortality rate of 25 per cent, including examples of last-minute care) www.nytimes.com/interactive/2014/07/31/world/africa/ebola-virus-outbreak-qa.html (all accessed 4 December 2015).

Contagious vulnerability

On the night of 23 October 2014, I was in Philadelphia for an event sponsored by MSF. Held at the television station WHYY-TV, the occasion sought to highlight the public release of a series of internal case studies that examined the organization's history of 'speaking out' in response to humanitarian crises.[17] The director of the organization's US branch had planned to attend, but at the last minute remained in New York to deal with a sudden emergency: an MSF doctor, recently returned from Guinea, had just been diagnosed with Ebola. That evening I watched in disbelief as the media storm burst. Multiple channels broadcast non-stop on the topic, including a news conference where a battery of New York health officials and politicians repeatedly sought to reassure the public that doomsday had not yet arrived. Their efforts did little to quell the hysteria, or calls for quarantine. Hasty provisions enacted in New Jersey and New York soon provoked a second controversy, when a healthy MSF nurse protested her confinement at Newark airport. Rather than seeking media outlets for its message, MSF found itself under siege, simultaneously protesting the new orders and explaining why its network of volunteers should not be seen as a stealth vector for infection.[18]

The organization's concern was not only a matter of protecting its personnel and image, unexpectedly exposed to public suspicion. It also worried about the damping effect indiscriminate quarantine would have on the effort to recruit new volunteers to head to the outbreak zone, putting its stretched resources under further strain. The relative vulnerability of caregiver bodies, even the most privileged, transnationally mobile ones, became a focus of debate about risk and containment, along with associated personal worry and political theatre. Would medical professionals agree to put their own lives on the line? If they did, would they endanger those around them, family, friends, neighbours and fellow citizens?

The media glare surrounding the small number of Ebola patients who began receiving care in wealthy countries had other effects. By raising the stakes of their treatment, it also served to highlight the deeper inequities coursing through the disease. Not only did these individuals benefit from evacuation, they also received expansive and expensive individualized care, with an impressive array of specialists and material resources devoted to their treatment. Beyond experimental drugs, this involved an inverted ratio of personnel from the apocalyptic scenes playing out in West Africa: the many caring for the few, rather than the other way around. In contrast to those expiring at alarming rates in the overwhelmed Ebola Treatment Units – including many African health care providers who succumbed to the disease – patients in more-privileged

---

[17] http://speakingout.msf.org (accessed 4 December 2015).
[18] www.doctorswithoutborders.org/article/q-msf's-ebola-response-and-protocols (accessed 4 December 2015).

settings largely survived. Perhaps nothing symbolized this inequality of lives more clearly than an upgraded evacuation plane the Germany government acquired from the carrier Lufthansa at the end of November. Removed from regular air transport, rechristened after the medical hero Robert Koch and newly retrofitted with state of the art equipment to maintain a flying isolation ward, this wide-bodied jet promised to serve as 'the world's only evacuation facility for highly contagious patients'.[19] Associated press releases cheerfully overlooked the question, however, of who would likely benefit most from this enhanced transport.

Even as MSF continued to berate the larger apparatus of global health for its laggard and insufficient response to the crisis, its own projects and protocols faced increasing questioning. The fact that patients arriving at West African treatment centres received only minimal supportive care came under increasing scrutiny, particularly as it began to appear that quality of care might affect survival rates. A diverse array of actors (well beyond the humanitarian field, and with multiple potential motives) began to clamour for fast-track research on potential tests, drugs and vaccines. Others called for an expanded treatment protocol, including greater use of intravenous hydration therapy. When Partners in Health (PIH) joined the cascade of organizations arriving on the frontlines, their iconic leader Paul Farmer suggested that Ebola's deadly aura was partly a result of insufficient care: 'MSF is not doing enough', he was quoted as saying in the *New York Times*. 'What if the fatality rate isn't the virulence of disease but the mediocrity of the medical delivery?'[20] Farmer and PIH called for an effort to lower mortality rates to 10 per cent, a figure others found wildly optimistic.

Criticism also came from within MSF itself. Although the organization had a long tradition of fostering internal debate, when a group of prominent senior figures wrote a provocative internal letter to their colleagues in December it struck a raw nerve. Dismissing the current approach as inadequate, the document's authors charged that MSF had failed to live up to its own commitment to provide quality care for patients, being too worried about staff safety and thus too timid about experimenting in the midst of the maelstrom. They called not just for greater use of IV

[19] http://worldairlinenews.com/2014/11/30/lufthansa-hands-over-an-airbus-a340-300-for-the-transport-of-ebola-patients (accessed 4 December 2015).

[20] www.nytimes.com/2015/01/02/health/ebola-doctors-are-divided-on-iv-therapy-in-africa.html. Farmer would later qualify his remarks in an editorial in the *Washington Post* that emphasized an inclusive obligation for improvement: 'When I noted to the *New York Times* recently that Doctors Without Borders wasn't "doing enough," what I meant was that we *all* need to provide better supportive care to increase survival. Double standards between such settings as Atlanta and Freetown are also harming efforts to find all patients with Ebola, which hampers efforts to isolate them from uninfected family members. Could there be a relationship between poor-quality care and people's reluctance to seek it in hot and raggedy Ebola units, where patients are interned until death or until blood tests show no circulating virus?' www.washingtonpost.com/opinions/paul-farmer-the-secret-to-curing-west-africa-from-ebola-is-no-secret-at-all/2015/01/16/658a6686-9cb9-11e4-bcfb-059ec7a93ddc_story.html (both accessed 4 December 2015).

hydration, but also the rapid development of new medical tools and a general change of mindset. The response to this letter was rapid and vociferous. Many closer to the frontlines found its tone harsh and its depiction of the situation unrealistic and unfair, particularly the charges that MSF had effectively institutionalized a form of 'non-assistance' and over-prioritized staff safety and security. A flood of rebuttals ensued, some responding point by point in detail, others levelling counter-charges that the open letter risked damaging operational morale, as well as returning the organization to an earlier era of open internal strife between its different sections.[21]

Whatever the specific merits of these controversies, it was clear that the West African outbreak reopened assumptions about Ebola, revealing just how little was known about either the disease or its treatment. The epidemic evoked a wave of innovation large and small, from the above mentioned plane to a solar-powered 'mobile suitcase laboratory' developed at the Pasteur Institute in Dakar, and an improvised version of personal protective equipment created by a Liberian nursing student.[22] For its part MSF mounted a variety of novel efforts, distributing home disinfection kits in Liberia, and agreeing to host clinical trials in the middle of the emergency. The experimental mode remained far from triumphant, however, focused less on best procedure than 'an imperfect solution in a situation that is far from ideal'.[23]

By March of 2015 the situation had stabilized enough for MSF to issue a retrospective report. Entitled 'Pushed to the Limit and Beyond', it detailed the events of what it called 'a sadly unique year' (MSF 2015: 4).[24] Despite having helped control outbreaks in nine countries over the previous two decades, the group had never experienced quite such a catastrophe of epidemic death, including fourteen of its own staff. Nor had it ever diverted so many resources, trained so many people, agreed to trials and vaccines amidst an outbreak or imported incinerators to cremate bodies. Never had it turned Ebola patients away, making horrendous decisions between those most likely to survive and those who were most contagious. The scale of the epidemic had also exposed

---

[21] Since this debate involved internal exchanges I will not quote them directly; Farmer's public remarks can serve as a rough proxy for the line of questioning. From an external perspective one meta-observation would be that many of MSF's most difficult experiences had been marked by heated exchange. See the now-public Speaking Out series: http://speakingout.msf.org (accessed 4 December 2015).

[22] See www.dw.de/germany-unveils-ebola-evacuation-plane-in-berlin/a-18092535 and www.bbc.com/news/health-30243636 and Sung-Joon Park & René Umlauf, Caring as Existential Insecurity: Quarantine, Care, and Human Insecurity in the Ebola Crisis, 24 November 2014 http://somatosphere.net/2014/11/caring-as-existential-insecurity.html (all accessed 4 December 2015).

[23] www.msf.org/article/liberia-distributing-home-disinfection-kits-west-point-suburb, see also www.msf.org/article/first-trials-ebola-treatments-start-msf-sites-december (both accessed 4 December 2015). On trials see Kelly (2014).

[24] MSF (2015) available at www.msf.org/article/ebola-pushed-limit-and-beyond (acces bride 29GROOM bride29GROOM sed 2 December 2015).

a human resource challenge. As the group's director of operations noted: 'MSF does not have an Ebola army with a warehouse of personnel on standby. We rely on the availability and commitment of our volunteers.' (MSF 2015: 9). When the outbreak began the group could only count about forty Ebola veterans. Although the number deployed over the course of the year would mushroom into 1,300 international and 4,000 national staff, it would still remain inadequate for the problem at hand. As MSF's Emergency Coordinator in Monrovia observed in August 2014: 'I think it's fair to say we are Doctors Without Borders, but we are not without limits. And we've reached our limit. It's very frustrating, because I see the huge needs, but I simply don't have the resources.' (MSF 2015: 10). Local personnel faced fear and rejection by kin and neighbours, even more than international volunteers. Both soldiered on, wearing eight-piece suits within which temperatures could rise to 46 degrees Celsius.

As the report makes clear, concern over safety was not only a matter of safeguarding the individual bodies of staff. MSF remained acutely aware of potential adverse publicity stemming from volunteer deaths, and its impact on the group's ability to recruit additional personnel and enrol other organizations in the struggle. Although not all the work involved exposure and full protective gear, fear proved contagious with each new infection. From this perspective the margin of error remained razor thin. At the same time, the façade of certainty masked continuing doubts, as post-mortem discussions revealed. Many of MSF's personnel chaffed under the security restrictions, feeling constrained and wondering whether they might offer more to their patients. The exhausting conditions that dictated a rapid turnover of staff – exceptional even by the group's mobile norms – also impeded learning and information transfer between teams. As noted above, some both in and out of the organization questioned received wisdom about existing medical protocols and technical planning, asking, for example, why the design of Ebola Treatment Units did not include climate control. In public discussions, other actors expressed frustration with MSF's tradition of independence, complaining of inadequate cooperation and tensions with national governments.[25]

One item in MSF's Ebola report list of 'firsts' for the organization deserves special mention: the address by MSF's international president to the UN member states at the UN General Assembly.[26] When the situation on the ground in West Africa spun out of control, it was the ceremonial head of a private voluntary organization who briefed and berated the assembled leaders of the world. In this moment of crisis, both the prominence of humanitarian aid and its incapacities proved undeniable. Most profoundly, Ebola exposed the deep vulnerability of the current

[25] www.nature.com/news/ebola-outbreak-thrusts-msf-into-new-roles-1.17690 (accessed 4 December 2015).

[26] MSF (2015: 4). See also www.msf.org/article/msf-president-urges-un-general-assembly-act-now (accessed 4 December 2015).

configuration of global health care, torn between national security and a moral economy of compassion. Thus I will close with a frank summation given by MSF's president Liu in the organization's later report: 'For months, ill-equipped national health authorities and volunteers from a few private aid organizations bore the brunt of care in this epidemic. There is something profoundly wrong with that.' (MSF 2015: 21).

Bibliography

Abu-Lughod, Lila. 1993. Finding a Place for Islam: Egyptian Television Serials and the National Interest. *Public Culture* 5 (3): 493–513.

——2004. *Dramas of Nationhood: The Politics of Television in Egypt.* Chicago, IL: University of Chicago Press.

Adams, Vincenne. 2012. The Other Road to Serfdom: Recovery by the Market and the Affect Economy in New Orleans. *Public Culture.* 24 (1): 185–216.

Alcock, Peter. 2011. Voluntary Action, New Labour and the 'Third Sector'. In *The Ages of Voluntarism: How We got to the Big Society,* edited by Matthew Hilton & James McKay. Oxford: Oxford University Press.

ALMA. 2011. Four African Leaders Honored for Accelerating Access to Life Saving Malaria Prevention and Treatment. Press Release, 31 January. www.mmv.org/sites/default/files/uploads/docs/press_releases/ALMA_AU_2011_press_release.pdf (accessed 29 November 2015).

Allahyari, Rebecca A. 2000. *Visions of Charity: Volunteer Workers and Moral Community.* Berkeley, CA: University of California Press.

Andaya, Elise. 2009. The Gift Of Health: Socialist Medical Practice and Shifting Material and Moral Economies in Post-Soviet Cuba. *Medical Anthropology Quarterly* 23 (4): 357–74.

Anderson, David M. 2000. Master and Servant in Colonial Kenya. *Journal of African History* 41 (3): 459–85.

——2010. Sexual Threat and Settler Society: 'Black Perils' in Kenya, c. 1907–30. *Journal of Imperial and Commonwealth History* 38 (1): 47–74.

Anderson, Warwick. 2003. How's the Empire? An Essay Review. *Journal of the History of Medicine and Allied Health Sciences* 58: 459–65.

Angell, Marcia. 1997. The Ethics of Clinical Research in the Third World. *New England Journal of Medicine* 337: 847–9.

Appelbaum, Paul S., Loren H. Roth, Charles W. Lidz, Paul Benson & William Winslade. 1987. False Hopes and Best Data: Consent to

Research and the Therapeutic Misconception. *Hastings Center Report* 17 (2): 20–24.

Archambault, Edith & Judith Boumendil, 2002. Dilemmas of Public/ Private Partnerships in France. In *Dilemmas of the Welfare Mix: New Structures of Welfare in the Age of Privatization*, edited by Ugo Ascoli & Costanzo Ranci. New York: Klewer Academic/Plenum Publishers: 109–34.

Arendt, Hannah. 1958. *The Human Condition*. Chicago, IL: The University of Chicago Press.

Arnold, David. 1994. Public health and Public Power: Medicine and Hegemony in Colonial India. In *Contesting Colonial Hegemony: State and Society in Africa and India*, edited by Dagmar Engels & Shula Marks. London: British Academic Press: 131–51.

Aubrey, Lisa. 1997. *The Politics of Development Cooperation: NGOs, Gender and Partnership in Kenya*. London & New York: Routledge.

Barkan, Joel D. & Frank Holmquist. 1989. Peasant-State Relations and the Social Base of Self-Help in Kenya. *World Politics* 41 (3): 359–80.

Barkan, Joel D., Michael L. McNulty & M. A. O. Ayeni. 1991. 'Hometown' Voluntary Associations, Local Development, and the Emergence of Civil Society in Western Nigeria. *Journal of Modern African Studies* 29 (3): 457–80.

Bar-Tal, Daniel. 1986. Altruistic Motivation to Help: Definition, Utility and Operationalization. *Humboldt Journal of Social Relations* 13 (1–2): 3–14.

Banatvala, Nicholas & Len Doyal. 1998. Knowing When to Say 'No' on the Student Elective. Students Going on Electives Abroad need Clinical Guidelines. *BMJ: The British Medical Journal* 316 (7142): 1404–5.

Bang, Y. H., F. M. Mrope & N. G. Gratz. 1973. Mosquito Control Service in Tanzania: II. Evaluation of 10 Urban Mosquito Control Programmes in Tanzania. World Health Organization. WHO/VBC/73.439.

Bech, Margunn M., Yusufu Q. Lawi, Deodatus A. Massay & Ole B. Rekdal. 2013. Changing Policies and their Influence on Government Health Workers in Tanzania, 1967–2009: Perspectives from Rural Mbulu District. *International Journal of African Historical Studies* 46 (1): 61–103.

Beck, Ann. 1970. *A History of the British Medical Administration of East Africa, 1900–1950*. Cambridge, MA: Harvard University Press.

Becker, Felicitas. 2015. Obscuring and Revealing: Muslim Engagement with Volunteering and the Aid Sector in Tanzania. *African Studies Review*. 58 (2):111–33.

Beecher, Henry. 1966. Ethics and Clinical Research. *New England Journal of Medicine* 274 (24): 1354–60.

Benthall, Jonathan. 2012. Charity. In *A Companion to Moral Anthropology*, edited by Didier Fassin. Chichester: John Wiley: 359–75.

Berg, Elliot J. 1965. The Development of a Labor Force in Sub-Saharan Africa. *Economic Development and Cultural Change* 13 (4): 394–412.

Berlant, Lauren 2004. Introduction: Compassion (and Withholding). In *Compassion: The Culture and Politics of an Emotion*. New York: Routledge: 1–13.

Berry, Nicole S. 2014. Did We Do Good? NGOs, Conflicts of Interest and the Evaluation of Short-Term Medical Missions in Sololá, Guatemala. *Social Science & Medicine* 120: 344–51.

Bezruchka, Stephen. 2000. Medical Tourism as Medical Harm to the Third World: Why? For whom? *Wilderness and Environmental Medicine* 11 (2): 77–8.

Biehl, João & Peter Locke. 2010. Deleuze and the Anthropology of Becoming. *Current Anthropology* 51 (3): 317–51.

Bloom, Gerald & Peroline Ainsworth. 2010. Beyond Scaling Up: Pathways to Universal Access to Health Services. STEPS Centre: www.steps-centre.org/publications.

Boesten, Jelke, Anna Mdee & Frances Cleaver. 2011. Service Delivery on the Cheap? Community-Based Workers in Development Interventions. *Development in Practice* 21 (1): 41–58.

Bohannan, Paul. 1955. Some Principles of Exchange and Investment among the Tiv. *American Anthropologist* 57 (1): 60–70.

Boltanski, Luc 1999. *Distant Suffering: Morality, Media, and Politics*. Cambridge: Cambridge University Press.

Bolten, Catherine E. 2012. *I Did It to Save My Life: Love and Survival in Sierra Leone*. Berkeley, CA: University of California Press.

Bolton, Adia. Forthcoming. Risky business: Race, Nonequivalence and the Humanitarian Politics of Life. *Visual Anthropology* 29 (2): 187–203.

Bond, Virginia Anne. 2010. 'It is Not an Easy Decision on HIV, Especially in Zambia': Opting for Silence, Limited Disclosure and Implicit Understanding to Retain a Wider Identity. *AIDS Care* 22: 6–13.

Bond, Virginia & Kwame Shanaube. 2005. Making Sense of Satanist Accusations in Zambia: A Modern Witchhunt against Exploitation and Disorder? Paper presented at the conference 'Locating the Field: The Ethnography of Medical Research in Africa', Kilifi, Kenya, 4–9 December.

Bonneuil, Christophe. 2000. Development as Experiment: Science and State Building in Late Colonial and Postcolonial Africa, 1930–1970. *Osiris* 2nd Series, Vol. 15 (Nature and Empire: Science and the Colonial Enterprise): 258–81.

Boesten, Jelke, Anne Mdee & Frances Cleaver. 2011. Service Delivery on the Cheap? Community-Based Workers in Development Interventions. *Development in Practice* 21 (1): 41–58.

Bornstein, Erica. 2003. *The Spirit of Development: Protestant NGOs, Morality, and Economics in Zimbabwe*. New York & London: Routledge.

Bornstein, Erica & Peter Redfield (eds). 2010. *Forces of Compassion: Humanitarianism between Ethics and Politics*. Seminar Series, Sante Fe, NM: SAR Press.

Brada, Betsey. 2011. 'Not *Here*': Making the Spaces and Subjects of

'Global Health' in Botswana. *Culture, Medicine and Psychiatry* 35 (2): 285–312.

Brogden, Mike & Clifford D. Shearing. 1993. *Policing for a New South Africa.* London: Routledge.

British Medical Journal. 1902. Mosquitoes and Malaria, 13 September: 809–810.

Brown, Hannah. 2013. 'Home-Based Care is Not a New Thing': Legacies of Domestic Governmentality in Western Kenya. In *Making and Unmaking Public Health in Africa: Ethnographic and Historical Perspectives*, edited by Ruth Prince & Rebecca Marsland. Athens, OH: Ohio University Press.

Brown, Hannah & Maia Green. 2015. At the Service of Community Development: The Professionalization of Volunteer Work in Kenya and Tanzania. *African Studies Review* 58 (2): 63–84.

Brown, Hannah & Ruth J. Prince. 2015. Introduction: Volunteer Labor – Pasts and Futures of Work, Development, and Citizenship in East Africa. *African Studies Review* 58 (2): 29–42.

Brown, Phil, Stephen Zavestoski, Sabrina Mccormick, Brian Mayer, Rachel Morello-Frosch & Rebecca Gasior Altman. 2006. Embodied Health Movements: New Approaches to Social Movements in Health. *Sociology of Health & Illness* 26(1): 50–80.

Burton, Andrew. 2003. Townsmen in the Making: Social Engineering and Citizenship in Dar es Salaam, ca. 1945–1960. *International Journal of African Historical Studies* 36 (2): 331–65.

——2007. The Haven of Peace Purged: Tackling the Undesirable and Unproductive Poor in Dar es Salaam, ca. 1950s–1980s. *International Journal of African Historical Studies* 40 (1): 119–51.

Burton, A. & M. Jennings. 2007. Introduction: The Emperor's New Clothes? Continuities in Governance in Late Colonial and Early Postcolonial East Africa. *International Journal of African Historical Studies* 40 (1): 1–25.

Butt, Leslie. 2002. The Suffering Stranger: Medical Anthropology and International Morality. *Medical Anthropology* 21 (1): 1–24.

Caldeira, Teresa P. R. 1996. Fortified enclaves: the new urban segregation. *Public Culture* 8 (2): 303–28.

——2000. *City of Walls: Crime, Segregation, and Citizenship in São Paulo.* Berkeley, CA: University of California Press.

Calkin, Sydney. 2014. Mind the 'Gap Year': A Critical Discourse Analysis of Volunteer Tourism Promotional Material. *Global Discourse* 4 (1): 30–43.

Callaway, Helen. 1987. *Gender, Culture and Empire: European Women in Colonial Nigeria.* Chicago, IL: University of Illinois Press.

Campbell, C., C. A. Foulis, S. Maimane & Z. Sibiya. 2005. 'I Have an Evil Child at my House': Stigma and HIV/AIDS Management in a South African Community. *American Journal of Public Health* 95 (5): 808–15.

Carrier, James. 1995. Maussian Occidentalism: Gift and Commodity

Systems. In *Occidentalism: Images of the West*, edited by James Carrier: 85–108.

Chaki, Prosper P., Nicodem J. Govella, Bryson Shoo et al. 2009. Achieving High Coverage of Larval Stage Mosquito Surveillance: Challenges for a Community-Based Mosquito Control Programme in Urban Dar es Salaam, Tanzania. *Malaria Journal* 8: 311.

Chaki, Prosper P., Stefan Dongus, Ulrike Fillinger, et al. 2011. Community-Owned Resource Persons for Malaria Vector Control: Enabling Factors and Challenges in an Operational Programme in Dar es Salaam, United Republic of Tanzania. *Human Resources for Health* 9: 21.

Chaki, Prosper P., Khadija Kannady, Deo Mtasiwa et al. 2014. Institutional Evolution of a Community-Based Programme for Malaria Control through Larval Source Management in Dar es Salaam, United Republic of Tanzania. *Malaria Journal* 13: 245.

Chambers, Robert. 1994. Participatory Rural Appraisal (PRA): Challenges, Potentials and Paradigm. *World Development* 22 (10): 1437–54

Chambers, Simone & Jeffrey Kopstein. 2001. Bad Civil Society. *Political Theory* 29 (6): 837–65.

Clyde David F. 1967. *Malaria in Tanzania*. London: Oxford University Press.

Coe, Cati. 2011. What is Love? The Materiality of Care in Ghanaian Transnational Families. *International Migration* 49 (6): 7–24.

Coertze, R.D. 2001. Ubuntu and Nation Building in South Africa. *South African Journal of Ethnology* 24 (4): 113–8.

Cohen, Jon. 2006. The New World of Global Health. *Science* 311 (5758): 162–7.

Coleridge, Peter. (1993). *Disability, Liberation, and Development*. Oxford: Oxfam.

Collier, Stephen & Andrew Lakoff 2008. Distributed Preparedness: The Spatial Logic of Domestic Security in the United States. *Environment and Planning D: Society and Space* 26 (1): 7–28.

Colvin, Christopher J. 2012. True Believers or Modern Believers: HIV Science and the Work of the Dr Rath Foundation. In *Medicine and the Politics of Knowledge*, edited by Susan Levine. Cape Town: Human Sciences Research Council: 33–54.

Colvin, Christopher J., Joan Leavens & Steven Robins. 2010. Grounding 'Responsibilisation' Talk: Masculinities, Citizenship and HIV in Cape Town, South Africa. *Journal of Development Studies* 46 (7): 1179–95.

Comaroff, John L. & Jean Comaroff. 1999. *Civil Society and the Political Imagination in Africa: Critical Perspectives*. Chicago, IL, University of Chicago Press.

——2006. Law and Disorder in the Postcolony: An Introduction. In *Law and Disorder in the Postcolony*, edited by Jean Comaroff & John L. Comaroff. Chicago, IL: University of Chicago Press: 1–56.

Conran, Mary. 2011. They Really Love Me! Intimacy in Volunteer Tourism. *Annals of Tourism Research* 38 (4): 1454–73.

Cooke, Bill & Uma Kothari (eds). 2001. *Participation: The New Tyranny?* London: Zed Books.

Coovadia, H., R. Jewkes, P. Barron, D. Sanders & D. Mcintyre. 2009. The Health and Health System of South Africa: Historical Roots of Current Public Health Challenges. *Lancet* 374 (9692): 817–34.

Cornwall, Andrea & Karen Brock. 2005. What do Buzzwords do for Development Policy? A Critical Look at 'Participation', 'Empowerment' and 'Poverty Reduction'. *Third World Quarterly* 26 (7): 1043–60.

Council for International Organizations of Medical Sciences. 2002. International Ethical Guidelines for Biomedical Research Involving Human Subjects. Geneva: Council of International Organizations of Medical Sciences.

Craig, David & Doug Porter. 2006. *Development Beyond Neoliberalism: Governance, Poverty Reduction and Political Economy.* London & New York: Routledge.

Crane, Johanna T. 2010. Unequal 'Partners': AIDS, Academia, and the Rise of Global Health. *Behemoth* 3 (3): 78–97.

——2013. *Scrambling for Africa: AIDS, Expertise and the Rise of American Global Health Science.* Ithaca, NY: Cornell University Press.

Crump, John A. & Jeremy Sugarman. 2008. Ethical Considerations for Short-Term Experiences by Trainees in Global Health. *Journal of the American Medical Association* 300 (12): 1456–8.

Cunningham, Hugh & Joanna Innes (eds). 1998. *Charity, Philanthropy and Reform: From the 1690s to 1850.* London: Palgrave Macmillan.

Curtin, Philip D. 1985. Medical Knowledge and Urban Planning in Tropical Africa. *The American Historical Review* 90 (3): 594–613.

Dankoski, M.E., J. Bickel & M. E. Gusic. 2014. Discussing the Undiscussable with the Powerful: Why and How Faculty Must Learn to Counteract Organizational Silence. *Academic Medicine* 89 (12): 1610–13.

Davin, Anna. 1978. Imperialism and Motherhood. *History Workshop Journal* 5 (1): 9–66.

Dilger, Hansjörg. 2009. Doing Better? Religion, the Virtue-Ethics of Development, and the Fragmentation of Health Politics in Tanzania. *Africa Today* 56 (1): 89–110.

Davis, Mike. 1992. Fortress Los Angeles: The Militarization of Urban Space. In *Variations on a Theme Park*, edited by M. Sorkin. New York: Noonday Press: 154–80.

Davis, Robert C., Nicole J. Henderson & Cybele Merrick. 2003. Community Policing: Variations of the Western Models in the Developing World. *Police Practice and Research* 4 (3): 285–300.

De Boeck, Filip. 2011. Inhabiting Ocular Ground: Kinshasa's Future in the Light of Congo's Spectral Urban Politics. *Cultural Anthropology* 26 (2): 263–86.

DeCamp, Matthew. 2007. Scrutinizing Global Short-Term Medical Outreach. *Hastings Center Report* 37 (6): 21–3.

DeCamp, Matthew, Joce Rodriguez, Shelby Hecht, Michele Barry & Jeremy

Sugarman. 2013. An Ethics Curriculum for Short-Term Global Health Trainees. *Globalization and Health* 9: 5.

DeCamp, Matthew, Samuel Enumah, Daniel O'Neill et al. 2014. Perceptions of a Short-Term Medical Programme in the Dominican Republic: Voices of Care Recipients. *Global Public Health* 9 (4): 411–25.

Derrida, Jacques. 1992. *Given Time*. Chicago, IL: The University of Chicago Press.

de Soto, Hernando. 2006. The Challenge of Connecting Informal and Formal Property Systems: Some Reflections Based on the Case of Tanzania. In *Realizing Property Rights*, edited by H. de Soto & F. Cheneval. Zurich: Rüffer & Rub: 18–67.

Devereux, Peter 2008. International Volunteering for Development and Sustainability: Outdated Paternalism or a Radical Response to Globalisation? *Development in Practice* 18 (3): 357–70.

de Wet, Katinka. 2012. Redefining Volunteerism: The Rhetoric of Community Home-Based Care in (the Not So New) South Africa. *Community Development Journal* 47 (1): 111–19.

Dill, Brian. 2009. The Paradoxes of Community-Based Participation in Dar es Salaam. *Development and Change* 40 (4): 717–43.

——2010. Community-Based Organizations (CBOs) and Norms of Participation in Tanzania: Working Against the Grain. *African Studies Review* 53 (2): 23–48

Dongus, Stefan, Dickson Nyika, Khadija Kannady et al. 2007. Participatory Mapping of Target Areas to Enable Operational Larval Source Management to Suppress Malaria Vector Mosquitoes in Dar es Salaam, Tanzania. *International Journal of Health Geographics* 6: 37.

Dongus, Stefan, Constanze Pfeiffer, Emmy Metta et al. 2010 Building Multi-Layered Resilience in a Malaria Control Programme in Dar es Salaam, Tanzania. *Progress in Development Studies* 10 (4): 309–24.

Douglas, Mary. 1990. No Free Gifts: A Foreword. In *The Gift* by Marcel Mauss, translated by W. D. Halls. New York: W.W. Norton.

Drain, Paul, Aron Primack, D. Dan Hunt et al. 2007. Global Health in Medical Education: A Call for More Training and Opportunities. *Academic Medicine* 82 (3): 226–30.

Duffy, R. 2008. Neoliberalising Nature: Global Networks and Ecotourism Development in Madagascar. *Journal of Sustainable Tourism* 16: 327–44.

Dumit, Joseph. 2012. *Drugs for Life: How Pharmaceutical Companies Define Our Health*. Durham, NC: Duke University Press.

Durham, Deborah. 1995. Soliciting Gifts and Negotiating Agency: The Spirit of Asking in Botswana. *Journal of the Royal Anthropological Institute* 1 (1): 111–128.

Durkheim, Emil, translated by W. D. Halls. 1993 [1893]. *The Division of Labor in Society*. New York: Free Press.

Edmondson, Laura 2007. *Performance and Politics in Tanzania: The Nation on Stage*. Bloomington & Indianapolis, IN: Indiana University Press.

Eide, A. H. & B. Ingstad. 2011. *Disability and Poverty: A Global Challenge*: Policy Press.

Englund, Harri. 2006. *Prisoners of Freedom: Human Rights and the African Poor*. Berkeley: University of California Press.

Eliasoph, Nina 2011. *Making Volunteers: Civic Life After Welfare's End*. Princeton, NJ: Princeton University Press.

Elliott, Carl. 2010. *White Coat, Black Hat: Adventures on the Dark Side of Medicine*. Boston, MA: Beacon Press.

Emanuel, Ezekiel J., Xolani E. Currie & Allen Herman. 2005. Undue Inducement in Clinical Research in Developing Countries: Is it a Worry? *The Lancet* 366 (9482): 336–40.

Epstein, Steven. 2007. *Inclusion: The Politics of Difference in Medical Research*. Chicago, IL: The University of Chicago Press.

Erickson, Jennifer. 2011. Volunteering With Refugees: Neoliberalism, Hegemony, and (Senior) Citizenship. *Human Organization* 71 (2): 167–75.

Etherington, Norman. 1988. Natal's Black Rape Scare of the 1870s. *Journal of Southern African Studies* 15 (1): 36–53.

Ezra, Peter Marwa. 2013. Host Community Perceptions of Volunteer Tourists in the Northern Tourist Circuit, Tanzania. Master of Tourism Management Thesis. Victoria University of Wellington.

Fassin, Didier. 2005. Compassion and Repression: The Moral Economy of Immigration Policies in France. *Cultural Anthropology* 20 (3): 362–87.

——2007. Humanitarianism as a Politics of Life. *Public Culture* 19 (3): 499–520.

——2012. *Humanitarian Reason: A Moral History of the Present*. Berkeley, IL: University of Chicago Press.

Faubion, James D. 2001. Towards an Anthropology of Ethics: Foucault and the Pedagogies of Autopoisis. *Representations* 74: 83–104.

——2011. *An Anthropology of Ethics*. Cambridge: Cambridge University Press.

Fechter, Anne-Meike. 2012a. 'Living Well' while 'Doing Good'? (Missing) Debates on Altruism and Professionalism in Aid Work. *Third World Quarterly* 33 (8): 1475–91.

——2012b. The Personal and the Professional: Aid Workers' Relationships and Values in the Development Process. *Third World Quarterly* 33 (8): 1387–1404.

Feldman, Ilana 2008. *Governing Gaza: Bureaucracy, Authority, and the Work of Rule, 1917–1967*. Durham, NC: Duke University Press.

Feldman, Ilana & Miriam Ticktin (eds) 2010. *In the Name of Humanity: The Government of Threat and Care*. Durham: Duke University Press.

Ferguson, James. 1992. The Cultural Topography of Wealth: Commodity Paths and the Structure of Property in Rural Lesotho. *American Anthropologist* 94 (1): 55–73.

——1994. *The Anti-Politics Machine: 'Development', Depoliticization, and Bureaucratic Power in Lesotho*. Minneapolis, MN: University of Minneapolis Press.

——2006. *Global Shadows: Africa in the Neoliberal World Order.* Durham, NC: Duke University Press.

——2007. Formalities of poverty: Thinking about Social Assistance in Neoliberal South Africa. *African Studies Review* 50 (2): 71–86.

——2013. Declarations of Dependence: Labour, Personhood, and Welfare in Southern Africa. *Journal of the Royal Anthropological Institute* 19 (2): 223–42.

——2015. *Give a Man a Fish: Reflections on the New Politics of Distribution.* Durham, NC: Duke University Press.

Ferguson, James & Akhil Gupta. 2002. Spatializing States: Toward an Ethnography of Neoliberal Governmentality. *American Ethnologist* 29 (4): 981–1002.

Fillinger, Ulrike, Khadija Kannady, George William et al. 2008. A Tool Box for Operational Mosquito Larval Control: Preliminary Results and Early Lessons from the Urban Malaria Control Programme in Dar es Salaam, Tanzania. *Malaria Journal* 7 (1): 20.

Fischer, Karin. 2013. Some Health Programs Overseas let Students do Too Much, Too Soon. *Chronicle of Higher Education* Nov 4: 4.

Fisher, Jill A. 2013. Expanding the Frame of 'Voluntariness' in Informed Consent: Structural Coercion and the Power of Social and Economic Context. *Kennedy Institute of Ethics Journal* 23 (4): 355–79.

Fisher, William F. 1997. Doing Good? The Politics and Antipolitics of NGO Practices. *Annual Review of Anthropology* 26: 439–64.

Fleischer, Friederike. 2011. Technology of Self, Technology of Power: Volunteering as Encounter in Guangzhou, China. *Ethnos* 76 (3): 300–25.

Foucault, Michel. 1975 [1973] translated by A. M. Sheridan Smith. *The Birth of the Clinic: An Archaeology of Medical Perception.* New York: Vintage.

Fourshey, Catherine C. 2012. *Karibu* Stranger, Come Heal Thy Host: Hospitality as Historical Subject in Southwestern Tanzania, 1600–1900. *African Historical Review* 44 (2): 18–54.

Fox, Renée. 2014. *Doctors Without Borders: Humanitarian Quests, Impossible Dreams of Médecins Sans Frontières.* Baltimore, MD: Johns Hopkins University Press.

Freeman, Dena (ed.). 2012. *Pentecostalism and Development: Churches, NGOs and Social Change in Africa.* (Non-governmental Public Action Series). New York & Basingstoke: Palgrave Macmillan.

Freston, Paul. 2005. The Universal Church of the Kingdom of God: A Brazilian Church Finds Success in Southern Africa. *Journal of Religion in Africa* 35 (1): 33–65.

Gardner, Katy, Zahir Ahmed, Fatema Bashir et al. 2012. Elusive Partnerships: Gas Extraction and CSR in Bangladesh. *Resources Policy* 37 (2): 168–74.

Garland, Elizabeth. 2012. How Should Anthropologists be Thinking about Volunteer Tourism? *Practicing Anthropology* 34 (3): 5–9.

Gathorne-Hardy, Jonathan. 1977. *The Public School Phenomenon.* London: Hodder & Stoughton.

Gawande, Atul. 2002. *Complications: A Surgeon's Notes on an Imperfect Science.* New York: Picador.

Geissbühler, Yvonne, Khadija Kannady, Prosper Pius Chaki et al. 2009. Microbial Larvicide Application by a Large-Scale, Community-Based Program Reduces Malaria Infection Prevalence in Urban Dar es Salaam, Tanzania. *PloS one* 4 (3): e5107.

Geissler, P. Wenzel. 2005. 'Kachinja are Coming!' Encounters Around a Medical Research Project in a Kenyan Village. *Africa* 75 (2): 173–202.

——2011. 'Transport to Where?' *Journal of Cultural Economy* 4 (1): 45–64.

——2012. 'We Are Not Paid – They Just Give Us': Liberalisation and the Longing for Biopolitical Discipline Around an African HIV Prevention Trial. In *Rethinking Biomedicine and Governance in Africa*, edited by P. Wenzel Geissler, Richard Rottenburg & Julia Zenker. Bielefeld: Transcript Verlag: 197–227.

——2013. Public Secrets in Public Health: Knowing Not to Know While Making Scientific Knowledge. *American Ethnologist* 40 (1): 13–34.

Geissler, P. Wenzel & Catherine S. Molyneux (eds). 2011. *Evidence, Ethos and Experiment: The Anthropology and History of Medical Research in Africa.* New York: Berghahn Books.

Geissler, P. Wenzel, Ann H. Kelly, John Manton, Ruth Prince & Noémi Tousignant. 2013. Introduction: Sustaining the Life of the Polis. *Africa* 83 (4): 531–8.

Geschiere, Peter, Miriam Goheen & Charles Piot. 2007. Introduction: Marginal Gains Revisited. *African Studies Review* 50 (2): 37–41.

Gikonyo, Caroline, Philip Bejon, Vicki Marsh et al. 2008. Taking Social Relationships Seriously: Lessons Learned from the Informed Consent Practices of a Vaccine Trial on the Kenyan Coast. *Social Science & Medicine* 67 (5): 708–20.

Ginsburg, Rebecca. 1996. 'I Now Stay in a House': Renovating the Matchbox in Apartheid-Era Soweto. *African Studies* 55 (2): 127–39.

Godelier, Maurice, translated by Nora Scott. 1998. *The Enigma of the Gift.* Cambridge: Polity Press.

Goldstein, Daniel M. 2010. Toward a Critical Anthropology of Security. *Current Anthropology* 51 (4): 487–517.

Gouldner, Alvin Ward. 1973. *For Sociology: Renewal and Critique in Sociology Today.* New York: Basic Books.

Green, Maia. 2000. Participatory Development and the Appropriation of Agency in Southern Tanzania. *Critique of Anthropology* 20 (1): 67–89.

——2003. Globalizing Development in Tanzania: Policy Franchising through Participatory Project Management. *Critique of Anthropology* 23 (2), 123–43.

——2010. Making Development Agents: Participation as Boundary Object in International Development. *The Journal of Development Studies* 46 (7): 1240–63.

——2012. Anticipatory Development: Mobilizing Civil Society in Tanzania. *Critique of Anthropology* 32 (3): 309–33.

——2014. *The Development State: Aid, Culture and Civil Society in Tanzania*. Woodbridge: James Currey.

Green, Tyler, Heidi Green, Jean Scandlyn et al. 2009. Perceptions of Short-Term Medical Volunteer Work: A Qualitative Study in Guatemala. *Globalization and Health* 5 (4): 1–13.

Greene, Jeremy, Marguerite Thorp Basilico, Heidi Kim et al. 2013. Colonial Medicine and its Legacies. In *Reimagining Global Health: An Introduction*, edited by Paul Farmer, Jim Yong Kim, Arthur Kleinman et al. Berkeley, CA: University of California Press: 33–73.

Grillo, Ralph. D. & Roderick L. Stirrat. 1997. *Discourses of Development: Anthropological Perspectives*. Oxford & New York: Berg.

Guyer, Jane. 2004. *Marginal Gains: Monetary Transactions in Atlantic Africa*. Chicago, IL: University of Chicago Press.

Hall, B. 1992. From Margins To Center? The Development and Purpose of Participatory Research. *American Sociologist* 23 (4), 15–28.

Handler, Richard. 2013. Disciplinary Adaptation and Undergraduate Desire: Anthropology and Global Development Studies in the Liberal Arts Curriculum. *Cultural Anthropology* 28 (2): 181–203.

Hansen, Karen Tranberg. 1997. *Keeping House in Lusaka*. New York: Columbia University Press.

——2005. Getting Stuck in the Compound: Some Odds Against Social Adulthood in Lusaka, Zambia. *Africa Today* 51 (4): 3–16.

——2008. The Informalization of Lusaka's Economy: Regime Change, Ultra-Modern Markets, and Street Vending, 1972–2004. In *One Zambia, Many Histories*, edited by Jan-Bart Gewald, Marja Hinfelaar & Giacomo Macola. Leiden: Brill: 213–39.

Hanson, Lori, Sheila Harms & Karina Plamondon. 2011. Undergraduate International Medical Electives: Some Ethical and Pedagogical Considerations. *Journal of Studies in International Education* 15 (2): 171–85.

Harder, Ben 1980. The Student Volunteer Movement for Foreign Missions and its Contribution to 20th Century Missions. *Missiology* 8 (2): 141–54.

Hardt, Michael 1999. Affective Labor. *Boundary 2* 26 (2): 89–100.

Harper, Ian. 2007. Translating Ethics: Researching Public Health and Medical Practices in Nepal. *Social Science & Medicine* 65 (11): 2235–47.

Harper, Ian & Melissa Parker. 2014. The Politics and Anti-Politics of Infectious Diseases Control. *Medical Anthropology: Cross-Cultural Studies in Health and Illness* 33 (3): 198–205.

Haski-Leventhal, Debbie. 2009. Altruism and Volunteerism: The Perceptions of Altruism in Four Disciplines and Their Impact on the Study of Volunteerism. *Journal for the Theory of Social Behaviour* 39 (3): 271–99.

Haugerud, Angelique. 1993. *The Culture of Politics in Modern Kenya.* Cambridge: Cambridge University Press.

Hearn, J. D. 1998. The NGO-isation of Kenyan Society: USAID and the Restructuring of Health Care. *Review of African Political Economy* 25 (75): 89–100.

Heggenhougen, Kris, Patrick Vaughan, Eustace P.Y. Muhondwa et al. 1987. *Community Health Workers: The Tanzanian Experience.* Oxford: Oxford University Press.

Herbst, Jeffrey. 1996–1997. Responding to State Failure in Africa. *International Security* 21 (3): 120–44.

Hewlett, Barry S. & Bonnie L. Hewlett. 2008. *Ebola, Culture, and Politics: The Anthropology of an Emerging Disease.* Belmont, CA: Thomson Wadsworth.

Heywood, Mark. 2009. South Africa's Treatment Action Campaign: Combining Law and Social Mobilization to Realize the Right to Health. *Journal of Human Rights Practice* 1 (1): 14–36.

Hill, Martin J. D. 1991. *The Harambee Movement in Kenya: Self-help, Development and Education among the Kamba of Kitui District.* London School of Economics Monographs on Social Anthropology no. 64. London: Athlone Press.

Hilton, Matthew & McKay, James (eds). 2011. *The Ages of Voluntarism: How We got to the Big Society.* Oxford: Oxford University Press.

Hinchliffe Steve, Matthew B. Kearnes, Monica Degen & Sarah Whatmore. 2005. Urban Wild Things: A Cosmopolitical Experiment. *Environment and Planning D* 23 (5): 643–58.

Hirschkind, Charles. 2001. Civic Virtue and Religious Reason: An Islamic Counterpublic. *Cultural Anthropology* 16 (1): 3–34.

——2006. *The Ethical Soundscape: Cassette Sermons and Islamic Counterpublics.* New York: Columbia University Press.

Hoeyer, Klaus. 2003. 'Science is Really Needed – That's All I Know': Informed Consent and the Non-Verbal Practices of Collecting Blood for Genetic Research in Northern Sweden. *New Genetics and Society* 22 (3): 229–44.

Holden, Daphne 1997. 'On Equal Ground': Sustaining Virtue Among Volunteers in a Homeless Shelter. *Journal of Contemporary Ethnography* 26 (2): 117–45.

Holmquist, Frank. 1984 [1979]. Class Structure, Peasant Participation and Rural Self-Help. In *Politics and Public Policy in Kenya and Tanzania*, edited by J. D. Barkan. New York: Praeger.

Hornberger, Julia. 2011. *Policing and Human Rights: The Meaning of Violence and Justice in the Everyday Policing of Johannesburg.* New York: Routledge.

Huish, Robert. 2009. How Cuba's Latin American School of Medicine Challenges the Ethics of Physician Migration. *Social Science & Medicine* 69 (3): 301–4.

——2012. The Ethical Conundrum of International Health Electives in

Medical Education. *Journal of Global Citizenship & Equity Education* 2 (1): 1–19.

Hulme, D., J. Hanlon & A. Barrientos. 2010. *Just Give Money to the Poor: The Development Revolution from the Global South*: Stylus.

Hunter, Emma. 2008. Revisiting *Ujamaa*: Political Legitimacy and the Construction of Community in Post-Colonial Tanzania, 1965–2004. *Journal of Eastern African Studies* 2 (3): 471–85.

———2015. Voluntarism, Virtuous Citizenship, and Nation-Building in Late Colonial and Early Postcolonial Tanzania. *African Studies Review* 58 (2): 43–61.

Hutchinson, Sharon E. 1996. *Nuer Dilemmas: Coping with Money, War, and the State*: Berkeley, CA: University of California Press.

Hyden, Goran. 1995. Bringing Voluntarism Back In: Eastern Africa in Comparative Perspective. In *Service Provision under Stress in East Africa: the State, NGOs and People's Organizations in Kenya*, edited by Joseph Semboja & Ole Therkildsen. Centre for Development Research: Copenhagen; London: James Currey: 35–50.

Ibbott, Ralph 1969/70. The Origin, Growth and Disbandment of the Ruvuma Development Association, 1960–1969. Unpublished manuscript.

Iliffe, John. 1998. *East African Doctors: A History of the Modern Profession*. Cambridge: Cambridge University Press.

Ingold, Tim. 2000. *The Perception of the Environment: Essays in Livelihood, Dwelling and Skill*. London: Routledge.

Ingstad, Benedicte & Susan R. Whyte (eds). 1995. *Disability and Culture*. Berkeley, CA: University California Press.

Jeeves, A. 2000. Health, Surveillance and Community: South Africa's Experiment with Medical Reform in the 1940s and 1950s. *South African Historical Journal* 43: 244–66.

Jennings, Michael 2002. 'Almost an Oxfam in Itself': Oxfam, *Ujamaa* and Development in Tanzania. *African Affairs* 101 (405): 509–30.

———2003. 'We Must Run While Others Walk': Popular Participation and Development Crisis in Tanzania, 1961–6. *Journal of Modern African Studies* 41 (2): 163–87.

———2007. 'A Very Real War': Popular Participation in Development in Tanzania during the 1950s & 1960s. *International Journal of African Historical Studies* 40 (1): 71–95.

———2008. *Surrogates of the State: NGOs, Development and Ujamaa in Tanzania*, Bloomfield, CT: Kumarian Press.

———2013. Common Counsel, Common Policy: Healthcare, Missions and the Rise of the Voluntary Sector in Colonial Tanzania. *Development and Change* 44 (4): 939–63.

Johnson-Hanks, Jennifer. 2005. Uncertainty and Intentional Action in Contemporary Cameroon. *Current Anthropology* 46 (3): 363–85.

Jones, Andrew 2008. The Rise of Global Work. *Transactions of the Institute of British Geographers* 33, 12–26.

——2011. Theorising International Youth Volunteering: Training for Global Work? *Transactions of the Institute of British Geographers* 36 (4): 530–44.

Jonsen, Albert R. 1998. *The Birth of Bioethics.* New York: Oxford University Press.

Jordan Smith, Daniel. 2003. Patronage, Per Diems and the 'Workshop Mentality': The Practice of Family Planning Programs in Southeastern Nigeria. *World Development* 31 (4): 703–15.

Kalofonos, Ippolytos 2014. 'All They do Is Pray': Community Labour and the Narrowing of 'Care' during Mozambique's HIV Scale-up. *Global Public Health* 9 (1–2): 7–24.

Kanogo, Tabitha. 1987. *Squatters & the Roots of Mau Mau 1905–63.* Nairobi: East African Educational Publishers.

Katz, Jay with Alexander M. Capron & Eleanor S. Glass. 1972. *Experimentation with Human Beings: The Authority of the Investigator, Subject, Professions, and State in the Human Experimentation Process.* New York: Russell Sage Foundation.

Keane, Webb. 2010. Minds, Surfaces, and Reasons in the Anthropology of Ethics. In *Ordinary Ethics: Anthropology, Language, and Action,* edited by Michael Lambek. New York: Fordham University Press: 64–83.

Kelly, Ann H. 2014. 'Ebola Running Ahead'. *Limn* 5, 2014. http://limn.it/ ebola-running-ahead (accessed 2 December 2015).

Kelly, Ann H., David Ameh, Silas Majambere et al. 2010. 'Like Sugar and Honey': The Embedded Ethics of a Larval Control Project in The Gambia. *Social Science & Medicine* 70 (12): 1912–19.

Kelly, Ann H. & P. Wenzel Geissler. 2011. The Value of Transnational Medical Research. *Journal of Cultural Economy* 4 (1): 3–10.

Kelly, Ann H. & Javier Lezaun. 2013. Walking or Waiting? Topologies of the Breeding Ground in Malaria Control. *Science as Culture* 22 (1): 86–107.

——2014. Urban Mosquitoes, Situational Publics, and the Pursuit of Interspecies Separation in Dar es Salaam. *American Ethnologist* 41 (2): 368–83.

Kennedy, Dane. 1996. *The Magic Mountains: Hill Stations and the British Raj.* Berkeley, CA: University of California Press.

Kimble, Judy & Elaine Unterhalter. 1982. 'We Opened the Road for You, You Must Go Forward': ANC Women's Struggles, 1912–1982. *Feminist Review* 12: 11–35.

Kimmelman, Jonathan. 2007. The Therapeutic Misconception at 25. Treatment, Research, and Confusion. *Hastings Center Report* 37 (6): 36–42.

Kingori, Patricia. 2013. Experiencing Everyday Ethics in Context: Frontline Data Collectors Perspectives and Practices of Bioethics. *Social Science & Medicine* 98: 361–70.

Kironde Lusugga, J. M. 1995. Access to Land by the Urban Poor in

Tanzania: Some Findings from Dar es Salaam. *Environment and Urbanization* 7: 77–96.

———2006. The Regulatory Framework, Unplanned Development and Urban Poverty: Findings from Dar es Salaam, Tanzania. *Land Use Policy* 23 (4): 460–472.

———2007. Race, Class and Housing in Dar es Salaam: The Colonial Impact on Land Use Structure 1891–1961. In *Dar es Salaam: Histories from an Emerging African Metropolis*, edited by James Brennan, Andrew Burton & Yusuf Lawi. Dar es Salaam & Nairobi: Mkuki na Nyota & British Institute in Eastern Africa: 97–117.

Kirsch, Thomas G. 2010. Violence in the Name of Democracy: Community Policing, Vigilante Action and Nation-Building in South Africa. In *Domesticating Vigilantism in Africa*, edited by Thomas G. Kirsch & Tilo Grätz. Woodbridge: James Currey: 139–62.

Kirsch, Thomas G. & Tilo Grätz (eds). 2010. *Domesticating Vigilantism in Africa*. Woodbridge: James Currey.

Kombe, Wilbard J. & Volker Kreibich. 2000. Reconciling Informal and Formal Land Management: An Agenda for Improving Tenure Security and Urban Governance in Poor Countries. *Habitat International* 24: 231–40.

Kyessi, Alphonce. G. 2002. *Community Participation in Urban Infrastructure Provision: Servicing Informal Settlements in Dar es Salaam*. Dortmund: Spring.

———2005. Community-Based Urban Water Management in Fringe Neighbourhoods: The Case of Dar es Salaam, Tanzania. *Habitat International* 29:1–25.

Lacey, Anita & Suzan Ilcan. 2006. Voluntary Labor, Responsible Citizenship, and International NGOs. *International Journal of Comparative Sociology* 47 (1): 34–53.

Lachenal, Guillaume. 2014. Chronique d'un Film Catastrophe Bien Préparé. *Libération*, 18 September.

Lakoff, Andrew. 2010. Two regimes of Global Health. *Humanity: An International Journal of Human Rights, Humanitarianism, and Development* 1 (1): 59–79.

Laidlaw, James. 2000. A Free Gift Makes No Friends. *Journal of the Royal Anthropological Institute* 6 (4): 617–34.

Lal, Priya. 2012. Self-Reliance and the State: The Multiple Meanings of Development in Early Post-Colonial Tanzania. *Africa* 82 (2): 212–34.

Lange, Siri. 2008. The Depoliticisation of Development and the Democratisation of Politics in Tanzania: Parallel Structures as Obstacles to Delivering Services to the Poor. *The Journal of Development Studies* 44 (8): 1122–44.

Leach, Melissa & James R. Fairhead. 2011. Being 'With the Medical Research Council': Infant Care and the Social Meanings of Cohort Membership in Gambia's Plural Therapeutic Landscapes. In *Evidence, Ethos and Experiment: The Anthropology and History of Medical*

Research in Africa, edited by P. Wenzel Geissler & Catherine S. Molyneux. New York: Berghahn Books: 77–98.

Lehmann, Uta, Princess Matwa, Helen Schneider et al. 2009. A *Map of Community Care Giver Programme Practices in Provincial Health Departments: Report to the Health Systems Sub-Committee of the South African National AIDS Council.* Cape Town: University of the Western Cape.

Leigh, Robert, David Horton Smith, Cornelia Giesing, et al. 2011. *State of the World's Volunteerism Report: Universal Values for Global Well-Being.* Denmark: United Nations Volunteers.

Le Marcis, Frédéric. 2012. Struggling with AIDS in South Africa: The Space of the Everyday as a Field of Recognition. *Medical Anthropology Quarterly* 26 (4): 486–502.

Lewinson, Anne S. 2007. Viewing Postcolonial Dar es Salaam, Tanzania through Civic Spaces: A Question of Class. *African Identities* 5 (2): 199–215.

Lewis, Bradley. 2007. The New Global Health Movement: Rx for the World? *New Literary History* 38 (3): 459–77.

Lewis, David 2005. Globalisation and International Service: A Development Perspective. *Voluntary Action* 7 (2): 13–25.

Lewis, Joanna. 2000. *Empire State-Building: War and Welfare in Kenya, 1925–52.* Athens, OH: Ohio University Press.

Lipsky, Michael. 1979. *Street-Level Bureaucracy.* New York: Russell Sage Foundation.

Little, K.L. 1965. *West African Urbanization: A Study of Voluntary Associations in Social Change.* Cambridge: Cambridge University Press.

Livingston, Julie. 2012. *Improvising Medicine: An African Oncology Ward in an Emerging Cancer Epidemic.* Durham, NC: Duke University Press.

Lock, Margaret. 2001. The Tempering of Medical Anthropology: Troubling Natural Categories. *Medical Anthropology Quarterly* 15 (4): 478–92.

Lodge, Tom. 2004. The ANC and the Development of Party Politics in Modern South Africa. *Journal of Modern African Studies* 42 (2): 189–219.

Lorimer, Jamie. 2010. International Conservation 'Volunteering' and the Geographies of Global Environmental Citizenship. *Political Geography* 29 (6): 311–22.

Lovan, W. Robert, Michael Murray & Ron Shaffer. 2004. *Participatory Governance: Planning, Conflict Mediation and Public Decision-making in Civil Society.* Aldershot & Burlington, ON: Ashgate.

Low, Setha M. 2001. The Edge and the Center: Gated Communities and the Discourse of Urban Fear. *American Anthropologist* 103 (1): 45–58.

———2003. *Behind the Gates: Life, Security and the Pursuit of Happiness in Fortress America.* New York: Routledge.

Lugalla, Joe L. P. 1997. Development, Change, and Poverty in the Informal Sector during the Era of Structural Adjustments in Tanzania. *Canadian*

Journal of African Studies 31 (3): 424–51.

Lyons, Kevin Joanne Hanley, Stephen Wearing & John Neil 2012. Gap Year Volunteer Tourism: Myths of Global Citizenship? *Annals of Tourism Research* 39 (1): 361–78.

Mackay, R. 1937. *Second (Final) Report of the Malarial Unit, Dar es Salaam, for the Period November 1934 to December 1936.* Scheme GBCDFMR, editor. Dar es Salaam: Government Printer.

Maes, Kenneth C. 2012. Volunteerism or Labor Exploitation? Harnessing and Sustaining the Volunteer Spirit for AIDS Treatment Programs in Urban Ethiopia. *Human Organization* 71 (1): 54–64.

Maes, Kenneth & Ippolytos Kalofonos 2013. Becoming and Remaining Community Health Workers: Perspectives from Ethiopia and Mozambique. *Social Science & Medicine* 87: 52–59.

Mahmood, Sara. 2005. *Politics of Piety: The Islamic Revival and the Feminist Subject.* Princeton, NJ: Princeton University Press.

Malinowski, Bronislaw. 1922. *Argonauts of the Western Pacific: An Account of Native Enterprise and Adventure in the Archipelagoes of Melanesian New Guinea.* London: Routledge.

——1926. *Crime and Custom in Savage Society.* London: Routledge & Kegan Paul.

Malkki, Liisa. 2010. Children, Humanity, and the Infantilization of Peace. In Ilana Feldman & Miriam Ticktin: 58–85.

Manton, John. 2013. 'Environmental Akalism' and the War on Filth: The Personification of Sanitation in Urban Nigeria. *Africa* 83 (4): 606–22.

Marks, Monique. 2005. *Transforming the Robocops: Changing Police in South Africa.* Pietermaritzburg: University of KwaZulu-Natal Press.

Marks, Shula. 1997. South Africa's Early Experiment in Social Medicine: Its Pioneers and Politics. *American Journal of Public Health* 87 (3): 452–9.

Marks, Shula & Neil Andersson. 1992. Industrialization, Rural Health, and the 1944 National Health Services Commission in South Africa. In *The Social Basis of Health and Healing in Africa*, edited by Steven Feierman & John M. Janzen. Berkeley, CA: University of California Press: 133–62.

Marsland, Rebecca. 2006. Community Participation the Tanzanian Way: Conceptual Contiguity or Power Struggle? *Oxford Development Studies* 34 (1): 65–79.

Martens, Jeremy C. 2002. Settler Homes, Manhood and 'Houseboys': An Analysis of Natal's Rape Scare of 1886. *Journal of Southern African Studies* 28 (2): 379–400.

Marx, Christoph. 2002. Ubu and Ubuntu: On the Dialectics of Apartheid and Nation Building. *Politikon* 29 (1): 49–69.

Mattingly, Cheryl. 2012. Two Virtue Ethics and the Anthropology of Morality. *Anthropological Theory* 12 (2): 161–84.

Mauss, Marcel 2002 [1967]. *The Gift: Forms and Functions of Exchange in Archaic Societies.* New York: Routledge [W.W. Norton].

Maxon, Robert. 1995. The Kenyatta Era 1963–78: Social & Cultural

Changes. In *Decolonization & Independence in Kenya: 1940–93*, edited by B. A. Ogot & W. R. Ochieng. London: James Currey: 110–49.

Mbembe, Achille 2001. *On The Postcolony*. Berkeley & Los Angeles, CA: University of California Press.

McClintock, Anne. 1991. 'No Longer in a Future Heaven': Women and Nationalism in South Africa. *Transition* 51: 104–23.

McFalls, Laurence. 2010. Benevolent Dictatorship: The Formal Logic of Humanitarian Government. In *Contemporary States of Emergency: The Politics of Military and Humanitarian Interventions*, edited by Didier Fassin & Mariella Pandolfi. New York: Zone Books: 317–33.

McLennan, Sharon. 2014. Medical Voluntourism in Honduras: 'Helping' the Poor? *Progress in Development Studies* 14 (2): 163–79.

McWha, Ishbel. 2011. The Roles of and Relationships between Expatriates, Volunteers, and Local Development Workers. *Development in Practice* 21 (1): 29–40.

MSF. 2015. 'Pushed to the Limit and Beyond'. Médecins Sans Frontières. Available at www.msf.org/article/ebola-pushed-limit-and-beyond (accessed 2 December 2015).

Mercer, Claire. 2002. Deconstructing Development: The Discourse of Maendeleo and the Politics of Women's Participation on Mount Kilimanjaro. *Development and Change* 33(1): 101–27.

Mercer, Claire & Maia Green. 2013. Making Civil Society Work: Contracting, Cosmopolitanism and Community Development in Tanzania. *Geoforum* 45: 106–15.

Merson, Michael H. & Kimberly Chapman Page. 2009. *The Dramatic Expansion of University Engagement in Global Health: Implications for U.S. Policy*. Washington, DC: Center for Strategic and International Studies.

Meyer, Birgit. 1998. 'Make a Complete Break with the Past': Memory and Post-Colonial Modernity in Ghanaian Pentecostalist Discourse. *Journal of Religion in Africa* 28 (3): 316–49.

Michigan State University. 2012. Taking the College of Medicine to New Heights. *MD: Michigan State University College of Human Medicine* 32.

Miller, David. 2001. *The Dialectics of Shopping*. Chicago, IL: University of Chicago Press.

Milligan, Christine. 2007. Geographies of Voluntarism: Mapping the Terrain. *Geography Compass* 1 (2): 183–99.

Milligan, Christine & David Conradson (eds). 2006. *Landscapes of Voluntarism: New Spaces of Health, Welfare and Governance*. Bristol: Policy Press.

Mindry, Deborah 2001. Nongovernmental Organizations, 'Grassroots,' and the Politics of Virtue. *Signs: Journal of Women in Culture and Society* 26 (4): 1187–1211.

Mitchell, Timothy. 2002. Can the Mosquito Speak? In Timothy Mitchell, *Rule of Experts: Egypt, Techno Politics, Modernity*. Berkeley, CA:

University of California Press: 19–54.

Mittermaier, Amira. 2014. Beyond Compassion: Islamic Voluntarism in Egypt. *American Ethnologist* 41 (3): 518–31.

Mogensen, Hanne Overgaard. 2000. False Teeth and Real Suffering: The Social Course of 'Germectomy' in Eastern Uganda. *Culture, Medicine & Psychiatry* 24 (3): 331–51.

Molé, Noelle J. Precarious Subjects: Anticipating Neoliberalism in Northern Italy's Workplace. *American Anthropologist* 112 (1): 38–53.

Molyneux, C. S., N. Peshu & K. Marsh. 2004. Understanding of Informed Consent in a Low-Income Setting: Three Case Studies from the Kenyan Coast. *Social Science & Medicine* 59: 2547–59.

Morris, Norma & Brian Bàlmer. 2006. Volunteer Human Subjects' Understandings of their Participation in a Biomedical Research Experiment. *Social Science & Medicine* 62 (4): 998–1008.

Mosse, David. 2005. *Cultivating Development: An Ethnography of Aid Policy and Practice.* London & Ann Arbor, MI: Pluto Press.

Mostafanezhad, Mary. 2013a. 'Getting in Touch with Your Inner Angelina': Celebrity Humanitarianism and the Cultural Politics of Gendered Generosity in Volunteer Tourism. *Third World Quarterly* 34 (3): 485–99.

——2013b. The Geography of Compassion in Volunteer Tourism. *Tourism Geographies* 15 (2): 318–37.

Muehlebach, Andrea. 2011. On Affective Labor in Post-Fordist Italy. *Cultural Anthropology* 26 (1): 59–82.

——2012. *The Moral Neoliberal: Welfare and Citizenship in Italy.* Chicago, IL: University of Chicago Press.

——2013. On Precariousness and the Ethical Imagination: The Year 2012 in Sociocultural Anthropology. *American Anthropologist* 115 (2): 297–311.

Mufamadi, Sydney. 1994. *Statement by the Minister of Safety and Security.* Conference: Media Conference, 22 August 1994, Pretoria.

Mukabana, W. Richard, Khadija Kannady, G. Michael Kiama et al. 2006. Ecologists can Enable Communities to Implement Malaria Vector Control in Africa. *Malaria Journal* 5 (9).

Mulder, Silvia Salinas, Susanna Rance et al. 2000. Unethical Ethics? Reflections on Intercultural Research Practices. *Reproductive Health Matters* 8 (15): 104–12.

Murphy, Keith M. & C. Jason Throop (eds). 2010. *Toward an Anthropology of the Will.* Stanford, CA: Stanford University Press.

Murray, Martin J. 1989. 'The Natives are Always Stealing': White Vigilantes and the 'Reign of Terror' in the Orange Free State, 1918–24. *Journal of African History* 30 (1): 107–23.

——2004. The Spatial Dynamics of Postmodern Urbanism: Social Polarisation and Fragmentation in São Paulo and Johannesburg. *Journal of Contemporary African Studies* 22 (2): 139–64.

——2011. *City of Extremes: The Spatial Politics of Johannesburg.* Durham,

NC: Duke University Press.

Musambachime, Mwelwa C. 1988. The Impact of Rumor: The Case of the Banyama (Vampire Men) Scare in Northern Rhodesia, 1930–1964. *International Journal of African Historical Studies* 21 (2): 201–15.

Muthuri, Judith, Dirk Matten & Jeremy Moon. 2009. Employee Volunteering and Social Capital: Contributions to Corporate Social Responsibility. *British Journal of Management* 20 (1): 75–89.

Nading, Alex M. 2012. 'Dengue Mosquitoes are Single Mothers': Biopolitics Meets Ecological Aesthetics in Nicaraguan Community Health Work. *Cultural Anthropology* 27 (4): 572–96.

——2013. 'Love Isn't There in Your Stomach': A Moral Economy of Medical Citizenship among Nicaraguan Community Health Workers. *Medical Anthropology Quarterly* 27 (1): 84–102.

Ndegwa, Stephen N. 1994. Civil Society and Political Change in Africa: The Case of Non-Governmental Organizations in Kenya. *International Journal of Comparative Sociology* 35: 19–36.

Ndlovu-Gatsheni, Sabelo & Gwinyayi A. Dzinesa. 2008. 'One Man's Volunteer is Another Man's Mercenary?' Mapping the Extent and Impact of Mercenarism on Human Security in Africa. In *Elimination of Mercenarism in Africa: A Need for a New Continental Approach*, edited by Sabelo Gumedze. Pretoria: Institute for Security Studies: 75–98.

Nenga, Sandi Kawecka. 2011. Volunteering to Give Up Privilege? How Affluent Youth Respond to Class Privilege. *Journal of Contemporary Ethnography* 40 (3): 263–89.

Newell, K. (ed.). 1975. *Health by the People*. Geneva: World Health Organization.

Nguyen, Vinh-Kim. 2011. Trial Communities: HIV and Therapeutic Citizenship in West Africa. In *Evidence, Ethos and Experiment: The Anthropology and History of Medical Research in Africa*, edited by P. Wenzel Geissler & Catherine S. Molyneux. New York: Berghahn Books: 429–44.

Nguyen, Vinh-Kim., C. Y. Ako, P. Niamba et al. 2007. Adherence as Therapeutic Citizenship: Impact of the History of Access to Antiretroviral Drugs on Adherence to Treatment. *AIDS* 21 Suppl 5: S31–35.

Noble, Michael & Phakama Ntshongwana. 2008. *No Sign of a Dependency Culture in South Africa*. Human Sciences Research Council.

Ntarangwi, Mwenda. 2010. *Reversed Gaze: An African Ethnography of American Anthropology*. Champaign, IL: University of Illinois Press.

Nuffield Council of Bioethics. 2002. The Ethics of Research Related to Healthcare in Developing Countries. A follow-up Discussion Paper. London: Nuffield Council on Bioethics.

Nyerere, Julius K. 1968. *Freedom and Socialism: Uhuru na Ujamaa – A Selection from Writings and Speeches 1965–1967*. Dar es Salaam: Oxford University Press.

——1973. *Freedom and Development: Uhuru na Maendeleo – A Selection from Writings and Speeches 1968–1973*. Dar es Salaam: Oxford University Press.

——1983, 'A Guest Always Brings Cheer', speech quoted in brochure compiled by Tanzania Tourist Corporation (TTC) Public Relations, Karibu Tanzania (Dar es Salaam, Tanzania Tourist Corporation, 2983): 2.

Ollwig Heinrich. 1903. Die Bekämpfung der Malaria. *Zeitschrift Hygiene und Infektionskrankheiten* 43: 1–4.

Ondrusek, Nancy Katherine. 2010. Making Participation Work: A Grounded Theory Describing Participation in Phase I Drug Trials from the Perspective of the Healthy Subject. PhD dissertation, Institute of Medical Science/Joint Centre for Bioethics University of Toronto.

O'Neil, Edward, Jr. 2006. *Awakening Hippocrates: A Primer on Health, Poverty, and Global Service*. Chicago, IL: American Medical Association.

Orenstein, A. J. 1914. Contribution to the Study of the Value of Quininization in the Eradication of Malaria. *Journal of the American Medical Association* 58 (22): 1931–3.

Padarath, Ashnie & Irwin Friedman. 2008. *The Status of Clinic Committees in Primary Level Public Health Sector Facilities in South Africa*. Durban: Health Systems Trust.

Parkin, David 1978. *The Cultural Definition of Political Response: Lineal Destiny among the Luo*. London: Academic Press.

Parreñas, Rheana 'Juno' Salazar. 2012. Producing Affect: Transnational Volunteerism in a Malaysian Orangutan Rehabilitation Center. *American Ethnologist* 39 (4): 673–87.

Parry, Jonathan & Maurice Bloch (eds). 1989. *Money and the Morality of Exchange*. Cambridge: Cambridge University Press.

Perlin, Ross. 2012. *Intern Nation: How to Earn Nothing and Learn Little in the Brave New Economy*. London & New York: Verso.

Perold, Helene, Salah Elzein Mohamed, & René Carapinha. 2006. *Five-Country Study on Service and Volunteering in Southern Africa: South Africa Country Report*. Johannesburg: VOSESA.

Petryna, Adriana. 2002. *Life Exposed: Biological Citizens After Chernobyl*. Princeton, NJ: Princeton University Press.

——2005. Ethical variability: Drug Development and Globalizing Clinical Trials. *American Ethnologist* 32 (2): 183–97.

——2006. Globalizing Human Subjects Research. In *Global Pharmaceuticals. Ethics, Markets, Practices*, edited by Adriana Petryna, Andrew Lakoff & Arthur Kleinman. Durham, NC: Duke University Press: 33–60.

——2009. *When Experiments Travel: Clinical Trials and the Global Search for Human Subjects*. Princeton, NJ: Princeton University Press.

Pfeiffer, David. 1993. Overview of the Disability Movement: History, Legislative Record, and Political Implications. *Policy Studies Journal* 21 (4): 724–34.

Pfeiffer, James & Rachel Chapman. 2015. An Anthropology of Aid in Africa. *The Lancet* 385 (9983): 2144–5.

Philpott, Jane. 2010. Training for a Global State of Mind. *Virtual Mentor* 12 (3): 231–6.

Pinker, Robert. 2006. From Gift Relationships to Quasi-Markets: An Odyssey along the Policy Paths of Altruism and Egoism. *Social Policy & Administration* 40 (1): 10–25.

Piot, Charles D. 1991. Of Persons and Things: Some Reflections on African Spheres of Exchange. *Man* 26 (3): 405–24.

Porter, Dorothy. 2011. *Health Citizenship: Essays in Social Medicine and Biomedical Politics.* San Francisco, CA: University of California Medical Humanities Consortium.

Prainsack, Barbara & Alena Buyx. 2011. *Solidarity: Reflections on an Emerging Concept in Bioethics.* Nuffield Council on Bioethics.

Prince, Ruth J. 2012a. HIV and the Moral Economy of Survival in an East African City. *Medical Anthropology Quarterly* 26 (4): 534–56.

——2012b. The Politics and Anti-Politics of HIV Interventions in Kenya. In *Rethinking Biomedicine and Governance in Africa: Contributions from Anthropology,* edited by Paul W. Geissler, Richard Rottenburg & Julia Zenker. Bielefeld: Transcript Verlag: 97–116.

——2013. 'Tarmacking' in the Millennium City: Spatial and Temporal Trajectories of Empowerment in Kisumu, Kenya. *Africa* 83 (4): 582–605.

——2014. Precarious Projects: Conversions of (Biomedical) Knowledge in an East African City. *Medical Anthropology* 33 (1): 68–83.

——2015. Seeking Incorporation? Voluntary Labor and the Ambiguities of Work, Identity, and Social Value in Contemporary Kenya. *African Studies Review.* 58 (2): 85–109.

Proudlock, Paula. 1999. Licence to Kill: Police Use of Force. *Crime and Conflict* 15: 28–32.

Putnam, Robert D. 2000. *Bowling Alone: The Collapse and Revival of American Community.* New York: Simon & Schuster.

Rajak, Dinah 2012. Platinum City and the New South African Dream. *Africa* 82 (2): 252–71.

Rajan, Kaushik Sunder. 2005. Subjects of Speculation: Emergent Life Sciences and Market Logics in the United States and India. *American Anthropologist* 107 (1):19–30.

——2006. *Biocapital. The Constitution of Postgenomic Life.* Durham, NC: Duke University Press.

——2007. Experimental Values. Indian Clinical Trials and Surplus Health. *New Left Review* 45:67–88.

——2012. *Lively Capital: Biotechnologies, Ethics, and Governance in Global Markets.* Durham, NC: Duke University Press.

Redfield, Peter. 2010a. The Impossible Problem of Neutrality. In *Forces of Compassion: Humanitarianism between Ethics and Politics,* edited by Erica Bornstein & Peter Redfield. Santa Fe, NM: School of Advanced

Research: 53–70.

——2010b. The Verge of Crisis: Doctors Without Borders in Uganda. In *Contemporary States of Emergency: The Politics of Military and Humanitarian Intervention*, edited by Didier Fassin & Mariella Pandolfi. New York: Zone Books: 173–96.

——2012. The Unbearable Lightness of Ex-Pats: Double Binds of Humanitarian Mobility. *Cultural Anthropology* 27 (2): 358–82.

——2013a. Commentary: Eyes Wide Shut in Transnational Science and Aid. *American Ethnologist* 40 (1): 35–37.

——2013b. *Life in Crisis: The Ethical Journey of Doctors Without Borders.* Berkeley, CA: University of California Press.

Redfield, Peter & Erica Bornstein 2010. An Introduction to the Anthropology of Humanitarianism. In *Forces of Compassion. Humanitarianism Between Ethics and Politics,* edited by E. Bornstein & P. Redfield. Santa Fe: School of Advanced Research: 3–30.

Reuters. 2005. 'Zambia Bans Brazilian Church in Satanism Row.' Accessed 13 Feb. http://wwrn.org/articles/19706/?&place=southern-africa (accessed 7 December 2015).

Reverby, Susan M. 2009. *Examining Tuskegee: The Infamous Syphilis Study and Its Legacy.* Chapel Hill, NC: University of North Carolina Press.

Reynolds, Lindsey. 2012. Vulnerability, Eligibility, and the 'OVC': The Local Lives of Policies and Categories. Unpublished PhD, Johns Hopkins University, Baltimore, MD.

Rieffel, Lex, & Sarah Zalud. 2006. *International Volunteering: Smart Power.* Brookings Policy Brief Series. Washington, DC: Brookings Institution.

Riles, Annelise. 2006 (ed.). *Documents: Artifacts of Modern Knowledge.* Ann Arbor, MI: University of Michigan Press.

Riley, Kathy A. 2009. Participation and the State: Towards an Anthropological View of the 'New Participatory Paradigms'. *New Proposals: Journal of Marxism and Interdisciplinary Inquiry* 2 (2): 24–30.

Robins, Steven. 2004. 'Long Live Zackie, Long Live': AIDS activism, science and citizenship after apartheid. *Journal of Southern African Studies* 30: 651–72.

——2006. From 'Rights' to 'Ritual': AIDS Activism in South Africa. *American Anthropologist* 108 (2): 312–23.

Rose, Nikolas 1996. The Death of the Social? Re-Figuring the Territory of Government. *Economy and Society* 25 (3): 327–56.

——1999. *Powers of Freedom: Reframing Political Thought.* Cambridge: Cambridge University Press.

——2000. Community, Citizenship, and the Third Way. *American Behavioral Scientist* 43 (9): 1395–1411.

Rothman, David J. 2003. *Strangers at the Bedside: A History of how Law and Bioethics Transformed Medical Decision Making.* New York: Aldine de Gruyter.

Rottenburg, Richard 2009. Social and Public Experiments and New Figurations of Science and Politics in Postcolonial Africa. *Postcolonial Studies* 12 (4): 423 – 440.

Roy, Ananya 2012. Subjects of Risk: Technologies of Gender in the Making of Millennial Modernity. *Public Culture* 24 (1, 66): 131–55.

Samoff, Joel. 1973. Cell Leaders in Tanzania: A Review of Recent Research. *Taamuli: A Political Science Forum* 4 (1) 63–75.

———1974. *Tanzania: Local Politics and the Structure of Power.* Madison, WI: University of Wisconsin Press.

Samsky, Ari. 2011. 'Since We Are Taking the Drugs'. *Journal of Cultural Economy* 4 (1): 27–43.

Scheper-Hughes, Nancy. 1990. Three Propositions for a Critically Applied Medical Anthropology. *Social Science & Medicine* 30 (2): 189–97.

Scherz, China. 2014. *Having People, Having Heart: Charity, Sustainable Development, and Problems of Dependence in Central Uganda.* Chicago, IL: University of Chicago Press.

Schneider, Helen, Hlengiwe Hlophe & Dingie van Rensburg. 2008. Community Health Workers and the Response to HIV/AIDS in South Africa: Tensions and Prospects. *Health Policy and Planning* 23: 179–87.

Schneider, Leander. 2004. Freedom and Unfreedom in Rural Development: Julius Nyerere, *Ujamaa Vijijini,* and Villagization. *Canadian Journal of African Studies*: 38 (2): 344–92.

Scott, James C. 1998. *Seeing Like a State: How Certain Schemes to Improve the Human Condition Have Failed.* New Haven, CT: Yale University Press.

Scott, R. R. 1963. Public Health Services in Dar es Salaam in the Twenties. *East African Medical Journal* 40: 339–53.

Semboja, Joseph & Ole Therkildsen (eds). 1995. *Service Provision under Stress in East Africa: The State, NGOs and People's Organizations in Kenya.* Copenhagen: Centre for Development Research; London: James Currey.

Shah, S. & T. Wu. 2008. The Medical Student Global Health Experience: Professionalism and Ethical Implications. *Journal of Medical Ethics* 34 (5): 375–8.

Shakow, Aaron & Alec Irwin. 2000. Terms Reconsidered: Decoding Development Discourse. In *Dying for Growth: Global Inequality and the Health of the Poor,* edited by Jim Yong Kim, Joyce V. Millen, Alec Irwin et al. Monroe, ME: Common Courage Press: 44–61.

Shapiro, J. P. 2011. *No Pity: People with Disabilities Forging a New Civil Rights Movement.* New York: Crown Publishing Group.

Shaw, Mark & Monique Marks. 2002. *Policing and Crime in Transition in South Africa.* African Abstracts 351. Durban: University of Natal, Economic History Department.

Shaywitz, D. A. & D. A. Ausiello. 2002. Global Health: A Chance for Western Physicians to Give — and Receive. *American Journal of*

Medicine 113 (4): 354–57.

Shipton, Parker. 1989. *Bitter Money: Cultural Economy and Some African Meanings of Forbidden Commodities*. Arlington, VA: American Anthropological Association.

Shivji, Issa G. 2004. Reflections on NGOs in Tanzania: What We Are, What We Are Not, and What We Ought To Be. *Development in Practice* 14 (5): 689–95.

Shutt, Cathy. 2012. A Moral Economy? Social Interpretations of Money in Aidland. *Third World Quarterly* 33 (8): 1527–43.

Silver, Mark. 2015. If You Shouldn't Call It The Third World, What Should You Call It? *Goats and Soda: Stories of Life in a Changing World*. Available at www.npr.org/sections/goatsandsoda/2015/01/04/37268 4438/if-you-shouldnt-call-it-the-third-world-what-should-you-call-it (accessed 17 November 2015).

Simone, AbdouMaliq. 2004. People as Infrastructure: Intersecting Fragments in Johannesburg. *Public Culture*, 16(3): 407–429.

Simpson, Kate. 2004. 'Doing Development': The Gap Year, Volunteer-Tourists and a Popular Practice of Development. *Journal of International Development* 16 (5): 681–92.

——2005. Dropping Out or Signing Up? The Professionalisation of Youth Travel. *Antipode* 37 (3): 447–69.

Smith, Janice K. & Donna B. Weaver. 2006. Capturing Medical Students' Idealism. *Annals of Family Medicine* 4 (Supplement 1): S32–S37.

Smith, Matt Baillie & Nina Laurie. 2011. International Volunteering and Development: Global Citizenship and Neoliberal Professionalisation Today. *Transactions of the Institute of British Geographers* 36 (4): 545–59.

Stallybrass, Peter & Allon White. 1986. *The Politics and Poetics of Transgression*. Ithaca, NY: Cornell University Press.

Stamp, Patricia. 1986. Kikuyu Women's Self-Help Groups: Toward an Understanding of the Relation between Sex-Gender System and Mode of Production. In *Women and Class in Africa*, edited by Claire Robertson & Iris Berger. New York: Africana.

Stewart, Sheelagh 1997. Happily Ever After in the Marketplace: Non-Governmental Organizations and Uncivil Society. *Review of African Political Economy* 71:11–34

Stirrat, Roderick L. & Heiko Henkel. 1997. The Development Gift: The Problem of Reciprocity in the NGO World. *The ANNALS of the American Academy of Political and Social Science* 554 (1): 66–80.

Stirrat, R. L. 2008. Mercenaries, Missionaries and Misfits: Representations of Development Personnel. *Critique of Anthropology* 28 (4): 406–25.

Stoler, Ann Laura. 1989. Rethinking Colonial Categories: European Communities and the Boundaries of Rule. *Comparative Studies in Society and History* 31 (1): 134–61.

——2002. *Carnal Knowledge and Imperial Power: Race and the Intimate in Colonial Rule*. Berkeley, CA: University of California Press.

Stones, M. & J. McMillan. 2010. Payment for Participation in Research: A Pursuit for the Poor? *Journal of Medical Ethics* 36 (1): 34–6.

Street, Alice. 2014. *Biomedicine in an Unstable Place: Infrastructure and Personhood in a Papua New Guinean Hospital.* Durham, NC: Duke University Press.

Sullivan, Noelle. 2011. Mediating Abundance and Scarcity: Implementing an HIV/AIDS-Targeted Project within a Government Hospital in Tanzania. *Medical Anthropology* 30 (2): 202–21.

——2012. Enacting Spaces of Inequality: Placing Global/State Governance within a Tanzanian Hospital. *Space and Culture* 15 (1): 57–67.

Summers, Carol. 2011. Boys, Brats and Education: Reproducing White Maturity in Colonial Zimbabwe, 1915–1935. *Settler Colonial Studies* 1 (1): 132–53.

Sutter, Paul S. 2007. Nature's Agents or Agents of Empire? Entomological Workers and Environmental Change during the Construction of the Panama Canal. *Isis* 98 (4): 724–54.

Svendsen, Mette N. & Lene Koch. 2011. In the Mood for Science: A Discussion of Emotion Management in a Pharmacogenomics Research Encounter in Denmark. *Social Science & Medicine* 72: 781–8.

Swan, Eileadh. 2012. 'I'm Not a Tourist. I'm a Volunteer': Tourism, Development and International Volunteerism in Ghana. In *African Hosts & their Guests: Cultural Dynamics of Tourism*, edited by Walter van Beek & Annette Schmidt. Woodbridge: James Currey: 239–55.

Swartz, Alison. 2012. Community Health Workers in Khayelitsha: Motivations and Challenges as Providers of Care and Players within the Health System. Unpublished MS, Masters in Public Health. Cape Town: University of Cape Town.

——2013. Legacy, Legitimacy, and Possibility: An Exploration of Community Health Worker Experience across the Generations in Khayelitsha, South Africa. *Medical Anthropology Quarterly* 27 (2): 139–54.

Swidler, Ann & Susan Cotts Watkins. 2009. 'Teach a Man to Fish': The Sustainability Doctrine and Its Social Consequences. *World Development* 37 (7): 1182–96.

Takahashi, Hiroshi, Yujiro Handa & Yoichi Yamagata. 2006. Japan's Experiences in Urban Malaria Control in Tanzania: Fifteen-year Progress and Future Challenges. *Technology and Development* 19.

Thomas, Barbara P. 1985. *Politics, Participation and Poverty: Development Through Self-Help in Kenya.* Boulder, CO & London: Westview Press.

——1987. Development Through Harambee: Who Wins and Who Loses? Rural Self-help Projects in Kenya. *World Development* 15 (4): 463–81.

Thompson, Lisa & Chris Tapscott. 2010. *Citizenship and Social Movements: Perspectives from the Global South.* London: Zed Books.

Ticktin, Miriam. 2011. *Casualties of Care: Immigration and the Politics of Humanitarianism in France.* Berkeley, CA: University of California Press.

Tilley, Helen. 2011. *Africa as a Living Laboratory. Empire, Development and the Problem of Scientific Knowledge, 1870–1950.* Chicago, IL, Chicago University Press.

Titmuss, Richard M. 1964. *The Health Services of Tanganyika: A Report to the Government. African Medical and Research Foundation.* London: Pitman Medical.

——1971. Why Give to Strangers? *The Lancet* 297 (7690): 123–5.

——1997 [1970]. *The Gift Relationship: From Human Blood to Social Policy.* New York: New Books.

Tollman, S. M. & W. M. Pick. 2002. Roots, Shoots, but Too Little Fruit: Assessing the Contribution of COPC in South Africa. *American Journal of Public Health* 92 (11): 1725–8.

Tousignant, Noémi. 2013. Pharmacy, Money and Public Health in Dakar. *Africa* 83 (4): 561–81.

Tsing, Anna 2000. The Global Situation. *Cultural Anthropology* 15 (3): 327–60.

——2005. *Friction: An Ethnography of Global Connection.* Princeton: Princeton University Press.

UN-Habitat. 2009. Tanzania: Dar es Salaam City Profile. Nairobi: United Nations Human Settlements Programme, Regional and Technical Cooperation Division.

——2010. *The State of African Cities: Governance, Inequality and Urban Land Markets.* Nairobi: Kenya.

Urry, John. 2002. *The Tourist Gaze.* 2nd edn. London: Sage.

van Ginneken, Nadja, Simon Lewin & Virginia Berridge. 2010. The Emergence of Community Health Worker Programmes in the Late Apartheid Era in South Africa: An Historical Analysis. *Social Science & Medicine* 71 (6): 1110–18.

Vigh, Henrik. 2009. Motion Squared: A Second Look at the Concept of Social Navigation. *Anthropological Theory* 9 (4): 419–38.

Vodopivec, Barbara & Rivke Jaffe 2011. Save the World in a Week: Volunteer Tourism, Development and Difference. *European Journal of Development Research* 23 (1): 111–28.

Wakeford, John. 1969. *The Cloistered Élite: A Sociological Analysis of the English Public Boarding School.* London: Macmillan.

Wall, L. Lewis, Steven D. Arrowsmith, Anyetei T. Lassey et al. 2006. Humanitarian Ventures or 'Fistula Tourism?': The Ethical Perils of Pelvic Surgery in the Developing World. *International Urogynecology Journal* 17 (6): 559–62.

Watkins, Susan Cotts, Ann Swidler & Thomas Hannan. 2012. Outsourcing Social Transformation: Development NGOs as Organizations. *Annual Review of Sociology* 38 (1): 285–315.

Watts, Michael. 2002. Should they be Committed? Motivating Volunteers in Phnom Penh, Cambodia. *Development in Practice* 12 (1): 59–70.

Wearing, Stephen. 2001. *Volunteer Tourism: Experiences that Make a Difference.* NY: CABI Publishing.

Wearing, Stephen & Jess Ponting. 2009. Breaking Down the System: How Volunteer Tourism Contributes to New Ways of Viewing Commodified Tourism. In *The SAGE Handbook of Tourism Studies*, edited by Tazim Jamal & Mike Robinson. London: Sage: 254–68.

Weinstein, Laura. 2011. The Politics of Government Expenditures in Tanzania, 1999 2007. *African Studies Review* 54 (1): 33–57.

Wendland, Claire L. 2010. *A Heart for the Work: Journeys through an African Medical School.* Chicago, IL: University of Chicago Press.

———2012. Moral Maps and Medical Imaginaries: Clinical Tourism at Malawi's College of Medicine. *American Anthropologist* 114 (1): 108–22.

Werner, D. 2009. *Disabled Village Children: A Guide for Community Health Workers, Rehabilitation Workers and Families* (2nd edn. First published 1987). Palo Alto (CA): Hesperian Foundation.

White, Luise. 1993a. Cars out of Place: Vampires, Technology, and Labor in East and Central Africa. *Representations* (43): 27–50.

———1993b. Vampire Priests of Central Africa: African Debates about Labor and Religion in Colonial Northern Zambia. *Comparative Studies in Society and History* 35 (4): 746–72.

Widner, Jennifer. 1992. *The Rise of a Party-State in Kenya: From Harambee! to* Nyayo! Berkeley, CA: University of California Press.

Wig, Ståle. 2013. *Awareness, Morality and Agency in Development: New Lessons from Lesotho.* Unpublished Master's Thesis, University of Oslo.

Wilson, John. 2000. Volunteering. *Annual Review of Sociology* 26: 215–40.

Wilson, Richard. 2001. *The Politics of Truth and Reconciliation in South Africa: Legitimizing the Post-Apartheid State.* Cambridge: Cambridge University Press.

Wipper, Audrey. 1975. The Maendeleo ya Wanawake Organization: The Co-optation of Leadership. *African Studies Review*, 18 (3): 99–120.

WHO. 2006. *Malaria Vector Control and Personal Protection.* WHO Technical Report 936. Geneva: World Health Organization.

———2008. *World Malaria Report 2008.* Geneva: World Health Organization.

Whyte, Susan Reynolds. 2011. Writing Knowledge and Acknowledgement: Possibilities in Medical Research. In *Evidence, Ethos and Experiment: The Anthropology and History of Medical Research in Africa*, edited by P. Wenzel Geissler & Catherine S. Molyneux. New York: Berghahn Books: 29–56.

World Medical Association. 2008. Declaration of Helsinki: Ethical Principles for Medical Research Involving Human Subjects. Ferney-Voltaire: World Medical Association.

Yhdego M. & P. Majura. 1988. Malaria Control in Tanzania. *Environmental International* 14 (6): 479–83.

Zelizer, Viviana. 1997. *The Social Meaning of Money* Princeton, NJ: Princeton University Press.

Zigon, Jarrett. 2007. Moral Breakdown and the Ethical Demand: A Theoretical Framework for an Anthropology of Moralities. *Anthropological Theory* 7 (2): 131–50.

———2010. Moral and Ethical Assemblages: A Response to Fassin and Stoczkowski. *Anthropological Theory* 10 (1–2): 3–15.

Zimmerman, Jonathan. 1995. Beyond Double Consciousness: Black Peace Corps Volunteers in Africa 1961–1971. *The Journal of American History* 82 (3): 999–1028.

Zink, Sheldon. 2001. 'Maybe We Should Pay Them More.' *The American Journal of Bioethics* 1 (2): 88.

Index

Lightning Source UK Ltd.
Milton Keynes UK
UKOW06f2022070616

275846UK00002B/5/P